Studies in

SEVENTEENTH-CENTURY POETIC

Studies in

Seventeenth-Century

Poetic

By Ruth Wallerstein

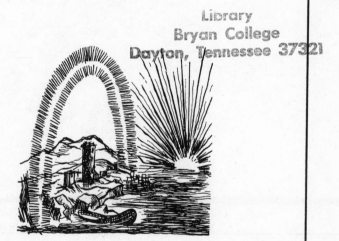

Madison and Milwaukee, 1965

THE UNIVERSITY OF WISCONSIN PRESS

Published by
The University of Wisconsin Press
Madison and Milwaukee
Mailing Address: P. O. Box 1379, Madison, Wisconsin 53701
Editorial offices: 430 Sterling Court, Madison

Reprinted 1961, 1965

Printed in the United States of America

PREFACE

T HESE STUDIES HAVE been very long in the making. And because of this, in part, it is impossible to make specific ac-
knowledgment either here or in the notes of all that, while teaching the writers of this period over some years, I have come to owe
to the general mass of very energetic scholarship and criticism in
the field. That debt will be manifest to my readers. For the same
reason, I owe more to my colleagues in the Department of English than I can possibly say. Certain specific thanks I can give,
with warm gratitude. Merritt Hughes of my own department
and Louis Wright, now of the Folger Library, read the second
part of my book in its first draft, and each made most valuable
suggestions. Professor Ronald Crane of Chicago read the first
chapter of the first part and also made valuable criticisms and
suggestions.

Because of my own slowness in preparing my final manuscript, and because of great, and unavoidable, delays in the production of the actual book, important work by other scholars
has appeared too late for me to take account of it. Though to
have gone into this scholarship and criticism would extend and
enlarge my views, I am not aware of any work that would
negate anything I have said or alter my point of view, and I have
therefore, for the most part, put it aside. It is perhaps invidious
to single out any studies to mention. But I am particularly sorry
that Miss Tuve's book appeared after my manuscript was com-

plete, and above all that I have not been able to avail myself
except in superficial retrospect, of the comprehensiveness, the
perspective, and the penetrating individual judgments of
Douglas Bush's *English Literature in the Earlier Seventeenth
Century,* or of Mr. Wolfson's great study of Philo.

The Research Committee of the Graduate School of the University of Wisconsin granted me from special funds voted by
the state legislature sums which enabled me to have two sum-
mers and a semester free, leisure without which I could not
have rounded out my studies into this book. To them I am
profoundly grateful. I have also received unstinting kindness
from the librarians of the British Museum, The Henry Hunting-
ton Memorial Library, The Newberry Library of Chicago, and
the Widener and Houghton Libraries of Harvard, as well as
from our own librarians. Thanks are due to the Henry Hunting-
ton Memorial Library and the Newberry Library for supplying
photostats for some of the poems reprinted in the Appendix.

In relation to family responsibilities and opportunities, my
sister Eve (Mrs. Samuel Fernberger) has guarded my leisure as
watchfully and generously as she has that of her husband, also
a teacher and scholar, with a most complete understanding of
a professional woman's life.

R. W.

Madison, Wisconsin
April, 1948

CONTENTS

Part One

THE LAUREATE HEARSE

---

*The Funeral Elegy and
Seventeenth-Century Aesthetic*

Chapter One

INTRODUCTION

Of THE POETIC art of the seventeenth century we have still too little understanding, despite the great scholarship which is illuminating our knowledge of the literature and thought of the age. We do not yet pick up most seventeenth-century poems with that sense of being at home in their modes and patterns which would give us a unified impression of their substance and their beauty. This lack of sure and ready sympathy and judgment prevents our entering fully into the humanistic value of what we read. For it is only in logic that our experience of the beauty and of the moral or intellectual intention of a poem or of the substance of life in it can be really separated. Much of the present uncertainty and disagreement as to Donne's significance arises from lack of precise insight into his poetic method and intention, no less than from our own divergences in values and in aesthetic approach. Dryden even more than Donne illustrates our condition.

There has been such illuminating comment on Dryden as much of Mr. Eliot's, and as Mr. Tillyard's criticism of *Religio Laici;* there has been Mr. Bredvold's basic exposition of a large area of his thought. But on the whole the quarrel between those who see Dryden as a stylist only, with a true and a false style, those who stress the scope and sincerity of his ideas, and those who too angrily or partially condemn his heart or character has not been brought to any common terms in a single view of his art.

Some failure to understand the art of the past is of course inevitable with changing philosophies, changing taste, a changing pressure of life upon us. And of us today it is particularly true that our failure to clarify and unify our views of the seventeenth century has been due in part to our own shifting views of poetry and more generally to our preoccupation with reconstituting our own intellectual and moral worlds in a number of ways. We are concerned each of us to use the seventeenth century after our own lights, to make it yield depth of perspective, tradition, and definition to our own views. And in so far, as a sign of the vitality of our own context, the quarrel may be a healthy function of our growth. Yet on the whole such a misunderstanding is apt to be a mark of the blinding limitations in our point of view rather than of its creative force. And in fact the present critical quarrel as to the place in the historic organism of English culture and the significance of the great line of seventeenth-century English poets is due largely to a confusion of issues springing from our ignorance.

It is often through his sense of the evolution of seventeenth-century poetry as a whole, rather than in concentration upon a single poet or a single line of poets that one becomes most vividly aware of the distortion of our vision. This suggests that the further knowledge we need may be got, not from the more intensive study of any one poet, but from the very close examination of a number of poems which together illustrate in some special way the development of seventeenth-century poetry, and which are related essentially enough to lend themselves to comparative analysis.

Our choice of theme and poems for such a study is inevitably suggested by the circumstances. Dryden is our terminus for the form we are to study, and Dryden's first published poem was his elegy *Upon the Death of Lord Hastings*. Written in

1649, just as he was leaving school, his poem was, nevertheless, no trifle, but a major essay in which, it would seem, he accepted a full and public challenge to his powers. It may yield us therefore an idea of the early conception of poetry instilled in him by Busby or drawn from his own reading. And his maturity is represented by two such considered and representative elegiac poems as his ode on Mistress Anne Killigrew and *Eleanora*. Turning back to the beginning of the century, again, Donne's elegies are among his major poems. Between Donne and Dryden, *Lycidas* in mid-century is the climax of Milton's maturing. Nor do the great elegies stand alone; Milton's on King and Donne's on Prince Henry are each, like Dryden's on Hastings, part of a collection or group. The elegy is a distinctive seventeenth-century form. No theme takes us more deeply into the temper of the seventeenth century than its attitude toward death, and these poems, which all seek to grasp the significance of death and in some form to reconcile us to it, ought to reveal the age as centrally as Bossuet's *Oraisons Funèbres* define the sensibility of his age. From the large body of elegy literature, the elegies which I have chosen to consider are the groups I have already named: the elegies on the death of Prince Henry in 1612, those on Edward King in 1638, and those on Hastings. The poems of all three groups are occasional poems written on the death of a gifted young man of public promise or at least, in Hastings, of public prominence; almost all are literary in the sense of being formal literary celebrations and not merely of that class of admonitory consolation which Mr. Draper describes among his mortuary elegies. All represent the poetry of the period characteristically, and each collection represents the work both of a number of widely different poets of importance and also of poetasters, so that the schools of poetry as well as the originating geniuses are seen. We find thus illustrated in this series the temper and design of seventeenth-century poetry from its earlier years until the form it had taken in the models probably known to Dryden at the end of his school days. And finally we may round out our impressions with poems in the same kind which show Dryden in his mature classicism.

It is less easy to define one's method of analysis than it is to select the body of poems which shall bring into sharp focus one's sense of seventeenth-century poetic. The over-all impression the elegies give one is of the continuity of seventeenth-century poetic form and of its evolution despite radical changes of program. To the seventeenth century itself, though there were profound shifts in philosophic view, keen literary quarrels, and far-reaching changes in taste and in deliberate literary program, its own development yet seemed integral. Nor was it the mere charm of the new or renewed concept of progress which favored that view, but rather a living connection from poem to poem. Dryden, for instance, regarded the body of English poetry before him as a progressive whole which reflected much of Nature, though he thought it needed that perfecting which he could give it in the light of the larger sanity of his own society, and of a fuller understanding of ancient and modern poetic theory and a more instructed taste. Dryden, of course, brought a mind predisposed to believe in the evolution of any art. But certainly he himself more than we have always realized read and reread the poets of the English line, analyzed them so far as his own difference of assumptions and of temperament allowed, and filled his imagination with their images, their rhythms, and their larger designs. And though we should not accept Dryden's interpretation of the great historic episode which he concluded— for he is the *pithecanthropos erectus* of the Renaissance and the Age of Reason—his art and his matter are in many essential qualities continuous with those before them, the differences and the common elements defining the qualities of each. He and they constitute an evolution of poetic form, moving forward as a continuous tradition of craft, though it was a very complex tradition. For it early embraced within itself a radical conflict of aims; and later it was modified by radically new attitudes and methods which drew from both wings of the earlier conflict. There was an unbroken tradition of poetic craft, with new streams entering it; there was a continuous tradition of poetic matter and the treatment of it. And back of form and theme there was the great evolving body of general knowledge, of philosophy, of social and moral attitudes—of temper, in a word—which gave life to each, and which transformed and reconditioned the art in which it was expressed. Of this evolving temper, taste and the theory of poetry are themselves parts. It is accordingly this change in climate of opinion and these inter-relationships as well as individual poems which we must analyze.

It is relatively easy to bring the form and substance of a single poem together into working terms; much more difficult when we are looking at an evolving series of poems. Roughly in order to understand the underlying spirit of the poems and their aesthetic, one has to describe a succession of attitudes toward death, and a succession of poems on death; then one has to consider each of the two groups as a series and at the same time to consider the two series, of attitudes and of poems, to-gether. Or to put the point in another way which brings out this third factor, one is by implication bringing together a series of attitudes toward death and a series of views of poetry and of poetic methods in order better to understand a number of particular poems.

My approach has been to analyze the series of poems them-selves, primarily because our chief interest is to understand these poems as aesthetic wholes and to feel their forms just as the forms of what they "say." But also from the point of view of understanding the poetic principles they illustrate, or by which they were written, such an approach seems to me in-evitable. For creative activity is always transcending the pat-terns it inherits, and it always overleaps theory even in those sophisticated ages which take much conscious account of theory. And if both theory and descriptive analysis of contemporary poetry are difficult, even more when we write of poetry in the seventeenth century, it is by way of the poems that were actually created that we have to find our path into what was felt and intended about the art of poetry.

But in analyzing the particular poems, we must still start with at least some tentative ideas about our third term, the poetic method which is active in them. With what working conceptions of their own art, we ask, did these seventeenth-century poets write, conceptions held either at the level of skill or at that of philosophy of art? We may find in the explicit poetic theory of the age and in the method in which schools taught the practice of poetry an answer upon which we can start to work, bearing in mind, however, that we shall test and modify this answer through our study of the poems themselves.[1]

There is no adequate or complete history of seventeenth-century poetic theory, and one can do no more really than to suggest how many theories of poetry were current at that time.[2] Our present analysis of the critical documents which give explicit expression in part to that theory is unsatisfactory because it has not probed deeply enough into the specific meanings of the terms they use, terms which shifted from one school of thought to another and from time to time. One corrective for this failure must lie in checking the theory with the poems. The other lies in relating the criticism to its backgrounds in general philosophy, as many scholars are now leading us to do. If we start with seventeenth-century theory at its most general and philosophic level, to take one most important instance, Mr. McKeon's essay on mediaeval rhetoric points out how two widely different views of the place of rhetoric in the scheme of thought and learning ran clear through the Middle Ages into the Renaissance, one stemming from the point of view which reached a culmination in Aquinas, another theory Augustinian in its roots. These views had two widely different consequences for expression. A third less clearly traceable sophistic tradition ran beside them.[3] This approach of Mr. McKeon's, though he has as yet given us only a sketch of it, proves very fruitful when it is brought to bear on the material to be considered in this essay. If, on the other hand, we try to understand casual seventeenth-century comment on poetry, we are forced into an awareness of these underlying philosophical differences and of the divergences in meaning arising from them. For instance, if we compare the discussions of imagery in the commendatory verse prefixed to Cartwright's works in 1651 with each other and then with the actual styles of the poets expressing these views, we seem to meet a chaotic crossing of the lines of criticism, and a chaotic inconsistency between theory and practice. Vaughan can condemn excessive wit. But he himself utters his views in a poem which is a tissue of emblems such as the age which was fast overtaking him would reject as totally lacking in lucidity; and it would attribute this lack to its false wit. For in the judgment of the new age, both the play of fancy with ornament and language in one poetic style and the solemn intuition of metaphysical truths through difficult symbols in another failed of the perspicuity which would enable even Lady Falkland's maid to understand what oft was thought. We, like that later age, have been too inclined to lump together the poets of the earlier seventeenth century according as they had many or few figures, and were analytical or descriptive. The age itself saw clear differences in what we confuse. And John Donne would have heard with horror Bishop Burnet's identification of Donne's own "strong lines" with the zealous imagery of the homely preachers. A final understanding of seventeenth-century critical dicta requires a comprehensive view of underlying philosophical and psychological principles, such as has not yet been written. Pending that, I offer only examples to suggest the multiplicity and variety of approaches in that age to the art of poetry. Perhaps taken together with the poems themselves they will give a bird's-eye view of what still needs to be done.

In our final view we must bear in mind, or I at least must remind myself of, one significant limitation on the importance of these conceptions of poetry I am about to describe. I shall seem to speak as though the theory of poetry taken in isolation created a formula by which the poet wrote. But it is only as a poet's theory of poetry is a living function of his larger philosophical attitude that it enters effectively into his poems. That is one of the crucial differences between poetry which has form and that which is engulfed in mere formalism. Poetic theory and larger philosophy define each other, and both are terms in the artist's sensibility. This truth I hope I have borne constantly in mind in my criticism.

First then, I purpose a tentative sketch of the poetic of the age, and following that the analysis of the three sets of elegies I have named.

Chapter Two

SCHOOLING AND
APPROACHES TO THEORY

IN THINKING OF the poetic of the seventeenth century, it is important to remember both by what means the writing of poetry was actually taught in schools and how varied were the approaches to a theory of design and style. In an age in which to write verse might almost seem as much a part of a cultivated gentleman's equipment as to take part in song, and in which so many hours of a schoolboy's week went to the writing of verse, classical and English, one must never forget the part which the character of his training had in forming his habit of expression.

"Imitation" was the word which resounded constantly in his ears. But what his master taught by this pedagogical method must have varied according to a wide range of theories of poetic. At its largest it implied the imitation of the general form and spirit of the great masters. In this view imitation was originally conceived to be as free as that copying of monuments of the soul's own magnificence which William Butler Yeats had in mind when he raised his thought to the great mosaics of Ravenna and spoke of the Sages standing in God's holy fire as in the gold mosaic of a wall. But such a view, under the dominance of neoclassical theory, passed gradually during the Renaissance, as Spingarn showed, into the familiar concept that Nature was closely and formally embodied in the great masters and that these masters accordingly must be our precise models in all detail of design.[1] Meanwhile, in daily teaching and practice, under the influence of a pedantic humanism, of drilling by the little endowed, administered to the immature and prevailingly less endowed, and of the theory of rhetoric as an art of ornament, imitation soon became a slavish imitation of themes or motives and of incidents and then of images and phrase patterns, made available not only in the poets but in *florilegia* and commonplace books.[2] Presently not only classical examples, Petrarch, the Latin-writing humanists, but new writers such as Donne, became models and quarries. Yet imitation, though sometimes so debased, remains a great and creative force. And in our contempt for the rigid verbal imitation of Cicero by a Rainolds, we must not forget the quality of a Milton's or a Fielding's imitation of Homer and Virgil. We must not forget the very principle of continuity and tradition in form. The quality of imitative teaching varies in character as the training in poetic of which the imitation is a part is more rhetorical or more philosophical in view; and the effects of imitation on different poems reflect the poet's teaching. We have only to recollect high school and freshman English today to realize that this must be so.

The "rhetorical" teaching of poetic, training the student to use the formulas of figure and patterns set forth in the rhetorical compendia was very widespread. As this rhetoric was taught in the common rhetorics and school books based on the mediaeval arts of poetry and on classical and postclassical rhetorics, the tropes, the figures of thought, and the schemes of sound were reduced to a common and often indiscriminate storehouse of dry forms to be used for ornamentation, the places of invention or thought being sometimes added to the "figures" as if members of the same category. These forms the pupil used to turn prose into verse and to create feeling. Such was the pedagogical fact. Mr. McKeon suggests, if I understand him, that much in the view underlying such teaching goes back to the theory of rhetoric as a purely verbal art, without place in a fundamental system of intellectual disciplines.[3] Such a view was implied also in the postclassical definition of poetry as matter in verse richly ornamented by figures, and came down through the Middle Ages in that form.[4] Whatever the philosophical context, in fact the long practice by school and college youths in the formulas, and in the art of naming the same simple object or concept in the widest possible variety of ways, tended to make expression formalistic.

Sometimes in the best mediaeval tradition the figures of thought, personification, and the rest, were kept distinct from the others—the figures of elocution—and were regarded as modes of "amplification," a process which precedes elocution in the structure of a poem or oration. But already in rhetorical teaching of postclassical times these figures of thought were viewed as elements of decoration; and they too in mediaeval arts of poetry had been adopted from rhetoric into poetic and had become formulas for poetry-writing.[5]

But though we must imagine the young versifier of the sixteenth and seventeenth centuries to spend many hours in the exercise of such crude imitation, we are not to suppose that his spirit, even at such moments, was unilluminated by a larger understanding of the structure of a poem worked out in its parts. Miss Sweeting has shown how early in England the influence of Quintilian operated to keep current a larger idea of imitation.[6] Perhaps our understanding of what the writer was taught in this age is hindered by a misunderstanding of his critical vocabulary.

In formalistic teaching the tropes and figures are referred to as "ornament" and "color." But the concepts of "ornament" and "color" must not be understood to be wholly covered by such use, as some modern historians of the period have supposed; nor must we lightly dismiss the words in any context as implying an entire divorce of style from thought, or of amplification for more essential meaning. Nothing could be less true.

Indeed, the significance of those terms in any discussion of rhetoric or poetry up to the eighteenth century is a clue to the whole scheme of thought involved in the discussion.[7] And as more philosophical views of poetry take the place of the narrowly "rhetorical" conception, the idea of ornamentation takes on a new meaning, or returns to an old. Dante, with both Aristotle's rhetoric and the tradition of allegory in mind, thinks of eloquence as the most persuasive aspect of speech or poetry. Boccaccio, explicitly raising with himself the question whether such ornaments are not inorganic, answers that they play in poetry the same part which columns play in architecture. His comment is but an echo of Cicero's ampler statement; surely in that answer is implicit the whole humanistic feeling for poetry as a fine art. Fracastoro in his *Navgerius,* enlarging Boccaccio's argument, makes ornaments the very stuff of that imaginative observation of experience and that expansion of it in which art consists. His psychology is strongly empirical. His conception of the imagination as a creative force in art has much in common with that of Leonardo da Vinci.[8] To Sperone Speroni, again, polished beauty of expression is as it were the very idealization by which the orator and the poet find the truth and teach in delighting us. After waiving as uncertain the solution to the question (which had developed as between the Platonic and the Aristotelian traditions) whether oratory—and the same holds true for poetry—represents ideal truth and beauty in the absolute, or whether it is an art of opinion representing truth and beauty as these are judged by men making a society under the imperfect conditions of our temporal life, Sperone says:

La Rhetorica non e altro, [the same applies to poetry] che un gentile artificio d' acconciar bene, & leggiadramente quelle parole, onde noi homini significhiamo l'un l'altro i concetti de nostri cuori. Diremo adunque, che le parole nascono al mondo dalla bocca del volgo, come i collore dalle herbe, ma il grammatico dell Orator famiglare, qua si fante di dipintore, quelle aconcia, & polische, onde el maestro della Rhetorica dipingendo la verita, parle, et ori a suo mode. Che cosi come col pennello materiale i volti, et i corpi delle persone sa dipingere il dipintore la natura imitando, che cosi fatti ne genero; cosi la lingua dell' Oratore con lo stile delle parole ... ci ritragge la verita: la quale proprio obietto delle dottrine speculative, non altrove che nelle schole, & tra philosophi conversando; finalmente dopo alcun tempo a gran pena con molto studio impariamo. ... Puo ben essere, et spese volte adiviene, che la ignorantia del volgo l'Oratore ascoltando, colga in scambio cotale effigie dipinta, lei istimando la verita; non altramente peraventure, che l'idolatra plebeio, le dipinture et le statue, nostre humane operatione, faccio su Dio, & come Dio le riverisca.[9]

In the thinking of these centuries, one developed new concepts not by starting afresh and changing one's vocabulary but by redefining old terms and modifying old concepts in the light of new assumptions. The term "ornament" itself changes with the changing view of art. Boccaccio uses the architectural figure as the core of a humanistic definition of the art of poetry. Ficino regards the temporal world itself as ornament, in the sense we shall presently see. Fénelon transforms the figure and uses the same word to reaffirm in neoclassical terms St. Augustine's view that great expression springs directly from thought and to side with Plato against the Sophists, and the rhetoricians who were their heirs:

L'érudition, autrefois si fastueuse, ne se montre plus que pour le besoin; l'esprit même se cache, parce que toute la parfection de l'art consiste à imiter si naïvement la simple nature, qu'on le prenne pour elle. Ainsi on ne donne plus le nom d'esprit à une imagination éblouissante; on le réserve pour un génie réglé et correct qui tourne tout en sentiment, qui suit pas à pas la nature toujours simple et gracieuse, qui ramène toutes les pensées aux principes de la raison, et qui ne trouve beau que ce qui est véritable. On a senti même en nos jours que le style fleuri, quelque doux et quelque agréable qu'il soit, ne peut jamais s'élever au-dessus du genre médiocre, et que le vrai genre sublime, dédaignant tous les ornements empruntés, ne se trouve que dans le simple.

On a enfin compris, messieurs, qu'il faut écrire comme les Raphaëls, les Carraches et les Poussins ont peint, non pour rechercher de merveilleux caprices et pour faire admirer leur imagination en se jouant du pinceau, mais pour peindre d'après nature. On a reconnu aussi que les beautés du discours ressemblent à celles de l'architecture. Les ouvrages les plus hardis et les plus façonnés du gothique ne sont pas les meilleurs. Il ne faut admettre dans un édifice aucune partie destinée au seul ornement; mais, visant toujours aux belles proportions, on doit tourner en ornement toutes les parties nécessaires à soutenir un édifice.[10]

Remembering then to redefine our terms where necessary, we may turn from the teaching which inculcates verbal imitation and the sophistic theory it implies and even from direct imitation of the spirit of another author to a second type of poetic.

Of broadly philosophical conceptions of poetry, we may take Scaliger's *Poetics* as one important statement, Alessandro Lionardi's treatise as another, to remind ourselves of the wide variety of views which prevailed.[11] In Lionardi's theory, from the point of view of rhetoric, the ornaments are the detailed explication by which we work out the accidents of our subject or substance and realize it to the full. But the real approach to poetry is through philosophy. In this approach Lionardi uses both Aristotle's *Poetics* and Plato. Verse, he proclaims, is one of the distinctive elements of poetry; but its essential element is imitation, the fable. Heroic poetry or drama may start either with history or with a feigned action, but the poet must render his action verisimilar: that is, the epic or the drama must represent the true coherence of an action, the true operation of the causes of all its elements. This ideal action is the central invention. It must be "adorned and enriched"; but these words are an awkward instrument to express Lionardi's meaning. The adornment and enrichment he conceives are in no sense extrinsic. It is they—the elaboration of particular details, of time, of place, of operations, above all, of the passions—which give the poem its verisimilitude; the best imitation is one which rests on the truth (factual history) but is adorned and enriched with those verisimilitudes which reveal the springs of human action and the color of human experience. Such is Virgil's elaboration of the Sinon incident from a detail of history. These ornaments express the poet's invention as the painter's colors develop his design. The delineation of passion is important both from the point of view of the imitation and from that of the reader's total aesthetic experience. In the imitation, the passions and the accidental causes which arouse them constitute those actualities in the life of man in which the ideal realities are embodied. They are also the principal source of that delight in the reader which it is the function of poetry to create. Petrarch's *Nel dolce tempo* is a supreme representation of those passions and accidents which are the chief ornament of poetry and through which the ultimate activity of love is shown.[12]

Underlying Lionardi's interpretation of Aristotle there is thus a Platonism of a Florentine cast; poems are shadows and images of *il vero,* they are representations in the realm of time, place, and the senses of the world of ideas. And we are, very likely, close to the core of his thought if we turn for a moment from his own work to Chapter III of the first speech of Marsilio Ficino's *Commentary on Plato's Symposium:*

And that not yet formed essence we call chaos. Its first turning to God is the arising of love; the infusion of his ray, the food of love; the enkindling which follows we call the increasing of love; the drawing nigh, the onset of love; the formation which results from this drawing near we call in Latin *mundum* [world] in Greek κόσμον, that is, ornament. The grace of this ornament is beauty. And the love which is straightway born draws the mind to it and leads the mind which had been hitherto formless to become straightway a beautifully informed [*formosam*] mind. . . . And the mind turns to God just as the eye turns to the light of the sun. . . . And in the same way as the mind just born and without form is turned to God by love and is formed; so the soul of the world is turned to the mind [or, intelligence] and to God whence it was born. And though at first it was formless and a chaos, when by love it is directed to the intelligence, receiving forms therefrom, it becomes a world. And not otherwise also this our world, though it lies at first as a formless chaos, without the ornament of forms, yet love being born within it, it directs itself to the soul of the world and renders itself obedient to that. And this love uniting them, it receives from the soul of the world the ornament of all the forms which we see born in this world, and of a chaos is made a world.

The synthesis of Aristotle and Plato may be seen again in Lionardi's statement of causes. Under natural causes he lists material and formal causes of things, and of these the fable or action is constituted. Under supernatural causes are efficient and final causes; and these may be represented in the gods. Though a poem need not represent them, it is the ultimate and final perfection of the mind to do so. Then there are the accidental causes; and in these the poet represents the actual mutations of the mind. It is from the point of view of Platonic ethic and aesthetic as well as of religion that it becomes the function of tragedy to show how dangerous are the affections and perturbations of the soul and how unstable and various the state of things human. Allegorized myth finds a place in Lionardi's poetic as a representation to the senses and imagination of natural causes.[13] Metaphors, similes, descriptions both of persons and of places and times are especially important, as are also epithets, because they represent the verisimilar.

In putting so great an emphasis on description as he does, and in elaborating the types of description, Lionardi might very likely be influenced by the importance given in mediaeval treatises on poetry to description as a method of amplification; if so, he is assimilating their material to his neo-Platonic view, and thereby giving description a more organic place in poetry.

The verisimilar is to Lionardi both a representation of the actions and characters of persons and of the qualities of men and objects in their ideal or typical character, "showing causes"; and it is the detail, the moment of experience which identifies the ideal and the actual.

Scaliger's is a radically different synthesis of Aristotle and Plato. Aristotle is for Scaliger, he states in his *De Subtilitate,* the supreme and sufficient philosopher except that he does not pay adequate regard to Plato's conception of order. But to this exception may be attributed, probably, that element in Scaliger's *Poetics* which is most truly an aesthetic theory. For Scaliger, verse is what constitutes poetry. This definition he gets at from three very different points of view. First, historically it was so. Men created and cultivated verse first, he tells us, for its delight, a view which he would find in Aristotle; and it was only later that a didactic or moral purpose entered it. This historic view is fundamental in Scaliger, I think, though at a number of points in his book he seems to deny it. In the afterthoughts which he had not time to integrate with his main chapters he asserts with vehemence that the function of poetry is to teach and delight, but primarily to teach. Yet the two attitudes are partially reconciled in his conclusion that the moral meaning delights by offering the soul an object worthy of its contemplation. His second approach is Platonic. Song is order, he tells his son in his preface; it is the special element of order in poetry. Scaliger's third approach is again Aristotelian. Verse is the matter of poetry on which is imposed the form of its teachings, and its types or genres. For in his section on *Idea* he considers not only action and character, which we should expect to find in that book, but also elaboration of incident and the genres. Perhaps the idea of order is paramount in determining his view, as indeed in his preface it receives special stress. Verse remains for Scaliger an entity by which we are given an immediate intuition of beauty and thereby, as one side of him would assert, of goodness. Presently the Jesuit Pontanus, who is a professed follower of Scaliger, will insist that verse is the essential factor in poetry, because it is so integral a part of the ornament by which poetry performs its special function.

Scaliger is driven to these positions about verse not merely by his sense of history but by the fact that on another side his Aristotelianism and his Platonism are destructive of each other. He modifies Aristotle's essential conception of a work of art as an imitation in favor of a more strictly moralistic view. With the superficial or at least very incomplete and puzzled comment that the idea of *katharsis* represents the mean (possibly as "all passion spent"), he passes over Aristotle's theory of tragedy. Poetic imitation is not, for him, as Mr. Weinberg has pointed out, a representation of life in an artifact;[14] it is, like history and rhetoric, a direct representation in words of life, and of moral life. Lionardi accepts the Aristotelian dictum that a fable may be developed without manners. Not so Scaliger. For him, imitation is action representing moral character in a literal sense. The lyric and several other forms of poetry are not, in Scaliger's view, imitations at all; and they are poetry simply because they are verse. Again, there is some reflection in Scaliger of the scholastic conception of a work of art as an object made for its own end, as distinct from a work of prudence.[15] But in the main analysis he passed over this view too, in favor of a didactic interpretation of poetry.

Indeed, the influence of Aristotle upon Scaliger does not derive solely from the *Poetics,* but rather from the logical and perhaps the scientific works and from the *Rhetoric.* He would seem, in his *De Subtilitate,* to have been in the line of that school of Aristotelians who, first at Paris and later in the universities of northern Italy, by critical interpretation and development of the scientific and logical works of Aristotle helped to found the methodology of modern science by defining the process of thought from object to general principle and back to object. That Scaliger belongs to this school, one may infer from the account of its work and the extracts from its members reprinted by J. H. Randall.[16] In any event, however the tradition of Aristotelian interpretation came to Scaliger, he defines the scientific "regress" from effects to causes and back to effects, as effects will now be seen in their essential character. Nature, indeed, is fixed; but things and artifacts are multiple. And dialectic is an art bringing nature and thought together. Reason, or discursive thought, is the means by which we understand things, using the instruments of resolution and composition, the method of definition being only a form of resolution. By this discourse we arrive not at certain demonstration but at the probable truths of science.[17] It is surely under the influence of these conceptions of the study of type forms of things that Scaliger erects Virgil into the supreme poet whose work represents a truer Nature than any we shall observe for ourselves in casual experience; and it is thus that he lays the foundations for the neoclassicism which triumphed in the later seventeenth century over other elements in Renaissance criticism at a time when Platonic criticism, at least of a Florentine sort, had disappeared and the Platonic elements in Scaliger had ceased to be emphasized.

Haec persona quae natura ita constant, in Naturae sinu investiganda, atque inde eruta sub oculis hominum subiicienda erunt. Id quod ut quam commodissime faciamus, petenda sunt exempla ab eo, qui solus Poetae nomine dignus est. Virgilium intellego: e cuius divino Poemate statuemus varia genera personarum.[18]

Another important statement is to be found in the passage in Chapter xxv of Book III of the *Poetics* on the representation of the typical form. Here it is hard to distinguish between the supposedly Platonic conception, widely current in the Renaissance, of the artist's abstraction of the ideal from many particular instances, and the Aristotelian view that art creates the type form. As painters take from things themselves the notions by which they represent lineaments, light, shade, perspective, so do poets. But they transfer their notions from many objects to one picture, seeming thus to give laws to nature.

Nam tametsi in ipsis naturae normis atque dimensionibus universa perfectio est: tamen utriusque parentis, mistio, tempus, caelum, locus multa afferunt impedimenta. Itaque non ex ipsius naturae opere uno potuimus exempla capere, quae ex una Virgiliana idea mutuati sumus.

In keeping with these conceptions, Scaliger proceeds to his well-known logical analysis of types and typical aspects of character.[19] Here again, he is developing Aristotle's logical works, though in making the types so strongly moral and social he departs widely from Aristotle. It is at this point of departure that he swings again to Platonism and to the conception of order. Poetry delights not only or chiefly by the order of its verse, but by presenting to the mind a picture of that perfect moral order which supplies the will an object worthy of her contemplation. It is, however, a Platonism widely different in emphasis from that of Lionardi. For in it, the stress falls not upon the immediate reflection of the ideal in the particular created thing, but upon the ideal as an abstraction.

So also the two critics differ in explaining how to elaborate the detailed incidents and descriptions of a poem, which Scaliger, properly following Aristotle, considers under invention, as part of *Idea,* and not under ornament. It is the logical character of their relation to the central conception which he emphasizes, an insistence on logic which exaggerates Aristotle to the point of producing a difference in kind rather than degree, and which must certainly tend to make the development of detail static and formalistic. Would it not, as compared to a more Platonic or creative view, produce in imagery, for instance, just such differences as that between Milton's images in *Comus,* on the Platonic side, and on the Aristotelian Ben Jonson's in the masques, or between the imagery of *Paradise Lost* and that of *Annus Mirabilis?*

Ornament in expression, or elocution, Scaliger, like other critics of the Renaissance, regards as having sprung from man's creative expansiveness, seeking to realize a full order; also from the wish to give due splendor to highest things. In so far, in the conception that the splendor of order is realized in elaborate expression, he derives from Platonism. But in the treatment of style he is broadly Aristotelian, in the purely formal treatment of the elements of style as self-existent entities. And again it is upon the logical categories of figures of thought that he dwells.

The genres he develops at considerable length. As we have seen in his comment on tragedy, he does not consider their forms in organic relation to their function. He considers solely their material, their parts, the decorum of their style, their meters, as tradition has handed these down to us. It is again a view which approaches them as literary types, and which leads to formalistic development.

Finally, in the realm of psychology Scaliger, like Pomponazzi, simplified the multiplication of subtle steps by which psychology had often sought to explain the transition from sensation to concept. For him, judgment, an immediate intuition, simply recognized the whiteness of white and the difference of whiteness in relation to different objects. This view of the activity of the mind accords well with his strong emphasis on perspicuity as a prime virtue of style. *Judgment* as applied to poetic invention and to elocution closely parallels *judgment* as a general function of the mind.

The tendency toward formalism in Scaliger is caricatured in his professed disciple Pontanus. It is on the very grounds that verse is the implicit ornament of poetry and that verse requires ornament of elocution that this famous Jesuit teacher refuses the title of poetry to fiction in prose, though imaginative fiction is the essence of poetry. It is by ornament that poetry fulfills its special function of teaching through delight. By rich and subtle variation of verse and richness of image and figure it both represents the emotion it imitates and awakens in us an emotion, extrinsic to the action, which carries its teaching home to our hearts and memories. Poetry, in a word, represents the insights of moral philosophy and psychology in terms that are "sensuous, and passionate" though doubtless the terms, had he used them, would not have meant to him quite what they meant to Milton. The poet must know all that moral philosophers have taught. "Compositissima oratione, exemplisque pulcherrimis a se vel primum excogitatis, vel ingenuosis fictionibus amplificatis & illustratis, & quodam modo conditis, etiam diversos animi motus misceat, & lectores sive spectatores vel alliciat, vel rapiat quo placuerat." Thence wise men have called poetry philosophy veiled in fables.[20]

Pontanus avowedly derives much from Scaliger, for him the outstanding master, with incidental draughts from Horace, from Robortelli, from Vida, from Minturno, and from others. But well within the Renaissance view as he is, there is in him a profound difference of emphasis from that of the humanists. For him poetic is not, like rhetoric and the other liberal arts, a discipline; it is only one of the pleasantest of human activities, and one particularly suited to the habit of our man and times. Hence, paradoxically, though he is fundamentally more rigidly moralistic in his view of the human personality than they, his treatment of the materials of invention is more sheerly literary and more divorced from Christian or humane intention than theirs. The delight at which he aims is a psychological instrumentality to fix truths in one's mind, or to dispose us pleasantly towards them, rather than an experience of truth as beauty, though he quotes the Renaissance commonplace on inspiration. He sends forth many glances which look both ways. He is aware of the purely creative delight of the imagination in making a more perfect world; and his statement on imitation, though it gives instructions for verbal imitation, gives also an admirable definition of the more fruitful imitation which consists in steeping one's imagination in earlier authors. But in the main his treatise—which is a textbook—becomes a formal and categorical account of the content of the genres and of the elements of expression by which truth is rendered poetry. In this, his relation to Scaliger is clear. As one would expect from Pontanus' milieu and his Jesuit point of view, the categories of the emotions represented or appealed to are listed at length in his treatise.[21] The formal character of his treatment and also at the same time the primacy of his interest in doctrine are very well shown in his long section on the epigram, a form in which the Jesuits were such copious writers. Particularly worth our noting are the eleven chapters (14-24) on funerary poetry, on which, as he observes in his preface, he found no previous guide. He is so germane to our purpose that it is worth resuming a good bit of what he says, since his book is not readily available. The epitaph or funeral poem should represent the name, age, merit of the dead, should express praises of soul and body, should often give an account of the kind of death, together with a commiseration and something on the significance of grief. Enlarging in the next chapter, he goes on to list ten general points which such a poem can well consider: signify our grief and that of others; inveigh against death which has despoiled us of so constant friends, etc.; detest the cause of the death; weep the misery of human life; urge even inanimate things to grief (*vide* Virgil, of course); compare ourselves with others who lie in grief; console relatives by reminding them that the merits of the beloved will live on, and so forth; pray for the dead; urge passersby to pray; remember the resurrection of the body and beatitude; praise. On kings and other notables, there are special themes. Pontanus' mingling of Christian and purely ornamental or inventional literary elements reflects the whole character of his work.

In one particular Pontanus is in sharp contrast with other poetics, though only by silence or implication. Jesuit doctrine rejected with a smile the syncretism of Ficino, and neither allegorized myth—except in the simplest didactic form as it appeared in emblem books—nor the Pantheon appear in Pontanus.[22]

Despite their profound differences, the points of view I have sketched may all be grouped together within one Renaissance view, accepting the doctrine of ornament in a Renaissance sense, though different writers stress the elements of ornament very differently. For all these writers poetry is a mediate expression of truth to the imagination in sensuous terms, through a richly elaborated beauty. Such an ideal of poetry it was that William Drummond appealed to against the rising popularity of metaphysical poetry when he said, writing to Arthur Johnston, probably some years before 1637:

In vain have some men of late, transformers of everything, consulted upon her [poetry's] reformation, and endeavored to abstract her to metaphysical ideas and scholastical quiddities, denuding her of her own habits and those ornaments with which she hath amused the world some thousand years. Poesy is not a thing that is yet in the finding and search, or which may be otherwise found out; being already condescended upon by all nations, and as it were exhibited *jure gentium* amongst Greeks, Romans, Italians, French, and Spaniards. Neither do I think *that* a good piece of poesy which Homer, Virgil, Ovid, Petrarch, Bartas, Ronsard, Boscan, Garcilaso, if they were alive and had that language, could not understand, and reach the sense of the writer.[23]

It is true that in the great prominence which Pontanus gives to epigram and to emblem as a form of epigram, both peculiarly didactic forms of verse, he reveals his fundamental center of balance to lie in the doctrine of poetry rather than in its delight, and in the direct expression of its moral rather than the narrative. And his view of the creative process would differ radically from that of, say, a Fracastoro, or a Milton feeding on thoughts that voluntarily move harmonious numbers. It is true also that in what he has to say on the form of the epigram he betrays a bias in favor of logic by insisting upon *argutiae* and by his selection of intellectual figures, and of supporting figures which play upon antithesis and upon sound, such as the "echo." Thereby he and the Jesuit practitioners helped to flood Europe with a stream of aridly witty poetry at the expense of the immediately descriptive and imaginative. But his general doctrine for the elaboration of poetry and his treatment of verse and of resonance as a prime beauty of poetry fall within the humanistic view.

There was current, however, a radically different approach to the problem of expression, an approach which altered the conceptions of ornament and invention and the choice of image and diction.

This was the view of expression developed by St. Augustine and modified before it reached the seventeenth century by many intervening conceptions of the cosmos and of art.[24] It was a view which came to the seventeenth century not only thus indirectly, but probably directly also. Augustine's theory was, of course, a theory of prose and particularly of the style of the sermon. But it was a view which might readily be transferred to verse, not only because of the connection between rhetoric and poetic in the Middle Ages and the Renaissance but because, like a parallel if widely different literary movement today, it involved a basic view of the nature of speech, of fundamental human values, of the function of eloquence. Since this Augustinian view must certainly be considered in thinking of the poetry of John Donne, I must here speak of it briefly. Donne's general debt to early Christian and mediaeval thought has of course been defined by Sir Herbert Grierson, and Merritt Hughes has pointed out his references on "wit."[25] St. Augustine—and the other primitive Fathers who were in large measure the models of the rhetoric of Andrewes and his school of preachers—rejected pagan stories along with pagan deities and pagan life. Pagan rhetoric they did not reject but transformed.

Augustine viewed style from the point of view of theology and of one confronting the rhetoric of Rome with the Latin versions of the Bible. For him rhetoric is the art of expressing clearly, ornately where necessary, persuasively, and fully, the truths which thought has discovered acutely (*argute*). But language is primarily the immediate embodiment of thought. Concepts arise as pure mental activities, and words are symbols to express them; the essential quality of expression must be its effectiveness in embodying a chain of thought. The concrete images of the Bible are symbolic expressions of metaphysical and moral truths. One may find there all the schemes of thought and all the tropes, and one must know them in order to interpret the Bible just because they are integers of thought. They are in a sense arguments which explicate the truth and show as figures how reason has reached that truth. It is perhaps worth noting that Scaliger explicitly takes account of this view of speech as *logos,* but only in order to reject it.[26]

St. Augustine's view is made more clear by his discussion of the three styles and his transformation of that theory from what it was in classical rhetoric and would be again in Scaliger. The low style is that to be used in teaching; its place in expressing thought is obvious. The middle or temperate style, which Augustine considered as the most amplified and ornate style, and the style richest in schemes, served only to delight. Only, that is, when it was necessary to catch the attention of one's auditory. The high style, the style which persuades, the style, one might say, which saves men, is created by the ardor of thought itself, by the ardent contemplation of truths seen as value, as a motive to the will. In this style the Bible abounds. Such a style springs from the mind's spontaneous and unconscious activity upon the elements of experience, and thence arise its abundant images; for the modes of logic, the topics and the tropes of oratory and rhetoric, are but explications of the mind's natural working. And if the high style exhibits all the ornaments, it can exist

equally well without them. In his letter to Cresconius, who
fears the subtleties of dialectic and of rhetoric, Augustine defends dialectic on the ground that traditional dialectic is the
very mode of thought; rhetoric on the classic ground that
abusus non tollit usum. But in his treatise *On Catechizing the
Uninformed,* he warns against those sophisticates who look
more to refined correctness and elegance of expression than to
the truth. The Bible, even in the Latin version he used, came to
seem to him greater in expression than classical writers; and
though he himself loved the schemes of sound of the rhetoricians, he points out that the Bible, in passages where it might
have secured such schemes by no more than a simple change
of word order, yet often avoided them rather than disturb its
meaning. When to this view of style is united the symbolic or
allegorical interpretation of the Bible, metaphors, similes,
parables have become elements in the system of symbols by
which the book of the creatures reveals its Maker, and "ornament" hardly exists in serious literature.

The conception that style takes its form immediately from
thought was, of course, not original with St. Augustine, but he
gave it special Christian application and authoritative definition
for the Christian centuries.[27] Certain elements which mark the
distinctive Christian life of the idea had, however, already taken
shape before him, by the close of the second century. In the
evolution of the idea of symbolic thought, an evolution built
upon the study of the Bible, there were two forces which were
at first radically opposed to each other. One, the conception and
example of Tertullian, sprang from the direct study of the
parables and images of the Bible, and its conception of style may
be called strictly symbolic; the other came from the allegorical
interpretation of the Bible, particularly of the Song of Songs
and of Genesis, or the Work of the Six Days, the Hexaëmeron.
The allegorical interpretation, as Origen in his Platonism prac-
tised it, was not without some contempt for the simplicities of

the literal text which was the subject of its exegesis. Origen's interpretation of the Bible does not in itself constitute a theory of style; but it makes important assumptions as to the relation of word and thought. It is preoccupied with meanings, not with style, and its principles for interpreting allegory concentrate upon the logical implications of images and of the elements of words. Hence both its own nature and the fact that many of the elements of its system of symbols or its allegorical foundations were absorbed into the Augustinian tradition make it important to consider here.

The first of these two methods, that which cleaves to the text of the Bible, is central to the habit of thought and speech of Augustine's great predecessor in the African church, Tertullian. Fénelon was to call him perfectly Augustinian in the basic texture of his writing, if one removed the schemes, paradoxes, and *jeux d'esprit* which Tertullian inherited from the schools of rhetoric. The root of Tertullian lies in his view of the relation of the parables and symbolic images of the Bible to the essential logic of the mind, a view which, as we have seen, Augustine was to define so precisely. The matter is not one of interpreting the Bible but of applying the symbolic method of Biblical thought to the development of Christian theology. He opposes the Biblical method of thought to a prevalent type of ascetic neo-Platonic Christianity. Defending the intuitions of the senses against ascetic "idealism" because these intuitions are essential to the doctrine of the Incarnation and the Resurrection and because they are the necessary foundation on which rests the witness of the Gospels and the Acts as to the life of Christ, Tertullian says:

Say if you will that the intellect is more powerful than the sense, and more powerful in understanding the sacraments, if only you allow that it is also yet only one particular force of the soul, even as the senses are. It makes no difference to me how you put it unless you mean that the intellect is preferred to the sense for the reason that by the same token as it is held to be stronger, it is held also to be more separate. . . . For although those things which touch the intellect are more powerful, since they are spiritual, than those which touch the sense, since these are corporeal, it is the things which are being compared, sublimer things with those more humble; it is not intellect contrasted to sense. For how shall the intellect be preferred to the sense by which it is informed for the understanding of truths? If indeed truths are apprehended through images, invisible things known, that is, through visible, as the apostle has written to us: *invisibilia enim eius a conditione mundi de factitamentis intellecta visuntur,* and Plato the heretic: *facies occultorum ea quae apparent,* and if it is necessary altogether that this world be as it were an image of some other, and if here the intellect seems to use the sense as its leader and author and principal foundation, and not to be able to reach truths without it.[28]

Symbolic thought is thus rooted for the Christian tradition in the epistles of Paul. It will be noted that Plato stands beside Paul. But in this reference to *Timaeus* and in others elsewhere, Tertullian is only calling for the reluctant witness of his opponents, as befitted a Christian who had once been a student of the great schools of oratory. For he is in this passage answering an extreme form of ascetic idealism current as Platonism in the second century, that of his great opponent Marcion, who conceived Christ as a spirit avatar. He is laying his finger on the paradox at the heart of the *Timaeus,* that paradox of the two aspects of God as the self-contemplating and withdrawn One, and as the loving and self-multiplying creator. In one aspect, the ascetic aspect of the paradox, God is conceived as absolutely transcendent and all life as a falling away into darkness; and against this view Tertullian directed his chief energies. His thought owes much to the other aspect of *Timaeus,* that in which Plato gives meaning to the book of the creatures by conceiving all particular life as a shadow of eternal ideas, showing it as an extended parable of religious and ethical truth, and making possible, too, an immediate relation between the soul and God. In his meditation on sleep as the image of death he says:

If in truth Adam gave a figure concerning Christ, the sleep of Adam was that death of Christ which he should sleep to death, that from the injury to his side the true mother of all living things, the church, should be figured. And so sleep, so healthy and so reasonable, becomes the public and common exemplar of death. For God wished, creating nothing in his disposition without exemplars, especially to remind us daily of the lines of our human beginning and end, in a Platonic paradigm, stretching out his hand the more easily to aid faith through images and parables no less of things than of words.[29]

In this passage, it is important to note, the impulse towards symbolic thought does not rest directly on the metaphors and parables of the Bible alone. To the literal reading of the Bible is added the doctrine that Old Testament history is a symbolic prefiguration of the life and ministry of Christ. That doctrine was a second major force in establishing the belief that the creatures are the symbolic alphabet of God, and in developing the mode of writing which sprang from that belief in the book of the creatures.

Finally, answering directly Marcion's extremist denial that the world we know is the work of the good God whose spirit descended in Christ, Tertullian maintains that this very world is not unworthy of God. For God made nothing unworthy of himself though he made the world for man: a world so fair that the Greek philosophers made gods of its elements, the Persians and Greeks of its substances.

Shall I come to its lowliest parts? unus, opinor, de sepibus flosculus, non dico de pratis, una cuiuslibet maris conchula, non dico de rubro, una tetraonis pinnula, taceo de pauo, sordidum artificem pronuntiabit tibi creatorem?[30]

Though this last passage occurs, like the others, in a dispute upon the interpretation of Plato, clearly the springs of its thought and feeling lie in the sayings of Christ, in the Psalms and Proverbs and Prophets, and back of them all in the ineluctable first affirmation, "In the cool of the evening God walked in the garden."

Tertullian seeks, then, by the method of thought of the Bible —in which he included, of course, the view that the Old Testament may be a symbolic prefiguration of the new—to explicate and demonstrate the emerging dogmas of Christianity. Many of the images through which he reasons have the simple quality, the naïve juxtaposition, of poetic metaphor; but it is metaphor just gliding into symbol. For it is never the outward look of things which his images describe, even when they are most simple, nor even the outward relationships and connections of the objects pictured, but something in their inner organic nature, some value or quality, some science of their being. Others of his figures, more extended in their analysis, in the detailed application of them, that is, to the dogma or conception they support, we might assign to the formal class of analogies, were it not that the term *analogy* has fallen for us into a logical context alien to Tertullian's purpose. The principle of his images is that if we look closely at the organic nature or the functions of any object or fact, we shall feel and find in its essential being, in the relationships by which it is unified, the principles and patterns on which the whole universe is constructed, and the principles by which man's thought comes to understand that universe. It is perhaps not superfluous to stress the seriousness of analysis in Tertullian's analogies in contrast with the gross and facile popular analogies that fill such a book as Raimond of Sebonde's *Natural Theology*. Both Tertullian's metaphors and his analogies are more justly seen as *symbols* in the modern sense. To set a few of Tertullian's figures immediately before us, I have chosen several whose manifest parallel with seventeenth-century poetry my reader will immediately draw.

[Defining how the soul may be said to grow, not indeed in its substance but in the development of its power.] Imagine a certain weight of gold or of silver, as yet a rude mass; its habit collected within it is less than it will be in the future; yet it contains within the limit of its mass all that is the nature of gold or silver. Then when the mass is beaten into plate it is made greater than it was in its beginning, through the dilation of its fixed weight; not through addition, since it is extended but not increased! Although in another sense it is increased also while it is extended, for it is increased in habit though not in state. Then is brought forth the very splendor of gold or silver, which was in truth something in the mass, but obscurer; yet not nothing. Then other and other habits [states of being] come to it through the facility of its material, by which he who controls it leads it, though he brings nothing to the mass except form.

[On the naturalness of sleep, the symbol of death.] Reasonable is the nature of sleep, so apt, so useful, so necessary, that no soul is sufficient without it, recreator of bodies, restorer of strength, establisher of healths, peacemaker of works, medicine of labors, to whose legitimate enjoyment day yields, night makes the law, carrying away even the color of things.

[Arguing for the resurrection of the flesh.] I mean that unique bird of the East, so famous for his singularity, so wondrous for his posterity, who freely burying himself renews himself, in his natal end dying and coming to life [*natali fine decedens et succedens*], *iterum phoenix ubi nemo iam, iterum ipse qui non iam, alius idem*, what more express and signal image for such an argument? Or for what other thing such a document. For God, even in his writings, says, "And ye shall flourish like the phoenix," that is concerning your death, your funeral, that you may believe the substance of your body also can rise from the fire.

For if God valued us, he goes on, above many sparrows, surely also above the sole phoenix. For as God exhibits the lineaments of divine things not less in parables than in speech, so through them we come to his edicts and decrees.[31]

Thus by an obvious connection is the *Physiologus* drawn into theology. Of number symbolism also there is some trace in Tertullian.

The paradoxes and plays on word which Fénelon drives out as excrescences upon Tertullian's style we cannot so readily dismiss. Stamped on his imagination from youth were the great concinnities and ornaments of the schools of rhetoric. And even the jejune scholar of Latin of today who may emerge from a college major in Latin with little conscious sense of Latin composition and little familiarity by ear with the language will hear in Tertullian's most moved or most bitterly ironic passages the long roll and intricate patterning of their syllabling and rhythms. But these patterns too had become part of the habit of Tertullian's thought no less than tools of his style. Like the images, they are transmuted into thought symbols. It is in the fiery assertion of the paradox between the worldly and the devout that they most constantly recur. One example may be given from his *Apology:*

Sed et iudicatos in partes secari a creditoribus leges erant, consensu tamen publico crudelitas postea erasa est, in pudoris notam capitis poena conversa est. Bonorum adhibita proscriptio suffundere maluit hominis sanguinem quam effundere.[32]

One further habit of Tertullian's thought calls for comment in this place though not directly a question of imagery. In rejecting at once both the dialectic of the schools and academic skepticism, he turns for a rational basis to the Stoics—*Seneca ipse noster*—for the conception of natural law; not natural law as it appeared in Stoic science or metaphysics, but natural law as it appeared in Stoic ethic and common sense. Dogma finds its proof in natural religion and in the *anima naturaliter Christiana.* The plants know by nature their function and habit and infants think naturally, however confused mature man becomes with his burden and gift of free will. "Out of the mouths of babes and children." The inference from this view to a natural, symbolic, logic of the mind is clear.

Though in the later history of symbolism and of the reading

of the book of the creatures the streams of Tertullian and of Origen were often to flow together, they started as I have suggested at radically opposite sides of the great ridge of neo-Platonism.

Before we take up Origen, however, we may look at one image from St. Augustine's own writing, to remind ourselves how close it is to the symbolism of Tertullian. Writing in his *Confessions* against the absolute idealism of the Manicheans, whose spirit universe would deny any reality to the incarnation of the creatures, and any meaning to individual experience, and in particular who in denying any reality to history sweep away the Old Testament, Augustine is defining the organic unity of the universe and of God's purpose in history, manifest both in the immediate teaching of the Old Testament and in its symbolic anticipation of the New. He says:

Measuring by their own petty habits, the moral habits of the whole human race. As if, in an armory, one ignorant what were adapted to each part should cover his head with greaves, or seek to be shod with a helmet and complain that they fitted not. . . . These things I then knew not nor observed; they struck my sight on all sides, and I saw them not. I indited verses in which I might not place every foot everywhere, but differently in different metres; nor even in any one metre the self-same foot in all places. Yet the art itself by which I indited, had not different principles for these different cases, but comprised all in one.[33]

The term Augustine used for his comparisons or parables was *emblem*.

Tertullian emerged out of the ashes of Roman rhetorical teaching and philosophy into Christianity. And much of his work was devoted to refuting the radical Platonic asceticism and idealism of Marcion as well as more generally the Platonic heresies of preëxistence and the transmigration of souls. For him keeping the classical heritage was a question of bending the essential moral and psychological intuition of Socrates, and to some extent of the Stoics, to the vision and habit of thought of the Bible, and to the teachings of the New Testament, to the doctrines of the Incarnation and Resurrection and the salvation of the individual soul. For Origen, in contrast, Christianity came first, followed by lessons at the feet of Alexandrian systematic neo-Platonism, to which he bent Biblical story. But before looking at Origen's formulation of the principles of allegoric and symbolic interpretation of the Bible, we shall find it helpful to glance at the chief concepts and principles of allegorization which emerge in the work of Philo Judaeus. Through the principles of interpretation of these two writers, emphasis upon the logical meaning of figures is firmly established. In the writings of Philo, the revelation of the Law of the Old Testament, as interpreted in the tradition of Rabbinic thought, is philosophically developed and explicated, and the psychological bases of its ethics are defined in the light of the Greek philosophies of Alexandria. It is Mr. Wolfson's view that Philo, in the principles by which he related philosophy to revelation and in the philosophy which he constructed through a criticism of Plato, Aristotle, and the Stoics, laid down the essential pattern for the method of Jewish, Christian, and Mohammedan theology until the later seventeenth century.[34] To Philo's own philosophy, the concepts and methods of Plato contribute far more than those of other Greek thinkers, but with radical original development. The entire structure of Philo's work is based upon the conception that all religious and philosophical truth is one, not only in its essential spirit and vision, but in its explicit meaning, whether we are to suppose that a Plato, for instance, had access to the teaching of Moses, or that his wisdom was directly inspired by God. It is a conception which we find dynamic in all European thought up into the seventeenth century, often latent when philosophy is inactive, but emerging again into dominant significance in such thinkers as Giovanni Pico della Mirandola.

The great instrument for the relation of revelation and

philosophy is the method of allegorical interpretation, deriving its authority from the belief, already deeply established in Greek and Jewish thought, that the highest philosophical knowledge was esoteric, in this sense a mystery, and that it was hidden from those who are not students, in myth, metaphor, and allegory. It is my purpose only to describe the principles of allegorical and symbolic interpretation, considered as principles of expression, not the religious or philosophical structure of Philo's thought.[35] These principles derive largely from Rabbinic thought and Jewish mysticism, from Platonic allegory and the symbolism of the *Timaeus;* and in addition perhaps they owe something to Stoic allegorization of myth, though not to the Stoic view of the world which underlies it. In drawing forth these principles, I have depended chiefly on Philo's *De Mundi Opificio* and *Treatise on the Laws.*[36] Mr. Bentwich in his study of Philo defines three strands in the work of Philo of which the second and third are important in developing the theory of expression. These strands are a setting forth of Mosaic law; an elaborate moral exegesis (of the story of the Bible) giving typical moral significance to each character in the Pentateuch and an allegorical meaning to each ordinance; an elaborate metaphysical, or theological, and psychological allegorization of the text as a whole.[37] Philo applies to his interpretations the terms metaphor, allegory, symbol, and type. These symbolic interpretations are, he says in his *De Opificio,* no poets' or sophists' myths, but the means of making ideas visible: "signs of types, revealing in allegory according to the signification of hidden meanings."[38]

Implicit in his commentaries are two theories of language, the distinctly Jewish theory of names to which his moral interpretations owe so much, and the conception of the *logos.* Philo's conception of the *logos* in its entirety is a part of his whole conception of the nature of God and of the mode of his wisdom in creating and sustaining the world.[39] As a theory of language, it conceives that speech issues concretely from the thought of man in a mode which parallels and reflects the creation of ideas and thence of particular things by the One, through the Word, or the divine wisdom. God, Philo says, brought the animals to man, to name, as Lord of all, in order as his teacher to test Adam; he kindled Adam's innate capacity to give them suitable names, bringing out clearly the traits of the creatures who bore them; "for the native reasoning power [λογιχή φύσις] in the soul being still unalloyed, and no infirmity or disease or evil affection having intruded itself, he received the impressions made by bodies and objects in their sheer reality, and the titles he gave were fully apposite, for right well did he divine the character of the creatures he was describing, with the result that their natures were apprehended as soon as their names were uttered." On this doctrine is grounded the symbolic interpretation of the names in the Bible through their etymologies.[40] Thus Reuben is "the son of insight," and so forth.

Philo's philosophy as a whole involves the radical division between the ideal world and changing things, but at the same time it involves the complete dependence of changing things upon the ideal world whose shadows they are in the procession from God of the ideas, of the *logos* of the cosmos. In this sense, things are the words of ideas, their concrete statement; and Philo's allegorical interpretation of the works of the Six Days is systematically built upon the principle of correspondence. In his interpretation of Creation and the Laws, the doctrine of numbers and the conception of man as a microcosm reflecting the macrocosm in all the detail of his being plays a large part. Philo uses the theory of numbers both in its most serious sense, which explicates the numbers from the integer one, derives time from space, and asserts the quantitative nature of the creation or the mathematical structure of the world, and also in all the magical formula of numerology and arithmetical pattern.

Philo's text is fixed on the one hand. On the other hand, his

moral and philosophical system is ethically and rationally determined by its own principles of thought in which the tradition
of Jewish belief and Greek philosophy come together. Hence
the particular allegorical interpretations by which he brings
text and philosophy together are necessarily arbitrary, and arbitrary also are the particular correspondences which he fastens
on for his symbols and to determine how he will work out the
analogy. Thus there is not in him, as there is in Tertullian, an
organic, what one might call a scientific, relation between symbol and reality symbolized.

Another element in his thought important for later thought
is his treatment of the characters of the Bible not as moral in-
dividuals who become also moral types, whose significance is
drawn from their history, but rather as general representatives
of the ethical views of the Bible and of Judaism in general.

Now men who have lived irreproachable lives are these laws and
their virtues are recorded in the Holy Scriptures not only by way of
eulogy, but in order to lead on those who read about them to emu-
late their life. They are become living standards of right reason....[41]

One final aspect of Philo's thought is of significance for the
complex science of the book of the creatures and all that it
contributed to the theory of expression. This is the emphasis
which he places upon contemplation of the order and structure
and beauty of the cosmos as proof of the existence of God.
Philo suggests that philosophy originates in man's deep joy in
watching the heavenly bodies and seeing their ordered movements. Thus early through Jewish religion and through Greek
philosophy and science, the interpretation of the creatures
through their structure and order is brought into direct connection with the interpretation of them in allegory and parable.
That man might see their order and know how his own life
should be lived, says Philo, did God create them. And the passage goes on even more significantly to apply the idea of the

lessons of the stars to the notion that man is a microcosm, and to bring it back explicitly to the view that man's thought is the special instrument for reaching the creator through the creatures. Man was created last that heaven and man, the two best things in creation, might be the beginning and the end. Man bears within himself, like holy images, endowments of nature that correspond to the constellations; capacities for science, art, love of the virtues.[42] In such allegorical statement there can be no room for elements of expression which are not directly meaningful.

Like Philo, Origen thinks of a threefold revelation· of the Bible; to all simple men, a not very full revelation; to the morally disciplined an ethically complete but still partial revelation; and a complete revelation to the philosophically instructed. To the last two, it speaks in enigmas. With no interest in the Jewish heritage and no sense of the development of Judaism, and condemning the Law as such, Origen is chiefly interested in systematic theology and in a psychology grounded in it. He, even more rigidly than Philo, conceives of the Bible as one single book, using one continuous and unified symbolism. Being at once an acute and precisely trained scholar, with the inexhaustible drive of the devotee, and a man lacking in any historical sense, not to say sense of humor, he has an eye even too sharp in finding the "impossibilities" of the Bible, as for instance when he remarks that the earth was too large for Satan to have shown Christ all the kingdoms of it. Like Tertullian, he draws his authority for allegorical interpretation from St. Paul. Origen defines his theory in the fourth book of his treatise *On First Principles* and in his homilies and commentary on the Song of Songs. There must be in the Bible, he assumes, a complete doctrine of the spiritual life of man as Paul defines it. And the incoherencies and impossibilities of the book are but intimations calling the attention of the informed reader to the fuller interpretation by letting him see the defect of its literal import. What the Bible says to the simple man is, as it were, the meaning of the senses; what it says to the more educated is the soul; what it says to men of spirit, men enkindled by a full spiritual love and despising carnal things, is the spirit. The correspondence of this with neo-Platonic psychology based on a concept of man as body, soul, and mind is clear. Put in another way, there are three disciplines by which men come to knowledge: ethical or moral, dealing with the habits and institutions of life and tending to virtue; physical or natural, which discusses the nature of things; and theoretical or speculative, which goes beyond the visible and contemplates with the mind alone things divine and celestial. Some writers, he notes, have added a fourth discipline, logical or rational, but others regard logic not as a separate discipline, but as woven through the other three. And so he himself must regard it, for in his scheme of interpretation he gives it no special place. The great testimony to these modes of understanding the Bible is that Solomon wrote one book in each discipline, Proverbs in the moral, Ecclesiastes in the natural, the Song of Songs in the speculative. So in Proverbs are found various tropes and various kinds of speaking, parables, *obscura dictio, aenigmata,* sayings of the wise; and so Solomon explains great and complete meaning in succinct and brief sentences.

Following out his theological system in his interpretation of Canticles, Origen describes the general plot of the epithalamion; the persons are Christ and the individual soul, the souls of believers (the chorus of maidens), and the angels and others who have come to the perfect life (the men). Among the modes which he uses for his detailed analysis are, first, the interpretation of an image by comparing its use in a particular passage with all the metaphorical uses of the term elsewhere in the Bible. Then in discussing that imagery drawn from natural objects in which the Song so abounds he uses what might be called a scientific analogic analysis. The eyes of the dove are pure, and he who has them in his inward eye shall see rightly and is promised mercy: the cedar is noted for never decaying, the cypress for the wonderful odor which it sends forth, and these gifts are applied to Christ. The presence in the Song of Songs of so much natural imagery must have helped to integrate this whole system of allegory with the symbolic use of natural history drawn from the habits, or supposed habits, and the structures of the creatures. Place names Origen interprets etymologically. In all this interpretation Origen regards the Bible as a unified work, a work containing in all its detail a tissue of absolute meanings, so that a figure used in one book is an absolute guide to its meaning in another.

From another point of view, he was shocked by the rudeness of its language and the naïvete of its attitudes. And this criticism led him to a concept of how God's verbally expressed meaning in descending became less potent, in a way parallel to the operation of his spirit, a concept which may have had great future significance. In his treatise *On First Principles* he introduces his theory of Biblical allegory by saying:

[If the superhuman element of the thought is not always clear, that is not wonderful.] For with respect to the works of that providence which embraces the whole world, some of these works show with the utmost clearness that they are the works of providence, while others of them are so concealed as to seem to furnish ground for unbelief with respect to that God who orders all things with unspeakable skill and power. For the artistic plan [τεχνικὸς λόγος] of a providential ruler is not so evident in those matters belonging to the earth as in the case of the sun and moon and stars; and not so clear in what relates to human occurrences as it is in the souls and bodies of animals. . . . But as providence is not at all weakened . . . once accepted, so neither is divinity of Scripture, on account of the inability of our weakness to discover in every expression the hidden splendor of the doctrines veiled in common and unattractive phraseology.[43]

With many differences of temper and of thought from

Origen's, the patterns set by him descend through the commentaries of the other early Fathers. In different men we find ethical and philosophical interpretations that are more systematic or more broadly ethical, more detailed and technical in exegesis or more free and imaginative: in all, a concentration upon the element of thought in figure.

Gregory of Nyssa, for instance, citing the objections of those who deny the enigmas, allegories, arcane meanings of the Bible, calls upon St. Paul as his authority for contemplation through analogy, or tropology, or allegory, even of historical passages. In a figure which is to recur later, he draws a parallel which has immediate bearing on the theory of expression. Speaking of the three works of Solomon, he notes that in Ecclesiastes youth is led by the flame of desire to hear greater things:

> But in the art of painting there is a wooden tablet all in different colors which carries out the imitation of the animal. But he who looks at the resemblance which is carried out by the art through the colors does not rest his gaze on the colors laid on the wooden tablet but looks only at the form which the painter has represented through the colors. So we look in present Scripture not to the matter in the color of the words but to the form as it were of the King which in them is expressed through pure conceptions of the mind.[44]

In Sermon VI, one of the most systematic of the sermons, he explains in full how the doctrine of the literal and the allegorical senses of the Bible correlates with the Platonic doctrine of the ascent of the mind to knowledge, from imagination to thought.[45]

One type of detailed interpretation in Gregory is worth illustrating. Commenting on the passage, "how fair is thy collar," he develops a very elaborate play upon the derivation of words, an etymology less technically accurate and more imaginative than those of Origen. Deriving the Greek from ὅρμος, a bay where ships lie quiet, he interprets the collar as an ornament signalling order; and as a collar keeps the horse rightly on its way, so Christ keeps the soul free of temptations, tranquil in quiet, not agitated by waves, and so forth.[46]

Gregory's sermons are not primarily theological. They are moral and devotional. The fact that he bases his reflections on the Song of Songs gives them a symbolic cast and accounts for the flow of their allegory. But he does not cleave to his metaphysical system, and his figures are applied and developed with great imaginative freedom. They are more apt to be pure allegory in our modern sense than close interpretation. Such is the elaborate allegory of the pillars of the tabernacle in Sermon ii, which carries the mind of the student of seventeenth-century literature forward to Herbert's poems such as *Sunday*. Or he loves parable and fable such as the parable of the bee, called forth by the passage, "Thy lips distill sweetness."[47] Gregory is already full of the emblems of natural history. In general both his didactic intention and the descriptive elaborations of his figures carry him far from Biblical metaphor and parable.

The "Commentary" of Ambrose of Milan is not a unified book but simply a collection of passages from his works.[48] He repeats the view of his predecessors that Solomon has given three pictures of the world. But in Canticles itself, also, all three meanings are to be found. Ambrose's interpretations are moral rather than doctrinal, abounding at appropriate places in unnatural natural history. Yet a single passage illustrates how closely wrought into his system was technical and close etymological analysis and how such analysis had become bound up with symbolic paradox. Writing on the verse, *Nardus cypri consobrinus meus in vineis Engaddi,* he designates its place as the place where the *opobalsamum* grows, and gives as the interpretation of its Hebrew name the meaning, *temptation*. Among those vines, he goes on, is a wood that gives forth an unguent if touched, but no such redolence if not cut and broken. And so Christ, crucified on that wood of the temptation, shed tears over the people and poured forth unguent from the bowels of his pity. So God, bound in when the Word was made man, was poor and was rich, and we are made rich by his poverty.[49] Amidst the broader flood of allegory which developed in the Middle Ages, the current flowing from the interpretation of the Song of Songs will still be visible miles out to sea.

This allegorical interpretation of the Bible played its part in St. Augustine's reading of the Bible. But I do not find it affecting his basic definition of expression, or his most basic interpretation of Biblical thought. Rather we may remind ourselves again of his relation to Tertullian, as Fénelon defined that relation. And from this very cursory examination of the early allegorical interpretations of the Bible we may turn to Hugh of St. Victor and Bonaventura, the especial heirs of Augustine.

They are greatly influenced by the rediscovery of Origen. But Origen is absorbed into their system. And it will help us to see their relation to him and to Augustine in the right perspective for us to recall Bonaventura's comment on Bernard of Clairvaux, whose sermons on the Song of Songs are so free and imaginative and so much closer to early allegory than Hugh's and Bonaventura's own systematic thought, the comment that Bernard is full of inspiration but lacks science. We find in them the modes of allegorical translation, such as etymological analysis; and such modes unite in them with Tertullian's paradoxical development of word balances and parallelisms. The Platonic conceptions assumed by Origen are present in a philosophical and disciplined form characteristic of the distinctive thought of these later Platonists: the trinitarian and mathematical structure of the cosmos; the conception of the three symbolic modes of Biblical statement, corresponding to the three aspects of the human personality, sense, soul, and mind; the patterns of the microcosm-macrocosm and of the book of the creatures, in full flower. But these elements are present also in Tertullian in less fantastic form than in Origen. And in Hugh's and Bonaventura's fully developed principles of epistemology, in their closeness to the Bible and in the influence upon them of the direct, literal texture of Biblical thought and image, in the completeness, depth, and unity of their system, and in the strictness and restraint with which they apply it, they evolve from St. Augustine. In them, the theory of style based on the principle of symbolic thought, only implicit and almost overlaid in Origen, again becomes explicit and complete.

Hugh of St. Victor's *Didascalia*[50] is a plan of education directed toward the contemplation of God through an analysis of the systematic symbolism or the systematic design on which the world is constructed; and it leads up in the last book to a survey of the symbolism evident in the book of the creatures. Logic, the fourth great discipline, which embraces grammar, dialectic, and rhetoric, is not an independent discipline but the handmaid of the other three, speculation, ethics, and natural science. Man discovered logic *propter eloquentiam,* that the other three might be developed and expressed. The universe and the human mind are constructed on a trinitarian principle and it is on the principle of the symbolism inherent in this construction that the imagery of the Bible is to be understood. In the interpretation of the Bible Hugh lists the three symbolic senses in which it is to be understood (the literal sense he takes for granted); the historical sense, according, that is, to the anticipation of the life of Christ in the Old Testament; the allegorical or ethical; and the tropological. His definition of symbolism is applied to Scripture, but it serves equally well for the book of the creatures. In the divine writing, *res* as well as words have something to signify. Philosophers know only the meaning of words, but truly more excellent is the signification of things:

For use only has instituted the word [the name of a thing], nature decreed the thing; the first is the voice of men, the second the voice of God to men. That being only brought forth, perishes; this being created, endures. "The word is the slight notation of the senses; the thing is the image of the divine reason." As for the sound of the mouth, therefore, which in the same instant begins and ceases to exist, it belongs to the reason of the mind; the thing endures through all the space of time to eternity. The reason of the mind is, accordingly, the intrinsic word which is made manifest by the sound of the voice, which is the extrinsic ·word; and the divine wisdom, which the Father has uttered from his heart, in itself invisible, is known through the creatures and in the creatures.[51]

Book VII of the *Didascalia* is the application of this principle of symbolism to the larger scripture of the creatures. For God, who made the world, is seen when the world is contemplated. And as was said in the Epistle to the Romans, the *invisibilia* of God are by the creatures of the world understood through things made. The principles for our understanding derive from the three invisible powers of God, his potency, his wisdom, and his benignity. These *invisibilia,* shown all at once in the immensity, the beauty, and the usefulness of the creatures, Hugh systematizes and divides by schemes which unite Platonic and Aristotelian classes, the Aristotelian categories as known through Boethius. Hugh's is no casual allegory or symbolism, but systematic and scientific in principle. But into the general development of the principles of science in the Middle Ages we must not here try to push our way further. Hugh's science in itself makes the principle clear so far as serves our purpose.

The pattern outlined in Hugh receives in Bonaventura its full development, from a mind of grander scope and a profounder spirit.[52] Bonaventura builds his science on the two principles of Augustine, first that the individual soul is the medium or mean of all things, through which all things are brought back (reduced) to God; and that all things are constructed on the pattern of the Incarnation. Bonaventura, then, interprets all the disciplines, all psychology, all ethic as symbols of that origin of things in the Word. Thus, for instance, in his *Breviloquium,* he tells how the elements are conciliated in forms of varying equality up to the human body, in which they reach a perfect poise.[53] All things are created according to the exemplar of God, which each receives in varying degrees as it can. His symbolism may be characteristically represented in brief in the following segment. The wisdom of God manifested itself in three forms: uniform in the divine laws (the principles, that is, of philosophy and of abstract thought in general); multiform in the mysteries of the divine Scripture; omniform in the book of the creatures. The book of the creatures is the supreme revelation to human consciousness of the Divine Essence, perfectly manifest to Adam until sin blinded him and made necessary the special manifestation of that essence in the Scriptures.[54] Bonaventura's sermons on the Hexaëmeron become thus not a particular commentary on Genesis but an exposition of his entire philosophy, through which play symbolic references to the work particularly of the sixth and seventh days and to the *enclosed garden* of the scriptures planted in the Paradise of the soul. Thus the essential symbolism of the Song of Songs becomes inwoven with that of the creation, if we study the mode and the attitude through which the human consciousness may have insight into the creation. Bonaventura's tone is paralleled, to take an instance of symbolic thought in the seventeenth century, in Donne's reflection in his sermon on Sir William Cokayne on the wonders of the Divine as revealed in the human body, which illustrates all that was done in the six days.[55]

The place of the mind in this scheme has already been suggested. As the Word became incarnate in Christ, the rainbow, so our degree in the hierarchy had to be sensate in order that our threefold knowledge might develop: to comprehend all that we can know by habit of mind through innate wisdom; to comprehend the infinite through infused wisdom; to comprehend by devotion all that it is possible to us to know of eternal wisdom. Bonaventura's theory of speech makes his concept of the nature of learning and thought more manifest. The light of the soul is truth, which is never lost. Truth is divisible into words (grammar), arguments (logic), and persuasions. But though he allows to persuasion that art of moving the affections deeply which is necessary to a system in which all things must be known by love, and although he accordingly introduces a perfunctory outline of the traditional parts of rhetoric, it has no real place in his scheme, and in a moment he condemns the colors of rhetoric along with sophistry. The real art of persuasion is in symbols. For the word is the direct outcome of the truth.[56] In the *Breviloquium* and in Sermon XIII of his *Hexaëmeron* he develops his theory of the interpretation of the Scripture, that *silva opaca,* given to man to illuminate him after Adam's sin, and filled with likenesses, proprieties, metaphors of things written in the *liber mundi.* Into his development of the four senses of the Scripture in accordance with his system of symbolic thought we need not go further than I have already intimated it. But I should like to illustrate in a single particular example how he often handles *words* and how the play upon words is a part of logic and of symbolic thought. Speaking of the application of geometry to Christ, Bonaventura argues: The earth is spherical, low, mean (*modicum*), and hence it is subject to the influence of all the heavenly bodies; spherical and low (*infimus*) in place, mean in circumference. So the Son of God is spherical in his poverty, *infirmus* [sic: *infimus?*] in his poverty, mean in his humanity, "limum nostrum suscipiens, de humo factus, non solum venit ad superficiem terrae, sed in profundo centri, 'et in ventre centri, in corde terrae,' salutem operatus est: quia per crucifixionem anima sua ad infernum descendit et restauravit coelestium sedium vacationes."[57]

I have suggested that the distinctive conceptions of the Augustinian tradition of style are to be borne in mind in understanding seventeenth-century poetry. It is not enough merely to think in general of the persisting mediaeval habit of allegory; that will give us no clue to the difference between a Lydgate or a Spenser or a Giles Fletcher on one side, and a Donne or a Marvell on the other. To name Lydgate and Spenser is to remind ourselves that allegory in its widest use merely supplied didactic purpose and a schematic structure in which to show concepts and type forms personified—it supplied plot, that is; but it did not determine invention or expression. It is the conception of the identity of thought symbol and word which in these views of Augustine and his followers significantly determines style.[58]

But the question arises how directly the Augustinian tradition can have been known to seventeenth-century England. Of indirect knowledge through sixteenth-century movements I shall speak in a moment; it is here a direct acquaintance with which I am concerned. Of Donne's familiarity with much of Augustine there can be no question. The Victorines and Bonaventura, according to Mullinger,[59] were well established in Cambridge at the close of the fifteenth century, particularly the Victorines; and when Erasmus came there, to his distress he found Hugh, with Nicholas de Lyra, the author most diligently studied. By Wilkins in the mid-seventeenth century, whom we may take as a moderate and rationalist, they are still cited in his *Ecclesiastes* among the great authorities. The great editions of their collected works had been published in the sixteenth century. Large excerpts from their writing were included in the popular compendia of Biblical commentary. And one may take as symptomatic of the interest in their sort of views Gale's addition to the title of his *editio princeps* of the *De Divisione Naturae Libri Quinque,* of Scotus Erigena, published as late as 1681, that it was "long called for."[60] That was partly because non-Catholics wished to explore for themselves what a suppressed work had to say, but they would hardly have done so had its whole method been alien to them. In Italy, in the Renaissance, there was a distinctive renewal of Franciscan Platonism through Nicolas of Cusa as a medium, a fact later lost sight of.

And H. B. Gutman has recently shown that the so-called "School of Athens" in Raphael's *Stanza della Signatura* is in fact part of a representation of Bonaventura's complete scheme of knowledge.[61] Would not Donne very possibly and Marvell very probably have known this?

Finally, since Ficino was so pervasive an influence in the sixteenth and seventeenth centuries, and since he is so directly in the line of St. Augustine and of the wing of mediaeval thought we have been exploring, we should consider for a moment the handling of symbols in his *Theologia Platonica*.[62] Though he does not discuss the principles of style, the symbolic habit of his thought will contribute to reinforce an already existing principle of style which is symbolic in essence. The conception of the various degrees of being and in particular the idea that man is the mean of those degrees, and of participation in the Divine Being, is most important in his thought. In the light of that principle he interprets many aspects of man's nature, many theological issues, so that he keeps symbolism as an instrument of thought constantly before us. To this type of comprehensive symbolic principle he further assimilated also in some degree quite simple and naïve analogies drawn from natural history. Thus in a passage on God's will toward the creation of the universe he says:

The more strongly He wills, the more powerfully He operates. And this in a certain way the eye of the sparrow intent upon its egg indicates. If the intelligence of God is more efficacious in creating than the eye of a sparrow in nourishing, nay if its efficacy is immense, . . .

Such uncritical images springing up amid the close-woven logic of his system of correspondences and derivations show how steeped in mediaeval thought as a whole his imagination was as well as in Augustine, Bonaventura, and Duns Scotus, and in just those aspects of it which made symbolism the core of expression. More particularly, S. R. Jayne, in his edition and translation of Ficino's *Commentary on the Symposium,* shows that in the very important passage on aesthetics in Chapter III of the fifth speech Ficino probably owes his concept of beauty and his vocabulary (*ordo, modus, species*) to Bonaventura's *De Reductione Artium ad Theologiam.*

Another aspect of the thought of Ficino, half scientific, half symbolic, derives from Plotinus. When Plotinus is developing a point in his thought by redefining an already existing conception, as for instance in his definition of the union of body and soul in *Ennead* IV, iii, 18, he will analyze the objects which have served to figure the thought, the analogies drawn by his predecessors, that is, and the concrete relationships previously used to formulate the concepts; in other words, he is analyzing the metaphors or symbols in terms of which his predecessors have thought. He treats them as genuine symbols in his mode of analysis, not as mere imaginative resemblances. He begins his own theory of light and theory of vision by just such an analysis of metaphor and analogy.[63] His whole psychological theory is bound up with the concept that vision does not originate in the object, deriving instead, from the mind's action through the eye upon light as that light illumines the object. And this view in turn integrates with his distinction between light and its opposing negation, darkness. Ficino, developing this conception of Plotinus still further, rests his ultimate argument for the spiritual nature of a reality on a closely considered analysis of light, color, mirrored reflection, which leads to his absolute distinction between *light* (a term which may be enlarged to include *heat* and in broad terms almost what we should call *energy*) on the one hand, and on the other that which we should call *extension*. The kinship of this system of relationship with Bonaventura's symbolic principles is clear.[64]

So do the Bible, theology, ethics, and scientific speculation each contribute to round out symbolic thought; and symbolic thought directs or determines the means of expression in the same way as had Augustine's view and particularly his conception of the high style as the immediate reflection of the thinking mind.

For the humanistic neo-Platonist who is enkindled by classical literature and art as literature and art no less than as philosophy, the temporal world as directly intuited by the senses in its very forms as they stand, shows the divine creation to man's sensibility in its eternal types; all the more vividly if it be understood and properly ordered in a work of art. Hence he loves simile, metaphor, description, qualifying epithet; and he delights in the allegorized myth because it allows him to possess himself of classical sensuousness and imagination no less than of classical thought. Such a man is a Lionardi, a Spenser (alive also with symbolisms), a Milton. The passage in Ficino to which I have just referred is perhaps midway between him and the Augustinian. To the Augustinian, on the other hand, this temporal world is always symbolic of moral and speculative truth. He would not deny that truth has power also to employ the imagination to give us a direct representation of the sensate world; but it is a dangerous and relatively insignificant subject. And it is not the ornaments of rhetoric swelling invention which the true writer uses, but the ornaments wherewith God has ornamented the creation and has revealed himself to human discourse of thought in the Bible.

In the development of Augustinian style which I have sketched were involved two concepts historically unfolding together at this time and in these writers, but not necessarily logically connected. The view of style as the immediate expression of thought which found its first clear expression in Socrates' and Plato's criticism of the Sophists was in the course of this development worked out in terms of an allegorical and schematic view of the Bible, a symbolistic view of nature and of human reason. But Augustine helped to enkindle in the sixteenth and seventeenth centuries a view of the integral relation of expression to the movement of the thinking mind which was quite independent of symbolism and allegory and quite critical of it. Fénelon, writing on the other side of Galileo and after rationalism had taken shape (a rationalism noted particularly for putting aside the schematic interpretation of the Bible), rejected the work of Origen as no more than pleasant and insubstantial play of the mind. He rejected, as we have seen, in such a writer as Tertullian the point, the paradox, the *jeu d'esprit,* elements which had become in Tertullian a part of his symbolic thought, and which the early seventeenth century in England loved, but which Fénelon deemed mere manifestations of temporary fashion; he praised only the fundamental integrity of style underlying these elements. Erasmus' fierce attack on the literary humanism of the Renaissance and on its pagan heart in his *Ciceronianus,* and his defense in contrast to it of the style which rises directly from thought, has no connection with symbolism or with the allegorical interpreters of the Bible; like Tertullian and like Augustine in their attacks upon mere rhetoric, he does find the ideal of style in the expression and habit of thought of the Biblical writers.

This whole anti-Ciceronian or Senecan movement of which Erasmus was a part has been defined by Morris Croll.[65] Its deeply conceived and widely influential effort to make style once more the direct expression of thought took shape on other lines than the impulse stemming directly from St. Augustine which I have tried to sketch above. It went back independently to classical sources; and though both it and the symbolic movement emphasized figures of thought, the handling of those figures in the two theories of style was necessarily different. Croll suggested that this anti-Ciceronian movement, too, passed from prose into poetry; and when the poetry of Donne—whose poetry is so like what his prose was to become—is considered, Senecanism must be borne in mind, though I do not believe it was a chief influence.

Still another theory of speech and style which owed much to Augustine is to be found in the logic and rhetoric of Ramus, which took hold with the Puritan divines and which profoundly influenced those of New England. Perry Miller has defined the character of Ramus' thought and his influence on expression in the chapter on "Knowledge" in his *The New England Mind;*[66] and he finds the chief effect of Ramus on the prose of the New England writers, where his influence can be most certainly identified and most extensively observed, to have been the separation of style from substance and the reduction of all elaboration to mere "rhetorical" pattern. Miss Sweeting, on the other hand, notes that the introduction of Ramus strengthened the influence of Quintilian. I do not know more than fleetingly the New England literature which Mr. Miller discusses, a literature so different in the scope of its thought and in its feeling for life from the writers whom I have been discussing. But a casual glance at its images, as they are cited by him, suggests that these divines owe very much in actual use of specific images to the earlier tradition of symbolic thought, despite the great difference in their use of the Bible as a whole. Such a relation would not quite sustain Mr. Miller's view. Miss Tuve, finally, has discussed the possible influence of Ramus in creating Donne's poetic mode. But I shall comment upon her suggestion when I come to speak of Donne himself.

In this rough and tentative sketch of Augustine's view of style and of the effect on later styles of the integration of his thought with symbolic thought, I have gone far afield from the poetic which may be found in the critical works, the rhetorics, or the handbooks of sixteenth- and seventeenth-century England. But it is precisely the significance of Augustine's and of the symbolic views that they reduce rhetoric in the traditional sense to quite secondary importance. How I think the Augustinian conception would actually affect the form of a poem, I shall show in discussing the elegies themselves.

The views and practices I have run over in this chapter may suggest then, the variety of views of the nature of a poem and of the art of expression which a seventeenth-century poet might have held, and which his readers have to bear in mind. Of course, many of the poets and versifiers whose work we are to consider merely learned from other poetry. They were not all conscious masters of a philosophy, nor of its application to poetry, any more than we who write of them are masters of philosophic criticism. And we shall, often enough, have to look for and find in the seventeenth century conflicting tendencies of thought and eclectic philosophies and views of expression. A pointed example of such eclecticism is Sir John Beaumont, who may point our moral though he is not one of our group of poets. Sir John Beaumont, as his recently published *Theatre of Apollo* shows, is an extreme Platonist from whom we might expect either a style rich in symbolic imagery or one rich like Spenser's in sensuousness combined with allegory. But in fact he accepts the French program for a rational style. And he directs against Donne and the wits about him in the court of James a criticism which he may well have derived from the views of the Pléiade or their predecessors on Spanish *argutezza* and on the symbolism or emblematism of Maurice Scève.[67] His own expression is as arid and "rational" as a Restoration improvement of Shakespeare. It is only from a Donne, or a Milton, or in less ambitious terms from a Marvell, a Denham, or a Herrick that we can look for a completely conscious and organic view of his art.

Finally, a style and a view of literature are formed, as a personality is formed, in imagination and thought not only by our conscious judgments, definitions, and decisions, but by all the forces that play upon us. And in poetic no less than in philosophy, the climate of opinion of the seventeenth century was remarkable for its power to absorb imaginatively a number of points of view not easily reconcilable if we look too closely to their ultimate implications. Hence the distinctions of theory among the various poets will not always be hard and fast. And hence, as we turn to the elegies themselves, we must keep our ear open to the whole complex sensibility of the seventeenth century as well as to the wide variety of its distinct ways of thinking about literature or the poet's art.

Chapter Three

THE DEATH OF PRINCE HENRY

AMONG THE POEMS on the death of Prince Henry, we may consider first those which follow the tradition of Spenser and of aureate poetry either in their entire design or in their ornament. Of these laments the five which are oldest in temper and style are no more than slight verses, but they show some interesting aspects of the teaching of poetry in 1612. The poems of the two Scots, James Maxwell and Sir William Alexander, are mediaeval in the tone of their feeling, yet each unites to a mediaeval reflection on death a later motive, and each has a mixed style.[1] Maxwell's theme is the nothingness of life; and the three simple symbols which express this theme, the lily, the star, and the gem, are as mediaeval as the feeling they embody. God has plucked a lily which grew in his garden. Men grieve, but the angels rejoice at the dissolution of a soul and body and at the coming of this soul among them.

> Mans life full well is likened to a flower
> Which growing up doth grace a Gardens aire.

Yet elements of Renaissance humanism and political consciousness qualify this otherworldly view of the universe and this simple symbolism. Henry is praised as son, as public servant, and as student, and to these virtues is added special praise of him as patron of the arts. The development, too, of this second theme no less than its content reflects literary humanism;

God is Jove, and the arts derive from Pindus and Helicon. Over-laying the simple mediaeval symbolism of the lament and disturbing the contemplation to which this symbolism invites us is a pattern of ornament and of special poetic diction such as the Elizabethan rhetorics and Spenser had popularized anew. There are archaisms such as *wight* and *choysest child,* and a figure of asyndeton further enriched by alliteration and assonance supports the climax of the poem. Maxwell evidently accepts the rhetorical conception that the theme is to be made beautiful and affecting by elaborate ornament.

Alexander's is a much drier literary exercise. His main theme is the fall of princes and the tragic stage of life; but at the close a sudden expression of personal reflection intrudes upon the impersonality of the verses. "My affections free till then," says Alexander with a shrill wit, "when Virgins first enjoyed him." He has a deeply traditional attitude, expressed in its own customary ritual. But, like a Norman cathedral modernized with new Gothic transepts, he accepts both the Stuart conception of the splendor of the state and the ceremony which supports that splendor. His poem seems an imitation in the most superficial sense, a pastiche of familiar motives, the mediaeval theme which, as we may suppose, was most familiar to him being paired with another in the wit fashonable in 1612. Each motive is expressed by such devices as he found expressing it in the models he imitates; the witty figure having an obvious resemblance to the metaphysical. But it is purely an ornament, neither paradoxical nor in any way dialectic and accordingly without that unity of purpose and tone which characterizes the metaphysicals even when most deliberately obscure.

Richard Niccols in his *Three Sisters' Teares*[2] has a more coherent design, though his style, like that of Alexander, lacks distinctiveness and unity of· tone. His verses, which might be called a masque or pageant rather than an elegy, are diffusely allegorical, recollecting Spenser and perhaps the *Induction* to

the *Mirror for Magistrates.* They mingle four themes, grouped
in two inventions. In the first invention, he depicts the Lord
Mayor's pageant which was going on at the time of Henry's
death as the rioting of the wicked Babylon insolent in its contempt of fate, but suddenly overwhelmed by providence with a
storm. The significance of the scene is specifically pointed up
by a comparison to Spenser's Idle Lake and by a reference to
the artifice which has here overlaid nature. From this scene he
passes in the second invention to Westminster, where the three
sisters, England, Scotland, and Wales, allegorized as the daugh-
ters of Albion, issue a gusty call to repentance for the sin which
has caused them to be deprived of Henry and an outcry against
Rome's rats. The first part mingles a general cry against worldliness with a lament for the falls of great ones; in the second
an outcry against death, rising in sharpness, yields to a call to
repentance for specific sins and an attack on Rome. As a whole
the verses reflect the mediaeval sense of fate and the Tudor
wish to find a moral interpretation of history and politics much
as these had been blended years earlier in the *Mirror for Magistrates,* with which Niccols' connection will be remembered.[3]
The fact that the poem appeals particularly to the city might
explain the introduction of the attack on Rome, and there is a
specific reference to Protestant hopes that Henry would take
a strong stand for the Protestants on the continent. But the
temper in which the call to repentance and the attack on Rome
are united is traditional in Puritan protestantism and not called
forth in special by the advance of the Catholic power on the
continent. Perhaps we need seek no further than Spenser for
the introduction of the motive here and the view common not
only in Ascham but, as Mrs. Bennett has recently shown,[4] in the
religious treatises which formed Spenser's background—that
Rome was anti-Christ, standing in the way of the heaven on
earth that reform had seemed to promise. The attack on Rome
is expressed in the image of the shepherd and the wolves, which

was a traditional symbol for the abuses of the church, but which perhaps came to Niccols through pastoral allegory.[5] The lament for patronage which precedes the chief passage recalls Spenser. James is the Kingly Shepherd who with his care doth keep the flock of Israel from the raging ire of ravening wolves.

Niccols' speech is in general rough and literal, but he has some attempt at aureate diction. His poem is not a mere collection of motives or verbal imitations. Moral theme and attitude are primary in him. Then he perhaps conceives, in a remote imitation of Spenser, that the invention in any specific passage, descriptive or lyric on the one hand, or denunciatory on the other, would determine diction and ornament. But though in his conception of the invention and of the elocution befitting it Niccols has some idea of poetry as a fine art, he has, I think, an underlying allegorical conception in virtue of which he regards the expression, even the elocution, as symbolic of the thought.

The sixains of Robert Alleyne and the altogether more accomplished laments of Henry Peacham represent a formalistic view of style from almost opposite approaches.[6] Alleyne's substance is chiefly a very literal, didactic outcry against Rome and an assertion of confidence in the gospels. But if he is to teach, he must delight, a task which may be performed by decorating his lines with established details of "amplification" and "elocution." A touch of the pastoral lament of nature, mixed with a ludicrous phoenix image, and a little mellifluous diction, together with the verse, are all which constitute his words as a poem. In Peacham's poems, on the other hand, the emotion rising from the style is in itself the substance of the lament. His verses are mere sentimental expressions of grief, closely imitating the texture of Spenser's style, with its nouns and adjectives of sentiment and its delicate and mellifluous sound patterns. They serve to illustrate very clearly the spiritual magic which was felt to reside in the mere voice of Spenser, in the "color" created by image and sound, even apart from Spenser's thought or design: and this exactly exemplifies Scaliger's view that the sheer pattern of sound and image give us an intuition of beauty, independent of the thought, though Scaliger would have said also that this pattern must closely reflect the form of the thought.[7]

In the laments of Drummond of Hawthornden and of Giles Fletcher, and to some small extent in *Great Britans Mourning Garment,* we come to poets of distinction and to a living Spenserianism.[8] In the first two the neoclassical and humanist ideal of the genre is realized, and each creates a single, unified effect. In the third, the well-filed line, the diction, and the fluidity suggest Spenser as the chief model, but there are other models too, and the sequence of sonnets lacks unity of design and temper.

Within its carefully limited scope, the young Fletcher's brief pastoral elegy may stand as a perfect example and defence of mediate and ritualistic poetry. The substance of his poem is a bare statement of the pastoral-Christian view of death expressed in Spenser's *November.* Many of the elegists fail in their statements of grief and of faith, through aridity. Fletcher, with Spenser as his model, translates the mingling of grief and otherworldliness into a lyric expression which makes it an immediately felt reality. He does not elaborate pastoral detail and imagery and Spenserian diction beyond what his feeling will support; but it is these media which manifest his feeling, this imagery and diction in which the seed of grief flowers.

Drummond's *Teares on the Death of Moeliades* imitated continental models of the pastoral elegy and perhaps Sidney's lament for Basilius in *The Arcadia,* not Spenser's laments; and these models are perhaps reflected in the severity of Drummond's style and the discipline of his line in this poem as compared with style and music in his later work.[9] He combines a selection of the motives of grief drawn from the humanist pastoral laments with a realistic comment on the contemporary political situation and with a long philosophical consolation not explicitly Christian but such as had become a traditional Christian addition to the lament after finding its first expression in Virgil and Cicero, who drew on the tradition of Socrates and Plato.[10] Though it is easy to point out his exact imitation of particular motives in his models, he works with freedom, proportioning his material to his own needs, unifying his poem and giving it the cast of his own sensibility. The lament of nature and the praise of the dead, both of which he reduces to brief proportions, voice our first sense of death and grief, intensified and universalized by being stated in traditional terms. The lament for death thus prepares the way for the visionary consolation, a type of consolation which, from the early days of Christianity, had constituted man's chief reflection on death. The lament for the times, or more generally for the world, was a natural and traditional part of this view of death, bearing also on the questions of Providence and sin and on the value of the single life; in purely mediaeval terms it would have been a *de contemptu mundi*. As a literary motive, it is true, it had been more fully developed in the pastoral political allegory than in the pastoral elegy. Drummond, however, brings the two elements of grief for the world and of political censure together harmoniously under the single allegorical theme. He thus by his combination of motives perfected the genre of the elegy as he had received it from his models, even while at the same time he transformed it to create an ideal imitation of his own feeling about the death of Prince Henry. His poem suggests that he thought of the genre both as a literary form with due allegory and motives and as a pattern of thought.

The elocution of Drummond's elegy offers, however, a special problem. Unlike the language of conventional pastoral which he much later used in his elegy on Sir Anthony Alexander, *Teares* is unclassical, witty, and, if we use the term very loosely, "metaphysical."[11] This is the more striking because we have from Drummond the explicit statement on poetic style, directed against the then fashionable metaphysical mode, which I have already quoted. Poetry was to give an ideal imitation of life in beautiful and traditional design and color such as Petrarch had used.[12] But *Teares on the Death of Moeliades,* in its temper and in the relative proportions of its elements, is much rather a metaphysical speculation than a pastoral lament; and the *witty* figure has come to be the form prescribed by decorum for such speculative substance, as I shall show more fully in some of the other elegies. In this association of speculation and "wit" Donne is only profounder and more original, more integral than others but not at all unique. This habitual association of style and matter, we may surmise, explains Drummond's choice of that style as the appropriate "color" for his poem; his wit is, however, far closer to that of the neo-Latin epigram and of Marini than it is to the wit of Donne, and Drummond is true to his own ideals in being neither obscure nor rough. The principle, if I interpret it aright, is an interesting intrusion into the more familiar idea of ornament and of the genre. Imagery is not determined by its decorum as suited to a high, mean, or low style in Quintilian's sense; but the character of the individual images bears a direct relation to the class of thought each clothes; and the imagery fitted to a philosophical or religious thought would be conceived of as St. Augustine conceived it.

I have listed *Great Britans Mourning Garment* among Spenserian poems. In themes it is perhaps only dimly so, and rather to be seen against more general backgrounds of the Renaissance humanism to which Spenser owes so much. To the materials of the pastoral elegy it is related by its sonnets of outcry against Saturn and the Fates, by the lament of the nymphs and of the rivers, by its expression of the pathos of youth untimely dead, while evil remains abroad in the world, by the flower image in which this theme is several times embodied. And it concludes with the promise of enduring fame in verse, subordinating to a less prominent place within the sequence Henry's ascension to heaven. With these familiar motives are others more sombre in tone, more directly dependent upon thought, less upon classical trapping and upon the amplification of traditional metaphor and prosopopoeia; one places Henry among the great untimely dead; one is a vision of melancholy, and one a meditation upon tears and man's capacity to feel grief that strikes a surprisingly analytical note among the more formal and ritualized themes.

The imagery of the sonnets as a whole is highly ornamented, full of direct address, of personification and sustained simile, rich in epithet and balanced lines. In the more deeply meditative sonnets, the diction and the handling of the line are more severe. But it would perhaps be pressing a point too far to find that their author consciously felt that their more intellectual treatment of theme demanded a plainer style. One can more safely note a deepening of temper which perhaps carried the author to continental models of the sonnet as well as to Spenser and which left him open to the influence of their styles.

In the poems we have so far discussed, there are apparent three levels of a poet's working view of poetry. In some we see the "poetry" to reside largely in the style, in the special diction and in variety of figure, a view likely to be the immediate outgrowth of the widely studied rhetorical handbooks and of school practice, but which had also a philosophical basis in the concept of rhetoric as pure style and of poetry as an art close to rhetoric. In others of the laments there is an imitation not of the expression alone of current models, but of the elements of their invention. And in this imitation there is on the one hand some sense at least of the distinctive quality of poetry as an imitation of life in a definite form, and on the other an idea of the relation of ornament to genre. But only in Drummond and Fletcher do we find the view that a poem is a unified, objectively definable form, as this view was conceived by Scaliger and the neoclassicists, such a view as may be restated in terms such as follow.

The pastoral elegy is a form to express man's experience of death and his interpretation of it. Its parts are a lament for death, a philosophic question on the meaning of life and on the moral pattern of the world (a question asked by Drummond, as by Niccols, in political terms), a consolation, found by these poets in contempt of the world. At the same time, Drummond reduces to a minimum the Greek naturalistic feeling out of which the pastoral convention had arisen and allows the lament of nature to become transmogrified into witty bravura. In doing so he is controlled by another widely prevailing view of the genre, in which certain types of invention are consecrated to certain types of theme, and certain types of elocution to certain types of thought or invention. This idea of the genre others share. On the surface it is a view which seems to arise from thinking of poetry as an art of giving pleasure through beautiful patterns of style, but in reality it reflects also a primary concern with poetry as moral or speculative doctrine, symbolized by the style in which it is expressed, or using images as logical counters to express itself. Here we are moving close to metaphysical poetry. I have already suggested in my introductory chapter the movement of thought and the philosophy of speech which may lie behind the style which we call "metaphysical." For the study of metaphysical poems we must turn now to Donne and to some of his imitators and to poets who wrote in the same tradition, in his time and after.

Before leaving the first group of poems, however, let us glance back at the general feeling about death expressed in them, an attitude which I have perhaps not sufficiently emphasized in my concentration on their form and method. In very many of them, the pressure of social and political unrest and of anti-Roman anxiety breaks in upon traditional religious and philosophical themes. Contempt of the world, celebration of the good man's virtue as it stands forth against the evil background of the life from which he has been released, had been the center both of Christian thought on death and of that which Cicero had garnered from the ancient world. But now the evil is seen in less absolute and more local and political terms. Again, hope of reform through religion had never been absent from meditation on the sinful condition of the world. But now, reformation optimism, in the pattern so clearly defined by Ascham, fixes upon Rome as the sole obstacle to the coming of a pure society. These views, more narrow and bitter than classical thought, but not unassociated with temporal hope, often receive an emphasis that alters the tone of the elegy entirely.

Nothing in the age is harder for us to recapture than the tone of Donne's elegy on Prince Henry.[13] We are today put off by the gross exaggeration of its adulation. Its ideas on reason and faith represent Donne's maturest spirit, but they are applied to Prince Henry's death in a manner at once overingenious and cursory, as though Donne were either ashamed or impatient of his task, so that when the first splendor and sweep of his statement fades, we are left with an impression of insincerity and even triviality. To overcome these impressions, we have to remember how far men of that day still believed in the historical force of the great, good man, and how much real hope England set on Prince Henry. We must remember, too, that Donne believed implicitly in the hierarchy of the state and in the unction of its leaders, despite the mixture of personal disillusion and deep religious pessimism which made him so bitterly cynical of the actual court world and so contemptuous of its hypocrisy. Thus the extreme compliment must be taken as one side of a paradox such as often renders Donne's voice so harsh compared with Spenser's visionary power to sing of reconciliation between the ideal and the real. Or if it is Donne's exaggerated expression which repels us, we have to recall Jonson's report that Donne was exaggerating his method and gratifying his egotism by trying to outdo Sir Edward Herbert in obscurity. But, and this is the more significant fact, to Donne the witty joke for God's sake was a thing of the most serious import, deeply related to the intellectual habit and the religious practice of many in that age, and it is possible that he tried to outdo Herbert, not in mere pride, but in a mocking wish to show how the type of *argutiae* which Herbert handled so jejunely might be seriously used by a man who understood them. The central theme of Donne's elegy, stripped to its barest intellectual terms, appears to be the same as that treated by the other major elegists: the meaning of death, the significance, for our view of the universe and of society, of the death of a young and noble man. And the exaggerated compliment which pictures the grief unto death of all England is not singular to Donne, but replaces in half the poems the universal lament for death which is the theme of the pastoral elegy. Not the newness of the theme but the view from which Donne attacks it, the depth of his interpretation, the mode of his expression and the completeness with which he developed the techniques of that expression distinguish the poem.

On the significance of death, Donne could not give the simple answer of classical-Christian feeling and assured faith which had been given by the pastoral elegists. The *contemptus mundi,* in its full religious bearing and with its metaphysical assumptions, is implicit from the first moment in his poem, and his metaphysical statement of this position leaves no room for a first naturalistic realization of death. Prince Henry becomes at once in actuality a symbol of the dependence of the life of man and nature on the divine intelligence, and a dialectic image through which to develop that theme. The main issue for Donne is not Providence but the grounds of knowledge and the methods by which man achieves it, with the twin issue of saving faith in the individual. To that saving faith, materialism and indifference are the great obstacles. This concern with intellectual doubt is the more urgent to Donne because he takes the position of Augustine that it is in the mind's own awareness of its operations, and in its primary love of God and virtue, that we find the grounds not only of faith but of reason as well. But it is an Augustinian outlook profoundly modified by Donne's own time and self. To comprehend it, one has to have in mind the subtleties of Donne's exercises in dialectic; his view that he who would find religious truth must go about it and about it as around a craggy mountain; and further his struggle with pathological hindrances to reason, a struggle which he expressed in one of his sermons in his cry that a man in sickness or melancholy might be uncertain of his own reason, but he could always believe in Christ's passion.

To Donne these issues were so serious, and the dangers of complacency and of intellectual and spiritual formalism at all times and in all men so great, that he must make his poem an intellectual discussion. But it must also be a meditative exercise, applying the discussion to his own state of mind. As a "devotion," the poem was an imitation of an emotion; by this imitation it became a poem, and Donne was made in writing it an angel singing.

The structure of the poem is determined by these two aspects of its matter, metaphysical and devotional. The opening line is at once the statement of a thesis and a prayer: "Looke to mee, faith, and looke to my faith, God." It is no less a conclusion than an opening and is meant to embrace and explain all the subtleties that ensue. The theme is then developed in the logical structure which Donne was presently to use for many of his sermons:[14] a statement of text, in this case a reflection on the relation of faith and reason and on their bearing on the death of Henry; definition and division; proof of each division; conclusion in the form of an application of the lesson. But in the poem the application becomes as we have seen a dramatic invention through which Donne resolves the emotion and answers the opening prayer by an act of faith: it is through love, he says, that the problems of limited reason and failing faith are solved. And so, though Donne cannot contemplate the essence of Prince Henry or of his worth in the world, if he can but contemplate the ideal human love through which Henry embraced absolute love, and can praise Henry and his beloved, he the poet will become—and in the poem he is—an angel singing before the throne of God.

The form of the poem is thus directly determined by the dialectic of its reflection on death. Yet Donne was intensely conscious of the further instruments of design and expression by which his experience was transmuted into a poem. Though in the last analysis he was contemptuous of much concern with beauty, he was intensely, even medically, aware of the art of persuasion, oratory; and equally aware, one must infer, of the art of poetry. In his rejection of softness and decoration in his sermons, he is not condemning rhetoric but appealing to a more philosophical view of it in its psychological function, within a basically Augustinian scheme. It is the function of rhetoric by ordered beauty to appeal to the imagination, if necessary to purge and reorder it tempestuously, and thereby to combat false opinion; and also it is its function to give ceremonious ornament to great things.

The distinctive elements of the poem as a poem are, then, these. First is its imitation of an emotion, including the development of that emotion through prayer to contemplation. Second is the application of its general theme to a particular occasion, namely, to discuss faith by considering Henry's place in the world, and the nature of the world; to discuss reason by the chain of reasoning in which Henry is a link; to round out the discussion by the fantastic love incident. All these incidents, if one may so call them, are symbolic in character and they are more fantastic, more extended, and more bold than what Donne would have used in prose. They are the distinctively poetic invention. Third are the imagery and the verse. It is the application of these elements of imagery and verse, and of these incidents to Donne's reflection and prayer which gives the poem its character. But before we consider his imagery in this poem, we ought to look at his general program for poetry so far as we know it or can infer it.

The most explicit statement we have on Donne's program is that of Carew, a statement carefully made and likely to be well informed. Donne's program included the rejection of the classical deities, a rejection which meant not only casting them out as type forms and as ornament, but casting out with them humanist and neo-Platonic allegory. Second, the binding together of great thoughts in the imaginative form of poetry, and, to effect this, the use of "strong lines." And last, discarding an enriched and Latinized diction for one English, normal, and toughly intellectual. So far Carew. From Donne himself we have, with regard to prose, the statements on the imagination and on ceremony to which I have just referred. Both apply equally or more strongly to poetry. Then from Drummond of Hawthornden we have the general complaint against those at court who of purpose abandoned traditional ornament and beauty for metaphysics and obscurity, a bill in which Donne must certainly be regarded as one of the chief offenders; for it defines Carew's picture in a reverse view.

This program can be readily related to the conception of style which derives from St. Augustine and which I have described in the preceding chapter. Within that tradition, one has to allow for broad differences of temper and of time, and one will not expect Donne, in whom sharpness of intellect is much more developed than sensibility, to sound at all like Hugh of St. Victor. Donne again is not one of the allegorizers of the Bible. Like Aquinas, and like St. Augustine in good measure, as well as like the modern school of Protestantism, he never turns to an allegorical interpretation of the Bible where a literal one can be found to have an ethical and pregnant meaning. But he does habitually think in terms of symbols, and of the application to ethics and psychology of the great structural principles of the cosmos derived by Christianity largely from Plato's *Timaeus:* trinitarianism, number symbolism, the relation of the microcosm and the macrocosm. But the influence of St. Augustine upon Donne's thought no longer needs to be demonstrated. Our concern is rather here to point out particulars of that influence as it affected his poetic and his view of style in general. If one looks at a sermon such as that on Christmas Day, 1624, one finds in it indeed the formal organization, the division, and the invention taught by conventional rhetoric. But that scheme is imposed upon a deeper form of thought. Donne's fundamental and underlying logic is to derive his points by drawing out in a circling movement the symbolic and sacramental or schematic implications of his Biblical text and of the whole structure of faith. Mitchell[15] has set forth the numerous parallels and allusions in Donne to Tertullian and other early symbolic writers. Their symbolic explication of faith is the core of Donne's method both in verse and prose. Donne defends his own wordplay and schemes of words by the authority of St. Bernard, thus relating himself explicitly to the tradition. Two of his most characteristic habits of expression are clearly grounded in the tradition. The first of these is "strong lines." "Strong lines," if I understand the term, must be considered primarily as a mode of thought, only secondarily as elocution.[16] As Mr. Mitchell has shown, the mode of statement known as "strong lines" seems to have come into English literature from Tertullian and kindred preachers. The term clearly corresponds to the strange metaphors, paradoxes, and points, all united often in a single vehement asseveration of which Fénelon makes Tertullian his first example, condemning them even while he praises Tertullian in general as an instance of the style defined by Augustine. Whatever the origin of these "strong lines," two qualities in them stand out. Their chief element is either a metaphor comparing a thought or a spiritual entity to a concrete object, or it is a paradox; and they are thus immediate instruments of dialectic, of symbolic dialectic as in general Bonaventura defined it. And they have a brevity and concentration which drives that thought home, leaving no room for extraneous amplification. They were therefore particularly fitted to express two central Christian realities: the essential paradox of Christianity, God in man, the finite from infinitude; and the symbolic character of the Bible, of nature, of the arts and sciences, of thought itself. The obscurity which sprang from their extreme concentration seemed, at least in Donne's age and to those of like mind, to befit the difficulty and darkness which attend the ascent to those mysteries of thought which are open only to the few. The difficulty in calling forth intellectual effort might also be held to create pleasure, as Augustine had held. What came to be considered their roughness may have been due in part to a refusal to distract attention or dilute thought by the concinnities, chiefly perhaps to an imitation of common speech patterns, in place of using the great conventionalized rhythms, by men concerned only with the truth, a concern such as led Augustine to prefer vulgar Latin syntax, idioms, and diction to the majestic speech of the great classical Latin writers. One may recall here Augustine's remark on the Biblical translator who deliberately stayed his hand from an easy scheme of sound. They should also be considered as examples of the high style as Augustine conceived it, thought quickened by emotion. Crashaw's single-lined paradoxes and ejaculations are one perfect type of the strong line.[17]

When Donne's poetry was taking shape, religion was not his subject, and in him the strong line is extended and complicated by many forces, intellectual, emotional, and literary. The essential paradox had been subtilized not only to express the

relations of the seen to the unseen, but to record the troubled
suspension of each particular human consciousness between two
worlds. In Donne this self-consciousness was exaggerated by
all the subtleties of his intellectual clarity amid intellectual confusion, his uncertainty of purpose. Among other literary influences, that of Spanish mysticism and Spanish *argutiae* must
be remembered, a development from the same sources as those
with which I have related Donne, but a development which
was already deeply differentiated and might exert an independent influence. Then too, Dante and his predecessors and
his circle had used "scientific" images.[18] And their point of
view and their themes helped to form the *Songs and Sonnets*.
But as Signor Praz has said, to read them and Donne together
is to feel almost shockingly the contrast between their single-
minded concentration upon the metaphysical realm and Donne's
doubt and self-absorption.[19] Love in the interval both had been
ungodded and had extended his prerogative as far as Jove. Meanwhile sophistic dialectic combat and Alexandrian wit-play had
become the fashion, and Donne used the sophistic paradox, the
animal poems, the emblems of the new Alexandrians.[20] But
R. C. Bald has shown in a study of the analogues to Donne's
Flea how that Alexandrian *jeu d'esprit* in erotics becomes in
Donne the focus to express an intense dramatic conflict of motive;[21] in like wise the arid paradox of Alexandrian and neo-
Latin humanist wit in praise of old age turns in Donne into the
relentless otherworldliness of his *Autumnal* to Mrs. Herbert.

Perhaps the literary influence which in temper and method
dominated all these turns of wit was the emblem. The emblem
had branched out from its earliest type, which presents a fairly
simple and obvious moral truth in fable, in parable, or in the
patent allegory of bestiary or of armorial symbol, to a later
kind which represented metaphysical truths in symbols that
use the world of appearance, the book of the creatures, to drive
our thoughts into theology and speculative cosmology. Such

emblems remind us of the nexus of the emblem with Egyptian hieroglyphics in the thought of this age, and of the fact that as early as Plotinus the connection had been made between symbolic thought, hieroglyph, and Platonic myth. But the roots of the emblem in the very sources of the theory of allegory and symbol are deeper than that. Signor Praz in his very important *Studies in Seventeenth Century Imagery* gathers together the statements on the theory of the emblem which make clear its direct and conscious connection with the theory of symbolic expression.[22] Erasmus in his preface to his treatise *On the Education of the Christian Prince* states succinctly the psychology underlying the theory of allegory, and in his epistle to Petrus Aegidius, cited by Praz, he defines the symbolic view of the metaphor: "Nihil autem aliud est παραβολή, quam Cicero collationem vocat, quam explicata metaphora." Emmanuele Tesauro reduces metaphysics, the book of the creatures, the starry heavens, to a book of heroical devices, witty symbols, *arguzie* and symbolic cyphers. Juan Eusebio Nieremberg in his *Occulta Filosofia* shows precisely how Alexandrian poetry with its figured verse and acrostics was in the emblems again linked to symbolic thought, though he puts the cart before the horse in finding in emblem literature the type for his own imagining that the world is a panegyric of God. And Gracian in his defense of the conceit and of figurative wit (*agudeza*) makes explicit the connection of the emblem with Ambrose and with Augustine. Giulio Cesare Capaccio in his *Trattato delle Imprese* traces out the theory of the relation of the hieroglyphs to the *Cabbala* and observes that the sole doctrine of the nature of animals and plants, gathered from Pliny or Albert is but common and trivial; if it is to make an *impresa* of perspicacious wit, it must appeal to the intellect and must be connected with the philosophy of a Plato or a Chrysippus. In general, the collection of emblems, which had been at the start the epitome of the doctrine of its day in ethics, in courtly manners and feel-

ing, in aesthetic theory, now became the compendium of philosophical and theological instruction. Emblems even took on a
further distinctive character, germane to their origins. They
were no longer intended merely or primarily to teach in the
ordinary sense of that word. They were instruments of contemplation, as is strikingly illustrated in the emblem of the eye
of God which Nicholas of Cusa sent along with his *Vision of
God* to the brethren who desired of him instruction in contemplation. It is for this philosophical geometry, whether of the
personal and secular life, or later of religion, that Donne used
the emblem. Mr. Hughes has shown the relation between
Donne's famous compass image and a Plantin title-page emblem, and the traditional character of that image has been
further shown by Mr. Lederer. Eleanor James has shown in an
unpublished thesis that the images which Donne names emblems in a number of his poems, as well as in some sermons, are
to be understood with specific reference to emblem techniques
and in the context of emblem literature.[23] And an increasing
number of articles is gathering parallels between Donne's symbols and analyses and those to be found in the emblem books.
Whether the emblem books are Donne's source, or he and they
and other poetry which drew on them are alike compendia of
older symbolism, does not here matter. But in Donne the emblem does not remain a mere statement of truth or even a mere
instrument for contemplation. Any specific emblem may have
been suggested to his imagination by the illustrations in the
emblem books and treatises. But his images are integrated with
the whole broad system of symbolic thought. In his mind, however, the symbolic science of the Middle Ages is itself modified
by the play of his mind over conflicting systems of thought and
the contrast between the values in which he has himself grown
up and those of the world into which he has cast himself adrift
from his moorings to make his way. It is modified no less significantly by a general shift in the emphasis of thought; by the

self-awareness, sometimes self-absorption, which arose from Renaissance stress on the individual consciousness, a stress apparent both in the form of Reformation insistence on saving faith and in renewed neo-Platonic awareness of man as the sole voice of nature rendering thanks to God for all creation. Thus in Donne the emblematic demonstration has not merely to lead our thought from sensible appearance to spiritual reality, but it has to lead us from outward fact to an individual's awareness of it; and it must express further the emotion a man feels when he finds two irreconcilable worlds impinging on his consciousness, or experiences how imperfectly he can immerse himself in either realism or idealism. Perhaps *imprese,* close kin of the emblem, which had early been used as symbols of personal condition and emotion, led the way to this use of the emblem. In the *Songs and Sonnets* these emblem-like images are infinitely complex and supple in their mediation between thought and feeling. In the religious and other later poems they are more traditional and rigid.[24] It is true that though I insist upon the fact that these *jeux d'esprit* could become such serious instruments of thought and emotion, in their very nature they tempted to restlessness and vanity of wit a mind not perfectly single or directed; they and the atmosphere in which they flourished helped to give to Donne's poetry the exaggeration of its wit and obscurity, the shrillness of the empty surprise with which some of the poems end. They are no less for that the expressive instrument of his most intense and piercing insights.

And if we are still inclined to give undue weight to the new philosophy in producing the seriousness of Donne's greatest poetry in contrast to his more flippant verse, despite Mr. Hughes's just estimate of the relation of his experience of science to the religious and mediaeval ground of his imagination, we should recall that symbolic thought in Hugh, Bonaventura, Ficino is itself scientific so far as the concepts of scientific method possible to their day allowed of science as we now think of it. Hugh clearly recognized the place of physics in the structure of thought. There can be no doubt that Donne's imagination was deeply affected by the science of the turn of the century. Whoever has seen the drawing of the brain and spinal cord in the great plates of Jan van Calcar for Vesalius' *Anatomy,* recently reprinted from the original blocks, or whoever knows contemporary medical works, with all their detail of color and form, as Don Cameron Allen has searched them out, will feel that here certainly is the inspiration for Donne's image of the sinewy thread. He will so, at least, unless he happens to recall the image the physician Ficino uses to illustrate God's love and provision for the world: the analogy that there is found in animals a certain nerve near the nape of the neck which whoever draws so moves all the members of the animal that each is moved by its proper motion; and with a like touch, writes Aristotle in his *Liber de Mundo,* are the members of the world moved by God. Or unless he happens to have stumbled upon the fact that early physiology actually believed the hair to grow upward from the brain, a physiological notion which Tertullian cites as the ground for some men's belief that the soul clings to the body for some time after death. Indeed, if one could always in speaking of Donne and science use the Latin term *scientia,* one would be helped to remember how closely the two, science and *scientia,* lay side by side in his mind. Despite the shock the "new philosophy" brought, it was still related to Platonism; and Galileo would still speak of *filosofia* as "written in the great book which stands here continually open before our eyes (I mean the universe)," though he believed it could not be read without the mathematics of Greek science, even that mathematics which might build the King of France's forts.

As I have already said in the preceding chapter, Mr. Croll has suggested that the Senecan movement in style or the development of Attic prose passed from prose into poetry, and in particular that it should be considered in relation to Donne.

The parallels in style and aim between that and the "strong-lined" movement, and the collateral connections between the two are manifest. But as I do not know of any contemporary comment which connects Donne with the Senecan movement, I have not made any attempt to find a way to test whether the heritage is direct or is collateral only.[25]

"Strong lines" are then a mode of thought which excludes further ornament or tropes or elocution, though they need not conflict with or reject patterns of sound. In Donne's poetry paradoxes and subtly analyzed figures are not only the stuff of his thought, but they are also the fables which unify it, the amplifications which give it power over the imagination. In the *Songs and Sonnets* and in the great religious poems, the dramatic themes and the emotion prevail over and control the dialectic which analyzes them. In the *Elegie on the Death of Prince Henry* considered simply as a poem for our delight today, the frigid theological discussion of faith and reason dominates the treatment of Henry's death; and the framework of that discussion is only harshly and meretriciously amplified by the inventions dealing with Henry and with Donne's share in grief. The deepest poetic reality is the prayer. But it was the lines on Henry and the elaborateness of the figures which, in the view I infer to have been Donne's, made his verses a poem.

Perhaps the symbolic method came easier to Donne because he had not the humanist's trust in beauty. The form of a poem was never for him primary. It was not for him, as for Scaliger, in itself an absolute element of the poem; nor, as for Lionardi, was the action a reflection in nature of ideal truth, reaching sensuous embodiment in image and description. His expression therefore does not, despite his defense of eloquence, aim at sustained splendor. His ground for rejecting the Pantheon is obvious. His diction too has nothing of mere beauty or of suggestiveness, save as a single word may invoke several conflicting philosophical concepts, and thereby arouse a widening circle of concern in us. Only the most direct, usual, nervous language will transcribe his thought. Epithets, which belong to such neo-Platonic schemes as those of Lionardi or Scaliger, have no place in it. His phrasing is usually in the idiom of speech, never in that of the well-filed line. Phrasing and music move directly with the ordonnance of thought and emotion, and the phrasing takes on just so much formal organization, just so much figure of sound, as will bring out this ordonnance. Wordplay in Donne is also dialectic rather than rhetorical, though sometimes it represents no more than the witty joke for God's sake. I refer my reader for parallels back to the passages in the last chapter from Tertullian and from St. Bonaventura, and to the examples cited in notes to that chapter. He may also consult examples of Spanish *argutiae* conveniently given in Praz. Repetition of word, on the other hand, Donne uses in a scheme of words or *schema verborum* to give grandeur and emotional energy to the thought, as in the opening of the *Elegie* or in the *Anniversaries*. Donne cited such a scheme from St. Bernard, as I have noted earlier, to justify his own use of similar ones in sermons. His great preference for it over other forms for heightening his style ought to be related immediately to St. Augustine's discussion of rhetoric, and to the emphasis which the rhetoric of Augustine's youth put on those schemes, so that to the end they came readily and functionally to Augustine's tongue just as still more exaggerated schemes came to the tongue of Tertullian. So also when Donne speaks of "height of metaphors and other figures" in justifying an appeal to the imagination, he implies a view of the high style akin to Augustine's and far from that which conceived of the highest style as the most ornamented.

The qualities of Donne's elegy are further defined for us by the other elegies which must be associated with it. With Donne's among the "surrepted" elegies in the third edition of Sylvester appeared several others which have a close connection with his in content and method, and which throw important light upon his point of view, his program and method, and his probable influence at least in shaping the common thought of his group. Sir Edward Herbert and Sir Henry Goodyere were so closely connected with Donne in friendship that we might almost certainly infer that he and they had discussed together the aims and methods of poetry, even if we had not Jonson's reported evidence that in this particular elegy Donne vied with Herbert. The character of their poems bears out the inference. With them also belong by their quality and method Cyril Tourneur's lament and that of Henry King.

Herbert's elegy is closely parallel to Donne's in its development of its subject, which is the consideration of Prince Henry as the soul of the world, interwoven with a metaphysical speculation on the nature of the world. But though Herbert shares with Donne the wish to reject the mere traditional elements and form of lament and to make his poem a speculative study, he is not an Augustinian, and his poem is not, like Donne's, contemplative as well as philosophical. It is significant that he begins with a question and not with a prayer. Within these limits, his rhetoric and expression parallel those of Donne. His deliberate statement of thesis in his opening line is like Donne's opening in its formal ordonnance. Like Donne, he chooses the stripped, analytical or emblem-like image to bring together and figure forth complex metaphysical questions. But the singular purpose for which Donne had perfected the emblem image is not in Herbert; he does not bring together the planes of metaphysics and the interior life, and he is in his poem more concerned with simple questions than with their relation to each other in a theory of knowledge. Hence his images, since they lack complex substance to express, tend to become merely ingenious.

Sir Henry Goodyere follows the same program, with less of literary play than Herbert, with perhaps more insight into the depth of Donne's conception of expression and logic than Herbert, though with less of natural literary virtue. His elegy is built upon the essential questions asked by so many of the elegies, the question whether such a grief and such goodness can be expressed, the larger paradoxical question whether we ought rather to consider our grief or his happiness. These considerations are elaborated and subtilized in a series of circling minor questions, answered by lawyer's argument or by the methods of *sic et non*. In these details there is much mere exaggeration of wit from which the whole is saved by the fact that each question is resolved by reference to a theological, metaphysical, or Biblical parallel, creating a texture of seriousness in the whole, a sense of the eternal world dominating the temporal. Thus in lines 21 to 26 his inability to express his grief is dissolved by the parallel that the sinner's grief at his inability to grieve is itself some token of grace, and the formalistic consideration of Henry as a soul or pattern of the world is in a degree saved from triviality by the context of the whole. The dominant invention which binds the parts together into a poem is an anatomizing of the relation of the poem itself to the experience it would express—a theme which reminds us at once of Donne's *Triple Fool*. This invention opens and closes the poem with question and resolution in lines 1 to 4 and lines 61 to the close. The larger issue of grief and joy is resolved within the figure of this invention, the elegy dispelling grief by preserving within its column those beauties which made Henry the pattern of our world. The emblematic character of the structure and of the logic of the poem is further illustrated in its detail, as, for instance, in lines 33 to 38. The poem is conventional in theme as we should never find Donne. Yet without anything of Donne's devotional passion, the verses do, like Donne's lines, by the genuine seriousness of their metaphysical consciousness, digest their own theatricality.

Among all the other elegies, Cyril Tourneur's stands with those of Herbert and Goodyere as closest to Donne's.[26] I shall therefore speak of it here before saying anything of G. G., who was also among the "surrepted" elegists. To understand the significance of this elegy fully, it is worth looking at an earlier poem of Tourneur's. In 1609 he had written a funeral poem upon the death of Sir Francis Vere. This poem cannot be too exactly compared with his later poem on the death of Prince Henry; rather it is in the tradition of Surrey's lines on Wyatt. For it must be remembered that a plain type of elegiac portrait, paralleling the character portrait in the funeral sermon, is very different from a royal elegy; and although a type of poem very common in the seventeenth century, it belongs outside the type we are considering. Yet to have in mind the plain moral lesson of Tourneur's lines on Vere illuminates by contrast what he did with his *Griefe on the Death of Prince Henrie.* Without anything of the special language of eulogy and without formal adornment, the earlier poem is a character study of Vere's virtue as a soldier, a virtue achieved through self-mastery. Vere was the pattern of a perfectly ordered and serious mind; and that ordering is described with the scholar's or the moralist's seriousness by Tourneur. His diction and phrasing are plain, direct, colloquial. The poem is akin to Jonson's poetry in moral tone and in fundamental idiomatic plainness of expression, though Tourneur does not try the formalized couplet which Jonson was already on the way to perfecting. In ethical substance, Tourneur's poem on Henry is an enlargement of the theme of the Vere poem. The praise of virtue is now set, however, in a broader context of spiritual drama. The poem plunges at once into a dramatic attack upon the actual world seen in that eternal light which the disaster of such a loss sheds upon it; in short, the poem is a *meditatio mortis,* followed by the personal corollary so important in the religious life of the age, the assertion that Henry died well.[27] Such a virtuous man is the center of well-being in the state. Old men grieve especially for him, for they had looked to him to guard their children when they were gone. Yet Henry did not die young, for only in those minutes that we give to virtue are we truly said to live as men. He loved arts and arms, and they will preserve his memory; if any painter who saw Henry draw an Alexander hereafter, his best imaginations will be so possessed with the remembrance of Henry that he will make the picture like him.

In throwing upon the moral reflection of his poem the light of metaphysical and dramatic contemplation, Tourneur is clearly in the same line as Donne, and the ordonnance, the abrupt prayer-like opening thesis and the following organization, relate form as well as substance to Donne: "Good *Vertue* wipe thine eyes. Looke up and see!" There are some who still carry on dancing. Was not Henry inclined to pleasures? Yes, but to pleasures fixed all above, of the sort that leave no repentance and do not waste one. Even his sickness was a pleasure to him, since he knew where it was taking him. Arts are so discouraged by his going

> That they would all leave *studie* and decline
> From *Learning;* if those *Naturall* and *Divine*
> Perswading *Contemplations,* did not leade
> The *One* to *Heaven,* the *other* to the *dead* ...

Tourneur's treatment of ethics is simpler than Donne's, and less metaphysical; and he is objective in his contemplation where Donne is concerned to assure the full participation of his own soul in the universal thought he contemplates. As a result, Tourneur's poem does not abound in paradox or emblematic figure, and his whole statement is more simply rational than that of Donne. But the resemblance to Donne in the organization and syntax of lines such as 103 and the following will be immediately felt. This is the passage which describes most directly the drama of man's suspension in two worlds. The poem also resembles Donne in two other points of expression. The opening lines use the scheme of repetition which Donne had used in the

Anniversaries. Then the rhythm of the couplet is also suggestive of Donne, the swing of the line over to the following line and the early caesura imposing on the verse the excited rhythm of speech. If we compare the whole ordonnance and rhetoric of the poem with the formal literary invention and pattern, and with the decoration that we find in many of the other elegies such as Drummond's or as Chapman's on the one hand, and on the other if we compare it with Tourneur's own earlier elegy and with the simple pattern of reflection in Davies' elegy on Prince Henry, which I shall consider presently, it will be seen clearly that Tourneur's poem to a degree parallels Donne's literary design and techniques.[28]

Henry King, the future bishop and friend of Donne, in 1612 just twenty years of age, besides two Latin poems in *Justa Oxoniensum,* composed an English elegy which was published later in his collected poems.[29] In it he develops two points: the power of shock and loss to confound heaven and nature as at the doom, and the inability of such a grief to find words, since Henry's death takes the light from the world and ends that invention which is highest wrought by grief and wit. King's poem, like Donne's, is speculative in theme, dialectical in structure, plain in language; it is not a personal meditation, and the thought of this youth is naturally very much simpler than that of Donne. The wit is finest and most Donnian in the image, "O Killing Rhetoric of Death" which is paradoxically developed into a meditation on man's speechlessness.

In the poems of Webster and Chapman there are elements of thought and expression which seem to place them in the line of Donne.[30] But the form of these poems, if we follow Pope's advice and look to the whole, is quite different from Donne's elegy. All have many images that are emblematic, analytical, "scientific." Both Webster and Chapman are speculative. The macabre element in Webster and his dramatic focus of universalized feeling upon particular passing circumstance show him quickened as Donne was by that fresh attention to the *meditatio mortis* and to the paradox of man's nature which had become a general part of the religious revival of the age.[31] But these images, marked also by the diction which expresses them, are only a few among many elaborate and rich images in the poems of Webster and Chapman; and the reflections on death form only a part of the many motives by which the poems are amplified, not their central and controlling theme.

Webster like Tourneur develops the theme of virtue, but he is more conventional than Tourneur, and he does not give the same sense of devotional urgency to his lines: Henry was virtuous and rewarded virtue; the world is nothing, and only virtue is significant; he was glad to die, for he has the triumph of immortality; from that view Providence is vindicated. But if Webster's handling of moral ideas is less absolutely serious than that of Tourneur, he brings to them a richer play of his imagination over the surface of the world's pain and anguish. The nothingness of the world and the vindication of Providence are developed in two elaborate inventions, the first an apologue in condemnation of worldly pleasure, an allegory of the type which was a conventional Renaissance vehicle for Platonic-Stoic ethic; the second a long emblem comparing Prince Henry in his life and death to a crystal glass accidentally broken in the furnace and blown anew in a better form to be sent to the lips of some great prince. A third invention is an illustration from heroic history in which the Black Prince is made the type of Prince Henry, this last developed with macabre realism. Not only the imagery used to express these inventions but other figures, too, aim at rich and high elocution. There is no aureate diction; but such well-filed lines as "Death with dart and ebon spade," or "And angry Neptune makes his palace groan/That the deaf rocks may echo the lands moan," or "Let the speed excuse/The zealous error of my passionate Muse" savor of Elizabethan rhetoric. Many figures of analogy in the early lines

of the poem reflect a somewhat more contemporary fashion of
didactic poetry. The macabre and grim figures are "realistic."
They come out of the world which had deeply touched Webster's imagination; they are contemporary and drawn from the
materials and experience that he was dealing with freshly and
passionately in the drama; the complex glass emblem in which
Webster embodies his reflection on Henry's translation to God
may well be an imitation of Donne; Webster's figure, however,
rather complicates and subtilizes the thought than expresses a
thought and feeling complex in themselves. We experience the
figure more fully than the idea. Music and schemes of thought
fall into and sustain the line movement, verse by verse, in patterns such as we find in the Elizabethan well-filed line, rather
than following the ordonnance of thought and sentence.

Chapman's grandiose and turgid poem unites metaphysical
speculation and literary humanism in a bold "imitation" of
grief for a death. Its two distinct parts are only artificially
brought together at the end. The first is an extended metaphysical lamentation, *a perturbatione,* as Chapman pedantically
sidenotes the grief on the state of the world and its renewed fall
into bestiality since Henry, the pattern of virtue and reason, has
been taken away in his youth, before his virtue has borne fruit.
Within this castigation of the world is included a formal praise
of Henry such as we have seen to be not uncommon in elegy.
The second section is the tears of the Muse, an elaborate *proso-
popoiea* describing the descent of the Fever and Henry's dying
days, closed by a dirge. This section, as Mr. Schoell has shown, is
taken with some few additions from an elegy of Poliziano; but
at the end, in place of Poliziano's description of the funeral
and of the young girl in death, Chapman returns to his castigation of the world.[32] The styles of the two sections differ widely,
and even the style of the first section itself is not all of a piece.
The conventional reflection on Henry's character and on the
world is embodied in neo-Platonic cosmology and psychology,

with a Christian view of Henry as a type after Christ of the perfect mind controlling the sense by which it is informed. This view is not far distant from that of Donne; but Chapman handles his theme very differently. His poem is much more discursive than Donne's and there is a distinctively humanist element in Chapman's insistence on the heroic pattern and in the tone of his discussion of fortune; purely in the tradition of courtly humanism, finally, is the passage on Henry's houses. The metaphysical and ethical argument is labored through a series of darkly stated figures of analogy, sometimes curiously wrought and elusive, yet not essentially emblem-like or symbolic in their intention and evolution; they are unfolded independently as ornaments and then applied flatly to the theme. These figures are noted by Chapman in his margin as similes, thus taking a place among the regular classes of amplification in rhetoric. That is to say, in the tradition of one set of rhetorics or poetics from Vinsauf on down, they constitute amplification (in poetic, *vice* invention in rhetoric) as distinct from the figures of elocution or ornament. They seem to me to show that Chapman in his poetic followed the old and essentially mediaeval theory of decoration. He is not touched at the core by his neo-Platonism and by the cult of darkness which is a part of that Platonism. Other examples of amplification in this poem not connected with darkness, are an *expostulatio,* an apostrophe, the designation of the moon, in a scientific figure, as Phoebe, and an elaborate simile drawn from the fall of Troy and containing a personification of the Furies. The diction is for the most part plain, Saxon, almost colloquial; yet as we should expect, there are a number of traditional poetic metaphors, personifications, compound epithets. The second section of the poem has all the classically elaborate imagery which it derives from its source and from its allegorical method, plus the ingenious amplification of detail common, as Miss Bartlett points out, to Chapman's translations, and indeed in some measure common to all Elizabethan and early seventeenth-century translations. At the close of the dirge, however, Chapman returns to heroic and to analogical figures.

In adding his moral and religious speculation to Poliziano's courtly dramatization of death, Chapman has, of course, destroyed the literary type and tone of the latter, without achieving any new synthesis. Chapman's epicede (he names it an *epicede* or funeral song, and perhaps thought of it as belonging to the class of ode rather than of elegy) is, like the first poems we looked at, not a unified poem, but an imitation of a number of inventions chosen from among many themes appropriate to death, and of ornaments whose number, boldness, and variety give it a high style.[33] This is true despite the neo-Platonic and moral episode which is so characteristic of Chapman. In general his strongly didactic nature prevents him from accepting implicitly the tone and the view of literature of Italian humanists such as Poliziano; yet on the other hand his philosophy is not so far reaching as to determine absolutely his theory of art and of expression as does Donne's. But at the same time it is clear that though most of Chapman's figures might be drawn from mediaeval and Elizabethan rhetoric books, reflecting Quintilian, the type of figures he uses in the metaphysical passage is due to a conception of style influenced by didactic or moral ideas: only by difficult speculation and only by darkening of the sensuous can one proceed on the philosophic way, and *argute* figures are therefore the becoming dress of speculation.[34] In Chapman's expression, then, and even more clearly in Webster's, one can see first a traditional classical view of decorum and the three styles. Then under the apparent miscellaneousness of imagery, one can trace a view in which didactic purpose, associating difficult and highly logical imagery with straining after metaphysical views, transforms the traditional rhetorical view. I have already referred to this conception of the genre of style in speaking of Drummond. Scaliger had said that different kinds of style, high, low, and mean, were used in the same poem in passages of different sorts. This idea now seemingly evolves under the influence of a half symbolic or allegorical view of style which transforms the idea of decorum.[35] In Webster, the character of the imagery and diction varies definitely with the type of substance it expresses; the mode of the imagery one might say is formally determined by the genre of the substance it clothes. Ethic uses allegorized myth or apologue and may use aureate diction and traditional schemes; metaphysic uses emblem-like or symbolic images, somewhat as Donne had developed them, with plain diction. We shall see further examples of this principle of symbolic style in both the later collections of elegies.

The infelicitous elegy of William Browne of Tavistock might well have been considered among those in the Spenserian tradition, but its eclecticism puts it more fittingly here.[36] For though it is predominantly in the mythological and allegorical tradition, and though it uses an elaborate stanza probably suggested by Spenser's *November,* it is essentially a rhetorical medley. Hope, Envy, Comfort gather to express man's endurance and his suffering; Helicon and the Muses, imps of memory, are called upon, proverbs abound, and Thetis raves; but from quite different quarries come the classical example of Caligula, the labyrinth and clue figure, an emblem though without symbolic content, and the churchyard conventions. Browne has followed the teaching of imitation at its most mechanical. The poem of Heywood carries it to an even more uninspired level, only its abundance of figures and the fact that it is in *ottava rima* giving it any claim to be called verse. King James, it may be noted, considered *ottava rima* a particularly solemn rhythm.

For Chapman and for a number of others the problem is to force speculative and moral themes into a distinctively poetic fiction or series of inventions. Sir John Davies in his elegy attacks his theme directly in a reflective poem that does not seek to rise to special invention until it elaborates a grief in the last section.[37] In impersonal and abstract terms, he meditates on Henry's departure from a world which by his Godlike character he transcended, discusses the ethics of kingship and of the ideal character in describing Henry, and decries the mutable world. His analysis is theological, dealing with such themes as essence and intelligence in God and man; his expression bare of images except occasional analogies, not complex or highly wrought, but full of such paradox focused in play upon word as belonged by long tradition to such themes. At the close of this long philosophical discussion, he enters upon a grief, chiefly notable for hyperbole; Saint James's palace is dedicated to spiders and bats, the death-day to darkness, the passion of grief rightly overwhelms reason as at the death of Christ. In expression this passage is chiefly heightened by an increase in the plays upon word, which do not now, however, support paradox, but are in artificial figured speech.

Davies' poem lacks structure, and it is not on the whole transformed by any ordered style. The quatrains are end-stopped, but they are sustained by no more positive metrical principle, no numerosity, no integration of metrical form and thought. The ethical paradox that passion here may rightly overwhelm reason is the nearest approach to fashionable wit. But the lament at the close and its figures of sound are chiefly what make of a reflective poem a courtly elegy. This is imitation at its most naïve, by a poet to whom such poetic invention cannot have meant much. At home in purely reflective or didactic poetry, Davies did not see how to give his reflections organic form within an elegy, nor to cast them into a suitably high poetic speech; and Ben Jonson had not yet supplied the model for such rhetoric. For this type of poetry a far-reaching discipline was yet necessary, in those forms which Rome had made especially her own. It would arise with a deeper sense of the genre in poetry, as yet fully understood by only a few writers, and not in all fields of poetry. It would arise only when, however much the moral end of poetry might continue to be stressed, men had a more distinct sense of even a didactic poem as a self-existent work of art. This sense I think Fletcher and Drummond clearly had. Donne also had penetrated to the conception of a poem as a work of art having a distinctive structure and being an imitation of an object or subject; but he had not an essential trust in beauty or in the artist's power of direct and imaginative re-creation of life. His compelling idea by this time was the theological one embedding within it a long Platonic tradition that the mind's sole concern was its ascent to speculation. To this end his artistic meaning was always subordinate, and from this view his style stemmed, though he, like his forerunners, took in much of rhetoric by the way.

The "elegy" of G. G. (who is identified by Sir Herbert Grierson as probably George Gerrard, Donne's friend) in Sylvester's collection of elegies is important not as an elegy, but because of G. G.'s statement of his literary aim, which forms the main body of the elegy, asserting his own disinterestedness and castigating the insincerity which allows others to flaunt their wit.[38] This contemptuous scorn of poetic sentimentality, so different in its self-dependent intellectualism from the "apathy" for which a Goodyere or a Davies pleads, is an attitude which will become as central in the later seventeenth-century temper as Goodyere's stoicism. We shall find the same attitude more dryly and narrowly expressed by Cleveland writing on Edward King. The poem then goes on to express Henry's quality in a dull phoenix image.

It is not easy to estimate the bearing of this brief critical statement out of the context of any other critical or creative work by its author. In his appeal from the common interested motives of grief and from the vanity of the wits to a more universal and serious view of Henry's death, G. G. shows something of Donne's temper. In his own style he is distinctly Donnian in the paradoxical boldness of deliberate aposiopesis; Donnian also in his burlesque punning protest against verbal ingenuity; and in his even violent directness of diction and syntax. *Curious* I take to imply an attack upon fashionable poetic elaboration, invention, imagery, diction; the meaning seems the same as in Donne's phrase, "So if your curiosity extort more than convenient ornament." *Wits* would not at this time necessarily apply to what we now call the witty school of poetry, but more generally to people who pretend to special energy of mind, though the lines on striving to outstrip each other's brain and the ironic pun seem to point to the witty school in so far as they in their turn were becoming conventional. Our reading of G. G.'s protest against insincerity ought to recall the parallel protest of the Pléiade against Petrarchanism. His own style and temper, however, so far as we can judge, place G. G. with Donne and not with the humanists. It is interesting for the history of critical comment later in the century that G. G. in his charges against the poetic coxcombry fashionable in 1612—charges which seem to include all forms of poetic ornament—uses the very language which will later be used on behalf of formal and ornamental poetry and of rational expression. But then the protest will be directed against realism and witty ingenuity imitative of Donne and of the neo-Latin epigrammatists and of Marinism, when these in their turn have become the fashionable formalism.

The remaining poems on Henry are not formal elegies. A few deserve comment because they represent a taste which reappeared in later elegies. Sir William Cornwallis wrote a simple reflective poem, in the tradition of Latin epigram and elegiac verse.[39] Its theme is the conflict of reason and passion, the subject with which Cornwallis is also chiefly concerned in his essays. Probably the author might have been influenced in the choice of form by Jonson, whose special friend he was, but his style has nothing of Jonson's formal order. Mr. Holland's *Elegie* is a reflection—really a series of epigrams—which suggests that the

Jesuit type of epigram, or the witty point familiar to us in the character of the day, was rising into popularity.[40] Among the Latin poems, we find a number in the elegiac and epigrammatic tradition.[41] Among the English poems there are several slight imitations of the Greek epitaph.

Whether we look at Drummond's elegy and other poems in the Spenserian and humanist tradition, at Donne and the theological school, or at "imitators" and rhetoricians like Chapman and Webster, we notice an effect upon literature which does not arise from literature itself. Two inner forces break and transform the old model of the elegy, the pastoral that is, or create new patterns: preoccupation with religion and philosophy, and a deeply troubled sense of unrest and disorder in society. The tradition of art, we are reminded again and again, is handed on through the forms of art, whether by a lisping child or by a genius, but these forms do not sustain themselves when deprived of emotions they are fitted to express. And if the soul can learn to sing only by copying monuments of its own magnificence, it must, when its time is ripe, turn to the holy city of Byzantium for its models. And it will, by its own vision, transform both what it brings and what it finds there.

The philosophical views and the religious passion of Drummond, as of Donne, end in a contempt of the world before which ultimately the claims of even the most ideal city of the earth wither. But yet through almost all the elegies runs an opposing desire not to meditate death but to concentrate on solving the problems of the active life. The solution is sought in the ethical triumph of reason over passion; but such a triumph may be sought on widely different planes. And in many of the poems, the temper of the solution is closer to a dependence upon Stoic poise and judgment than to Christian conversion, such a feeling as will in the end come to depend on human order more than on divine. And to the models of poetry which had in the past expressed such human order, to classical models rather than to metaphysical, mid-seventeenth-century poetry will turn.

Chapter Four

IUSTA EDOUARDO KING

As WE SHOULD EXPECT, Spenser with his Renaissance and humanist Christian Platonism, Donne with his theology, his dialectic, and his troubled devotion, dominate all that is most significant in the Prince Henry elegies. Spenser, pre-occupied with beauty and with art as basic human intuitions, as primary modes of inspiration, adjusted his moral aspiration and his religion to that vision of poetic creation; and he transmits an influence so unified in its single artistic form that in the age which follows, either his form of thought and expression is transmitted as a whole or, when Platonism fails, it fades entirely. The force of Donne, however, is divided. Donne's essential art form is subordinate to his theology, to his religious passion, to his direct intellectual activity. The accepted Renaissance view of poetry as residing first in the elaborate development of plot and expression triumphed over Donne's conception of poetry, even though his forms of expression exerted great influence. His theology, his critical intellectual force, his passion continued to influence those who followed him, either as a single complex force or separately, according as other men shared or lost something of his vision of the world, as they maintained or abandoned the tradition of thought which had created him. Ben Jonson, being out of England, wrote no elegy for Prince Henry; nor was his general influence yet felt in 1612. Humanist and not theologian, rational and not sentimental, devout but not other-worldly, with strict limits to the scope of his philosophical curiosity, critical intellectualist, but with absolute trust in art and in its forms, he will exert on the next generation a force that is reconciling but, on the whole, narrowing.

It must be remembered, in comparing *Iusta Edouardo King*[1] with the elegies on Henry, that the poets who wrote on the death of Edward King were a limited Cambridge group, among whom, besides Milton, only Cleveland and Joseph Beaumont of the English elegists later rose to any pretension as poets. And even they at this time were, like most of the contributors, not more than twenty-two to twenty-five years of age. Besides *Lycidas,* theirs are the only English poems which show any command of substance or style. The others, by and large, serve only to illustrate the literary fads then current at Cambridge. Even so, they bear some witness to the failure of the larger humanism. The general narrowing of vision, in their age illustrated in only one of its aspects—that of men's attitudes toward death—perhaps determined their choice of forms. I shall consider first the minor poets and versifiers, and speak of *Lycidas* against the background they form.

Joseph Beaumont has absorbed certain elements of the religious view and of the intellectual emphasis expressed by Donne into a formal and conventional poem, in which Donne's spirit is modified not only by the classical discipline and smoothness of Ben Jonson but by that blend of Latin temper and Anglican piety manifest in Jonson and central in mid-century orthodoxy. Cleveland is dominated by rationalism, by negating absence of religious feeling, and by repression of personal feeling. But he erects the intellectualistic elements of the style of which Donne is the great example into a clear-cut convention. There are some poems besides *Lycidas* in the Spenserian tradition. But there is no reason why at this date we should consider them first; and we can survey the other poems more quickly if we make essential definitions by looking first at those of Beaumont and Cleveland.

Beaumont joined a cosmological Platonic-Christian consolation which is essentially a meditation *de contemptu mundi* to a portrait of King as a type of virtue. Such a union, as we have already seen, is in direct continuity with the thought of earlier elegies. In tone, as in pattern, his poem is close to Anglican funeral sermons. His philosophy and religion, though often Donnian or Anglo-Catholic in their terms, lack personal passion. His very great emphasis on moral psychology relates him both to Spenser's Platonism and to the temper of Jonson and his sons. King, he says, was a perfect reflection of virtue. Why, since his art was perfect, did he seek the parts and graces of the arts (see Webster's elegy on Prince Henry), *the arts being only the means by which the world below strives to attain that perfection of nature which it reflects,* and since all that can be learned here is nothing? He was the pattern of self-controlled virtue and discretion, one in whom reason deliberately controlled the heart. He had the gift of friendship and was willing to point out a friend's faults. He was dutiful to his parents and to the large circle of his Mothers. Why then was he taken? He was an intelligence which needed a sphere, and heaven had need of him.

Before we consider Beaumont's ideas and attitudes further, however, we must understand the general aesthetic form of his poem, for that delimits the substance, as probably he intended that it should when he chose it. He opens with an expression of grief and closes with a formal consolation, and in this ordonnance his poem is shaped, like *Great Britans Mourning Garment* earlier, by the kind of pastoral elegy, though it is not a pastoral allegory. In place of the lament of nature more familiar to us, Beaumont describes in intimate and personal terms how word of the loss first came to him, a motive equally common in neo-Latin eclogue in Italy. The simple and poignant tone of this description suits well with the Roman temper of that ideal virtue to describe which Beaumont makes his principal theme. To this elegiac design, however, he has added the motive or invention of an allegorized myth, which is akin to the apologue in Webster's earlier elegy. In this myth he follows the common practice of Renaissance Platonism in using allegorized myth to make art the expression of truth; he is also thoroughly characteristic of himself in doing so. In all his poetry, Beaumont belongs to the school of allegorists and emblematists; and his definition of art as the means by which the sublunar world strives to imitate that Nature which it reflects might be taken as a summary of much in Lionardi's Platonic treatise.

The two elements of Beaumont's design, lament and allegory, are carefully and formally balanced, and his style has a Jonsonian classicism which is harmonious with the design and temper of his poem. It is restrained, lucid, and perspicuous, with succinct qualifying epithets and with no adjectives of sentiment such as one finds in writers of the school of Spenser.[2] His meter is the classical lyric tetrameter couplet, which is so distinctively a seventeenth-century form, and of which he had a clear model in Jonson and in the French poets. It is end-stopped, with strong medial caesura, firm half-line phrasing, and strong rhyme. Phrasing and versification, in fact, illustrate perfectly the principles set forth by Ronsard and by Scaliger. In the general aesthetic form of his poem, then, classicism and reason prevail.

The ideas and emotion accord with this artistic purpose and temper. The poem expresses a view of death seen in the larger theological light; then it defines the ethical consequences, both individual and social, which, in the *via media,* spring from that view of death—ethical consequences which, rather than any contemplative meditation, become the center of our thought, since we are placed in the sublunar world to lead the active life. But there is room also for intense individual devotion, at least evoking echoes of otherworldliness, as well as for active virtues. The poem unites with its metaphysical statement of the consolation a strong sense of the interior life in a way which suggests the influence of Donne or of Donne's models, though Beaumont has nothing of Donne's scope and dramatic tension. In referring to Donne, however, we must not forget the general influence at Cambridge of Laudianism and of the *devotio moderna*. For these devotional metaphysical elements of the poem, and for these alone, the special instrument of expression is the emblem-image, together with something of paradox and of wordplay, as in lines 55 and following. We have already seen examples in Webster and in Drummond to show that the emblem-image—an object drawn from the creatures or the arts and sciences and analyzed dialectically rather than described imaginatively—was becoming recognized as decorous for material which united the interior life with a metaphysical frame of reference. It was not only the instrument frequently used by George Herbert and other lyric poets, as by Donne before; it was chosen also, for instance, by Benlowes for his *Theophila,* with so disastrously little sense of distinction as to whether he intended his poem to be a philosophical analysis, a resumé of Platonic thought, or rather a series of meditative ejaculations towards the contemplative life. We may pause a moment to note further the contrast of this choice by Benlowes with Henry More's determination to use outmoded Spenserian expression when he wishes to add the force of poetic inspiration to a reasoned account of the philosophy of Plotinus.

Though Beaumont's emblem–image perhaps derives from Donne, who first in England fully transmuted emblem and paradox into the thought-laden and passionate forms which they wear in him, Beaumont, like George Herbert, makes no cult of the obscure or the difficult in his analytical images.[3] The element of wit game which is so important in Donne was not to any such extent a part of the background of Herbert and still less of

Beaumont. Nor did they participate in that vast attempt at intellectual disintegration and reintegration which made doubt, obscurity, and complexity almost inevitable elements of Donne's expression, even had he had no mystery to express. They were less concerned with mystery too, for they were deeply shaped by the Anglican ideal of reasonable order. Beaumont does not strive at all to be original, but to be expressive and representative—classical. In the passage I have cited, the emblem image sits easily with the classical image of the "well-immured mind."

Other elements of the *devotio moderna* may best be seen in Beaumont's diction, which needs brief comment. It is prevailingly Latin or French in that it defines the typical in general and traditional terms. But where the thought demands, there can be such a high concretization of the abstract as has been termed characteristically "metaphysical" in, for instance, a phrase like "And he/Be expectations treasurie." Besides the emblems themselves the most heightened passage in the poem is the allegorized myth (lines 39-44). Though the incident is humanist in its myth, its diction, like some of that in the previously cited passage, seems to draw from Marini; in this it resembles the diction of much of Crashaw, who was to be a very dear friend of Beaumont, and to be led by him to St. Teresa. There are, finally, several compounds which, seeing Beaumont's relation to Crashaw, we are tempted to derive, like similar diction in Crashaw, from "Sydnean showers."

I have dwelt so long on this quite slight poem because it illustrates so well the blending of Latin attitudes and of the Anglican ideal of social order with personal religious intensity. The religious intensity is real, but the character of it is at the same time deeply modified and limited by the concentration of the intellectual struggle and the narrowing of its scope. Beaumont's substance is well reflected in his form. Donnian intelligence and Latin reason together have triumphed over Spenser in imagery, diction, meter; but just as the Donnian psychology has been moderated by the whole of mid-century Anglicanism, there is present of Donne's style only what could be absorbed into the formal Renaissance ideal of poetry, now that that ideal has taken on so rational a tone and that neo-Platonism has been so chastened of its pagan exuberance, of its mediaeval schematic elaboration, and of its ascetic passion.

John Cleveland was not interested in either the speculative or the introspective aspects of the earlier seventeenth-century world. And his sense of order rested on intellectualism without the twin foot of personal piety. His poem offers neither consolation nor exemplification of virtue. This grief, he says, as G. G. had said of Prince Henry, is too great to speak in poetry. King was a very learned man. These thoughts Cleveland develops without play of idea or of sensibility, but with elaborate wit play. The elements of this wit play consist in an ingenuity of figure dependent upon verbal twist of meaning, but not symbolic or interpretive, figures drawn from "science" and from the marketplace, plain language with some deliberate and mannered use of familiar diction, paradox and wordplay, harshness.[4] Despite the harshness, however, Cleveland shows the influence of the formal poetic then just gaining control. Paradox and wordplay are adjusted to the formal metrical pattern of stopped line and half-line. "So that," as Dryden's penetrating eye perceived, "there is this difference between his *elegies* and Doctor Donne's; that the one gives us deep thoughts in common language, though rough cadence; the other gives us common thoughts in abstruse language." Yet we may find in the abstruse language and the convention of wit something a little more significant than Dryden found. In an age from which the subtler analysis of the consciousness and of its integration with the world was fading, Cleveland's wit does yet afford a kind of play of sensibility; such a play as was still possible to an intellectualist conservative who had not given up his strong individualism.

The other English poems to King belong to that class of

rhetorical poetry and imitation exemplified by Chapman in his epicede for Henry, though they are very much more limited than Chapman in range of thought and in scope and boldness of invention. Most of the versifiers, indeed, might have selected their reflections from among a text-book list of appropriate themes such as that recommended by the Jesuit Pontanus in his digest of poetic. These reflections are, however, given an Anglican cast, both in themes selected and in the emphasis with which they are developed. They say about what is said in the minor elegies on Prince Henry. Thus they assert Providence, the beauty of King's character, the social ideal, the punishment of our sins by our loss of King. The emphasis is, however, significantly different from that in the Prince Henry poems. Henry King, Edward's younger brother, in his English poem stresses his brother's serene faith in an age of difficult and imperfect belief, and he and Samson Briggs voice fears of rising atheism. The fear is more emphatically stated than the answering assertion of Providence or than the definition of virtue, though in both Henry King's English and his Latin poems there is a warm personal feeling and a warm sense of the family as a center of virtue. In the highly-colored expression which clothes these reflections and is meant to render poetic not only the poems of King and Briggs but the others as well, that medley of imagery which we have already noticed in Webster, Chapman, and Browne advances towards chaos. For instance in one poem the reflection that it is no private man who seems to die but a well-ordered university, shoulders a reference to Phoebus as a close mourner in a sable hood of clouds. Parallels to heroic or classical models of character also abound.

But, though all sorts of images still persist, the advance in the fashion of the witty image is quite clear. This is not, however, to be ascribed to the influence of Donne or of symbolic thought in any large and serious sense, but to general and purely literary influences and tastes. Among the images in these poems there are several echoes of Donne; but on the whole in their type of development they follow the fashion of that neo-Latin epigram which had been so strongly influenced by the rhetoric of Ovid. Among the Latin poems of the volume are several such epigrams. This type of epigram, it will be remembered, had under various influences made its staple of the ingenious figure and of wordplay in a spirit quite different from that of Donne. The identity in sentiment and figure of many of the longer English poems with these epigrams is clear. And, indeed, both their stylistic device and their substance are pretty well described in the sections on epigram and elegy in Pontanus. It is worth keeping in mind that Buechler's digest of Pontanus had become rather widely popular as a school text book. "Too much of water hast thou, dear Ophelia." The fact that King died by drowning made it inevitable that all the changes should be wrung upon this concept; and the stream of Jesuit repentance literature with the Magdalen as its grand type figure made it equally inevitable that every physical element should become ingenious symbol. An example may be given from W. Hall, who uses several concepts used by Cleveland and who had probably seen Cleveland's poem, but who writes in a very different spirit. I summarize to spare citing at length.

There is no use in our weeping. You already have brine. Many treasures are buried in the sea, but King is the only real treasure there. He was a jewel too precious to bury in marble; it is buried in the casket of the ship's cabin. He was allowed to be buried in the sea lest we had worshipped at his grave or wept ourselves to death there. [At the close comes the only real reflection.] The setting sun hides his evening light in the ocean; the world does not know where he is "Till with new beams from seas he seems to rise"; so King's soul to no dark tomb withdrew by nature's common law but set in waves and will rise more glorious than the sun.

Such images serve to channel significant changes in attitude. The last image, resting ultimately on Biblical texts, goes as far

back as the early church fathers, and it is, one supposes, in them
not only a Biblical symbol but also a deliberate appropriation
and alteration of the familiar pagan image of Catullus. From
earliest Christian times it is perhaps the central image of the
immortality of the soul and the nothingness of the world,
popularized by Boethius, offered by St. Augustine to Petrarch
as a basic analogy. It may be noted also in these poems that
Stoic-Christian condemnation of grief gets momentarily overlaid by Jesuit-fostered floods of repentance. And this alteration
is but a sign of the further rejection in the poetry of the mid-
seventeenth century of paganism, of the pagan sympathy of
nature, and of the neo-Platonized myth which is so vital in the
pastoral elegy. With the loss of the pathetic fallacy the elegy has
lost the sense of man's share in the temporal life of nature; and
the elegist no longer expresses the natural man's first immediate
and profound response to the fact of death. The contrast between
man's final death and the returning life of nature is not indeed
lost sight of; but it is appropriated and altered even before it
can bring the reader a full sense of death; nature dies, but, we
may hasten to add, man arises. Catullus' image of the setting
and rising sun had been used once or twice in Italian pastoral
elegy. In these English poems, the re-arising sun becomes the
sole image to express the whole motive so common in pastoral
elegy of the comparison of man and his fate to the life of nature.
This fact may be due to the increasing popularity of the Latin
elegists, a popularity which in turn had its share in the craze for
the neo-Latin epigram. And this popularity rendered it once
more necessary to combat the materialism of the libertines as
the fathers had combatted it by an appropriation of their art and
symbol. The theme of the resurrection in the same faddist
epigrams often appears in another analogy only less popular
than the sun image, a series of witty figures on the soul as a
jewel.[5]

Something of Donne, chiefly his dialectic wit, is merged in

this craze for the epigram, as distinct echoes of him prove. But there is clear evidence that the severer moral strain in his expression and the deeper purpose of his wit were also kept sight of. This is shown in the lines of W. More, who, like G. G., states his attitude to poetry explicitly, an attitude which runs sharply counter to most of the poems. He rejects all the display of wit and learning, the Stoicism, the confusion that talks of King as mortal. He rejects all passion of grief. King lived well, knowing how to die, and his calm at the moment of death finds its type in Christ on the sea. The poem reflects an important strain in the thought of the age which does not elsewhere appear among the elegies; the condemnation of elaborate imagery and poetic invention as a form of passion. In the critical discussion of the day this condemnation was usually expressed as a mere secondary note in the condemnation of religious zeal or enthusiasm, both image-making and zeal being forms of a delusion by the imagination. The paradox and wordplay in More's own statement connect his poem with that of G. G. Evidently More did not regard such forms of expression as rhetorical displays of wit. Rather his use of paradox and wordplay, while he condemns figures, seems to me to show clearly that in one stream of thought of the age the play of mind in Donne was far from being regarded as ingenious wit in figure. Rather the term or the conception of "ingenious wit" was attached to *mythology* and personification as part of paganism and rhetoric. Donne was still the model of the revolt against such wit, as in lines 9 to 12.

From the rhetoric of these minor elegies on King Spenserianism has practically gone. R. Brown alone among the English poetasters attempts something in the tradition of the pastoral elegy. He writes a stanzaic poem with initial refrain and filled with mythological figures. His imagery, however, is of the witty type. His Latin poem is much more consistently classical. And indeed one may note purity and distinctness of type in the Latin poems as a whole.[6]

Of *Lycidas* I shall say only so much concerning its form and structure, concerning the significance of Milton's choice of that form and structure, and concerning the elements which constitute the poem as illuminate this study and may be illuminated by it.

All that Milton shared with Spenser in Christian Platonism and in their views of art carried him back in this as in his other poetry to the tradition of Spenser; and even had there been no example in Spenser, his entire humanist training made the choice of the pastoral elegy for him at this mature period of his art and thought as inevitable as the choice of the later forms of *Paradise Lost* and of *Samson Agonistes.* At the same time he brings to final realization not only the forms and attitudes of Spenser and the continental humanists but much of the social and religious feeling that struggled for artistic embodiment in the minor elegies we have been examining. The literary humanism of Milton's first elegy on his sister's child is as jejune in its imitation of motives and in its mingling of classical god and legend with Christian consolation as the naïvest of the elegies on Prince Henry, however far removed from them it is in the genius of its detail, and of the as yet unfocused passion out of which the detail springs. The growth of his view of art obviously contributed as much as the maturing of his thought to the fusion he achieved in *Lycidas.* To approach his thought through his conception of his art helps us to understand how he brought the elements together and how he focused them all on that beatific vision which had been from early Christian times and earlier still the mourner's central theme of meditation, and which, as Mr. Hanford has said, filled Milton's imagination from the days of his first elegies on college dignitaries.

In Milton's famous sentence on poetry in his tractate *Of Education,* the word *simple* I take to mean *simplex,* that is, of a single, living, and unified essence, an essence which in poetry immediately reflects Nature and the divine essence behind

Nature; not divided and analyzed as discursive reason divides. Hence he speaks of poetry as distinct from logic (not from rhetoric, except as rhetoric is the open hand of logic). Much in Spenser's allegory is a direct and dry embodiment in concrete symbols of elaborate speculative thought. It is not strictly "simple." With Milton this is never so, and this conception of Milton's of the simple nature of a poem is probably what guarded him from going too far in that kind of allegorization and focused him upon the imitation of life; it kept him to the great type forms of *Comus,* the pastoralism of *Lycidas,* the figures of Sin and Death. Perhaps we are closest to his decision when we read his words on mythology and symbolism in his academic exercise on the music of the spheres; for it is likely that the essential character of one's imagination in its apprehension of symbols takes shape in the fluid and sensitive years of adolescence. Milton there protests, it will be remembered, against either the literal interpretation or the literal allegorization of a figure which he regards as an imaginative intuition of truth, a symbolic myth. Milton's literal view of the Bible and reverence for the text of it, so different from Donne's schematic and symbolic view of it, no doubt helped form his attitude. To one who holds such a conception, the whole of life is evaluated with the poet's intensest insight, in every poem. But the metaphysic, and the thoughts which make it explicit, must emerge from the story and interpret it rather than themselves supplying the inventions for the poem. And this view is reconcilable with Aristotle's *Poetics* read in the light in which it is closest to Plato. *Sensuousness,* if taken together with simplicity, would involve not merely the exquisite pictures and patterns of sound, and the dramatic completeness of symbols, but the immanent presence of the spiritual or otherworldly meaning of the story in the world which is known to man first through his senses.[7] And *passionate* then means, I suppose, that the whole is seen in the light in which it appears to man's rectified imagination and to his will, both those of the protagonist and those of the poet, so that the subject is affected by the poet's feeling of value and also affects his readers through his imitation.[8] This total view of a poem as simple, sensuous, and passionate would both have contributed to Milton's understanding of the pastoral elegy as a poetic form and at the same time have derived in part from it. But the depth of Milton's Christianity and of the fresh Platonism which penetrated it would keep him from the formalism of Scaliger on the one side and from Scaliger's too simple moral didacticism on the other.

Into the ultimate reconciliations of thought and feeling embodied in *Lycidas* we cannot probe fully. Naïve but sensitive readers are not, I believe, troubled by the conflict of traditions and implications in the poem which has sometimes momentarily checked scholars; such readers simply accept the great contrasting waves of emotion through which the single meaning of the poem is developed and which are so perfectly embodied in its music. And this immediacy of communication is the sign of the completeness of Milton's unification of *Lycidas,* to be felt in the poem itself, if we understand the idea behind the form. And without exploring Milton's soul with the aid of new or old psychological concepts we may ask ourselves how Milton in his design balances the principal elements of thought and feeling obviously present in the poem. In this analysis it should never be forgotten that though Milton necessarily was conscious in his designing of the poem of the separate elements and though we shall have to separate them still further in order to identify them, his feeling is simple and organic. The cry which seems to close the naturalistic grief, the cry beginning, "for so to interpose a little ease," is in reality the deeper cry of religious desolation and is filled with the music of that cry. But the two elements of "pagan" naturalistic feeling and of religion are not ultimately opposed in Milton. For the delight in nature is not merely naturalistic. It expresses a religious sentiment, though one remote from Donne's habitual thought and feeling as these appear in his poetry. By Donne, the creatures, the arts, the sciences were chiefly felt as symbols, as objects of speculative thought. If he reveals their splendors in his sermons, it will not be the pansy freaked with jet; it will be usually that splendor of the remote, radiant, and ordered heavens so loved by Plotinus. But Milton, like Spenser and Marvell, reaffirmed the holiness of "day and the sweet approach of even and morn, and flocks and herds and human face divine" in themselves and in their direct power to reveal God to man and communicate to him the divine love and goodness.[9] Another humanistic element is the lament itself. The pastoral gives voice to a universal rhythm of grief in a concentrated way paralleling the statement of it in the ritual and ceremony of funeral: the shock of death, the grief which must be realized, the stilling of that grief. The elegy, in clothing this rhythm in an allegorical convention, makes use of the power of ritual to absorb man into the experience of the race, to detach him from the disproportion of the moment and draw him into that larger experience which he shares with all men. Thus the convention is made to reflect and embody a conception of harmony and of the mind's control over feeling.

But the grief which Milton expresses is wilder, and the question it asks is of far wider import than any which naturalistic Greece and Rome had expressed. And like Cicero's lament for his daughter, it can be stilled by no human ritual. Hence it is from the last and deepest unassuageable wave of grief that we are swept out of nature into the transcendent consolation. For within that last cry, "For so to interpose a little ease,/Let our frail thoughts dally with false surmise," is a passion more profoundly troubled than any classical sense of transiency and human loss. And as the lines go on, we can feel the outward fact of final loss becoming a symbol. In the Christian experience of death as it was early formulated, there are two griefs, the personal grief which kills, the grief of repentance leading to

God. In the loss of a young man, the question of Providence arises out of the question inevitably raised as to the meaning of that fell sergeant death; and the contemplation of the Judgment prepares the way for the contemplation of the Resurrection. The passage in *Lycidas* beginning with Orpheus and ending with the rejection of earthly fame has already both realized an indefinable grief and prepared the way for the transformation of it. In that passage Milton, as man, has separated himself from nature and raised himself to grace. And in it are most perfectly reconciled the classical impersonality and the personal Christian passion of the poem. But to complete the theme, the idea of a Christian society, one other element is necessary, the attack on the church. In the development of this as of the personal theme Milton is at once traditional and highly individual.

In most of the elegies, it is to public repentance that we are called. In Virgil the pattern of associating the death of a young man with reflections on the state of the world was already present, if later ages needed an example for a theme which life itself is so apt to press upon each succeeding generation. Cicero had consoled himself for the loss of his daughter in a *contemptus mundi* which St. Augustine thought equal to all that Christian heart could feel. Milton's attack on the church with its image of the shepherd is, as Mr. Coffman has shown, in the direct tradition of the *contemptus*.[10] But Milton has given the theme a different context. In Renaissance and Reformation the call of the prophets to perfect our earthly life has reasserted itself above the more absolute rejection of this world. It has united itself with another thought both Christian and Greek, the sense of the unity of man's individual and his social being. One side of this sentiment is Ascham's and Hamlet's deep sense that all sound manners derive from a true religion and a just and religious government. The other is the passionate reaffirmation of the membership of the individual in the church. The comments on the times in most of the elegies we have read—Drummond is an exception—rest on the ideas of Providence, Judgment, and the state of the Church. No doubt not only pastoral elegy but the whole tradition of ecclesiastical and political allegory in the pastoral eclogue formed in Milton's imagination a single literary background. Richard Niccols had already shown in a crude way how to unite allegorical elegiac expression of grief and pastoral religious allegory. But Niccols had had none of the fulness of Milton's sense that man's religious and his social life were one. In Spenser's *Shepheardes Calender* Milton would have found a far surer though less explicit blending in pastoral poetry of social consciousness with the unfolding of the interior life. When we think of Milton's debt to Spenser in *Lycidas,* we have to think not of one dirge, but of the total effect on him of all of Spenser's pastorals. It is true, as Mr. Hughes has observed, that Spenser in his *Calender* destroyed the old pastoral gaiety in the treatment of love. But nothing Spenser sang deserves more attention than the way in which, in the feeling of these poems if not in their form, he has fused with social and moral allegory and with dirge and occasional lyric, a representation of the unfolding of his own sensibility as a lover and as a poet, and of the place of love and poetry in illuminating this harsh world. For love and poetry are forms of the religious inspiration supplying a vision on which all the rest depends. The pattern which is diffused through Spenser, Milton perfects and makes manifest.

In the opening of the third book of *Paradise Lost,* Milton perhaps gives expression to his maturest sense of the peculiar significance of the individual consciousness in the universe and in man's comprehension of God's nature. And so those lines shed light back upon *Lycidas.* The passage is often considered an intrusion, a glorious intrusion to be sure, of Milton's egotism into his epic story. But it seems to me rather that in ascending from the description of Hell to a contemplation of God, Milton feels himself compelled to ask anew for the infusion of grace and to give witness through his own passionate experience, of the means by which Nature and the Divine are united in this middle

creature. Thus the remembered song of the nightingale returning in the spring brings with it the whole image of the book of
the creatures, the pageant of the times and seasons, the beasts,
the human face divine; but that radiant book yields to a higher
vision as John Milton turns from nature now so bitterly denied
him and through grace accepts joyously the inner life of the
mind, in which religion and poetry are one.

That *Lycidas* should so overflow with personal passion, though
not with personal grief, is then no mere mark of Milton's own
nature but the impress of a whole age upon a genius. And
though *Lycidas* and Donne's elegy on Prince Henry differ in
that one is the drama of doubt and faith, the other the story of
man's transcendence from nature to grace, both are dramas of
the individual soul, each witnessing the terror of death, the personal experience of grace. In Donne the portrait of Henry becomes an instrument of contemplation; in Milton, by a profounder and simpler transfer of surface experience to the interior life, it is not King's character but his own which he defines in the lines beginning "Alas! What boots it." Giordano
Bruno, so much less a humanist than Milton, never so finally
rejected humanism as Milton rejected it in his dismissal of even
the most ideal earthly fame.

Donne makes his elegy a poem by applying his theology to a
particular occasion. His emotion still remains primarily an act
of devotion, though he turns it into an object of art by the formal
delineation of that emotion. Milton imitates the experience of
death and Christian acceptance of it not in a religious form but
in an artistic form in which, by the completeness with which
the entire experience is represented and by the sensuous and
representative quality of the imagery, the most personal experience of one man is universalized.

Milton's communication of his experience of the ideal in the
particular involves the total emotion and movement of *Lycidas;*
but among other elements the imagery is particularly important.
And I should like to say a word on the great depth, scope, and

complexity of Milton's imagery when compared to that of the early pastorals and on the relation of it to witty imagery. His depth of expression owes most to the whole quality of his mind, much to his keen sensibility to the classical and humanist poems which had impregnated his imagination, much to the penetration with which he sees in each detail both its sensuous immediacy and its ideal quality. One would like to study in detail how Milton's expression might be fitted to Lionardi's interpretation of ornament, for instance in the flower passage, with its beautiful epithets and qualifications. But Biblical symbol and emblem imagery also have contributed something to the deepening. Milton has assimilated the emblem to the imagery of sensuous, of classical, poetry. Of this assimilation the fullest example is the image of the setting and rising sun, in which, in addition to the obvious sense, we ought to be conscious also not only of Matthew's symbolic identification of Christ and the sun, but of the part played by the sun in Platonist thought as the symbol and instrument in this world of the divine energy. It is emblematic both in the sharp logic of its statement and in the way in which it serves to draw together and to transvalue all the matter of the poem. That it is a central, traditional Christian analogy, I have earlier observed. Not only is it used emblematically in the witty poems on King, but it is the subject of an elaborate elegy on Hope in the collection of emblems on Faith, Hope, and Charity by the Jesuit, William Hes, published almost as Milton was writing *Lycidas* and containing at its turn a line which is in movement a close analogue to Milton's "weep no more, woful shepherds, weep no more."[11] At the same time, the image is simply, sensuously glowing, so that it makes a direct, affective, aesthetic contribution to our dawning joy. But if to be "metaphysical" be to feel the objective realities and to contemplate their ultimate meaning chiefly as they transform the inner life of one sensibility and make him a part of his universe, then *Lycidas* is a metaphysical poem.

Chapter Five

HASTINGS AND DRYDEN

THE ELEGIES ON Hastings may be discussed more rapidly than those preceding both because the patterns are now clear to us and because a great number of the poems are available in modern editions.[1] The King volume is a Cambridge volume and represents, besides, only writers of about King's age. The Hastings volume, like the Prince Henry elegies, represents a wider range of poets. The dominant single influence is that of John Donne, an influence which has now clearly divided into three streams: devotional, in Pestell, Hall, and Marvell; theological in several minor poets; in Denham, moral and intellectual, the religious passion passing almost entirely into social emotion. Of Donne's conception of a poem, almost nothing remains or is recovered except the use of the emblem image to express metaphysical speculation. Yet wherever Donne's intellectual and moral tone still have force, they carry with them something of his ordonnance, his phrasing, and his rhythms. He still exerts an influence on the form of poetry where his thought is still felt.

We are ever conscious in the Hastings elegies that a tradition has been built. Whether the poets imitate a selection of poetic inventions from a collection such as that in the rhetoric of Pontanus, or whether they write with a deeper idea of the typical form of a poem as a whole, each poem has more singleness of effect than many of the Prince Henry elegies, less exuberant and undisciplined combinations of invention and imagery. Yet one is conscious, too, that the superior orderliness may be due less to artistic tradition than to limitation of imagination and vision. Poetry, in 1649, like thought, attempts far less daring flights of speculation and fancy than in 1612 or even 1638.

We have already seen in Beaumont's lines on King the shrinking of the bounds of contemplation, the dominance of a Latin ideal of order. In the poems on Hastings that note is very strong, and with it the Roman feeling toward death becomes common, the pity for what was so beautiful and has died. Order itself rests on a narrower basis than formerly, as religious vision fails and as social disaster emerges. Mediaeval schematism, scorn of the world, Platonism, symbolic thought, are yielding to rationalism. And over these poems in particular hangs the chill of the civil war, narrowing to its own bitterness the sense of sin and the call to repentance, never among the greatest emotions when felt of the second rather than of the first person. Poetry naturally sought models written in a kindred temper, both in the past and recently. It was around 1640 that Waller, working in contact with Falkland and his rational theologians at Great Tew, established his program for the imitation of rational thoughts and rationally defined emotions in clear and reasonable diction. Among other things, that program turned the witty or emblematic image into simple and lucid argument from analogy. And merely as a style, apart from all connection with modes of thought, the concept of literal and perspicuous expression had gained ground. Sir John Beaumont was an ardent neo-Platonist in his metaphysics and his ethics. But he had long before Waller accepted the ideal of French classical perspicuity, an ideal which he applied to judge the witty poetry of the court of King James. His own poetry was bare of any heightening except the simplest metaphors, and so scrupulously and merely perspicuous as to be wholly without tone. The sense of order, the fear of enthusiasm, the mood of common sense, and literary fashion worked together with deeper changes in philosophy and outlook. There was a great narrowing both in the scope of the experience which poetry sought to imitate and in the means by which it sought to imitate that experience and to affect its readers. When this sharply critical temper prevails, and with the establishment of a narrower taste, the mixture of tones and motives which often strikes one in the earlier elegies naturally no longer stands out.

Some reminiscence of older motives there is. Edward Standish builds his very inartificial couplets simply on the theme of the branch plucked by God. Sir Aston Cokaine's sweetest lines compare Henry to a river returning to the sea, the description of the river in its dainty epithets suggesting Spenser's or Drayton's river passages. In most of his verses, Cokaine is a mild and simple-hearted son of Ben, an orthodox man, untroubled by the "new" poetry. One can cull from his verses a view of the history of English poetry quite in the taste of the normal cultivated man of his day, praising in the drama the genius of Shakespeare and of Beaumont and Fletcher, and the judgment and art of Jonson; in poetry the achievement of Chaucer, Sidney, Spenser, well-languaged Drayton, and of Donne's wit in satire. One sees in his love of English history, towns, poets, what makes Spenser and Drayton dear to him; and one is conscious of a link of patriotism that will extend directly, by however thin a line, from them to Pope and *Windsor Forest*. But of their high flights he attempts nothing. In the whole Hastings volume, the only poems in Spenserian diction are a pair of sonnets submitted by Arthur Gorges the younger, of which the better of the two is, however, as Miss Sandison pointed out in her sketch of Gorges, conveyed from his father's tribute to Prince Henry.

Robert Herrick's choral song voices Christian classicism in the temper of Jonson. Herrick has a strong sense of the genre and of decorum of style in the traditional meaning of decorum. The prevailing detachment and impersonality of view and classical

simplicity of his poem blend, in the lines on Elizium, with the
sensuous radiance which is also typical of him. It will be remembered that he was not only the oldest of those who wrote
on Hastings, but older, probably, than any of those who wrote
on King. In substance his poem is very close to the epitaphs of
Jonson in its representation of an ideal and typical and classical
attitude toward death. It contains a brief expression of human
pity for human fate; an intuition of the swift merging of the
individual experience in the common lot:

> Eucosmia.   More let me yet relate.
> Charon.   I cannot stay; more souls for waftage wait,
>   And I must hence;

Christian ethic and consolation. In almost all Herrick's songs
for music there is a deliberate and fictional invention, and in his
choral songs the emotion is cast into formal story. In the choral
and antiphonal songs which he had written with Lawes a few
years before for the King's choir, he had drawn for such story
upon the meditations on the life of the Christ child which were
favorite religious themes at court. For an elegy so Latin in its
sense of life as this on Hastings, he inevitably chooses a classical
invention, a dialogue between Hastings' intended bride and
Charon. The vision of Elizium which he grants the soul which
has not become immersed in the world represents the beatific
vision in the old simple Elizabethan way of using the classic
myth—classical myth had already been so used in earlier pastoral elegy[2]—and leads the angel chorus in very naturally. Herrick's slight, exquisite poem, reflecting both the Elizabethan
world and the devotional tastes of the vanished court of Charles
and Henrietta is *sui generis,* outside the main stream of the
elegy.

Thomas Pestell was almost as old as Herrick. But he was the
child of Cambridge and the *devotio moderna* and with him we
come again to the "metaphysical" and to the direct influence of

*Non contriſtemini, ſicut & ceteri qui
Spem non habent. 1.Theſſ.4.*

EMBLEMA VIII.

*———— Spes lucis amœnior ipſo
Surgit ab occaſu. ————*

*———— Lucis occaſum tuæ
Natura quid fles? quaſque ſubduxit dies
Lacrymas reſumens, rore te mergis tuo,
Pariterque ſolem? lux ab occaſu amplior,
Magis ampla Spes conſurgit, & ſpondet diem
Iterùm ante noctem. Ploret occiduum iubar,
Sperare lumen quiſquis auerſum nequit.*

H 7 *Dolendum*

From the *Emblemata Sacra de Fide, Spe, Charitate*
of William Hes (Antwerp, 1636)
(See page 114)

Donne.[3] In most of his poetry Pestell is the Sir Fopling Flutter of the Clevelandists. Constantly proclaiming Donne as the prince of wits, but more sensible of Donne's egotism, as his editor remarks, than of the deep intellectual and emotional drama which impersonalized it, Pestell had written a number of occasional poems barren of everything but arrogance, and with fustian ingenuity of figure, devoid of Cleveland's incisiveness and skill of evolution. But he wrote also a few ritualistic meditative poems. These poems, by his calling them "strong lines," definitely connect him with the metaphysical and devotional aspect of Donne. On Hastings Pestell wrote two poems, one a devotional poem for Hastings' mother, the other an elegy proper. The devotional poem is an admonition to the Countess on the nature of her loss, showing how fruitful and even necessary the loss is for her interior life. The admonition is dryly neo-Platonic: her son's beauty, while he lived, bound her to the senses; now his soul will turn her mind upward. This idea he embodies in the Ulysses-Circe myth, a symbol as conventional in the Renaissance for the expression of the ascent of the soul from the senses as are the traditional symbols in mediaeval religious art. The general appeal to the interior life is expressed in emblem and paradox. In short, the poem is just in the genre of Beaumont's elegy on King; its kinship, in its stress on the interior life and in its use of emblem and paradox, with the school of Donne and at the same time with the more humanist neo-Platonic tradition is clear. Like Beaumont's, the poem is in tetrameter couplets and the diction plain and perspicuous, easily passing into the classical where it defines character: "He parted in perfection's time . . . and White Report Of Vertue." In contrast to this, the actual elegy is a fustian definition of Hastings' virtue, with Platonic frame of reference, but essentially empty. The figures are not integrated with the expression of the Platonic concepts. Its staple of expression is Cowley-like "boldness" rather than Donnian wit. If we set the two poems together, we see that Pestell owes his poetry to the imitation of the genre rather than to his own philosophy. The choice of elegy which shall serve as his model is a matter of literary taste rather than of philosophical view.

J. Hall, one of the most engaging of very minor poets, is both more deeply metaphysical than Pestell and more controlled in literary aim and method. His reflective poetry in general sets ethics against a cosmological background as Donne had set the devotional life. Hall is, however, only ethical and not devotional. In his lyric poetry, he analyzes his own experience of love and the neo-Platonic assumptions about love each in the light of the other in a way that clearly reflects the influence of Donne, though again his treatment is critical and not passionate. His elegy on Hastings is, however, not primarily theological or imitative of Donne, but an elegy in the Graeco-Latin tradition, treating the theme of death impersonally and almost naturalistically, and with stress on the social significance of the loss. In ordonnance, it is not, like Donne's elegy, a thesis but, like Jonson's reflective poetry, a discourse.[4] The flower springs anew, but pitiable man does not return; in Hastings the world has lost a model of virtue; his virtue is defined; the loss of his family and in their loss the loss of society is described; but, it is asserted, he is removed to the divine world and his ashes must be left to rest in peace.

Hall is, however, in all his poetry, speculative in his interests and hermetic or neo-Platonic in his view. In this poem, accordingly, he states the theme of the renewal of nature not in naturalistic but in metaphysical terms:

> A perisht Flower can from that Central fire
> That lurks within its seed, next Spring aspire . . .

And in defining he turns readily to scientific figure, used as a symbol, to express metaphysical truth:

> The Celestial Seed
> The Stars had shed into him, could not slow
> To Looseness, nor yet poorly undergrow.
> Nothing in him was crooked, lame, or flat,
> But Geometrically proportionate.[5]

Yet despite the supernatural frame of reference, we feel, if we compare this elegy not only with Donne's but with Beaumont's, a profound shift of emphasis. In Beaumont the purely religious view is already strongly modified by humanistic ideals of earthly order. In Hall the mediaeval-elegiac feeling for death, so deeply involved with the sense of decay and mutability and sin and pain, and with the escape from these into eternity, has shifted to the more normal classical one:

> But
> Pityable Man, when once his eyes are shut,
> Is seen no more; but past recov'ry lost;
> A tender fleeting Form, a Bloodless Ghost.

Otherworldliness has yielded almost entirely to the social sense. After the psychological and metaphysical cry that Hastings is moved to the Center of Light where his Love now tosses sublim'd intuitive species instead of having to use the objects of sense for thought, the poem closes with an *ave atque vale:*

> He's now at peace, disturb him not with Fears,
> Nor violate his Ashes with your Tears.

It is that classical feeling which determines the form of the poem. It may be in part due to the Donnian ideal of unmediated realism in speculative poetry or to writers in whose tradition Donne was, that Hall makes no attempt at formal poetic heightening of style or couplet. But I rather think he owes his plainness and his succinct epithets as much to the spirit of good sense and to Jonson as to Donne.

Marvell's lines on Lord Hastings were almost his first published verse, though some of his experimental lyrics may well have been written earlier. In these lines the union of a deeply bred classicism with a religious and speculative spirit influenced by Donne and by the larger forces of which Donne was in part a product, is already apparent. Like so many of the elegists, Marvell unites two forms of lament, but in him the two forms are fused as they are not in most of the elegies. Marvell had an intensity of sensuous endowment which Donne lacked; this together with his classical training gave him a vivid sensibility to aesthetic forms. A number of his verses which are evidently experimental show this sensibility very clearly, as I shall consider in chapter VII. His lines on Hastings unite integrally the two sides of his thought, a union well expressed in his fusion of the theological and the classical forms of lament in a poem of remarkable singleness of tone and expression and firm strength of movement.

The poem is classical in the development of its parts: lament, analysis of the meaning of this death, allusion to particular circumstance, and comfort to the mourners, acceptance of death. It is classical also in the smoothness and perspicuity of its expression, in its finality of definition, in the precise and ordered rhythms of its end-stopped couplets.[6] The firmness of ordonnance shown in the deliberate opening and close is classical too. But here Marvell and Donne are at one, perhaps because Donne was influenced by classical rhetoric. Marvell in his abrupt beginning states the essential thesis of the poem as had Donne, and resolves that thesis in his conclusion. This treatment corresponds to the essential intellectual tone of the poem, which is also Donnian. The meditation on the meaning of death is not simple, sensuous, and passionate, but theological and analytical; the thought is unfolded in emblems oversubtle and quaint, perhaps, but never merely witty like the images of Cleveland and like those of the neo-Latin epigrammatists; always, rather, genuinely metaphysical. These images have, however, become classical in the perspicuity with which they unfold, concentrating on a single point. Marvell's expression of grief has that sensibility which is not in Donne and which must have contributed along with Marvell's education and the spirit of the times to keep him a humanist; a sensibility which he devoted much of his later life to analyzing. But his lament, despite this sensuous alertness, is not naturalistic; it is dialectical and Marinistic:

> *Hastings* is dead, and we must find a Store
> Of Tears untoucht, and never wept before.
> Go, stand betwixt the *Morning* and the *Flowers*.[7]

I have said that in thus synthesizing two forms of elegy, two conceptions of a poem, Marvell united two sides of his nature. Yet it would be truer to say that he gave expression to a profound and never fully resolved tension in his life. The aesthetic tone of the poem is one; the double attitude it expresses toward death is unresolved. So perfectly tempered is the classical side of the elegy, not only in its form but in its detachment, in the whole sense of tradition which that form expressed, that the use of the classical figures of Hymen and Aesculapius to represent Hastings' marriage and the failure of medicine strikes with no harshness amid the Christian theology and the emblematic images. The theological assumptions in their turn are stated with what precise intensity! Yet the Christian view does not triumph in Christian acceptance. The images chosen to express the Christian view all show it as a negative, denying our desires. It is a Christian cosmos without a Christian heart. It is Heaven's jealousy that has taken Hastings. In the same tone the poem concludes in an outcry against fate and in a resolution of fortitude only, rather than in the Christian embrace of death. Conceivably, Marvell might have known and recalled the report that Cicero, whose lament for his daughter was so Christian in its contempt of the world and in its vision of the blessed, yet said of her death that in all things else he had mastered fate; in that, fate had mastered him. Marvell's whole poem might fall within the bounds of Cicero. But, whatever literary influences may have served to stimulate Marvell's feeling, the final effect of the poem is one of real conflict between intellectual acceptance and emotional denial. And it is that conflict which seems to justify Marvell's fusion of forms.

Jo. Joynes, John Cave, and S. Bold are more simply imitative of Donne's theological thought and manner, unmixed with classicism. None is a literary man. To see Donne, therefore, through their eyes corrects some of our distorted notions as to what is central in Donne. In them the genre of the theological elegy, already exemplified in Goodyere and Tourneur, continues. John Cave's elegy follows Donne in that it states a speculative thesis and resolves it:

> Teach me (dread Fate) out of thy strong-clasp'd book,
> Whose every Marble page as vast doth look,
> As th' immense volume of Eternity,
> Whereto for Index serves Mortality . . . .

The analysis of the thesis is, however, a purely abstract one and is bare of figure. The phrasing imitates afar Donne's compression, but certainly makes no cult of obscurity, though it refuses the cult of smoothness and perspicuity. The couplet, too, I suppose is Donnian in the negative sense of refusing the now fashionable balanced form; it is insignificant, for Cave has not a musical ear, and Donne's was not a couplet, like that of Waller and his group, to be sustained by metrical and rhetorical form apart from an energetic ear for auditory images in the individual poet. Cave probably owed what sense of form he had to Donne alone and not like Donne to a great tradition of thought and expression of which he was a conscious disciple. What Jo. Joynes feels most keenly is the civil war; in the early loss of a young nobleman he sees the confirmation of the destruction of the governing aristocracy. Hastings' learning in philosophy and the tongues would have enabled him to take his part in the great social scheme. But these reflections are still colored by the light of the eternal world and the *contemptus mundi*.

> Still stood
> In him (that Cypher for these many yeers)
> Th' opprest, and now quite ruin'd House of Peers.
> All these, not lost, but outlaw'd, did conspire,
> To him, as to their centre, to retire.
> But he is gone; and now this carcase, World,
> Is into her first, rude, dark Chaos, hurl'd.

The poem is perfectly sincere. There is nothing of Clevelandism, no imitation of Donne's pride of wit. But the intellectual passion and the religious intensity of Donne, the elements which had also inspired Tourneur, are quite gone. Gone also are the elements of formal poetic invention. The fading of the fires both of religion and of art is even more clear in the elegy of S. Bold. For his poem is a direct and painfully unpretentious statement of the decay of the times and an appeal to the better world where bishops are peers, and doctors, saints, and martyrs "have their Aureola's above the rest"; it does not venture to deal with any great ideas.

> For us, poor Dwarfs in Science, we thought fit
> To hold in Fee, of thy great Giant-wit,
> Those smaller parcels which we have of art.

These poets do admit mythological reference as ornament.

In the poems in the type of Latin reflective elegy and epigram the influence of Jonson and of neoclassicism clearly prevails. Such are the poems of young Charles Cotton, of Sir Aston Cokaine, and of the skillful journalist, turncoat, and flatterer, Marchamont Needham. Their reflection is tame; their principal decor is classical; but the classical tradition of the nymphs has given way to illustration from classical history.[8] This invention from classical history had been in the Renaissance one of many commonplaces. Now, as the speculative and ethical scope of the Renaissance narrows down, as Platonism and allegorical vision, as warm-spirited nationalism even, vanish, and interest centers in society in a more restricted sense, comparisons to Greek and Roman figures, which suggest that the great tradition is being perfected in contemporary life, become a principal means for heightening a poem.

Yet though these poems are primarily reflective, they are still in the genre of the formal aristocratic elegy. And in accordance with the tradition illustrated by Chapman or summarized in the instructions of Pontanus, therefore, the grief is a central motive in them, and must be formally expressed. Cokaine for his *grief,* as we have already seen, refers back to Spenser's and Drayton's river passages. Cotton and Needham prefer to imitate neo-Latin elegy and epigram. In the elegies on King, the *grief* had played upon King's drowning and the interchange of sea and tears. For Hastings the inevitable subject is the smallpox. Needham gives us

> Those eyes which Hymen hop'd should light his Torch,
> Aethereal flames of Fevers now do scorch,
> And *envious Pimples* too dig Graves apace,
> To bury all the Glories of his face;

Charles Cotton:

> Bathe him in Tears, till there appear no trace
> Of those sad Blushes in his lovely face:
> Let there be in't of Guilt no seeming sence,
> Nor other Colour then of Innocence.

In the "color" or "ornament" of the most minor poetasters, the ingenious image still prevails as in the poems on King, though in Bancroft, Paphian roses and nymphs shoulder flowers planted emblem-wise on the grave. Joh. Rosse and Alexander Brome most clearly represent the fashion of the "metaphysical" image, but Richard Brome's

> Now let Sigh-tempests and Tear-torrents rise
> To pour out Marble-hearts th'row melting Eyes

is obviously from the Donne scrapbook. On the other hand the epigrams, by Westmorland, Falkland, Millward, Higgins, Fairfax, are in the Jonsonian and classical tradition; they are plain though they do not copy the model for incisive definition and for the schooling of the couplet which had been set by Jonson and recently perfected in the taste of Waller and Denham.

Among all the men we have considered so far, only Marvell, and in slight measure, Hall have the power to carry the influence of Donne's speculative mind forward into a vigorous synthesis with changing attitudes. In general we seem to be in a world of failing faith and failing poetry. But Sir John Denham, living in a world of discourse utterly different from that of Donne, draws upon Donne for a renewal of seriousness. His is a world so altered from Donne's that he must in a sense refound poetry; but half his foundation rests upon Donne. Denham is not concerned with metaphysical speculation nor with the interior life, and his view of character is only a common-sense one, though deeply religious. His theme is the sacrificing of Hastings as an oblation for sin; and behind it, as behind Donne's *Anniversaries,* lies the day of Judgment and the sense of noble characters—for the poem is really a lament for Charles—as types on earth of divine love. Their loss is accordingly a warning to man through his senses of that which he refuses to see with his intellect. Every such death is a *memento mori*. Denham has, however, turned away from Donne's intellectual searching and doubt and personal passion. Instead of the great issue of saving faith, he turns with Jonson and with Davies and others to the ethical issue of the passions and of man's right to grief. And instead of the *contemptus mundi* he utters a lament for the destruction of that simple order which he believed *could* be established in this world, and which claimed his religious devotion. In both these orientations, his is the outlook of typical Anglicanism at this time.

Thus the feeling of Denham's poem becomes essentially social. But when we see the social emotion from the point of view of this world and not of the City of God, every aid of formality is needed to embody its ideal element. Denham's poem is permeated by a solemnity of feeling half reflective of its moral thought, half of reverence for the king and for the hierarchy of the state as symbols of order. The opening paragraph follows the pattern of Donne's ordonnance as closely as had Tourneur, stating the entire thesis in the opening couplet. The plainness of Denham's diction also is Donnian. But Denham accepts the view of poetry as an art of ornament, elevating its subject by incident, appropriate though not integral, and giving its style a formal poetic beauty. The solemnity of his feeling is reflected in the style which Denham chooses as decorous. He follows, in his basic thought and expression, the model of intellectual directness set by Donne, but he heightens his design with decorative forms. Like Tourneur, he follows Donne's rhetoric in the restrained use of repetition, of schemes of words, to express the climax of the loss. Like Donne and Tourneur he reflects in his verse the rhythm of speech, especially in his handling of the run-on line. In other respects, however, he subjected the couplet to the discipline of end-stopping and balance, and he merged his resonant speech rhythm in smooth lines. The emblematic images and paradox which expressed Donne's speculative conflict and his stormy interior life Denham with the rationalists has let fall. Instead, he has concentrated the social feeling of the poem in a simple, resonant, fully elaborated Virgilian image on Charles's death.

To judge from the state of the text, the poem of Marchamont Needham and an epigram by J. Harmar came in after the original volume on Hastings had been printed. And at that time was added also a little collection of poems by Hastings' schoolmates, written one surmises under the direction of Busby, the headmaster of Westminster School. In all three of the sets of elegies we have been looking at, close repetitions of invention and detail suggest that various writers in each volume had seen the poems of others writing before them on the occasion. And this fact, added to the seeming fact that the poems of Westminster boys went to the printer after the printing of the original little book had been completed, makes it not improbable that they saw the collection for which they were writing before they wrote their own verses. To the other boys, who were writing in Latin and on Latin models, this would have been unimportant.[9] But John Dryden wrote in English and was about to publish at eighteen a first poem most seriously undertaken, and to publish it among the work of experienced writers.[10] In his elegy, he collects together a large number of the themes and motives present in the lesser poems in the volume; and there is in it almost no theme or image not in some one of the earlier poems. But his lines are no mere pastiche, no mere aggregation of themes. He attempts a full-scale and independent elegy. In writing it, I think we may infer, as my analysis will show, he had in mind a whole and its parts, with structural relations as necessary as those of classical tragedy, such a whole as Scaliger might have described. To understand these parts, he had been studying the various existing English modes, in order to perfect the form.

In constructing this ideal elegy, Dryden combined three types: classical lament, theological elegy in the tradition of Donne, and praise of character; for the last of these, though often only a part of the other two, was also written as a separate type and may be considered a distinct element. He selects first the principal parts of the classical lament: the particular death, and the question it evokes as to the nature of the world; the grief, including a lament for the state of the world; consolation. These parts he divorces from pastoral allegory. With them he interweaves the speculative reflection of the theological elegy in a formal praise of Hastings' character. The forms of the two he also strives to unite; but it is the sermon-like organization of the theological elegy which dominates the whole, the classical harmony of the opening and close perhaps coming to him through the ideal of the classical oration, which he might have known in school studies and in sermons. This opening and close, together with the careful arrangement of material in the parts, give the poem its distinctive ordonnance. In the fact of Hastings' death, the circumstance which most deeply struck many of the older writers and all of his schoolmates was that he died just on the eve of his marriage. For, apart from the personal pathos of such a death, such an arranged marriage was an event of almost state importance, uniting two families for the continuity of each and of the society of which they were mighty branches. To the schoolboys it must have seemed in every way Hastings' coming of age. From this pathetic drama Dryden draws the framework of his poem, opening with the question, "Must noble Hastings immaturely die and change a wedding for a winding sheet?" and closing with the consolation not, as we should have expected, of religion, but of the promise that Hastings will live on in the thought of his bride. This consolation had, however, been used not long before, as Gwynne Blakemore Evans brings to my attention, in an elegy by the then popular Cartwright.[11]

Between the asking of the question and the final resolution of it Dryden, like Marvell, unfolds the religious theme.[12] This theme he organizes not on the logical pattern of Donne, but with the "natural" order of common-sense discourse familiar in the later seventeenth-century sermon, such as we might find it in the sermons of Tillotson, or in those of South, Dryden's younger contemporary at Westminster. Donne's poem, as we have seen, was a devotion, bringing his metaphysical and theological view of the world and man to bear on his own religious development. Within his prayer, he developed his theme by the traditional dialectic of statement of theme, definition, division, proof. A successful poem of such a sort could be the fruit only of mature intellectual life and of years of religious concentration. Later elegies by lesser men who followed Donne's as a model tended, therefore, to leave out the personal passion and to consist of abstract theological discussion only. Even less than these writers was Dryden ready for a devotional poem. But more important even than Dryden's youth is the fact that the whole emphasis and method of religious discussion had shifted in the interval between Donne and Dryden. Sermon and theological writing were shifting their dialectic to the "common-sense" pattern of rational thought, condemning successively the older rhetorical division of Donne and his age and the "method" of the Ramists.[13] Their persuasion had shifted its ground from the drama of the interior life and from argument based on the symbolic nature of the world to a reasoned affirmation of the moral order and of duty (a shift which, incidentally, Marvell was to express his contemptuous rejection of in his answer to Parker). Religious argument had ceased to concentrate on the mysteries and on the contempt of the world and had focused on the affirmation of the rational nature of the soul of man long since defined, but for a long time subordinated to an emphasis on the vision and grace by which that reason may be restored. The image of God, so ran the primary definition, is impressed upon the soul of man in two powers: first in the power for science or knowledge, though the limitation of that power, especially in the field of theology, was also stressed; second in ethical insight. Both powers were at the Fall thrown into confusion, both are restored to the individual only by grace through the orderly ministrations of the church. For the discussion of such issues, the essay type of development is needed. It is exactly in these prevalent theological terms that Dryden defines Hastings' virtue and that he discusses the whole issue of Providence. The organization of his poem suits this religious discussion. The neat transitions by which Dryden articulates the parts are characteristic of the essay sermon. Yet he still sets his rational argument against a background of mediaeval and Platonic cosmology. And this central metaphysical argument he develops through a metaphysical image obviously imitated from Donne, with more understanding of Donne's imagery than many people had:

> His body was an Orb, his sublime Soul
> Did move on Vertue's and on Learning's pole.

Dryden's grasp of the great themes of his elegy is necessarily limited. But if we read the poem in the light of his prescribed task, as he conceived it, we will be struck, I think, by his sincerity and by his sheer power of making, at least as much as by his inadequacy. The description of Hastings' actual virtue and learning is naïvely but honestly confined to a schoolboy's point of view. When Dryden passes from the account of Hastings' attainments to the more universal definition of his virtue, he is clearly thinking not of the real Hastings but of a pattern of the virtuous youth, and the portrait becomes accordingly unreal and exaggerated. This was inevitable, granted his models, granted the flattery in elegies by older men, and granted that he may well have had Donne's *Anniversaries* in mind. So far, Dryden has treated his thought boldly. But it is striking that the immortality of the soul, which is in Christian thought the chief answer to his question about death, he asserts only by implication. And over the twin issue of Providence he passes as swiftly. His answer, "it is our sin," is that most commonly given in all three sets of elegies, and is one common in all the more conventional sermons of the day. What is notable is that Dryden states this guilt only in general terms and without reference to the civil war. It may be that his sympathies were with Parliament; and this is probable from what we know of his background, despite the royalism of Busby and the school. But it is equally possible that Dryden would not risk an overt expression against Parliament in print when the school was under direct supervision of a parliamentary committee and Busby held his mastership under sufferance.[14] The impression the two passages make on us in their context lies between a sense that Dryden had an honest diffidence in speaking specifically on the speculative theme and a sense that he was experiencing an aversion of thought from that theme toward the visible experience of the world.[15] On the decay of the world Dryden gives a naïve imitation of naïve models; for Donne himself, though he resumes the encyclopedic wisdom of his world, is to our eyes naïve enough until we come to his astronomy passage. We should hardly be aware of the religious origins of Dryden's lines had we not the background of the elegy in mind. The close of the poem moves still further from religion to its classical peroration on social loss and on consolation in human thought; the latter is stated, however, in "Platonic" and "metaphysical" terms.

In comparing Hastings to the great figures of the past and in describing the *disease,* Dryden is likewise elaborating the formal and humanistic elements of his elegy. These motives, as the King volume has made clear, are principal ones in the classical elegy as it was then written. In his description Dryden imitates exuberantly the epigrammatic models of the King volume and of Hall and Needham in the Hastings volume. The imagery has nothing to do with the truly metaphysical as we know it in Donne. The roll of heroes from the past, an equally conventional invention, is related to the philosophical argument with a neatness characteristic of the ordonnance of the whole poem.

In the very logical completeness of the poem there is something young, and something inimical to its life as a poem. But this ordonnance is a creative thing, too, and suggests important considerations as to Dryden's poetic education. Clearly he had not only been subjected to notions of rational thought, but he had also undergone or had sought out for himself severe training in the designing of a poem, on principles very different from those of Donne's day. In reorganizing into a whole the

current fashionable motives which he found singly or in con-
glomeration in other poems of the volume and in trying to
bring together the three types of elegy, he shows a far deeper
sense of the elegy as a formal poetic genre than anyone who
wrote for the King volume except Milton, and than any other
contributors to the Hastings volume except Denham and Herrick
and Marvell. Between these mature poets and the boy Dryden
it is almost impossible to draw a comparison; but I think we
may say that his conception of the genre is more purely formal
and Aristotelian, as Scaliger interpreted Aristotle, and less determined by the immediate almost allegorical relation of form
to spiritual meaning than are theirs. Compared to Milton, on
the other hand, his form is external, his selection of material
more adventitious and imitative of models, less determined by
the integral nature of the experience it imitates. A few points
on the organization in addition to those I have already noted
bring out the deliberateness of his design. Noteworthy are the
fine rhetoric with which the closing consolation answers to the
opening question, and that clear grasp of the movement of
emotion which led him to put the lines on the tears just before
the consolation. This close of grief parallels the strewing of the
hearse in *Lycidas* and may well have been suggested by that
poem or by some of the neo-Latin Renaissance elegies; for it is
clear that Dryden had studied their design as well as that of
Donne.

His conception of a poem is no less clear in the style than in
the structure. He has rejected pastoral allegory, presumably for
a number of reasons. First, because he and his age in their stress
on the rational had lost Milton's Platonism and Milton's delight in the creatures as a revelation of God, in the naturalistic
sense of life which was a part of that Platonism. Then they had
lost also their view of poetry as something simple, sensuous, and
passionate, a symbolic reflection or a reflection of ideal truth in

the accidents of life, a view which depended on Renaissance psychology and philosophy. And finally they had lost vivid and personal interest in that interior life of which the pastoral elegy had been made an allegorical expression. To some extent Dryden's imagery varies in type with his themes, according to a formal law of decorum, as we have seen in other of the mid-century elegies such as Beaumont's. This explains his virtue image and his description of the disease. But over all he has thrown the Renaissance ideal of the poem as an art object which must be elevated by ornament. The allegorical conception of expression has yielded almost entirely to the idea of a high style which should give his poem a continuous ornamented texture. The fulness and resonance with which the images are elaborated and the sweep of the passage in which Hastings is compared to the men of the past show deliberate rhetorical amplification.

His diction is not like that of any of his models. It reflects with all allowance for his youth the masculine and intellectual expression of Donne, as compared with more feminine models, but it deals more in grandiose abstractions and generalities than Donne, a fact which fits Dryden's change of attitude and thought. Moreover, it is not only intellectually direct and rational, but at the same time "apt, sounding, and significant" to use Dryden's own formulation of the precept of Scaliger. Dryden has—and in this his view differs sharply from that of Donne as Carew reported it—a clear preference for sounding words of Latin derivation.

Scott commented on the tunelessness of the poem. And it is true that the versification lacks that resonance which "fortune rarely gives the young." But Scott, reading it with an ear attuned to the heroic couplet, saw only its defect. To me the rhythm suggests a probable attempt to mediate between speech rhythms and the formal movement of the new couplet. If so, it follows Denham, and it is Dryden's first try at the principle which was to create his great verse. He definitely gives more pattern to the opening and closing paragraphs than to the rest, a practice which he was to follow throughout his prose and verse and which would accord with the tradition of rhetoric as to proem and peroration. Dryden's *Hastings* has not the personal and emotional tone to win our interest as does, say, Shelley's early poetry: but in scope, in ordonnance, in its selections and rejections, in its wonderful sense of artistic purpose, it is the prophecy of a major poet and of a new age.

Between this callow poem on Hastings and Dryden's ode on Mistress Anne Killigrew thirty-seven years had elapsed. In spite of all that had happened between the two poems, in the consolidation of post-Restoration civilization and in Dryden's long life of thought, experience, and literary study and practice, it is still fruitful for our understanding of Dryden's approach to poetry to compare the two elegies. *Threnodia Augustalis,* though it includes the elements of an elegy within it, is for many reasons a state poem on a quite different scale, and I therefore pass it over. In the interval between the lines on Hastings and the ode on Mistress Killigrew Dryden's study of the great English poets before him, Chaucer, Spenser, Shakespeare, and of his elder contemporary Milton, was unremitting. This included also a renewed study of Donne, a study which may be related to Dryden's conversion and to the fact that he was giving serious attention to religious thought and to Catholic themes of devotion. Donne offered Dryden the sole great models in English of solemn verse of compliment in the religious field: and not only great models, but models Catholic in theme and spirit. Between the two poems had come also the major part of Cowley's work, and in particular the establishment by Cowley of the Pindaric ode as the form for high occasional poetry. The salient points of an ode upon which Cowley had seized had been its enthusiastic attack upon great concepts and intellectual events, the bold play of figures and ideas, and the large and varied metrical structure. Like Dryden, he believed in embellishing high poetry; and he gathers about his central theme a play not only of witty figures but of scholastic concepts such as Donne had loved to bring to bear on his experience. But to Cowley they are now obsolete as thought and exist only as the material of sheer intellectual game, useful for poetic amplification. Such was the embellishment suited to his extremely secular, rationalistic, and Epicurean temper; and the undisciplined energy of his meter does not come amiss to it. Very different is Dryden's conception of the Pindaric ode as a genre, though he acknowledges Cowley as the authoritative master of the form. Dryden sought to find its most universal forms of thought and structure, and regarded the embellishment as a branching out of these. He has left on record his criticism of Cowley's Pindaric measures, namely that Cowley did not find out the organic relation of his varied line lengths to each other. It is clear from his own odes that he did not believe that Cowley had adequately studied the structure of the ode either. Such a form he himself seeks to perfect in his ode *To the Pious Memory ... of Mistress Anne Killigrew.*

In this ode he seeks to unite once more the tradition of the Latin elegy, not excluding attitudes expressed in the pastoral, with the tradition of Donne—this time the Donne of the *Anniversaries*—both within the design of the Pindaric ode. The central theme is now not the theological one but that of the classical elegy. This time the theme is deepened by a closer study of *Lycidas* and behind *Lycidas* of the Sicilian elegies themselves, though Dryden still eschews a naturalistic and pastoral treatment. To this theme we are first awakened by echoes of the Greeks, of Milton, and intermediately of Cartwright's "To the Memory of a Shipwrackt Virgin,"[16] echoes as deliberately suggested to our ear as Virgil's echoes of Homer, or Milton's own of both poets.

> Whether, adopt'd to some neighboring star,
> Thou rollst above us in thy wandring race, . . .
> Cease thy celestial song a little space: . . .

But thus Orinda died.

If we look at the structure of Dryden's ode with *Lycidas* in mind we see clearly these following parts: the statement of the theme of death, here an address to the dead; the praise of the dead; a lament for the times (stanza IV); the admission of the ineluctable claims of fate, closing with a reference to an earlier poetess; the lament of the mourners (stanza VIII); the consolation. But in actual development Dryden's poem has nothing of Milton's sense of the mystery of death and decay; rather Dryden evokes that other classical humanist theme of the Renaissance, only partially submerged by the great impulses of the religious revival and of Platonism, the theme of order in a great society and of art as the ornament of that society. This difference between Dryden and Milton renders easier and more decorous Dryden's transformation of the pattern of the elegy into the form of the Pindaric ode. On a close consideration of the transformation Dryden's critical and social temper stands forth clearly. The Pindaric was a poem celebrating some great idea. And for this Cowley had used it. In Cowley's Pindarics, however, there is little movement aside from the development of this idea itself, no great lyric structure. Dryden imitated the structural parts of Pindar's odes more closely, adapting the parts of the elegy with amazing neatness to that form. The elegiac praise of the dead transforms itself into what is in the *epinicea* the praise of the victor. The lament for the times opens out in stanzas V, VI, and VII into the celebration of the idea, in this poem a critical definition of the new principles of painting, of which Mistress Killigrew was one of the first practitioners.

Thus in general, Dryden follows the invention of the classical elegy. The theme of contemplation, however, is drawn from

Donne and the theological elegy. The poem opens with a vision of Mistress Killigrew among the blessed, in which there is an echo of Milton, but which is also probably reminiscent of the ascent of the soul of Elizabeth Drury. It closes with a Last Judgment and with a Renaissance and classical coda on fame. Cowley had written a Pindaric on the Judgment, but Dryden is closer to Donne in his development of the theme than is Cowley. And yet despite the resemblance to Donne the two scenes by the two poets might be taken as typical of the difference between the ages of Donne and of Dryden. Donne evokes in the first eight lines of his Judgment sonnet the experience of every single soul surprised by the trumpets blowing at the round earth's imagined corners. In Dryden, the whole outline of the Judgment scene is blocked in, but the description is impersonal, general, not carrying us inward to one individual soul facing itself, but diffusing outward to social comment and to a defense of poesy.

This profound difference of temper explains the imagery of Dryden's poem. For Donne and for Milton, in different ways, this world is symbolic. For Dryden, despite his conversion, it is the essential imaginative reality. This is the fact which underlies any theory of elocution that helped to shape his poem. *Mistress Killigrew* is in essential social feeling and in discussion of ideas closer in temper to Dryden's lines on Oldham and to those on Congreve than to Milton and Donne; and the ode might well have been a reflective poem. But the poet has chosen to deal with the general idea of death, and accordingly to throw his emotion into the form of the Pindaric. He must, therefore, develop the poem in the high style especially suited to the Pindaric ode, a style which will harmonize all the parts, and which by its imagery will startle and command our passion suitably to the greatness of the theme. The stanzas dealing with the thought are sustained by the elaborate statement of that thought and do not need additional color. It is different with stanzas 1,

III, and IX, which express the lament. Since the lament is a ritual, these are the stanzas which in Dryden's view, as we may surmise, needed most amplification to sustain their passion and to elevate it to the level of the thought of death. Dryden, therefore, replaces the natural description which he has discarded by imagery drawn from elementary science and cosmic lore. These are just such amplifications as he had used many years before in his formal praise of Cromwell. Only the palms of Cromwell are become the palms of heaven. The image of the clustering bees had appeared in Beaumont's elegy on King James, a fact which reminds us of the deliberately traditional character of these adornments. Moreover, the play of ideas shown in amplification constituted the special character of the Pindaric. The ideas which Dryden brings into play are, unlike those of Cowley, of genuine interest to him and they bear a direct relation to his theme. He believed, at least at the end of his life, and already by this time, we may guess, in judicial astrology; and the discussion of the origin of the soul had still a recognized place in orthodox treatises on the immortality of the soul. Nonetheless, these images are the outpourings of discursive thought, not like those of Milton and Donne the substance of a concentrated intuition that draws thought and feeling inward to a center.

The music of Dryden's ode, like its invention and its imagery, is true to neoclassical principles of formal design. Its beauty is inherent in the pure metrical pattern of the ode itself, objectively conceived, in the varied cadences of the lines within the stanza. It is conceived and managed with perfect artifice. To my ear, despite its fine numerousness, it never, like his lines on Oldham, takes emotion from its theme.

The ode on Mistress Killigrew is at once illustrative of the grandeur of Dryden's analysis and reconstitution of the great formal genres of literature, and of the thin spiritual air he often had to breathe in his perennial struggle between the fading

mediaeval world and the rising world of science and social en-
lightenment, in the midst of the disillusion of the first restored
Stuart courts.

Finally, we may glance briefly at the elegiac verses Dryden
was asked to write toward the close of his life for members of
Catholic society.

Eleonora is much more formally a Donnian poem than is the
ode, though even less Donnian in spirit; and Dryden justly
speaks of Donne as his model. The poem laments as an ideal
pattern of virtue a lady not personally known to the poet, in
this following Donne. But Dryden's deepest religious feeling, as
we may judge from its finest expression in the opening of *The
Hind and the Panther,* is not ascetic or personal, it is formal
and ritualistic. And he had surrendered his skepticism and the
mysteries of his faith to authority. He did not, therefore, attempt to imitate the metaphysical discussion or the otherworldly
vision of the *Anniversaries.* Instead, he expressed that aspect of
religious experience to which we may surmise that, given the
temper of his mind and of contemporary religion, he had devoted most attention after his conversion, daily personal piety.
It is not an aspect of religion out of which the greatest poetry
has ever come even in the most experienced hands. And Dryden
was no expert in the direction of souls. This poem is in the
tradition of the didactic funeral sermon, as we know such sermons in Donne, in Taylor, and in the French preachers, the
sermon of good works.[17] Yet Donne's handling of the mysteries
must have challenged Dryden. And in the *Epitaph for the
Monument of a Fair Maiden Lady,* at the very end of his life,
he essayed the metaphysical flight. His plays show that he had
in later years been thinking about neo-Platonic metaphysic. As
Professor Grierson has noted, line twenty of the epitaph closely
echoes a line from Donne. But an even more significant imitation lies in Dryden's description of a soul-informed body, and
in the fact that the images which describe it are emblematic.

Dryden thus recognizes the relation of Donne's imagery to his thought in this type of reflection. But Dryden's emblem simply defines a single idea; and his speculation soon ebbs again into a few lines on holy living and holy dying.

Chapter Six

CONCLUSION

FROM THIS SURVEY of almost a century of elegies, nothing emerges more clearly than the significance of the Renaissance conception of the formal nature of poetry, of the genres and of the great tradition; and at the same time, equally plain is the absolute dependence of these forms upon the substance they embody. We have been apt to forget, in our criticism of the rhetorical character of Renaissance poetic and of the over-development in English educational training of the sixteenth and seventeenth centuries of a naïve theory of imitation, how important the formal tradition is; art is art, and the tradition of art is always handed on in the forms of art whether we view these forms as logic or as ornament. At the same time, the relation of form to substance is always integral in great art. These two facts determine the literary history we have been looking at. If we think of pure poetic, the struggle which took place throughout the seventeenth century was principally the struggle between formalism and a philosophic view of art, between rhetoric narrowly conceived and the great genres. But the struggle changes its nature with the great intellectual and spiritual changes of the age. As we pass from the Renaissance endeavor to refound the social order and religion by means of Platonic and mediaeval psychology and through the renewal of interior life, to neoclassical trust in the common sense, and to rationalism, symbolic intention departs from art and the purely structural and traditionalist conception of the genre triumphs over a more organic view of it. In a sense one might say that the humanism of Petrarch is now free to become neoclassicism. It is as though the art forms were the artist's matter, and his ideas were the forms he imposed upon them. So Milton, the Platonist, conceived the tradition of the pastoral elegy, studied its invention in relation to its spirit, and by the fulness of his mastery of a view of death perfected the genre in *Lycidas.* It is the form as he determined it that Shelley and Arnold later used. But the thought of these later poets shared something of the scope of Milton's. Dryden had a great structural view of the design of the genre, of the logical unity of a theme and of the subject matter of the great types of poem. But he does not consider the organic relation of a given form to the psychological, the emotional, the philosophical character of its substance. And where his thought and feeling are unequal to the thought and feeling which originally created the form he follows, his design becomes an inflexible burden upon what he has to say. Hence his adjustment of the traditions of the elegy to the Pindaric in *To the Pious Memory . . . of Mistress Anne Killigrew* is a structural and logical triumph, but poetically hollow. That failure is a part of the limitation of his fundamental outlook. When he chooses the social this-worldly emphasis in his poem on Hastings, and social and critical emphasis in the ode on Mistress Killigrew, he is bending the elegy in the direction of his real interests and those of his age, but away from the spirit by which the elegy had taken shape. His sincerest, most moving elegiac verse is the lines on Oldham, simple as they are; and in these he fulfills the direction not of the formal elegy but of Hall's poem and of Roman classicism. But Dryden is a child of the Renaissance, too, and highly touched by the great English tradition. He never ceases his endeavor after the great passions and the great ideas. In this, his age did not sustain him. Christian theology exists to interpret and support a tragic view of the twofold nature of the world. And mere theological concepts will hardly be great without that tragic sense. Swift, who barred the mysteries, had more of the Renaissance vision than Dryden. From Dryden's figures, too, all symbolism, religious or psychological, has gone. Milton and Donne share the essential sense of the spiritual significance of things seen. From Dryden's self-existent world, the immanence of God has departed. It is hard to include his humanism within the same view as Milton's Platonic humanism. Yet he too had humanism, a great tradition of ideas and art, to defend from the new barbarians. When in *The Hind and the Panther* he aroused all the anti-Catholicism of England, his enemies answered by attacking the whole achievement of the Renaissance. Prior and Halifax attacked in the poem the tradition of Spenser and allegory, or of Virgil and of splendid poetry. Tom Brown attacked the tradition of poetry itself, linking even with Dryden the old outcry against all figured thought, the condemnation of poetry as enthusiasm. And yet Dryden in *Mistress Killigrew* embodied and handed on to later poets the habit of contemplating great ideas; and he helped preserve in English verse the tradition of a poetry aiming at passion, rich in imagery and in the various play of the mind.

But, if I may turn back upon my own thought, though we must see Milton and Donne on one side of a basic division in man's sense of his situation, Dryden on the other, and though this radical structure determines the contour of poetry in the seventeenth century, the metaphor does not take account of the depth and complexity of the age and of the division within the earlier age itself. The humanism which unites Milton and Dryden separates both from Donne; the realism of temper in Donne precurses that of Dryden and separates both from Milton. The complex of intellectual, religious, and social forces which shaped John Donne created a special poetic event within the larger development toward classicism I have just summarized. It was a major force of thought, of which Donne is the

first major and shaping voice in poetry and which both contributed to the final outcome for thought and poetry, and yet
yielded to the development of classicism as a whole. In England, Dryden's appreciation of Donne may be held to be
analogous within its own context to Fénelon's praise of Tertullian and St. Augustine, however far Dryden be separated from
Donne by other poetic considerations.

Donne united the great realistic intellectual impulse of the
Renaissance, the religious and philosophical revivals of the
fifteenth and sixteenth centuries and of the Counter-Reformation, and the recessions of thought which arose from the inter-
play of these forces. His influence was twofold. He himself
created one form of poetry expressive of the singular place of
the individual consciousness in the universe and in the world
of thought; and his influence was fruitful so long as the poetry
of the interior life continued to be written. In addition he deepened the tone of the rationalism which was taking possession of
poetry as of thought. But his attack upon the humanistic aspect
of poetry, as the Renaissance had conceived it, ultimately fell
before rising classicism; it was within the neoclassical tradition
itself that much of his force was felt. His method for expressing
psychological experience and relating it to speculation, his symbolic view of life, were mental and creative habits able to be
assimilated to classical elements in the poetry of the first half
of the seventeenth century, to the deep enrichment of that
poetry. Of this force Marvell is a striking example, as I shall
in the second half of this book develop. But on the other hand
among the dry wits and rhetoricians of poetry who cared little
for the other world or the interior life, he was one chief source
for the fantastic convention against which classical order had
exerted its discipline in France and was to exert it in England.
For a time therefore, though it does not appear in these elegies,
he became the prime object of classical attack. But in Dryden,
Donne's intellectual power exerted again a positive force.

As a lesser result of the symbolic impulse of which Donne is one voice there arose also within the major evolution of style a minor but not unimportant poetic episode, the taking shape of a distinctive theory of style which helped to develop one strain peculiar to the age, and, so far as I know, to England. The theory of imitation in the narrowest view of it treated the genre or type as a mere gathering together of a collection of motives germane to a particular subject. The poet imitated the motives and the style of his models. But with the flourishing of Renaissance allegorical and symbolic art, and with the work of Donne and *devotio moderna,* the decorum of style came often to be thought of as symbolic; different *modes* of style were suited to the genre not of a poem but of the particular invention in a poem which they expressed. This conception for a time invaded the classical conception of the three styles. Of this principle of variation of style the elegies offer many examples. It was a view so assimilable to the teaching of rhetoric that it persisted when all memory of symbolism had gone from art. Perhaps this idea was associated with Scaliger's view that any poem might be written in more than one of the three styles, and that the three styles themselves varied in their characters in different poems. Perhaps, also, it helped to sustain that love of concrete and figurative statement which England never yielded in the face of French influence and which gave Dryden's narrative and heroic poetry so distinctive a cast. In the lines on Hastings, at least, it is present. And Pope's *Windsor Forest,* with all its organization of motives from many sources, gathered around the core of Denham's simpler design, and its many styles traceable back to those various sources, is in some sense a last great example of it. Milton and Dryden returned from it to the classical conception of the genre as a form, a single unified form, and of the ultimate and basic significance of plot. The greatness of that conception of the genre shows in the way in which it lent itself in Donne to a poetry which was the direct expression of prayer, and which yielded as little as possible to the idea of poetry as distinct from thought or feeling, and to man's aesthetic yearning; in Milton to a great aesthetic representation of man's view of death that is mediate, sensuous, but that is also, however, almost symbolic; in Dryden to the most purely formal embodiment of the type of society's lament for its lost members.

Part Two

MARVELL AND THE VARIOUS LIGHT

From the *Pia Desideria*
of Herman Hugo (Antwerp, 1645)
(See page 162)

Chapter Seven

THE STRUCTURE OF POETRY

THE WISH TO recapture Andrew Marvell more completely than has yet been done needs no excuse beyond his own greatness and the fascination of the seventeenth century. At every turn a half-veiled though infinitely suggestive image, a line a little muffled to a sensitive ear, a rhythm precisely intimating a feeling that is less completely delineated in the words on which it flows, as we now comprehend those words, calls on us to restore our power to understand the poems and to keep fresh our naïve aesthetic experience of them by the process of historical re-creation of the intellectual and imaginative world in which their maker lived.

To contribute to such a reading of Marvell is the single aim of this study, in which I purpose to consider so much of Marvell's background as will make possible an *explication de texte* of three poems, his *Horatian Ode, Upon Appleton House,* and *The Garden,* considering other of his poems as they illuminate or are illuminated by these three. Yet though my study might have existed quite independently, my approach to it and the form which it takes has inevitably been affected by the stream of contemporary criticism of Marvell. To such sensitive interpretations as Mr. Tillyard's comment on the plot of *Little T. C.*[1] and Eliot's essay on Marvell in the anniversary volume[2]—to name only two without invidiousness—any following insight into Marvell must be indebted. But, despite comment so informed as this, and despite the historical scholarship of which Mr. Margoliouth's edition is so distinguished an example,[3] Marvell has been no less barbarously kidnapped than Donne. And with much of recent criticism of him, my reader will see, I am in profound though for the most part tacit disagreement. Although, as he will also see, I owe to the saner elements of it many fruitful particular suggestions, much modern criticism has been so essentially preoccupied with its own psychological and epistemological aesthetics that it reads less like commentary on Marvell than like a palimpsest of fresh exercises in composition—often fascinating, I do not deny. Or if it has been at many points in touch with the seventeenth century and sensitive in particular *aperçus,* it has nonetheless been rash and inconsistent, swinging between historical fact and modernistic interpretation, irresponsible as to any consequences to be drawn from the historical picture in its entirety, heedless of the aesthetic of another age.

In endeavoring to be consistently historical, I would not of course bar to modern critics their views of human nature, of the poetic process and of the nature of a poem, or their application of these views to the criticism of seventeenth-century poetry. A modern reader of Marvell will inevitably see Marvell finally in the light of his own view of poetry, and of his own imaginative needs. For poetry, as Marvell would have said, is an art of the mind and not an impulse from the objective experience of life. This modern reader may wish consciously to ask himself how far and by what means the abiding activity of poetry has in Marvell operated in and through the local and temporary forms of his poetic technique, and how far it has been conditioned by the patterns of thought Marvell brought to bear on his experience. Or he may wish to consider how adequately Marvell's own view of life does, indeed, interpret his poems or the experience and the feeling expressed in his poetry, or on the contrary, what the poems owe to conflict between the poet's conscious intellectual and artistic intentions as he designed and completed the poems and the presence within the poems of elements of emotion and creative forces of which he has not taken account. For such criticism, the critic's own view of life and his own psychological and aesthetic assumptions will be his tools. But he is hardly wise to muddy the wells of inquiry and to stultify his own science by reading himself only in Marvell. And before one goes on to meanings of which it is "not clear that this is what the author thought he was doing," one would be wise to form as clear an idea as possible as to what, indeed, he did think was his aim, what he did think he was making.

Let me take one or two broad instances of failure to make such historical distinction. To find in *The Garden* a state of mind resembling immersion in the fifth Buddhist Heaven must be of extraordinary interest to the student of the psychology of religion who wishes to study parallel states of mind in men living at widely separated times under widely different cultures. But it will hardly conduce so much to an understanding of Marvell himself as an investigation into the philosophical milieu in which the experience realized in the poem had its local and temporal life. Or, to take another example from the brilliant but sometimes wayward study of Miss Lloyd Thomas and Miss Bradbrook[4] (who had so well checked the excessive fancy of Mr. Empson in their own most penetrating first analysis of *The Garden,* which preceded that book), to find in *An Horatian Ode* as in *To His Coy Mistress* "a triple movement, the Hegelian thesis, antithesis and synthesis" is to muffle our sight doubly. First, we block off our general perception that Marvell's habit of thought had deep roots not in Hegelian but in mediaeval and Renaissance logic. And then we prevent ourselves from seeing in particular that a man of the seventeenth century would not be likely to apply to the judgment of history the same logical method of analysis that he would be accustomed to use in solving and defining a specific value in ethics. A simple reading would tell us that in *To His Coy Mistress* Marvell indicates by quite explicit transitions the tripartite division of the poem and that in the *Ode* there is no such rubric. To be run away with by a modern theory of wit obscures this elementary and important fact as to the design of the *Ode,* which has profoundly interesting thought patterns of its own.

What we seek to recover, then, is that balance of substance and form which existed in Marvell's poems in his own day. Present distortion beyond what time renders inevitable rests on twofold historical ignorance: ignorance of Marvell's own conception of the nature of poetry and the techniques of his art; partial ignorance as to his ideas and attitudes and as to the meaning for him of his symbols. Any attempt to understand him must follow both lines of investigation until it reaches their meeting point. The only difficulty lies in knowing which line to follow first. For the evidence as to Marvell's forms of expression and as to the tradition of his thought are in a measure interdependent. The emblem images which involve both Marvell's figures and his wordplay are one of the most distinctive characters of his poetry. Often highly traditional, they are, as I shall show and as I have already maintained in regard to Donne, the direct fruit of his consciously held view of life no less than of his spiritual history. Thus they not only control his expression but are the clue to his whole intellectual context, frequently serving as an important guide to us in discovering among the many strains of thought in seventeenth-century England those which formed the matrix of Marvell's lyric sensibility. But it is from the philosophy itself that we understand the character of the images. Yet since the traditions of art are handed on in the forms of art, and the form of any poem is a prime determinant of its meaning, I shall consider first the structure of Marvell's poems, their imagery, and their diction, asking my reader to bear in mind that further corroboration for my interpretation of his symbols will be found in my discussion of the general backgrounds of his thought and the most definite evidence of all in my *explication de texte,* where the iconology should justify itself by making every word lucid and significant in an organic whole.

It is important to remember first that Marvell is a poet himself highly conscious of form and genre in the design of his poems and that he lived in an age much given to the study of forms in art. One early poem of his, his elegy on Hastings, I have already considered in the first part of this book, where I have shown its place among the poetic traditions of the age, and the part which seventeenth-century interest in the forms of art contributed to shape the poem and can contribute to our mastery of it. All Marvell's poetry must be read in the light of the seventeenth-century poetic I have there defined. But in that analysis I was considering only one poem of his and one type of poem illuminated by the general aesthetic of the age. Here we are concerned with Marvell's special vision and his aesthetic in the totality of his poetry.

In poets of supreme aesthetic gift like Marvell—as contrasted with those like Vaughan, whose constructive gift seems so largely the by-product of general vision—the sense of pattern, of intoxication with forms, rhythms, diction learned by imitation and gradually filling themselves with more and more original content, is in any age one of the first powers to awaken. In Marvell's day, when so much teaching was devoted to formal imitation, and when a highly complex and studied system of forms had arisen, the sense of art was bound very early to take possession of such a sensibility as his. And Marvell's early poetry gives clear evidence that he conceived his craft in terms of types in which in each poem treatment of subject, mode of development, and expression have a common traditional character. *Eyes and Teares* and *Mourning* are Marinistic not merely in their subjects and in their imagery at once witty and sensational, but in the handling of their tetrameters also. *Daphnis and Chloe* in subject and tone follows the cynicism of the court anti-Platonists. Its verse form also, the provenience of its images, its tough and familiar diction, its phrasing, clearly suggest Suckling, though it has more of image and paradox than one would find in Suckling, thereby revealing significantly Marvell's essential and ingrained habit of imagination. *Clorinda and Damon,* in marked contrast, reflects the older tradition of the pastoral elegy no less in its motifs and in its epithets than in its dialogue, its allegory, and its mythology.[5] It is less the imitativeness of this early verse which deserves our attention than that it imitates in each case the total structural character of the poems which are its models. Later, the *Horatian Ode* is notable for its combination of Horatian structure, meter and diction and, *mutatis mutandis—* for Marvell unites a transcendental view and transcendental images to express it with much of the Horatian sense of order and personal calm—of Horatian attitude. I shall point out in the proper place the formal emblematic structure as well as the emblematic content and dialectic in *The Drop of Dew* and *The Coronet.*

In speaking of the strong sense which Marvell and his age had of the distinctive poetic kinds, we think first of the aesthetic character of each genre as a formal type of poem expressive of its distinctive subject matter and artistic mode, and of the humanistic tradition of imitation by which the genre was studied in past poetry and responsibility to it was developed. But in fact among seventeenth-century poets, the idea of the logical character of a poem in the sense of its dialectic and the intellectual tradition embodied in it as well as of its artistic aim exerts a determining influence upon the development of its form and gives to the poet's conception of some of the genres a character quite other than the formal meaning the idea was to take on when classicism and neoclassicism triumphed.[6] Of the outcome of this view on style and the varied styles of different sections of a poem I have spoken in the first half of this book. But dialectic conceptions also affected the structural forms of poetry as well as their expression. At this point, then, I want first to consider as a background for our study of Marvell a particular design of poem which will illustrate the logical genre and which was common in the age. This is the form of poem created by the influence of the logical debate, which was still so prevalent an element in the education and thought of Marvell and his contemporaries, no less than of their sixteenth-century predecessors. It was a type which developed far beyond its simple form in the mediaeval *débat*. It is important to recognize to the full not merely the explicit paradox and conflict of definition and value which inform the metaphysical poems of the day—the paradox, at least, has not lacked attention in modern criticism—but the distinctive genre of the debate poem, and the poem of categorical definition. To be aware of this type of poem illuminates all of Marvell's poetry; it is essential for an understanding of *The Garden*.

The mediaeval schoolman's definition by the *sic et non*, reinforced by renewed struggle in the Renaissance between classical idealisms and classical materialisms, and by the Counter-Reformation's concerted effort to capture the world in the world's own terms, and deepened by wars, and by the dislocation of old social sanctions in the ruthless emergence of new economic patterns, exerted a strong influence on the poetry of the age. That influence gives their structure to entire poems, or to incidents in longer poems, or it supplies integral structural symbols. Mr. Tillyard has shown us how to understand the twin definitions of the gifts of the spirit in Milton's *L'Allegro* and *Il Penseroso* in the light of Milton's academic exercises in defense of a formal logical position.[7] And Mr. Sensabaugh has pointed out in how much detail Milton's *Comus* would supply a comprehensive formal refutation of the theories of Platonic love current in the court of Henrietta Maria.[8] Such formal ethical dialectic was the ancient prerogative of masque and

pageant, the very breath of their life. It filled other literature
no less widely.

Of the large literature of that symbolic rose which was the
prize in the debate between the worldly and the Christian views
of life, one need only recall Herrick's roses and Spenser's and
Tasso's rose song on the one hand and on the other, the rose of
Herbert's *Virtue* and Jeremy Taylor's enchanting rose newly
springing from the clefts of its hood and so soon to fall into
the number of weeds and outworn faces. Indeed, the whole
wanton and perverse beauty of Acrasia's Bower, which is contrasted on the ethical side with that simple and natural garden
not actually present in the poem but forever awaiting us beyond
the gate, and on the metaphysical side with the ordered Gardens
of Adonis whose place in the artifice of eternity Mrs. Bennett
has so well defined, that bower is an epitome of the dialectic
which runs through the heart of the *Faerie Queene*. And before
Spenser, Palingenius in his popular treatment of the neo-Platonic
view of generation had opened with an explicit invitation to the
Epicurean gardens of pleasure and materialism against which
so much of the thought of Florentine neo-Platonism was directed; an invitation given, however, only to be formally rejected first for virtue's garden and then for the neo-Platonic
cosmic gardens of creation. It was one of the triumphs of Jesuit
literature, as part of its larger transformation of the world of
art, to have seized upon the emblem literature of profane love
and reversed its meaning in the emblems of the art of divine
love. The emblem of the sunflower from Vaenius' *Amoris
Divini Emblemata,* illustrated and described by Signor Praz in
his *Studies in Seventeenth Century Imagery,*[9] affords in neat
space a precise illustration of the whole movement. Or another
parallel may be found in such a poem as the eighth elegy of the
third book of Herman Hugo's *Pia Desideria,*[10] in which the roll
first of classical heroines, weeping and tragic, and then of
maidens turned to water nymphs is called up to serve the uses

of repentance and to illustrate dissolution thereby into tears of contrition.

A theme hardly less commonly debated in individual poems than worldly and profane love or than the garnering or denial of the rose of the senses was the theme of hope, a theme of more subtle variation than the others, one's attitude toward hope being the index and symbol of views of life ranging from the most idealistic to the most crassly Epicurean, from the most ascetically devout and otherworldly through the stoically realistic to the most naturalistic. Cowley's and Crashaw's companion poems on hope are but two among dialectical pieces on the subject, numerous to the point of utterly jading the poets.[11] And we may round out our point by illustrating one type of these poems at some length from Marini's *Della Speranza,* a poem so germane to our purpose that it ought to be available to all readers of Marvell. The poem, one of three formal pieces on Faith, Hope, and Charity, is not manifestly a debate. Yet implicitly, in its use and transformation of the senses, it is a deliberate reversal of Marini's courtly work, and in its symbolism (which, though no more than a mere string of conceits, offers a striking parallel to the imagery of Marvell's *Garden*) it is no less significant and characteristic of debate poetry than if it were a full poem of debate expressing both sides. At the same time it is incidentally valuable to us as a vivid example of that sensuality in symbolism, so different from the symbolism of the mediaeval Latin hymns, for instance, which Marini threw into the stream of European literature.

> O Speme, ò vivo fiore
> Ristoro de gli spirti afflitti, & egri;
> Tu qual più tristo core
> T' accoglie frà i pensier torbidi, e negri,
> Riconforti, e rallegri;
> Tu colto in tua verdura
> Da man semplice, e pura;

O come belle, o come
Tessi ghirlande à te più belle chiome.

Fior vago, e vezzosetto,
A far di te prede amorose, e belle,
Gl' Angioli per diletto
Quasi di Paradiso api novelle
Volano da le stelle.
Fede vera, e zelante,
Zelo fido, e costante
Son tuoi veri cultori
De begl' Horti di Dio Zeffiro, e Clori.

Fior segnato, e dipinto
Non di note profane, ond' ancor serba
Aiace con Giacinto
Del suo nome real descritta l'herba:
Non qual rosa superba
Tinta del più bel sangue,
Non qual fù vista esangue
In mortal pallidezza,
Mà d'un color, che sol nel ciel s'apprezza.

Fior lieto, & amoroso....

Fior di frutti divini
Felice precursor, caro messaggio,
Che ne' vaghi giardini
Vien maturato da celeste raggio,
La dove a breve Maggio
Un Autunno immortale,...

Speri l'alma, e respiri,
Che di perir non teme
Mentre verde, e vivace è fior di speme.

It is against such a background that, as I shall try to show
presently, we must read Marvell's *Garden* and, to instance one
specific detail, that we must understand the symbolic use of

green in that poem. In *To his Coy Mistress* no lines more sharply focus the teeming implications of its debate than

> And yonder all before us lye
> Desarts of vast Eternity

evoking so concretely as they do the centuries of sermon and devotional admonition which in that moment throng through the poet's mind and give scope to his denial of their lesson.[12]

It is characteristic that the denial should turn upon an image. For the vision of the desert and of the handful of dust had been down through the Christian ages no mere metaphor, and no mere scientific assertion, either, of man's origin, but had been recognized as one of the basic analogies in that divine science in which the impress and shadow, the *vestigia* of the cosmic order were set visibly on the face of created things. And Marvell's imagery must be understood in the light of the revival of the philosophies which dwelt upon symbolic thought, neo-Platonism in various of its forms and the older symbolic interpretation of the Bible.[13] Not only is the substance of this literature essential to a full understanding of Marvell, but it supplies the technique of much of his imagery, that philosophical geometry which I have already discussed in relation to Donne and Donne's use of emblem techniques.

That Marvell was interested in the emblem proper seems certain. Misses Bradbrook and Lloyd Thomas have offered a probable identification of his strange *Unfortunate Lover* as an emblem and the same authors point out suggestive parallels, though analogues only, between the last stanza of *The Garden* and Jesuit emblem books. In that stanza he is perhaps rather indebted to a common source in the literature of the Song of Songs and to actual gardens suggested by it, than directly to Jesuit literature. But his lines,

> O who shall, from this Dungeon, raise
> A Soul enslaved so many ways?

> With bolts of Bones that fettered stands
> In Feet; and manacled in Hands

immediately evoke in our memories the pictures familiarized to seventeenth-century readers by such iconologies as Herman Hugo's plate for his elegy on "Who shall deliver me from the body of this death?"—a drawing in which the soul, not very dissimilar in appearance to a Van Dyke Baby Stuart, struggles to thrust apart the imprisoning bars of the skeleton torso within which it stands. *On a Drop of Dew* and *The Coronet* remind us of the work of George Herbert, whose poems like *The Collar* they closely resemble in their religious motif, in their treatment of image, and in metrical structure. Such poems of Herbert's have been shown to have a direct connection with emblem literature, and these of Marvell ought certainly to be thought of as emblem poems.[14] The relationship of Marvell's image of the dew to a broad philosophic background which we must be familiar with if we are to understand the image fully becomes clear if we analyze his poem in detail.

In its conception of the cosmos or its theology and in its imagery the poem is an expression of Renaissance neo-Platonism, in contrast to his *Dialogue Between the Resolved Soul and Created Pleasure,* the elements of whose Platonism had been long since woven into the texture of Christianity. The poem is a formal statement of the soul's place in the universe in the extreme neo-Platonic view. The soul of man, a ray of the clear fountain of Eternal Day, or in other words an emanation of the Divine Mind, enters reluctantly into the bodily life. To enter is a corruption, for to do so the soul leaves the world of pure intelligence and the contemplation of the One (or the Good), in whom are absolute Truth and Beauty, to become entangled in matter, which is nothingness. And it can have its highest life, even in bodily form, only when it turns away from sense and appetite and back to thought and through thought to God.

In this view of the one and the many, the Divine Intelligence is light, matter is darkness. And in the world of Nature which is created by the Soul of the World, the Sun is the immediate representation of the Divine Light and as an instrumentality creates the life of the particular things of this world which is below the moon and which is the scene of change and decay. The moon has her place between the sun and things, and she may turn her face to the world and be dark or to the sun and shine in brightness. She is, in Nature, the symbol of the soul of man. That soul is made dark as it turns to the life of the world and matter, through absorption in the senses and the life of the appetites, by which it may be destroyed; bright on the side which it turns to the contemplation of the Divine, and radiant in joy as it fulfills its true being and moves upward toward God. Such is the picture of the soul as it is imaged, to cite examples familiar to me, in Giovanni Pico della Mirandola's *De Hominis Dignitate* and in Leone Ebreo's *Dialoghi d'Amore* or in more general terms in an analogy drawn from the moon in the *De Rebus Coelestibus* of Pontanus. This view is I believe implicit to the full in Marvell's imagery.[15]

In the exquisite line on the "sweet leaves and blossoms green," the rose might seem to belong in the garden of Nun Appleton. But *purple* is symbolic of the pomp and luxury of the world. It stands in direct contrast with the adjectives *white* and *intire* applied to the manna, adjectives which have unmistakable religious and philosophical symbolism with reference to divine purity and to the circle or divine unity. This symbolic intention is even more clear in the Latin. In that version, the world is expressed by the terms of traditional association with the world and the flesh, *odoratum Ostrum, Tyria veste, vapore Sabae;* and the association of the purity of the soul with the religious concept of chastity is made explicit in the phrase, *Vixque premat casto mollia strata pede,* and in the simile of the young girl:

Qualis inexpertam subeat formido Puellam,

. . . .

Sic & in horridulas agitatur Gutta procellas,
Dum prae virgineo cuncta pudore timet.

These images by their explicit emphases on chastity as a symbol of purity (and of divine love, of course—see Milton's faith,
hope, and chastity) and by the associations of the terms *Sabae,*
and so forth, cast over the Latin poem a tone more traditionally
Christian than neo-Platonic, however.

The manna itself perhaps carries no more meaning than the
literal analogy. But since we are already in a symbolic world, it
may be that Marvell expected his reader to recall that manna,
like dew, is a symbol of grace, as it is defined by Ficino in his
De Amore and by Richard of St. Victor in his treatise on Canticles, or more particularly as Erasmus in his *Enchiridion* records
its traditional meaning, that as small it symbolizes the humility
of the speech of Christ, as white it symbolizes to all mortals
soiled with the blackness of error the saving doctrine of Christ,
snowy white and pure.

The abstraction and impersonality of the poem are a thing
rare with Marvell, but characteristic of emblem poems, which
are not in the ordinary sense mere lyrics but, like the bestiary
symbols of mediaeval sermon and sculpture, meditative exercises, useful in fixing true opinion upon the imagination.

In Marvell's poem on *The First Anniversary of the Government under O. C.* there are, I think, reminiscences of the same
strictly figured neo-Platonic imagery. Marvell by the time he
wrote this poem wished to show Cromwell as one divinely
gifted to restore to England an order reflecting the order of the
universe, one conceivably who may usher in the millennium. To
express this, three types of imagery are interwoven in the poem.
Puritan millennial hopes rest, of course, on the Old Testament,
and Marvell sets Cromwell in the context of Old Testament

prophecy. But this prophetic theme is not the opening theme of the poem, which begins with a general philosophical and symbolic portrait of Cromwell.

The common man and the common ruler eddy in time in this world of change and decay, like vanishing circles in water. Cromwell, unlike them, is no creature of the senses or of selfish ambition, but an intellectual being: a man, that is, living in the light of divine reason. He moves up into the unchanging celestial world. His cycle is the cycle of the sun and with the sun he becomes identified throughout the poem. This figure, as we have just reminded ourselves, suggests neo-Platonic cosmology in which the sun is to the world of Nature, to the visible cosmos, that is, the representative of the Sun of the Divine Light or Mind, and the central instrument by which the work of the Divine Mind is wrought. And the conception of order as musical harmony typified in the harmony of the spheres is in such symbolism integrated with that concept. The reference to the Platonic year fixes, at least, the context of thought at play in Marvell's mind.[16]

The next images comparing Cromwell to the great mythological founders of states are part of the same context, the two sets of images being interwoven through the idea of harmony. In neo-Platonism before the Renaissance the great exemplary heroes of Greek heroic legend, according to the pattern of Stoic thought, had, like allegorized myth, been synthesized with Platonism and made symbolic in it, in this synthesis following the habit which had existed at least from the time of Alexandrian civilization on down through the Renaissance, of conceiving all knowledge and all history to be truly one in both a literal and a symbolic way which is hard for our imaginations to compass. Mr. Hughes's study of Christ and the hero myth in Milton is extremely illuminating for Marvell's poem.[17] Of this symbolism the figures of the Old Testament are an integral part; and Marvell's association of Cromwell with Old Testament

prophecy is thus more complex than that in ordinary millen-
narian thought. It combines a rational ethical interpretation of
Old Testament history and prophecy with a Platonism both rational and symbolic that unite to give Marvell his sharp sense
of difference from the vulgar Fifth Monarchy men of his day.
Already in Philo Judaeus the Rabbinic view of Old Testament
heroes as moral types or rather as symbolic figures had been integrated with Platonic allegory, possibly under Stoic influence.[18]
And Leone Ebreo might have shown Marvell a great Renaissance endeavor in the same tradition to synthesize the newly re-
discovered and reinterpreted writings of Plato and Plotinus with
Judaism and to give once more a common allegorical or symbolic interpretation to them. In Leone also the cosmic symbolism
Marvell here uses is developed in detail. Parallel illustrations
of heroic legend are commonplaces in Castiglione's *Courtier*.

Marvell's imagination may have been set off on the imagery
in which he defines this heroic ideal by an actual historical fact
which reminds us vividly of the general prevalence of interest
in symbol and emblem in his England. Commenting on the line,

And shines the Jewel of the Yearly Ring

Mr. Margoliouth writes: "Cromwell's crest was 'a demi-lion
rampant argent holding in the dexter paw a gem ring or'. It
has been suggested to me that, as the sun was the tutelar planet
of the lion, there is here 'a twist of heraldic and astrological
figures'." And on the lines which apply to Cromwell the
Amphion image,

> Such was that wondrous Order and Consent,
> When *Cromwell* tun'd the ruling Instrument,

"Cromwell's Protectorate was established by the instrument of
Government, 1653."[19]

To this type of emblem image most of Marvell's figures belong, though not all are so strictly formal in development or so

serious. By Marvell's time many influences had come to bear upon the witty image. *Eyes and Tears,* the indebtedness of which to Crashaw Mr. Martin has pointed out, seems to represent mere experimentation in the stuff and techniques of poetry. But Marvell probably continued to feel the influence of Marini, which is here indirectly at work; for Marini's formula for poetry as a succession of witty images seemed more serious to the men of that day, who were accustomed to symbolic images, than it can to ours. Then Donne's delight in ingeniously witty comparison and in the sheer play of the mind had descended also both directly and through Cowley, to whom metaphysical ideas were no longer the very stuff of his imagination or views of life seriously to be reckoned with, but motifs to be woven into poetry. Yet what had become in Cowley merely witty geometry was by other poetry contemporary with Marvell constantly being called back into serious use as symbol. As Miss Bradbrook has shown,[20] it is almost certain that Marvell saw while he was at Fairfax's, the poems of Mildmay Fane, Fairfax's brother-in-law. Fane, like Marvell, as we shall see presently, was influenced by the feeling for nature in the French poet St. Amant, and Fane's poems may have been something of a model to Marvell. Many of them are a tumbling alphabet of emblems in little, or *argutiae,* as they would have been called by the Spanish sermon writers who pulled such conceits out of the tradition of rhetoric to put them to their own psychological uses, or of *imprese* as perhaps Lord Herbert would have named them.[21] In the same emblematic kind is the almost contemporary work of Benlowes. But of all the poets in the line of Donne, as it has been perhaps too narrowly called, Marvell was the one who grasped most fully Donne's use of symbolic image to analyze individual states of thought and feeling in dramatic lyrics in relation to the great patterns of moral and philosophical thought of his tradition, possibly because he of them all knew most of that tradition. Of that free and supple lyric use of the emblem,

The Definition of Love will spring to every one's mind as an example. Perhaps the imaginations of no other of the great poets of the age were so deeply penetrated by symbolism as Donne's and Marvell's or by a symbolism grounded in so wide a tradition. And this symbolism informs the imagery of all Marvell's chief poems outside the satires. Even there it sets its characteristic stamp on the wit.

When Marvell speaks, for instance, in *Upon Appleton House* of the "light Mosaick" of the leaves and of reading in "Nature's mystick Book," I do not know what specific meaning his words can have unless they are an explicit reference to symbolic interpretations of Genesis, conceivably cabbalistic ones such as Henry More brought into England but much more probably works like Bonaventura's *Sermons upon the Hexaëmeron,* in which man's immediate experience of God in the creatures is bound up with the whole system of symbolic thought upon his place in the creation and upon the scale of the soul's ascent to contemplation.[22] Earlier in the poem the "holy mathematicks" which Marvell prefers to worldly pursuits is surely to be understood in the light of the passage from Bonaventura I have already quoted. And in Bonaventura the image is significant because so traditional in symbolic or in allegorical thought. In *The Garden* as I shall show at length later, the "various light" is the light of the many springing from the One real light. There is no more central analogy in neo-Platonism and in the symbolism which arose from it and gathered about it.

Wordplay is integral to Marvell's imagery. Of it I must say something at length since it is important to recognize not only its general prevalence in the age but the logical and strict character of it in Marvell. Upon a mistaken interpretation of it depends much of the warping of Marvell in recent criticism. His images and plays upon word have been interpreted as free association, notably by Mr. Empson but by others also in Mr. Empson's school of criticism; and his puns and double meanings have been held to impart a light or cynical tone.[23] To these critics who have exploited Marvell's "ambiguity" we owe a fresh awareness of the great number of double meanings in him. But they have perverted both his substance and his tone. In his poems, though many emotional currents flow into the making of a poem and into the words of which it is made, the result is not a "stream of consciousness." In the finished poem a context has been set up which determines the specific meanings of the words, often suggesting several meanings but ruling out many possible others. And though, as in passages of *Upon Appleton House,* wordplay may be the instrument for conveying a fantastic half-seriousness of tone, it does so precisely because in a normal context in the seventeenth century and in Marvell such language has the utmost seriousness of tone, whether in tragedy or in the certainly not gay comedies of Ben Jonson. Wordplay is with Marvell so ever-present a habit because it expresses his philosophical irony and paradox.

So far as I know, no adequate history of the theories of the sixteenth and seventeenth centuries about wordplay and of its origins in the literature of that period exists. In speaking earlier of the symbolism of Tertullian, Philo, Origen, Bonaventura, I have suggested some of its backgrounds.[24] Since its character in seventeenth-century literature in general has been so widely disregarded in comment on Marvell, I shall not fetch too wide a circle if I say something of its character in the literature just preceding Marvell, before analyzing some of Marvell's own double meanings.

Wordplay was one of the recognized devices of ornamentation of poetry from the beginning of the re-creation of style in the Renaissance.[25] But even in Lyly, as Croll has best shown, though wordplay owed so much to the tradition of pure schemes of sound, it threw into prominence the underlying dialectic of thought. And in the grave passages of Sidney's *Arcadia* it is already again the tool of ironic paradox, though still elaborate in form and cast into *schemata verborum*. In *Hamlet* one finds almost an epitome of the development of wordplay. In Shakespeare altogether wordplay is so important and so various that to sketch a full analysis of it would be to have covered all that concerns the lesser issue of Marvell. But that I cannot do. Shakespeare, however, so perfects and reduces to their ultimate form the techniques of language which he uses that their nature is particularly easy to see in him; and the better to understand Marvell's tone we may take time to look at two cases from *Hamlet,* intimately related to each other. When Polonius says,

> Do you believe his tenders as you call them?
> . . . .
>
> That you have ta'en these tenders for true pay
> Which are not sterling. Tender yourself more dearly
> Or, not to crack the wind of the poor phrase,
> Running it thus, you'll tender me a fool

these puns are not intended by Polonius for mere decoration. They channel a clear meaning, though it is a meaning that flows out in very diffuse runnels. Their diffuseness is not, however, the significant fact about their method though characteristic of Polonius in his approach to senility. Shakespeare has used them as a typical means to define for us the instructed folly of Polonius. His development of his thought through puns marks the mere sophistry of his mind. Perhaps Shakespeare counted on his audience to remember specifically the tradition of Euphuism and the verbal intoxication of *Love's Labor's Lost* and thus to receive from the ring of these words a signal to take note in Polonius of the decayed dialectic which is one important element in Euphuism, and in *Love's Labor's Lost*. Or conceivably he might have counted that they would recollect the examples of the sophister and rhetorician on one hand and the thinker on the other in the trial scene of *Arcadia* and would judge Polonius accordingly.

In Hamlet's words to Gertrude, in contrast, the profoundest ironic movement of Hamlet's mind has taken the place of Polonius' sophistry:

> *Queen.*   Hamlet, thou hast thy father much offended.
> *Hamlet.*   Mother, you have my father much offended.
> *Queen.*   Come, come, you answer with an idle tongue.
> *Hamlet.*   Go, go, you question with a wicked tongue.

Here Hamlet suspends the same or parallel words in two contexts which give them in each case very precise meanings, and by this juxtaposition he makes them the focal point at which his universe is contrasted with that of his mother. Jonson's defense of the instructed pun as opposed to the clench in *Every Man in His Humour* is much in the spirit of these lines from *Hamlet*.

Though much less given to wordplay in his poetry than Marvell, Donne is probably his immediate forebear, both drawing, however, from the habit of thought of an age. To take his line,

> When thou hast done, thou hast not done.

The conceptions of the individual and his aloneness and recalcitrance and danger of damnation on one side, and on the other the sense of the ceaseless yearning and generosity of Christ's love, which lie back of that line, had been precisely defined by generations of experience and of precise logical thought before Donne wrote the line. That is why Donne can secure the effect he does secure through one bare word which suddenly precipitates the relationship of the two concepts in the drama of one soul. Between Shakespeare and Donne in these examples there is the notable difference that in Donne the two concepts or entities which are brought together belong to formal philosophical or theological thought, whereas in Shakespeare the contrasted elements arise immediately in the struggling mind from the action of life.

In Donne's pun and in the last plays on word from Shakespeare, the full irony of the tone owes something to the sense they awaken in us of the frail verbal instrument by which the tragic import is carried; something—the *Hamlet* line certainly very much—to his and our awareness of the contrast between the trivial and the serious significance of language, its merely rhetorical or its intellectual use. In this contrast is symbolized, explicitly in Hamlet's catching up of Gertrude's words, the whole contrast of two attitudes to life. The point is worth stressing; for it is almost like a specific statement by Shakespeare and by Donne on the issue as to the tone implied by punning. The tradition of pun and wordplay in symbolic poetry shows that the tone implied by them is oftenest tragic and in the strictest sense metaphysical.[26] Indeed, though we have no explicit statement from Donne on the joke for God's sake, the innumerable wordplays of his *La Corona* speak loud, and the European background upon which Donne draws so much in those sonnets offers abundant explicit comment.[27] The type of wordplay which Crashaw derived from European sources will also spring to mind.

Marvell's wordplays are just of this intellectual character we have been defining. But they often have their roots in even more formal concepts than that implied in the pun from Donne just cited, or in even more conventional systems of symbolic thought and representation. And from these they take their meaning.

In the lines on the Scots in the *Horatian Ode,* as Mr. Margoliouth says in his note, the pun on the derivation of *Pict* from *pingere* was a conventional figure, as is shown by the fact that it was used by Cleveland also. Miss Bradbrook and Miss Lloyd Thomas extend the figure and the play on words in Marvell by pointing out the color meaning as well as the sense of *steadfast* in the word *sad.* In this extended analogy between the dress and characters of the two sides, Marvell sets his political judgment against something of an eternal background. For the analogy belongs to that large mass of figures or emblems in which the seventeenth century was accustomed to see the world of things as a continued alphabet or symbol of its own mind and condition or of the world of ideas; and the very dress of Cromwell compared with that of the Scots becomes a symbol of his divine mission. This precise meaning leaves no room, I think, for such adumbrations attributed to Marvell as that "a civilized state can digest the forced power" though the poem as a whole defends force. Again, the heat pun in *The Garden,* "When we have run our passion's heat" draws upon the Renaissance analysis of the varied conceptions of love and perhaps upon the symbolic embodiment of that interpretation in allegorized myths and legends such as the tale of Atalanta. Mr. King has done useful work in reawakening our awareness of this and other double values by comparing the English and Latin versions of the poem,[28] though he overlooks the differences of medium in the two. But then as he pushes further his independent analysis of the English poem, he ignores what we have just learned of Marvell's method in those instances in which we can be almost certain as to the meanings of his words in their context. Having proved the existence of wordplay in the poem, he goes on to invoke from the implications of wordplay meanings and tones which bear no relation to those Marvell's known techniques habitually evoke. He is possibly still half-historical when he says that *"stumbling, Insnaired, flowers* would image sin to the Puritan in Marvell," though Puritan Marvell is not. But he is very imperfectly historical both as to Marvell's religious attitude or his attitude toward nature and as to the limitation of that conception as Marvell here used it to Puritanism. And when he goes on to say that by contrasting the normal sin-associations of these words with his safe helplessness now, Marvell presents the occasion as amiably ludicrous, he is worlds away both from the traditional frames of reference of the particular symbols and from the tone of puns in general in the seventeenth century. The tone of the puns in the *Ode* is tragic and ironic. In *The Garden* they convey the philosophy upon which the serenity is poised.

Marvell's wordplay is never used at random, or in casual free association. It is used at special points to bring out particular paradoxes or interrelationships. Or where the pun itself leads our thought, it is as part of an already established context of thought. And we in evaluating or taking in the wordplay should be guided by the context as a whole. For as I have already said, not all even precisely delimited meanings that we can find with the aid of a dictionary are to be taken as intended by Marvell in his particular use of any word, to say nothing of the further connotations, private to Marvell or public to the age, which we are able to think up. This point is perhaps important enough for our general reading of seventeenth-century literature to be worth laboring a little. In the line,

> The forward youth that would appear

Miss Bradbrook and Miss Lloyd Thomas interpret *forward* as "both precocious and brave." Lucan had said,

> Sed nescia virtus
> stare loco: solusque pudor non vincere bello.
> acer et indomitus, quo spes quoque ira vocasset
> ferre manum et nunquam temerando parcere ferro.

And this May had translated,

> But restlesse valour, and in warre a shame
> Not to be Conqueror; fierce, not curb'd at all,
> Ready to fight, where hope, or anger call
> His forward Sword; ...

The passage and its translation give us "the forward youth," and the "industrious valour" of line 33, as Mr. Margoliouth points out; also "restless Cromwell."[29] Marvell, barely touching, however, on the restless aspect of Lucan's Caesar—which indeed would ill serve as a model, despised as Caesar's restlessness is by Lucan—enlarges upon the concept of valour or *virtue*. This is the meaning of "forward youth" completed and delimited by the phrase "that would appear."

Wordplay and image in Marvell are closely involved with each other and are alike in method. They are equally precise. The *heat* image sets together a precise metaphor of the life of the senses and a precise criticism of it as the surrender to passion. And in such images we are carried back to the dialectical character of Marvell's poems in their entire design. I hope to show that the immediate experience which is interpreted in *The Garden* is sharpened and defined for Marvell by the poetry of other poets celebrating the way of life which Marvell there rejects.

In barring out too multiple association from the images, I do not suggest that only the images apparent on the surface to the reader of today make part of Marvell's poem. I think Miss Bradbrook and Miss Lloyd Thomas right in their interpretation of *The Picture of Little T.C.* in finding the theme of death appear in the third stanza through the *shade* image. This image has escaped many sensitive readers. It lies in a double meaning, not part of the primary surface statement of the poem at that point, though it comes to the surface in the last stanza. Yet once we have the clue to it, we find that the meaning of the image is completely delimited. Moreover, the double meaning does not depend on a personal association of Marvell's with the word *shade*, a personal symbolism. Rather, it has a general meaning, applied to an objective fact which the recipients of the poem would have recognized. For Mr. Margoliouth has rendered it probable that underlying Marvell's reflection on T.C. was the recollection of an elder sister who first bore her name and who died in infancy.[30] Nor does it depend upon sense association at either "conscious" or "unconscious" levels. It is a classical image, a conceptual image of precise and traditional meaning. It is because the contrast between the glories of our blood and state on the one hand and the grave on the other is so central and so omnipresent a thought to the Middle Ages and to the Renaissance, and because the thought is so traditionally represented in the two figures of a triumph and of a shade or spirit, that we understand it.[31] The plot of the poem is characteristic of the metaphysical spirit of the seventeenth century, as of the historical situation which had whetted that spirit, in making a sudden turn from life to the idea of death and in bringing the two ideas together in a double image of sense and of the eternal world. And if we may seek the first impulse of the image in the fact that Marvell in looking at this Theophila thought of the other nipped so early in the bud, it was yet not his one thought but a whole tradition of religion and of art which turned the intuition into a poem. For no age was ever more aware of possible conflicting schemes of value, of the many ways in which a man may organize his experience of the paradoxes and ironic frustrations of life. But to express this metaphysical insight the image itself must be as lucid and final as the often used classical

> On her buried body lay
> Lightly, gentle earth.

Indeed, multiple image and pun are not necessary to metaphysical poetry in the broader sense. What is essential is intellectual control: precision of picture in the primary sense image, a clear conception in the larger analogue, clear and usually traditional meaning in the symbol, if there be a symbol; a pivotal point, in sum, at which two clearly apprehended worlds are brought together. The roof image in the first and last stanzas of Hardy's "She hears the storm" is a striking illustration of this.

It is harder to be sure we catch many of Marvell's symbols that come from the mediaeval and Renaissance worlds than those which come from the Latin tradition more familiar to us. There must be many implications in him which I have entirely missed. Nor in those which I have drawn out do I suppose that I am always precisely right. I intend merely to draw the parallels and analogues in him to traditions of thought which it may be inferred from the poems themselves and then from general historical probability that Marvell knew. Others more widely read in patristic theology and neo-Platonic philosophy, in mediaeval and Renaissance literature, will correct and supplement what I supply. What is possible, however, despite the limitation of our specific knowledge, is for us to be guided by the total character of a symbol rather than by multiple meanings of single words, and to be led by it to the tradition from which it draws that character in which lies its very nature as a symbol, a tradition which then becomes hypothetically a part of Marvell's tradition; and also to be governed in our interpretation of detail by the structure of each poem as a whole.

I do not know, for instance, of anything in the demonstrated habit of Marvell's thought to indicate that *apple* in stanza III, and likewise *melon,* through the Greek meaning of that word, refer to the Tree of Knowledge, as Mr. Empson has suggested.[32] This could only be argued, I think, if every detail in that stanza, to begin with, fitted into the same scheme of symbols. And we must further be sure, even when we find a symbol commonly used in the seventeenth century, as these of Marvell's are *not* known to us to be, that it is distinctly enunciated in the particular poem we are considering, and at one with the method of the poem as a whole, before we declare it to be part of the meaning of any particular poem.

Still less does the fact that Marvell frequently used traditional images and used them in double statements warrant us in inferring that he intended—which is to say that the poem in its first meaning contains—images and double meanings of quite other types. The critics who assume a stream-of-consciousness progression in poetry and a universal symbolic psychology, without being very scientific in their use of these assumptions, sometimes float on a line of suggestion from image to interpretation to image in a way quite alien to Marvell's technique. And into the particular image, as into the word, they read a multiplicity of meanings which assume all conceivable associations. Yet if my interpretation of Marvell's poems is full and consistent, his imagery is clearly defined and each image focused by the intellectual character of its context upon one or two meanings. Marvell's plotting or structure as a whole is formal, often severely logical, though the emotion which is the subject of its plot may develop most subtly and delicately—dramatically—to its resolution. And whether the development of this emotion make use of a series of extended images controlling the main movements of the plot, of many and shifting images, usually within the controlling image, or of a single extended image, the total structure defines and limits the images which it encloses and upon which it depends. It is indeed upon this precision of reference that the ironic contrasts and the richness of juxtaposition depend.

What I have said may be drawn together by looking closely at one very complex image upon the detail of whose genesis in Marvell's experience and reading we have a good bit of information and which we may, consequently, analyze with a good bit of objectivity. The account of Charles's death in *An Horatian Ode* is so exact, as well as so intense, that Marvell must either have been present himself at the scene (though Charles's speech was inaudible) or have heard an account from a witness, or read with heartfelt interest some one of those pamphlets describing the scene and reporting Charles's last speech, which were published immediately after his death. While the king was speaking, an attendant officer moving across the stage carelessly brushed the edge of the axe with his cloak; at this Charles interrupted his last solemn exhortation to his people to beg the gentleman "not to hurt that lest it hurt me." From these words or from Charles's pause or glance must have arisen in the first place the image,

> But with his keener Eye
> The Axes edge did try

just as the clapping of hands by some of the soldiers standing among the multitude as in a pit around the platform or stage on which the execution was to take place probably precipitated in Marvell's imagination the sense of the visible drama of history, though the thought that this particular stretch of history *was* tragedy was already in men's minds and no doubt on their tongues. But as Mr. Margoliouth has shown, Marvell also had vividly present to his memory in writing the poem the scene of Pompey's death in Lucan's *Pharsalia,* both in the original poem and in Thomas May's translation of it. And this scene in which Pompey looks at the sword waiting to end his life and gathers himself together to meet death becomingly contains a not close parallel to the scene of Charles's death. Mr. Margoliouth asks, "Is there a reminiscence of the two meanings of the Latin *acies,* eyesight and blade?" If so, it may be remembered further that in neo-Platonic psychology, *acies* denotes not only the gaze of the eye, but the intention of the mind upon the image presented to it by the imagination. At any rate, the double sense of *keen* is certainly there, in a pun close to Charles's own words, and through it Marvell sharply juxtaposes Charles's glance and the axe in order to quicken our sense of that human experience which is so different from all that we suppose in the rest of nature, and to awaken us to the intersection of the plane of man's mind with the plane of things. One can hardly fail to notice at the same time how easy it would be to represent either this image or the images in the second Cromwell poem in line drawings such as are found in Capaccio or other treatises on emblem, *imprese,* heroic symbol. But collections of emblem, *imprese,* and heroic symbol are in many instances but the characteristic Renaissance encyclopedias of older and newer symbolic thought. And thus the form of Marvell's images no less than their content carries us back to a world of discourse which is a determining part of the content of his poems.

Chapter Eight

INTELLECTUAL BACKGROUNDS
AND CURRENTS

THOUGH MARVELL's greatest poems are lyrics of personal feeling, philosophical conceptions are an ever present element in his emotion. Neo-Platonic attitudes form, for one thing, a common ground of his reflection. In discussing his techniques I have said that the character of his images in general and many of the particular images themselves identify for us the world of discourse implicit in his poems, and that it is a world related to that tradition of symbolic thought and contemplation in which St. Bonaventura is a leading figure and in which in some form or other almost all later neo-Platonism is involved. That tradition is a very complex one to which many strands of thought have contributed; and even in its simplest form it involves complicated and paradoxical philosophical issues, so that in reading Marvell's poetry there arise for readers of a later age a number of questions about the precise significance of his words and about conflicts of value and intention within the poem as a whole, questions which only resolve themselves in the light of his tradition. One has to be constantly aware, that is, of Marvell's choices among the commonplaces of his day, and of the whole complex which he made of them. The most direct way of treating the concepts and attitudes involved in Marvell's poetry would be to handle each point in a strictly limited way as it presents itself to us in that poetry and with particular reference to the structure of the poem itself. But in attempting to do so, I find that the commentary overweighs the poem and thereby prevents us from experiencing that very sense of unity and complete activity in the poem which it is our aim to recover. Yet the mass of already existing interpretation is so great and so partial that a somewhat full discussion seems unavoidable. My best solution, therefore, in order to give more concentration to my *explication de texte,* is to precede it by a general survey of a number of these related attitudes. In doing so I am still asking my reader to take it upon faith that the views I describe are the attitudes involved in Marvell's thought. The parallels to Marvell's language and thought in what I have already said of symbolic thought in the first chapter of this book will be something of a verification. And my further discussion itself will have Marvell's poems constantly in mind and should therefore carry its own conviction. With criticism of the philosophical and theological assumptions involved in these attitudes, or of the ultimate logical and metaphysical problems they raise, as Mr. Lovejoy has analyzed and described them in *The Great Chain of Being,* I am of course not concerned. I am only attempting to describe the range of attitudes which were in Marvell's immediate background and to discuss the values and emotions with which such attitudes would color the imagination of a poet such as Marvell, the logical criteria they appealed to in him and the differences of tone and emphasis with which we may suppose they presented themselves to his mind and defined for him the experience realized in his poems.

A number of strands may be separated in this complex of ideas. First is the traditional attitude in neo-Platonism and in Christian Platonism towards the created world and the problem of ascesis. This leads to a consideration of the concept of the book of the creatures, for in that concept of the creatures, which is a special aspect of the idea of the great chain of being, and in formal representations of the book were embodied both those pictures of the cosmos and the theory of man's understanding of it and of his integration with it which most deeply influenced Marvell.

To both the question of the place of the senses in man's life and the idea of the book of the creatures as they appear in earlier Christian writers and as they re-arise in Marvell's day a very special character was, of course, given by the fact that the problem and the concept were conceived and felt in a Christian context, in relation to the Bible, to the theology of its revelation and to its imagery and immediate poetic insight. More particularly, the problem of psychology and of the life of the senses was deeply affected by the fact that the solution of it—or perhaps I ought rather to say the statement of the solution—was deeply involved with the Song of Songs. The allegorical interpretation of that very lyrical and sensuous poem as a type or pattern of statement of the central Christian significance of the individual soul's relation to God and of the visible church's relation to Christ helped, as has often been observed, to shape men's ideas of symbolism and of the function of the imagination. Simply as a poem, also, it contributed to the forming of their own imaginative attitudes. In cosmological theory the allegorical interpretation of Genesis also was an active agent. Of the contribution of the literature of the Song of Songs and of Genesis to the idea of symbolic thought I have said something in the first part of this work. Of its influence upon the reading of the *liber creaturarum* and upon the theory of the imagination and of contemplation I shall say more in describing some of the great forms those subjects took.

The tradition of the retired life might not seem at first glance to have an intimate connection with the nexus of ideas and attitudes I have just named. Actually and historically it is closely related to them. Its necessary connection with the extreme ascetic view is manifest. But even in less absolute views, even if we are dealing with mid-seventeenth century England and not with the century of the hermits or with mystical Spain, the issues between the claims of the active and the contemplative life involved in man's view of his place in the universe, the search for leisure and concentration of energy, will from time to time give renewed rise to the thought of retirement from the world. Then too the development or renewal of the tradition of neo-Platonism has often taken place not only in the Renaissance and in seventeenth-century England but also in earlier centuries in times of great social, economic, political, and intellectual upheaval. Then criticism of the world and despair of purifying or rectifying history in its own terms may give rise to contemplation and the idea of retirement as twin impulses. Stoic thought, finally, with its own emphasis on retreat, was from the first a chief ingredient in the neo-Platonic synthesis. Intellectually the pattern of criticism and synthesis set forth by Palingenius in the sixteenth century in his *Zodiac of Life,* that of rejection of the gardens of Epicurus, discipline in retired stoic virtue, instruction in the Platonic view of creation, is a very type of progress in the ideas we are concerned with. In the literary Christian tradition, the *hortus conclusus* is one of the central symbols in the imaginative vision of the soul's relation to God as sung in Canticles. It is a symbol with which the ideal of humility and a negative attitude toward ambition are closely interwoven.

Marvell's anti-intellectualism is part of the whole nexus of his neo-Platonic attitudes. But it calls for some special consideration in relation to the whole general temper of his own day. In discussing that general mood of anti-intellectualism, I shall limit myself to considerations affecting his poetry. It was probably his strong belief in religion as the foundation of society, together with his absolute distrust in the power of reason to arrive at dogmatic theological conclusions, and the strong sense, consequently, of the wickedness of endeavoring to compel thought, which determined his political views during the Restoration period. But that is not our concern, and I shall speak of his anti-intellectualism only as it illuminates his poetry from one more side.

It is a fact commented on by Mr. Legouis,[1] as by others in speaking of Spenser's gardens, that Marvell's rose is described with intense sensuous realization; and this actual sensuousness in a poem of ascetic theme has been held to show a fundamental contradiction in purpose in the poet or a fundamental failure in self-knowledge. The same might be said of Jeremy Taylor's rose, and it has been held that Milton's Comus no less in his poetic expression than in his philosophy transcends the poet's Lady. One's most immediate answer lies in recalling that rose and sorcerer belong to the literature of debate. The rose of the Renaissance is emblematic of the world of sense and in turning to Platonism as an answer to the problem of personality, Marvell would not have felt that he could make his market to himself or to others by minimizing or refusing to reckon fully with the allure of the appetites. Marvell knew the literature of Europe; he had travelled extensively in Italy, France, Spain; he had probably had through Lovelace some contact with many who had once formed the court of Henrietta Maria, with its preciosity and its raffish Catholicism, as a recent Catholic historian has called it;[2] he had thought about the Catholic use of the senses in devotion. Here were manifestations of human nature that he would not put aside without taking account of them and without reinterpreting them. Whether in reinterpreting his sensuous experience as a foundation for a higher intuition he merely rationalized his temperament and deluded himself; whether he was describing with subtle artistic precision an actual and hence very significant psychological experience, different from ordinary appetitive response to the sensuous, but was confusing as Mr. Panofsky says of Abbot Suger of St. Denis, an aesthetic with a religious experience;[3] or whether the metaphysical concepts to which he related a first sensory experience actually explained and created the larger experience by holding it in consciousness long enough to realize itself and by integrating it with an organic whole of thought large enough to give it creative force, each of us must decide according to his own views. But at least we shall be in less danger of failing to sense what Marvell says if we look at some of the traditional attitudes towards the created world and the senses in the neo-Platonism which probably formed part of his immediate background.

In Plotinus the issue is present whenever the philosopher speaks of the problem of evil; it is in that aspect rather than in its full metaphysical form that his view of man's use of his senses can perhaps be most easily seen; and at the risk of urging the commonplace, I will use him to define the question. Out of the soul's restless falling away from the Divine Intelligence toward *hyle* or nothingness springs all evil. And in that view all participation by the soul in the life of the senses is enthrallment to the rebel powers that it array. Yet in another point of view, since God's generous love participated himself to the ideas and the creatures, it is to share in that act of love and fulfill its own part that the soul descends, and in descending becomes a just part of the beauty of the created world. Metaphysically, of course, Plotinus emphasizes the idea of being and of that conceptual integrity in which all particulars are unified. And morally he lays his stress upon the soul's attention to philosophical union with its source through the knowledge won in ethics, cosmology, mathematics, music, metaphysics rather than upon its participation in created things even through a sense of their beauty.

He is clear, however, that it is right to live the normal, "natural" life of man, once the soul has ascended to its higher life and can participate in the life of the senses in that transmuted and proportioned way which is the fruit of its ascent. Plotinus is one of the philosophers of whom we are always conscious that much of his thought is an explication of psychological experience, whether he begin with defining the nature of thought by a subtle observation of its process in the successive phases of perception, conscious reflection upon perception and upon thought itself, absolute and absorbed concentration in thought without self-awareness; or whether he describes that state of mind in which, as distinct from more common perceptions, the external world and human relationships and ties are felt with a singular clarity, intensity, and yet detachment and self-possession. The experience which he tries with such delicate precision of language to describe could hardly have absorbed so much of succeeding attention and called forth so much redefinition had it not answered to something very real in human experience, however different interpreters may account for that something.[4] Hence his allowance of the life of the senses as the purged mind knows it, subordinate as is that permission to higher demands upon our time and attention, was no mere concession to the actualities of life. Moreover, though he thinks, when he speaks of the stars or of music, of their intellectual structure, it is in their beauty that he feels their structure; it is the fire folk sitting in order there whom he evokes; though he starts intellectually with the concept of the mathematical structure of music, it is our final aesthetic absorption in it that he has in mind when he cries that the musician must understand him. Moreover, one whole side of his argument, which explains the cosmos and defines the procession of the ideas and nature in the three hypostases, is a justification of the created world and of the soul's pleasure in the plenitude of things in the great chain of being. The famous image of the many-rainbowed lights into which the one light is divided is by the very substance of the figure an affirmation, not a rejection. But though Plotinus so movingly suggests the beauty as well as the science of the stars, and though he is explicit on the use of the senses by the purified mind, and though the ideas of the nature which reflects God and creates the world and of the great chain of being receive distinctive form in his writing, the overwhelming weight of his emphasis lies on the other side, on the side of psychological withdrawal into the conceptual and beyond it.

In the Hellenic and Roman worlds in Plotinus' time and centuries before him the extreme ascetic or idealistic view had prevailed in some forms of Christian thought, no less than among the ethnics. But that view had also evoked within Christian Platonism—for with other answers we are not concerned—a sharp criticism. That it was an extreme position had been early emphasized; and the lines of battle against it had been clearly drawn. Tertullian, before Plotinus, and St. Augustine contemporaneously with him, formulate the core of the answer. Tertullian's answer to the question, of which I have already spoken in speaking of his use of symbol,[5] is significant both because he was one of the Fathers widely read in the seventeenth century and because it is in itself a very important type of reaction to one extreme of neo-Platonism. Tertullian, critical at once of neo-Platonism and of neo-Stoicism as they existed in the schools of Africa, yet blends in his own way the neo-Platonic psychology of devotional love and the Stoic sense of nature with the Biblical intuition of God in nature. Asceticism and idealism such as he found them in gnostic interpretations of Plato and in Eastern idealisms, or in Marcion's interpretation of St. Paul, were to him denials of the Incarnation, of the historic evidences of Christianity in the miracles and in the gospels in general through denying the validity of sense perception, of the temper of Biblical literature, of its words.[6] That above all Genesis reveals the goodness of the creation is so intimately present to his thought, as it will be to that of Augustine, that he often neglects to say it explicitly. Or again approaching the Platonic tradition from the academic side, he speaks out contemptuously against academic stock examples of the errors of sense. Psychologically, in his wish to maintain the unity of man's being, he was led to insist that soul does all things indistinguishably through body. Stoicism he found saner than Platonism in its view of the senses, and so also Epicureanism. But to the separation of opinion from sense in both these philosophies, no less than to Academic distrust of sense, he replies by analyzing and reinterpreting the classic cases of deception by the senses, such as the oar bent in water or the square tower which appears round at a distance. It is not, he says, the sense which is deceived. But there is an objective, additional cause, such as the water or the air, which gives an object to sense as it is not in itself; sense itself gives trustworthy impressions. Upon it depends all knowledge, sense and intellect being really one:

> Between objects of sense and objects of thought we admit no difference but the diversities of things, some corporeal and some spiritual, some visible and some invisible, some common and some arcane, corporeal and visible things being presented to sense, the others to intellect; both these and those waiting upon the soul, which perceives bodily things through the body, just as it understands incorporeal through the mind, saving always that it perceives while it understands. For is not to sense to understand, to understand to perceive? What is a sensation unless an understanding of what is perceived? What is an intellection unless it be a perception of that which is understood?[7]

For St. Augustine as for Tertullian the crux of the matter lies in Genesis, in St. Paul's affirmation of the knowledge of God through his works, and in the principle of the Incarnation. With savage irony against the Manicheans in his *Confessions* he describes man's normal share in created life. And in *Of the City of God* the center of his attack against the neo-Platonists is their denial of the Incarnation and the principle of immanence. Sin is not in the nature of the flesh but in the soul's choice of evil. The corruption which sin has procured is not sin, but the punishment of sin, the evil not in the body but in its corruption. It is not the body, but the soul which makes the perturbations; for as the Bible says, envy and so forth are evils of the mind.[8] It is only that one must not use the body for the ends of bodily pleasure, but the senses to know through the creatures their creator. His is, in other words, the Socratic psychology modified by the Christian idea of the incarnate nature of the world. From the neo-Platonists—Origen included—he turns back to Plato, particularly to the Socratic books. For him the principle of the Incarnation is realized in the principle of being, all things deriving their essence from God and leading the mind back to God. No one expresses more vividly than he the natural creative urge in life. Hence the emphasis upon the plenitude of the creation falls in Augustine just opposite from where it falls in Plotinus. And no reader of Marvell should fail to have in his ears the great imaginative praises of nature in the *Confessions* or in *Of the City of God,* especially that so rich and immediate passage in Book XXII, chapter xxiv. From things that have multiple being, the mind is carried back to the simple being of God. And in the fulness of their created life are their beings known:

And then for the beauty and use of other creatures which God has set before the eyes of man (though as yet miserable, and amongst miseries) what man is able to recount them? The universal gracefulness of the heavens, the earth, and the sea, the brightness of the light on the sunne, moone, and stars, the shade of the woods, the colours and smells of flowers, the numbers of birds, and their varied hues and songs, the many forms of the beasts and fishes, whereof the least are the rarest (for the fabrike of the bee or pismier is more admired than the whales) and the strange alterations in the colour of the sea (as being in severall garments) now one greene, now another; now blew, and then purple? How pleasing a sight sometimes it is to see it rough, and how more pleasing when it is calme?

At this point he can synthesize Genesis and Plato. It is essentially through revelation that he reconciles his separation of sense and concept (a separation stated when he argues that the existence of the soul is proved by its thought; it knows that it is, and it rejoices in that knowledge independently of sensation) to his emphasis upon the emanation of the creation. But so great is his sense of the beauty of the world and its order that, though in his final view he believes that Plato in order to understand the universe must have had access to Genesis, yet at one point he speculates that Plato might have inferred his view of creation (God's love overflowing in the plenitude) merely from speculation on the creatures.[9]

Yet whenever Augustine speaks of the beauty and goodness of the world, whether with aesthetic delight in nature, with joy in the teleology or decorum of man's form or in the arts, or with praise of the crafts and science, always he stresses order and thought: order as in the order of science; or structural unity in diverse parts as in praising the enhancement of the beauty of the world by the fact that it is made of contraries; above all the mind's activity, as in the comment that music is motion (sensate and mutable) but that it is the judgment of the mind that makes the beauty of it.[10] This sense of the conceptual nature of our experience of a work of art—this "formism" as Mr. Pepper calls it[11]—is of the utmost importance in understanding St. Augustine's attitude toward the senses. Here we are carried back to the center of his thought, to his argument on the spirituality of the soul from the nature of the mind's activity, its awareness of itself free from activity of the imagination. Hence, for all the great beauty of the world, we are always carried back in Augustine to conceptual activity, to the contemplation of the cause of things. The beautiful things of sense are not properly our objects. And there is no more characteristic passage than that in the *Confessions* in which we are bid to turn rapidly from the creatures to him who is the beauty of all things beautiful.

The unresolved paradox of Augustine's view, the element of experience undefined in his view of man and the creatures by his mediation between sensate experience and metaphysics through his analysis of the mind, is apparent in his attitude towards poetry, and particularly in his comment on the Song of Songs, to which his ordinary view of art is not applicable.[12]

He accepted that book, of course, as an allegory, or rather as symbolic. At the same time, with the realism which is his genius, he recognized his extraordinary pleasure in it as a poem, in acknowledging that the ideas it contains would not give nearly so much delight if presented merely as concepts. To interpret this delight his ordinary theory of art, which would emphasize the mind's activity in unifying the immediate sensuous elements, does not apply. For he is focused upon the conception of the poem as symbolic theology and not as a poem. And its subject matter would have precluded it, if taken in its literal sense, from his canon of allowed art. He accounts for his pleasure, therefore, by assigning it to the intellectual activity called for in *interpreting* the poem. It is, I think, significant for the whole temper of Augustine's view of the creatures and the mind that he does not fall back upon a more shallow explanation which was common, one which distinguished radically between imagination and reason, and which, while fearing the imagination, allowed art to present truth to it in order that opinion might be therein rectified.[13]

Finally one may note the significance for Augustine's view of the creatures of his emphasis on a devotional and intuitive attitude, his anti-Stoic emphasis upon love, pity, righteous anger, above all upon love.

Of the import of Dionysius the pseudo-Areopagite it is hard for one to judge who looks on him from outside the tradition he made popular and solely as a scholar. For his is not, like the writing of St. Augustine, the work of a profoundly direct mind seeking a center of understanding in a crisis of civilization, and in that search probing every corner of his own deeply human experience. Of Augustine we feel that every line on the mind and the senses is a description of what he has observed in himself. Dionysius' is a study in pure symbolic theology and ritual based on the neo-Platonism of Alexandria and the eastern Mediterranean; and Origen and the allegorical interpretation of the

Song of Songs is at its core. In English poetry only Crashaw in some measure carries one to an understanding of him.[14] In the first five chapters of his Περί τῆς Οὐρανίας Ἱεραρχίας, or *De Coelesti Hierarchia*[15] Dionysius explains the system and conception on which he bases his account of the heavenly hierarchy. Its aim is not like that of St. Augustine to define and choose among the values of natural human experience and so by grace to use them for contemplation. Augustine seeks allegory only where it is needed for central belief, to absorb the Old Testament into the New or to give meaning as theological revelation to what we should call historical or primitive passages in the Old Testament. Dionysius' aim is to seize the senses in their entirety by giving them an overmastering association with a conceptual system. His scheme of symbolism has two parts. The first, to apply a system of theological or allegorical (anagogic is his term) meanings to the metaphors and symbols of the prophetic books of the Bible; the second to translate that primary natural sense imagery and emotion and aesthetic experience which is necessary to us as men by giving it conceptual associations and equivalents, leading up the scale of more and more perfect forms to the thought of God.[16] His central analogy both for the emanation of created things from God and for irradiation of the mind first by God and secondarily by things, is that image of light which had come into later Western thought from Plato and from Zoroaster and other Eastern thought about the energy springing from the sun, about the cleavage between immaterial light and the world which it renders visible, and about the activity of the consciousness in sensation.

In the commentary of John the Scot on Dionysius' *Concerning the Heavenly Hierarchy* in a famous passage, a naturalistic teleologic interpretation of the creatures is united with that of Dionysius:

If it be asked in what sense all things that are are lights . . . All things are established by the Father, through the Son and the Holy

Ghost . . . if the father of lights is in himself light (*lux*), and if he would not be the father of lights unless he were light in himself, then all things which he has made, he has made in his wisdom, which is light itself . . . through the things which his wisdom has made he can descend to the informing (*notitia*) of the intellectual and rational creation, as the Apostle taught. . . . For instance, let us take an example from the closely bound orders of nature. This stone or this piece of wood is a light (*lumen*) to me . . . considering that stone or this stone I think of many things which enlighten my mind. I notice that it is fair and good according to the analogy that befits it; that it is divided by genus and species from other genera and species; that it has in its structure (*numero*) that which makes it one; that it seeks its place according to the quality of its weight.[17]

The devotional emphasis upon man's immediate intuition of God in the beauty of the creatures and in the organic structure of the universe, when it was further winged by the idea that the total creation is an incarnation witnessing to the particular and all significant Incarnation of Christ, was a myth or intellectual structure of force sufficient to draw within the Christian sense of the creatures other intuitions of joy in the fertility of the world. And these other intuitions were sometimes guarded from too simply expansive an optimism by their incorporation in the structure of ethics or theology or of neo-Platonic thought; sometimes left in all their spontaneous dynamic. I have spoken earlier of the special energy which was given to the metaphor of the re-arisen sun by the fact that Christianity with deliberate imagination transmuted the pagan image of transiency, the *nox perpetua dormienda,* to its own use. It may well be that the same deliberate imagination transmuted also pagan elegiac broodings over the fact that nature returns while man returns not, into a metaphor of the Resurrection and such an imagination may thus have reinforced and sought to purify fertility myths by subduing them to Christian feeling. Miss Tuve, in her *Seasons and Months,*[18] has described the early and mediaeval Easter hymns, mingling the paean of spring with the joy of Resurrection, hymns into which the Lucretian Venus has also been absorbed. Miss Joan Evans in her *Nature in Design*[19] gives a fascinating account of the naturalism in art and church ornament which arose and spread across Europe almost contemporarily with Franciscanism, but quite independently of it. These appropriations of pagan feeling are movements very remote from Andrew Marvell in his Yorkshire garden in seventeenth-century England, useful only to show us all that is implicit in the Christian conception as it unfolded in history. And yet not too remote. For surely there is an invisible thread at least of feeling binding to them George Herbert's Easter song,

> I got me flowers to straw thy way;
> I got me boughs off many a tree:
> But thou wast up by break of day,
> And brought'st thy sweets along with thee.

Miss Tuve has described also the great encyclopedias, particularly of the school of Chartres, which centuries later gave the rationale in part for the inclusion of all the life of the creatures among the sculptures of Chartres and elsewhere in those great schemes of the world which led up to the Judgment door and in manuscript illuminations of the seasons' and the months' occupations. Taken over into Western Christian art from Greek and Byzantine chronologies in a humanistic spirit as early as the Carolingian renaissance, they developed with Christianity.[20] The orthodoxy of such encyclopedias, once suspect of pantheism, has been fully vindicated by the interpretation of such scholars as M. Gilson.

Our concern is with whole imaginative attitudes, with the organic concrete form in which patterns of thought took shape and were transmitted, rather than with their purely metaphysical and moral bases. And before we carry our illustration of the neo-Platonic concept of the senses and the creatures down to its Renaissance statement in Ficino we must look at the special intellectual and devotional structure which the idea of the great chain of being and the attitude towards the senses took when they developed as the book of the creatures, and at the distinctive literary and imaginative tone which was imparted to the representation of the world of sense by commentary on the Song of Songs. The two are often closely interwoven, and both deeply affect Ficino.

Ludovico Vives, commenting on a passage in St. Augustine's *De Civitate Dei* on the proof of God from the beauty of the world, says that all the Greek and Roman schools of thought that smelt of divinity held that nothing so much proved the world of God's creating as the natural beauty of it.[21] Those schools or philosophers he lists as the Platonists, the Stoics, Cicero, Plutarch, Aristotle. The term *beauty* is here used rather broadly, and the inference from beauty would cover both aesthetic intuition and theological and causal inference, as Vives' list of names shows. The idea of a book of the creatures, of the inference of God and of his nature from the structure of the universe and from the quality of its parts was not solely Platonic, though in its great mediaeval forms it was closely inwoven with the idea of the great chain of being, with the conception of the microcosm and the macrocosm, with symbolism and with the devotional temper. From Plato's *Timaeus* came the concept of the great chain of being, the *plenum formarum,* with some modifying contribution also from Aristotle; the concept of Nature, or in special form the cosmos with its planets, as an organism or comprehensive animal through whose instrumentality were created man and the lesser creatures; the idea of the microcosm reflecting the macrocosm; the idea central to the preceding one, of the mathematical structure of the universe; the beautiful picture of the procession of the seasons and the hours, creating and marking Time, but reflecting in its cycles the return of Time into Eternity. These ideas attracted others to them in the cosmopolitan intellectual world of the eastern

Mediterranean; and out of this union developed the doctrine of sympathies and symbolisms of various sorts, number symbolism in particular from Babylonian and Biblical sources as distinct from Plato's Pythagorean number theory. Already into Tertullian's use of the book of the creatures these various symbolic traditions have entered, though Biblical metaphor and analogy dominate his thought.[22]

But there was also a strong non-Platonic tradition. In Aristotle there was not only his cosmic structure, with its argument toward a first mover. There was his biological conception of the graduated series of forms, with its subsidiary conception of teleological consistency or integration in animal structure—an evidence for design and a manifestation of ordered beauty than which none was more frequently used down the ages, one on which Augustine glows, and one which was set forth with fresh zest, for instance, by the Protestant theologian Zanchius, following the anatomical work of Vesalius—and with its implications also that any given genus contained an inherent form evolving toward the fulfillment of its place. This last idea is present even in Aristotle's account of the evolution of tragedy.

The Stoic attitude to nature was both aesthetic or devotional and scientific, and in either aspect it contributed largely to the book of the creatures. The classic statement of the Stoic feeling, particularly in its aesthetic and teleological aspect, is the radiant description of the beauty of nature in Cicero's *De Natura Deorum,* a description taken over almost word for word into Christian literature by Minucius Felix. Something of its humanistic, its direct natural response perhaps inspires the simple delight of More's Utopians in the bounteous beauty of life. The strictly scientific impulse in Stoicism, the impulse to study natural law, is pervasive almost wherever Stoic influence is felt;[23] but that scientific impulse no less than the aesthetic impulse itself may become devotional, may be conceived as a way of knowing God. As early as Philo Judaeus, a neo-Platonic concept of emanation is mingled with a stoic sense of law, both awaking devotion.

This will be a convenient place to comment briefly on Thomas Aquinas' development of the book of the creatures, in which his attitude toward the senses—in themselves and without consideration of original sin—is implicit, as he sets it forth in his *Summa contra Gentiles*.[24] For though our concern is with the neo-Platonic form of the idea, yet Aquinas' massive elaboration of it may enter to some degree into all accounts which follow him, share in forming the later imaginative attitudes even of those who do not strictly follow the course of his thought. On the other hand, it serves by contrast to delineate and define the distinctively Platonic formulations of the idea.

Thomas holds it of central importance to understand to the full the book of the creatures, the entire structure, that is, of created things. For those who, like Augustine, incline to be content with a merely devotional attitude without comprehending the cosmos metaphysically leave the door open to a number of misconceptions and heresies which are banished if we see man clearly in his place in the rational structure of the universe,[25] and if we can see also the relation of all things in their cause, order, and beauty to God. We derive from that structure both the meaning of the other creatures and their relation to man, their goodness for his use; our comprehension, within the limits of our capacity, of the workings of Providence; and our knowledge of our own souls. Of Plotinus' sense of evil, the notion that there is a wilful and negative separation from God implicit in the mutable world, there can be no shadow in Thomas. The error of this view he demonstrates formally in a criticism of Origen.[26] Genesis and the Psalms offer the text which he has to interpret, confirmed by the proof text in the Epistle to the Romans; and like a shining thread through the texture of his argument runs the theme, "The Heavens declare the glory of God," with all its kindred verses. Plato's conception of the great chain of being, the idea that the One, in a love so great that it could not refuse to share itself, created the cosmos, is the philosophical instrument by which Aquinas interprets Genesis;[27] it serves, that is, as the axiom on which he builds his logical proof of the system of the world, his logical and functional analysis of its parts. The particular parts are types, concepts in the whole.

In this philosophical analysis we do not approach God through our own psychological experience; we do not reach out to him through the study of particular creatures as concrete symbols of his nature, but through a logical structure, and through the analogies of the relationships of things to each other within the system which that structure describes. Hence we are in no danger of pantheism, or of being seduced by the senses and the imagination in our relations to the creatures:

> For things made by an art are representative of that art, since they are made in the likeness of that art. And God made things (*res in esse produxit*) by his wisdom (Psalms, 103, 24). Whence from the consideration of things made we can gather the divine wisdom as in made objects through a certain communication of the likeness impressed upon them (texts). . . .
> Third, this consideration kindles the minds of men to a love of the divine goodness. For whatever of goodness and perfection is distributed to the different creatures, creature by creature, all is universally united in Him as in a fountain of goodness, as we have shown. If therefore the goodness of the creatures, their beauty and sweetness, so delight the minds of men, the fountain of that goodness, God himself, compared to these streams of the goodnesses found in the creatures one by one draws the minds of men totally enkindled to itself.[28]

The nature and consequences of the Fall do not here enter into Aquinas' reasoning. All creation is good, and the simplest man may start with an imaginative intuition of its goodness in particular created things if his clarity of vision, the order of his mind, be restored by theological instruction.[29] But the beauty we are asked to contemplate is always unmistakably the beauty

of the metaphysical structure and of the divine idea which it
shadows forth and from which it proceeds. It is above all the
beauty of order, the meanest parts taking their beauty from the
whole. In their way, also, they have beauty in themselves. For
the variety and the differences of degree are the necessary evidences of God's act passing into action, of the love which necessarily has created the best of worlds.[30] In this view there is a
rationale for direct aesthetic delight in the world's beauty, if
seen as order in its fulness. There is a place for literal, specific,
and not symbolic or emblematic representations of the creation
in artistic works, in the Thomistic tradition. But that is not
where the emphasis of the *Summa* falls. The two works derived
from Thomas which I shall describe presently are one doctrinal and one emblematic.

The mingling of a teleological view with a Platonist view
which emphasizes emanation is manifest in the passage I have
cited earlier from John the Scot. It seems clear that any scientific description of the cosmos, or of a part of it indicative of its
order, might be considered a book of the creatures; and perhaps
commonly the term would mean simply such a cosmology or
an element of it used in a particular science of generally accepted Aristotelian origin. But in a twelfth-century treatise on
the calendar we find a beautiful example of a scientific book
of the creatures just at the point where it is taking on also a
symbolic aspect. The *Livre des creatures,* written by the Norman
French poet Phillipe de Thuan for Henry I of England, and
published by Wright in 1841,[31] was designed to instruct priests
how to locate the festivals of the church, thus supplying one of
the necessary texts of ecclesiastical practice which had been
desired by Augustine. The main text of de Thuan's work is a
description of the procession of the seasons in the signs of the
zodiac and an account of the construction of the calendar in
relation to these. But from this scientific summary the author
then turns to an account of the higher significance of the zodiac,

a significance given in the symbolic, theological meanings of the signs. The poem, or our manuscript of it, is tantalizingly incomplete, but there is included in it as it stands a table of matters which guides us to de Thuan's inspiration: listed in the table of contents among the promised chapters, though not given in the poem as Wright printed it, is one on Dionysius the Old.

In two other creations at least of the twelfth century we can see an integration taking place of naturalistic aesthetic response and neo-Platonic tradition. Bernard Sylvester's *De Mundi Universitate*,[32] a humanistic work similar to those of the school of Chartres, describes the creation of the world in terms of neo-Platonic science. But the tone of that neo-Platonism is so deeply infused by the humanism of the Latin poets who are Bernard's artistic inspiration that the figures of the Venus of Lucretius and of the goddess of Nature tinge its expression deeply. Nature as a personification hypostatizes the calling forth of the forms of things from their seeds in first matter in their typical ranks. Spenser's introduction into the *Shepheardes Calender* of the ages of man is the very signature of a Platonic tradition. For long before, Bernard Sylvester had also set them as part of that ordered procession of time and the seasons, first described in this context by Plato in his *Timaeus*. Despite what he owes to neo-Platonism, Bernard is purely optimistic in hymning the joy of the creation and the life of the plenitude. But his is the Plotinianism of a mind certainly also steeped in Genesis. And, on the other hand, if his unbounded optimism, close to pantheism, startles us, we must remember that it is a world before the Fall that he pictures, a consideration which affords at least a technical saving of the facts. His symbolic implications and feeling tone are important.

In the same century falls the work of Abbot Suger of St. Denis, the building and adornment of his church and his account of that work. Mr. Panofsky has shown in the introduc-

tion to his recent edition of the writings of Abbot Suger that
Suger justified his stained glass and his jewels and the whole
great Gothic architecture of his building by appealing to
Dionysius the pseudo-Areopagite, of whose work, together with
the commentary of John the Scot, his abbey was the special
custodian. In those writers he found not only the "anagogic"
system for the use of the creatures according to the pattern laid
down in the symbolic interpretation of the prophets, but a
justification of immediate sensuous intuition through the absorption of our experience into our concept of God. And in
Dionysius' metaphysic of light, descending from God and
leading the mind back to its center in the divine creating light,
he found the inspiration for his use of windows. De Thuan's
Livre des creatures must have been written within twenty years
or so of the time when Suger was recreating St. Denis. Suger,
defending himself against those who criticized his use of gold
and jewels, of whom Bernard of Clairvaux was chief, appeals
for justification first to the use of jewels as symbols in Aaron's
breastplate. He then continues:

Thus when, springing from my delight in the beauty of the house
of God, the loveliness of the many-colored gems has called me away
from external cares, and worthy meditation has induced me to reflect, transferring that which is material to that which is immaterial,
on the diversity of the sacred virtues, then to me in truth it seems
that I see myself dwelling, as it were, in some unexplored region of
the universe which neither exists entirely in the slime of the Earth
nor entirely in the purity of Heaven; and that, by the grace of God,
I can be transported from this inferior to that higher world in an
anagogical manner. . . . The detractors object also that a saintly mind,
a pure heart, a faithful intention ought to suffice for this sacred function; . . . we profess that we must do homage also through the outward ornaments of sacred vessels. . . . For it behooves us most becomingly to serve Our Saviour in all things in a universal way—Him who
has not refused to provide for us in all things in a universal way and
without any exception; who has fused our nature with His into one
admirable individuality.[33]

The last sentence, with its reference both to the making of the whole creation for man's use and to the peculiar sanctification of the creatures in the Incarnation, deserves particular note.

Hugh of St. Victor in his *Didascalia*[34] made the classic formal definition of the book of the creatures as a systematic Platonic theology. In him, the symbolic and the naturalistic and aesthetic are intimately mingled. The naïve and ardent love which is the core of Bernard's *Sermons on the Canticles* is by Hugh absorbed into a systematic theology, from which stem the order and relationship of the intellectual disciplines, the plan of the long and arduous course of education by which man is led from grammar to speculative thought, by the *scala* or ladder of creation and of the successive functions of his own mind, through all the degrees or rounds from nature up to God.[35] In that ladder it is primarily by a scientific, a symbolic analysis of nature, based on the disciplines of the *trivium* and the *quadrivium* that man understands his creator. Yet the central energy for that understanding springs from love, and Hugh's survey of the book of the creatures in Book VII of the *Didascalia,* which is the keystone of his whole work, ends in the rapture of their immediate beauty. Beginning with the citation from the Epistle to the Romans out of which together with the Psalms arises the Christian conception of the book and on which is predicated every symbolic reading of it, "For the Word may not be seen itself, and he made that he might be seen, and is seen through that which he made," he goes on to analyze under divers aspects the wonder, utility, and beauty of the creation, the multiplicity and variety of this book written by the finger of God. A stupid man sees their species—forms and colors—without understanding their *ratio,* but even a witless fool sees their beauty. Then after speaking of the wondrous beauty of their order and continuity, he speaks of the great addition of the beauty of color to the loveliness of nature: light, the blue of the sky, the spheres and colors of the sun, moon, and stars; precious stones, the earth covered with flowers, that delightful sight which calls forth our feeling, the ruddy rose, the white lily, the purple violet, all as wonderful in their source as in their beauty: *Quomodo scilicet Dei sapientia de terrae pulvere talem producit speciem.* In the concluding one of the chapters on the beauty of the world he goes on especially to speak of the sensible qualities of things and the harmonies of these. God created the world for man, man for Himself. Man is in the middle post with the world outside to lead him to God, so that he should find in the things below him whatever he should seek above and that he should have no lack of visible things which are made to announce the inestimable affluence of eternal things. When God added what was fitting to what was necessary, he showed the wealth of his goodness, when to that he accumulated all that was harmonious (*commoda*) he showed the supreme abundance of the divine goodness, the *iucundia*.[36] So Hugh laid the foundations on which Bonaventura completed the building.

Bonaventura's work, we remind ourselves, is in its entirety a book of the creatures, though he does not, like Hugh, use that title; his most extended philosophical treatise on the universe and on the mind's understanding of its symbols is the series of sermons upon Genesis, the work of the Six Days or *hexaëmeron*,[37] a study supported by his condensed educational treatise on the *reductio* of the mind to God and by his shorter treatise on the mind's journey to God. It is developed from Hugh's *Didascalia.* But the central influence in its philosophy, as Professor Gilson has shown, is St. Augustine's approach to God through psychology and the nature of Being.[38] In Bonaventura's method of defining symbol the influence of Dionysius is primary. Throughout the work plays the idea of the *hortus conclusus* of the soul or the soul in contemplation, led by the symbols of the world to God, as in Canticles it is led by the symbols of one sacred writing. For Bonaventura that book is, in the furthest extent of his view, the larger revelation, the Bible offering only what has become necessary to man's salvation because of sin. Hence the book of the creatures is equated with the whole structure of cosmology as in Thomas (though not by the same method) and of theology too, and with the very method which defines that structure.

In Bonaventura the sense of the immediate beauty of the creatures is both more pervasive and more controlled than it is in Hugh, more involved in an indefinable discipline of sensibility in which intellect and feeling, symbol and natural delight, are one. It is therefore harder to illustrate. Its general intellectual structure may be illustrated in passages such as these: the face and form of wisdom (that is, the divine in all the creatures, whose special degree in the scale of being is to be omniform) is *omniformis* in *vestigiis divinorum operum.* Such wisdom is in the highways, yet we like the layman with a book care not to read it. It is diffused in everything because each according to all its proper being has the rule of wisdom and shows the divine wisdom. In man's use of reason (*ratio* as distinguished from intelligence) he distinguishes between a terrene regard and an animal regard towards the lower world.[39] Every creature, Bonaventura says in the eleventh sermon of the *Illuminationes in Hexaëmeron,* that on the Trinity, cries out the eternal generation and expresses it in twelve particular generations, by diffusion, as shining from light, as heat from fire, as rain from a cloud, as rivers from a fountain; by expression, as speech from the speaker, as thought from the mind; by propagation, as the germ from the seed, as the tree from the root, as the child from the womb, as the son from the father, though none of these is absolute.[40]

Just as you see that a ray entering the window is colored in various ways following the various colors of the various parts of the glass, so the divine ray shines forth variously in the individual creatures and in their various proper qualities. Every creature is a *vestigium* of the wisdom of God, a certain sculpture, and from them all a certain book is written externally. When then the soul sees this, it sees for itself that it must pass from the shade to the light, from the way to its end, from the footprint to the truth, from the book to that true knowledge which is in God.[41]

This book contemplatives alone can read, not natural philosophers, for they know only the nature of things, not things as the trace of God. But that other knowledge is the support of the spiritual creature "which is a light, as a mirror, as an image, as a book written within." And beautiful as are the beautiful things, the joyous radiation of the stars for one, that outward beauty is but an effigy.[42]

A somewhat different emphasis is given in his *Itinerarium Mentis ad Deum,* in which the actual aesthetic experience of the beauty of the particular creatures forms the second step of the six in the soul's progress toward the *apex* or *synderesis* in which it passes beyond the body to the perfect peace of contemplation. This experience Bonaventura explains in terms of St. Augustine's aesthetics, the sense of beauty arising from the mind's perception of order and number in the forms of the creatures.

His tone is manifest in passages such as those above, or in this one on the mind as the *hortus conclusus:*

In Paradise is no plantation save of eternal causes. . . . And the soul is a paradise in which is planted the Scripture. And it has innumerable sweetnesses and beauties, whence it is written "An enclosed garden, sister my bride." A garden in which are sacramental mysteries and spiritual intelligences, where flows a fountain of spiritual emissions; but the garden is enclosed and the fountain sealed, for it does not lie open to the sinful, but to those of whom "God knows that they are his."[43]

Bonaventura's specific use of the *hortus conclusus* as well as the implications and method of every page of his work remind us that the Song of Songs was profoundly important in affecting men's imaginations as well as in giving the intellectual form to the theological idea of the book of the creatures, as the book appears in any theology which owes much to neo-Platonism, and in attaching a nexus of associations to it. Hence we must pause a moment to look at the special influence of the Song of Songs upon men's apprehension, imaginative and intellectual, of the creatures. The renewed study of Canticles was always both a cause and an effect. The influence of this book of the Bible in its traditional interpretation was felt afresh only in periods when men's minds were particularly ready to receive it. And the thought and tone of each such age impresses itself in turn upon the renewed interpretation of the poem. Both individual sensibility and the broader patterns of ethical and psychological outlook determine how Canticles will be felt. Central in the work of Bernard, the Victorines, and Bonaventura, heirs in special of St. Augustine, is their psychology of the emotions, which stresses the energy of love (and of righteous indignation, too) first in its outgoing toward the world which immediately surrounds us, and then as it is transformed from imaginative to intellectual love, from perception to concept, from things to God. In the light of this psychology they read the Song of Songs. But the Song of Songs itself affected men's sensibility by its direct lyric force. At the same time, to minds so otherworldly its lyric form of statement had always to be explained. And by its character as an allegorical or symbolic revelation, it affected its readers' theory of knowledge and of devotional habit, their attitude not only towards itself but towards things and art; specific commentary on the Song of Songs almost always concerns itself with answering the special problem, what is the significance of the senses and of created beauty in the approach to conceptual truth and to the contemplative realization of it. These mutually interactive influences which create the meaning of the Song of Songs and determine how in general the reading of it shall open or close men's sensibilities become explicit in the commentaries from beginning to end. For close parallels in thought and phrasing in many introductions to commentaries mark the tradition of commentary as directly continuous from Origen through the Victorines and Bonaventura; and this continuity gives special significance to the differences among the commentators. I am concerned here not with the "meaning" of the Song of Songs as they read it, but with the significance of the imagination as they defined and felt it when they criticized the poem as an allegorical form of literature. Origen's attitude, his wish to give the poem purely intellectual force, I have implied earlier in discussing his theory of symbolism.[44] Gregory of Nyssa abounds in the fables of nature; with them, indeed, he is more at home than with the poetry of the Song of Songs itself. Marking the goodness of God in giving to our senses the allegory of the Song, he marks also the extreme danger involved in the reading of it. With the early Christian Platonist's stress on an absolute distinction between the world of thought and the world of sense experience, he comments that he who looks at a work of art carried out through colors laid on a wooden tablet does not gaze on the colors laid out but looks only at the form which the painter has represented through them. So in this book of the Scripture we do not look at the colors of the words but at what they symbolize. What is more wonderful, he asks, than that Solomon could make nature herself the purger of our affections, when by words that seem full of affection he teaches apathy? He so affects the mind that by words that seem unfitting he interprets the mind.[45] Thus Gregory remains close to ascetic neo-Platonism. We have already seen how directly Augustine felt and acknowledged the beauty of the poem, though he brought a pure activity of the intellect in to explain his pleasure. Richard of St. Victor, in his ethical treatise, *In Cantica Canticorum Explicatio* is closer to the older interpreters. But though he begins his preface with the analogy of the picture and its colors, and though he distinguishes elaborately between the evil imagination and the good, and praises the good imagination alone, and though in elaborating the distinction between the evil imagination and the good, he does not deny the wicked imagination its traditional power and does not cease to fear the dangers inherent in it, yet he affirms that the good imagination can drive evil from the soul. Nephtalie, the good imagination, is thus a conversion or comparison, converting the known nature of visible things to spiritual intelligence; she is especially apt to awaken minds inexperienced in contemplation through that which is easy to understand and joyous to hear. She is called the *cervus emissus* because she leaps from the ground but never really leaves it, drawing always the shadow of corporeal things with her. Of this eloquence of beauty, Canticles is the supreme example. *Sic novit Nephtalim carnalia cum spiritualibus permiscere et per corporalia incorporea describere, ut utroque hominis natura in ejus dictis inveniat unde se mirabiliter reficiat qui ex corporea et incorporea natura constat.* Yet if we embrace the literal sense only, the song says nothing worth wondering at; and perhaps this is what we so gladly embrace, that from the joy and, so to speak, the fatuity of the letter we are compelled to flee to spiritual intelligence.[46]

In later typical and popular works of devotion and exegesis, the influence of such commentary upon the imagination and upon literature can only be thought of as very indirect, as a thing which has contributed its share in the past to mold more immediately influential forms of Christian thought. Other modes of interpreting Biblical thought as a whole have replaced the schemata of patristic and mediaeval thought, and with other conceptions of human reason and of the normal life of man, radically different views of ceremony, ritual, and symbol have prevailed. Yet the Song of Songs and commentary on it are directly at work in centers like Peterhouse, through the Spanish mystics, and more generally in emblem literature and through the renewal of mediaeval types of devotion.[47] And the original commentaries are also still available as well as these indirect streams of influence and are evidently still read, as we may surmise from the attempt of George Wither, who is no mystic, to include the Song of Songs in his *Hymns and Songs of the Church* and from the defense which he makes of his proposal:

He that hath gayned his humble knowledge, both by hearing the Church, & observing the power which Gods word hath showne upon him, in his own affections, is persuaded that heavenly Poeme was composed & preserved for the pyous use of all men. & principally for yong lovers, inflamed with naturall love; that by their carnall affections they might ascend & be made capable of that which is spirituall. So other Allegoryes, are chiefly intended to stirr up those who are subject to other Affections. For little would it prevaile with an olde man, whose heart is settled upon riches and such like, to illustrate the pleasures he might receive in his communion with God, by setting before him mutual contentments enterchanged between two affectionat lovers; seeing those passages are usually derided by the elder sort. And less would it move that yong man who is delighted in beauty, and the perfections of his beloved, to expresse unto him the spirituall happines, by Tytles, Treasures, or the profites and pleasures of a vineyarde, which he meanely regardes.[48]

Literal as this is, in the spirit of its own day, and crude in its psychology when removed from the context of a whole philosophical scheme, the question asked by the Fathers and the echo of their answer may be clearly heard in it. Wither feels the poem also as a book of the creatures, describing the loveliness of God's workmanship. Vaughan's *Mount of Olives* is in large measure based on the Song of Songs in its allegorical interpretation, and Henry Reynolds in his *Mythomestes* appeals to Canticles to reinforce his plea for allegorized myth as the staple of great poetry.

To come back then to the book of the creatures with the influence of the Song of Songs fresh in our minds. In the whole tone and emphasis of the psychology of Hugh of St. Victor as well as of Richard, and of Bonaventura, there is room for the love of God in the immediate delight of the creatures such as Origen did not allow. Bonaventura, with his subtle and delicate introspection, is notable in stressing the unity of the mind and in refusing to separate intellect radically from imagination. It is in the corruption of the whole mind and will that evil exists, he says, following Augustine, not in the imagination.[49] The whole man is turned toward the sensate and carnal or toward the spiritual. Bonaventura has the genius and grandeur of mind which can speak its insight to us directly and across any barrier of ages and of differing rational structure. Hence his work is of major importance in carrying us into Marvell's world of discourse. But it will help our understanding of Marvell to hear also what is further said by a lesser man than St. Bonaventura, even though we find our way with difficulty through his logical distinctions and elaborations, his seeming faculty psychology. Richard of St. Victor, in his *Benjamin Major. De Gratia Contemplationis Liber,* distinguishes our intuition through cognition, meditation, or contemplation upon the same material. In cognition (which may be called *evagatio*) we are intent (sense, that is and identify), the mind going about as it will; in meditation (which may be called *investigatio*) we tear open or grub up, directing our minds to an end, often with great difficulty (in discursive thought, that is); in contemplation (*admiratio*) we wonder, the mind moving with free flight over the whole. Presently he distinguishes six kinds of contemplation: in imagination and solely according to imagination; in imagination, according to reason: in reason, according to imagination; in reason according to reason; above but not beyond reason; above and beyond reason. The first takes place when the form from visible things and their image is brought into consideration; when wondering we attend, attending wonder, when in admiration we venerate those corporeal things which we drink in with our corporeal sense, thinking how great, how diverse, how beautiful or joyous they are, and in all venerate and admire the power, wisdom, munificence of their superessential creator (*creatrix*). The second is at work when we seek and learn the reason of these things, their reason, order and disposition; the third when by the likeness, or likening (*simulatio*) of things visible we are raised to speculation on things invisible.[50]

I have discussed only those aspects of the book of the creatures, as conceived in the neo-Platonic tradition, which, so far as my limited knowledge of that great library goes, bear directly on Marvell. Other chapters develop the central theme of them all in different intellectual and imaginative tempers. A student of Donne, who uses so much of bestiary symbol and of the science of man as the microcosm, and whose imagination is so impregnated with the idea of the symbolic anticipation of the New Testament in the Old, but whose sense of the immediate beauty of the world seems not often called on, has to take into account not only Donne's temperament but also his particular intellectual tradition and has to recall his praise of Raimond de Sebonde. Vaughan's relation to the whole vast tradition of magical Hermeticism has been explored,[51] leaving the conclusion that much as in detail of particular poems he owed to it, his greatest poems owe their interpretation of nature not to the specific tenets of later Hermetic lore, but to the larger and profounder concepts which had been gathered into the warp and woof of the ancient *Hermetica* and of Florentine neo-Platonism, concepts arising from man's experience of thought and things, his ideas of the relation of light and darkness, of time and eternity, of motion and stillness; and that he owes even more to that great wellspring of the book of the creatures, the poetic intuitions and metaphors of the Bible. Into the strange chapters of vitalism, of Agrippa and magic, of alchemy or of the German contemplatives of the fourteenth century who, according to Rufus Jones and to H. O. Taylor, rested upon the structures of Thomas and Bonaventura,[52] but who experienced and who branched forth so freshly, I do not attempt to go. I surmise that they would not be fruitful for Marvell.

A particular chapter of the book of the creatures allegorically or symbolically conceived is to be found in technical com-

mentary on Genesis and in the reconciliation of the account of
the creation there given with neo-Platonic cosmology and theology. Of that chapter the extreme form, cabbalism, which so
attracted Giovanni Pico della Mirandola[53] and of which Henry
More was to be the English expounder, may well have been
known to Marvell at the time he wrote his garden poetry. Henry
Reynolds we know had been reacclaiming Pico and the *Cabbala*
twenty years before. That optimistic account is rather a substitution of *Cabbala* for Genesis than a reconciliation of the two,
quite incompatible with the story of original sin and raising no
question as to the validity of the senses. In 1672 in *The Rehearsal
Transpos'd* Marvell refers to cabbalism as a type of fantastic
speculation. Though he might have had it in mind in his garden
poems when he speaks of the light mosaic, it could, I think,
have been only as a passing recollection. He is concerned with
the individual personality, not with schemes of creation. Accordingly I shall say no more of it. Of the more normal tradition, Bonaventura's *Illuminations on the Hexaëmeron* is a sufficient example. And it is in his tone and the tone of the Victorines that we may anticipate to find Marvell's imaginative
temper.

Before, however, we leave our account of the book of the
creatures as a formal mediaeval neo-Platonic embodiment of the
idea of creation and of man's relation through created things to
God, we may glance at two versions of the book certainly current in Marvell's day, versions which further define the neo-
Platonism of the Victorines and Bonaventura by their contrast
with it. These are the version of Raimond de Sebonde, written
in the fifteenth century, translated by Montaigne, and published
in English in a digested form in 1550;[54] and the beautiful little
*De Ascensione Mentis in Deum per Scalas Rerum Creatarum
Opusculum* with which in 1615 Cardinal Bellarmine refreshed
himself from his long labors of fierce controversy, and which
was translated into English and issued at Douay in 1616 by

T. B. as *A Most learned and pious treatise, full of Divine and Humane Philosophy, framing a Ladder, Whereby our Mindes may ascend to God by the stepps of his Creatures.*[55] Both were almost certainly influenced to some extent in their primary conception by Bonaventura or the Victorines. But each in its own way they differ radically from the Augustinian tradition. Sebonde's rationalistic *Liber Creaturarum, sive theologia naturalis,* intended to support the dogmas of Thomistic thought and fortify instructions on the sacraments with natural arguments drawn from the design and order of the universe and the inferences to be drawn from systematic analysis of man's place in it, had nothing to offer Marvell, though it might well reproach and enkindle the mind of a Hamlet, brooding on the sanctions of human action and asking

> What is a man
> If his chief good and market of his time
> Be but to sleep and feed? a beast, no more.
> Sure he that made us with such large discourse . . . .

It contains the commonplaces drawn from Aquinas' *Summa contra Gentiles* on the wonderful variety of the creation and on man's unique place in rendering prayer and thanks to God for the whole bounty of the creation; but that is as the creation is useful to him, not as he is sympathetic to it. All its emphasis is thrown upon man's distinction from those that have only being, life, or sense; and his love manifests itself through orthodox moral sanctions and through the duties and offices of the church. Nothing in tone or image is suggestive for Marvell. Yet even here, if one traces through Jesuit emblem books, one can see a filiation which helps to connect Marvell to his larger tradition.

Bellarmine's work begins by distinguishing between the rare religious genius, a St. Paul, and the average Christian to whom his work is directed and who will ascend, as the Bible tells him that he may, by recognizing the power and greatness of God in the beauty of the creatures, and by being thereby helped to set little store on temporal things, knowing that he will see God fully hereafter. With a genial and loving sense of the beauty of things, and with language that suggests Francis of Assisi, Bonaventura, and the Victorines—it is the intrinsic end of a thing to reach its most perfect form, as of a tree to spread its branches, to produce leaves, and to be beautiful with flowers— yet all his emphasis is upon the transcendence of God, even in his sustaining immanence. In chapter v of Part II is a charming passage on the beauty of things, as distinct from their goodness, on the gardens, woods, rivers, the stars, the trees clothed with flowers, the forms of the beasts, the flight of the birds, the play of the fishes, the beauty of men and women, which has led to so much sin; but the treatment is general. Part III is more to Marvell's purpose, treating the instruction given by the world. The passage on water, among the four elements, may illustrate the character of the symbols or lessons Bellarmine draws. In its moisture and coldness, washing stains away, it reminds us that God is the water which completely washes away our sins. Water assuaging our thirst is the emblem for a little essay on the restlessness of the human heart. A spring of water is an image of God as the fountain of Being. As water does not come from the rivers but rivers from water, so do all things receive their proper being from God, and so man's reasonableness is his essence, but his existence depends always upon God. These are sufficient to show how the emblems of this orthodox and rational treatise of the seventeenth century are but illustrations or illuminations of its doctrine; they are rather aphorisms than devotional ejaculations, and if they were to be drawn, as well they might, in an emblem book, they would belong to the older type of didactic emblem, rather than to the more witty, "metaphysical" emblem which finds its counterpart in the verse of Donne, of Crashaw, of Herbert, and of Marvell.

And finally, there is a little book which is not strictly speaking a book of the creatures, but which is clearly related to that

of Bellarmine in the impulse of its thought and in a good bit of
its substance, the *Parthenia Sacra* of the Jesuit Henry Hawkins,
1633. This book comprises twenty-four emblematic devotions
to the Virgin Mary, each based upon a symbol or analogy such
as had been traditional types of her virtue in poem, sermon, and
tapestry since mediaeval times, all twenty-four drawn from
flowers, birds, trees, landscape, and bound together within the
hortus conclusus which is the most comprehensive type of her
soul. What relates the work in spirit to Bellarmine is the long
"Character" of each symbol, naturalistic, loving, vividly precise
in detail, if not always strictly accurate in science.

My reader will no doubt have been thinking all this while of
Marsilio Ficino as the great Renaissance expounder of neo-
Platonism, and as a writer closer to Marvell in time and likely
to be more accessible to him than the mediaeval writers. But as
I have said earlier, a large number of Marvell's images no less
than his specific reference to nature's mystic book seem to carry
us back to these older masters. Moreover, we should not so
readily define Ficino's attitude toward the senses and created
things if we did not have the older writers in mind. For though
Ficino is the great interpreter to the Renaissance of Plotinus,
and of Plato read in the light of Plotinus, seeking to build
Plotinus into the structure of Aquinas, an even more central
influence in his *Theologia Platonica* is that of St. Augustine and
his followers.[56]

The force of Plotinus is most apparent in Ficino's *Theologia
Platonica* in his ascetic or idealistic metaphysic and psychology.
In his theory of knowledge he draws precise distinctions between the successive steps from sense experience up to pure
intelligential concept. Yet Plotinus is deeply modified in him
by the pull of Christian thought—he assumes constantly the
unique significance of the individual soul and the doctrine of
the real unity of body and soul—and by the weight of the
Renaissance; and both these pulls are sharpened by the fact that

he is always conscious that he is answering Averroes' false interpretation of Aristotle on the doctrine of the single soul for all men. Thus the imaginative weight of what he says, even more than his logic, falls on the other side from Plotinus. To the reader of today, at least, the terms of his comment on the phantasy (*imagination* he uses as the function which calls up the images of things not present; *phantasy* is a higher function acting creatively upon these images and moving them up toward the spiritual realm) seem perhaps even more significant than his logic. When the clouds of phantasy obscure the intellect, he argues, then the will is affected by the perturbations. And the gift of knowing herself, on which Ficino rests so much of his argument for the immortality of the soul, the phantasy has not. Yet the general Renaissance idea of the creativity of the imagination affects him deeply. In the phantasy lies the power of making things greater than she receives them. Beginning with a hymn to light which praises the soul supremely as the shadow of God, distinct from all matter and independent of the body in her actions, he says:

The phantasy follows the external senses, the senses the disposition of their own body and of others. Wherefore we say that the judgment of sense and phantasy is a property of the disposition of bodies. When our mind desires to know from teachers of this sort what is the nature of God, the phantasy, a bold enough instructor and workman, contrives a statue, as it were from the five materials which the external senses supply her with as more beautiful than all other things, materials which she receives from the world indeed, yet in such a sort that she renders those materials more excellent than she has received them from the world through the senses. Phantasy then offers us a light so clear that no other can seem more radiant; a light so mighty that no other is ampler; a light diffused almost through the immense inane, which is made beautiful with innumerable colors, and turns in a circle; and by that revolution it sings in the sweetest modes, filling and softening our ears. It smells of most delightful odors. It abounds in all those savors which are sweetest. In touch it is wondrous soft, delicate, gentle, temperate. This the phantasy tells us is God. The body of the world gives us nothing more fair. The bodily sense finds nothing better nor reports anything more excellent. The phantasy, friend of the senses, creates nothing more sublime. But reason, meanwhile, from the highest watch tower of the mind looks down upon the tricks of the phantasy and speaks forth thus: Beware, little soul, beware the sleights of that sophister. Do you seek God. Receive a light as much clearer than the light of the sun as that light of the sun is more luminous than darkness.[57]

He goes on to show us how, in order to understand God, all specific properties must be subtracted from this vision. Yet surely the vision plays its part in our concept. The sharp distinction here between percept and concept is dialectical rather than experiential. Ficino constantly uses the theory of light and the distinction between light, which is immaterial, and the material things upon which it plays as his central argument by which he draws the line between spirit and matter. But one feels to the full in this passage the beauty of the rainbow creation which carries the mind up to God as the beauty of all things beautiful. In this aspect the sense of immanence and of man's sympathetic love of God through the creature is, as always in Platonism, stronger than in scholastic thought. And when Ficino speaks explicitly of man's place in the universe the transformation is complete.

The soul, he says, is the greatest miracle in nature. In it are all things, the images of the divine things on which it depends, the reasons and exemplars of lower things, which in a certain way it also reproduces. And since it is the mean of all, the center of the five degrees, it has the powers of all. And since this is so, it passes into all. And since it is itself the true bond (*connexio*) of all things, it may be called the center of nature, the medium of the whole of things, the series of the world, the face and juncture of the world. Thus though from the point of view of the theory of knowledge, man cannot know God through *naturalia,* and though the soul uses the *simulacra* of the phantasy to think only because it is in the body and not because of any inherent need, yet from the point of view of plenitude, through the soul of man—the particular among particular beings, which has entered into his body, that most beautiful of all terrene things—the divine ray which has gone forth and passed through Nature into the matter of the world returns to God. The idea that man alone of all the creatures renders back to God thanks for the whole creation, present throughout mediaeval Platonism and wherever any thinker dwells upon the book of the creatures, receives fresh stress in the Renaissance. Professor Cassirer felt its emphasis to be so important that in his *Individuum und Cosmos* he found in it the distinctive philosophy of the Renaissance.[58] And so contemplating all things beautiful, the disciplined sensibility will not be sharply aware of the distinction between the things seen and the ideas of them in the mind, or rather it will experience only a pleasure less and a pleasure more.

Ficino, then, never fully resolves his paradox. If, with Plotinus, in one aspect of his thought, he looks at the world not to explain the origin of evil but to contemplate creation by successive descents from the divine mind into nature, he paints the glowing beauty of it. In the vision of the plenitude neo-Platonism can best unite itself to humanistic joy in the beautiful world and can best assimilate the influence of classical art upon the Renaissance; witness Davies' *Orchestra,* Elyot's chapters on the dance, Michael Angelo's Sistine ceiling.[59] But in Michael Angelo's ceiling the neo-Platonic idea of God's unfolding into creation is profoundly affected by Genesis, and the problem of evil is solved in Christian terms. Abbot Suger found, as we have seen, in the principle of symbolic analogy the rationale for the jewels and jeweled windows of his church as well as for the representation of the creatures. And modern Thomistic thought has drawn forth to the full the sanctions to be found in Aquinas for artistic insight and creativity. But to place beside mediaeval sculpture or illumination such a poem as Davies' *Orchestra* or a Renaissance dance of the hours in painting speaks how different was the actual mediaeval sense of this creativity from modern feeling. Or to take an even closer comparison, to look at Spenser's pageant of the seven deadly sins side by side with one of its sources, as Lowes has done, is to see at a glance how different was the way in which early Christian neo-Platonism had met a dying Roman empire from the way in which its Renaissance counterpart evolved in a rising humanism. Could Renaissance neo-Platonism by emphasizing the creativity of the universe and man's share in it mediate between Christianity and the new expansion of the imagination? Could it transform and assimilate the living elements from a vast material, technical, and sensuous expansion, from streams of ancient philosophy of all sorts, from a great body of actual art both classical and contemporary, neither Platonic nor Christian? The neo-Platonic artist's attitude toward the senses is much more complicated than that of the philosopher or the theologian. And Spenser is for English poetry in his own time and after him the great pattern of the problem and of its solution.

Spenser's view of the senses is felt in terms both of his allegory and of his whole poetic effect and must be measured with a sensibility fully awake to both. Whether we name them or not, we are responding constantly both to his Christianized Platonism and to all that Ariosto and Tasso enkindled in him. In the Garden of Adonis passage, which we may take as our instance of his statement of theory,[60] the deep rifts in his neo-Platonism are apparent. The strictly neo-Platonic concept of evil, or at least of the participation in creation of a very reluctant and negative element, involved in the descent of the soul into the sensuous world, with all its implications as to the danger of a merely imaginative apprehension of that world of things that are begotten, born, and die—that sense of evil is surely intimated in stanzas XXII and XXIII. For the word *slime,* translating *limus,* is it is true a very much more neutral word in neo-Platonism than it is for us; nevertheless it carries the connotation of the negative, the inferior, that which hinders the ascent to God. But in a moment all the poetic weight of the poem is thrown upon the opposing definition of the beauteous pageant of created things and of the glorious fulness of love in the thrusting circles of creativity. This emphasis is thoroughly in keeping with Christian formulations of the idea of the great chain of being. But yet if we compare it with any of the other great Christian statements, or with Michael Angelo's half-Platonic representation of the creation, we feel at once how much more active is the sensuous energy of Spenser's imagination than its conceptualizing or symbolic force. Ignoring for our purpose the profound elements in Spenser's individual temperament which doubtless contributed to this effect, we may stress the fact that the poetic tradition of Italian romance epics which he sought to assimilate was a great force in determining his vision. And the lines on Time, though they are technically consistent with the neo-Platonic system—a system which Spenser defines more comprehensively in his mutability cantos—are actually so saturated with the vivid sense of time's enmity that they fall rather with Catullus, Ovid, and the other elegists than with Plato in his *Timaeus*. But if the logic of neo-Platonic thought yields at that point, it is not to sensuality that it yields; it is to that old and deep sense of the tragedy of man's situation which is always a significant tone in Spenser's art; a sense expressed by Erasmus in the *Enchiridion* and in which we see Christian thought again and again thrusting back to Socratic Platonism. Christian humanism in Thomas Aquinas or in Erasmus, at war with pagan humanism, restates it with fresh poignancy. In the actual embodiment of Spenser's idea, the pictures in the series of cycles of creation are too brief and condensed to embody the complex philosophy they imply. What is creatively realized is a diffuse sense of joy in the idea of life, shaded by a deep sense of yearning toward the imperfectly experienced actuality of that joy. The passage, though it is technically one of the most philosophical in content in the *Faerie Queene,* is one of the many in the poem which remind us that it is by a thousand filaments of moral sentiment attached to an innumerable gallery of traditional devotional images that Spenser's sensuous world is controlled, rather than by a clearly focused intellectual vision.[61]

For a consideration of Spenser's presentation of the senses in a dramatic passage, we may glance at Acrasia's Bower, taking for granted the ethical scheme and considering the problem of actual artistic realization. In that scene, besides the representation of ensnarement in sexual sensuality, the implicit theory of the significance of the senses comes to us also in another form, in the problem of man's experience of external nature and his shaping of it. With that experience, the nature-nurture or nature-artifice debate had become integrated. Underlying the passage and contributing to its tone is the view expressed in the book as a whole that man's erotic adjustment is both the determinant and the sign of his general relation to life.[62]

Every detail of nature in Acrasia's Bower is planned to suggest an exaggeration: nature not seen for herself, as the sum of the great types of life, but her surface excised and worshipped in itself, her abundance twisted to gluttonous and erotic enhancement. The air is fetid. In this world an evil artifice is set over against simple nature in her spontaneous bounty and variety and perfection of form. To feel the full import of the scene, we have to have fresh in memory such a contrasting passage as the betrothal masque of Una and Red Cross, contrasting not only in substance but in imagery and all detail of embodiment. The manipulation of nature by the senses immersed in their own life is evil; the awakening of the mind by the sensuous perception of nature to the ideal forms and order which nature mirrors is a joyous apprehension of truth, a frank aesthetic delight.[63] Yet it is the condition of our life here that in any form nature may charm our imaginations, as she charms Guyon's.

Such is the clear diagram. Creatively the matter is more in doubt, as contemporary criticism constantly assures us. Did Spenser, as has been held, on one hand unconsciously give expression to the unmediated sensuousness of his own nature enkindled to artistic expression in him by Tasso? Or did he on the other hand, in a struggle to repress that element in himself seek to destroy all art and beauty with a Puritan sword? The theoretic answer to the second half of the question I have already given. What of the whole effect of the passage?

It would be hard to argue that in the formal set concert of nature and art which precedes the famous rose song from Tasso and in the song itself there is, as compared to the tone of similar passages of a different intention elsewhere in the poem, anything of exaggeration which ought to let the reader into the irony of the import of these lines. And the experience of many readers as serious and as sensitive as Professor Grierson, for instance, extends the doubt to the whole canto. Yet I believe the more experienced we are in understanding Spenser's scheme of thought and in letting our imaginations be penetrated by his allegorical method (without necessarily accepting his world of discourse), the more fully we intuit his poem.

To train our imagination to read him is not easy. For to appreciate Acrasia's Bower depends, as I have said, on having other passages immediately in mind. And perhaps beyond all other major narrative poets Spenser witnesses to the cogency of Aristotle's observation that a plot cannot successfully exceed a certain magnitude; and if we include the magnitudes of doctrinal and formal complexity, as well as of external action, even the *Shepheardes Calender* may stand condemned. Yet broadly, though it is difficult to experience *The Faerie Queene,* or even a single book of it, as an imaginative whole, we do learn to be steadily responsive to the systematic allegory and to the modes

of its embodiment somewhat as an audience of Spenser's day
might be. Yet there is a still further veil of difficulty to be en-
countered. Not only did Spenser in his action syncretize the
schemes of both mediaeval and Renaissance allegory. But he
brought allegory also into his conception of style. He loved the
Renaissance theory and habit of elaborate ornament. He sought
to subordinate and digest that habit to his philosophical intention, I think, by making the varieties of style and its decorum
fill an allegorical function, so that the severe delineation of the
House of Holiness and the voluptuous elaboration of Acrasia's
Bower should symbolize in contrast the attitudes which each described. But Spenser had not the controlling intellectual focus
to achieve in that way what he intended. We are often lost in
the details. And in the aesthetic theory itself there is a confusion, though we cannot stop here to consider it. It is certainly a
method which allows the prevailing sensuousness of his temperament to express itself fully and to stir the reader's imagination
warmly. As Sainte-Beuve was to say long after of *Madame
Bovary,* Spenser can hardly stir Guyon to sensual impulse without a little stirring his reader. Yet we must never forget the perfectly clear impression his idealism made on readers of his own
day and of the seventeenth century. To them, he had made the
distinction between the use and the abuse of the senses in all its
aspects clear.[64]

Miss Bradbrook and Miss Lloyd Thomas rightly call our attention to the possible influence of Spenser's neo-Platonism on
Marvell. His statement on man's use of nature is most important
in defining the tradition of Marvell's thought. But if we place
the two poets side by side, it is rather the significant difference
between them that strikes us; it brings home to us the fact that
Marvell for the most part rejected the pantheon and the allegory of Florentine neo-Platonism and turned to the symbolic
thought which the Florentine Academy shared with an older
neo-Platonism. He is at once less systematic than Spenser and

in a way more intellectually direct and disciplined. His is the more pure and immediate reflection of sensibility and of devotional experience, and he turned directly to the masters of such experience. Spenser is for him a pattern of poetry, not a prime pattern of thought.

In bitter irony Satan says,

> My dwelling may not haply please,
> Like this fair Paradise, your sense.

How far Milton's conception of creation was neo-Platonic, and to what neo-Platonism it belonged has not yet been completely defined.[65] Clearly it belongs to that family of Platonic thought in which creation is the purely positive outflow of God's love, even to the uttermost particular thing, and in which it may be most perfectly equated with Genesis and the Psalms, when Genesis and the Psalms are read literally and not according to a schema, or symbolically. The cognateness of his paragraph on the hierarchy of the mental powers in Book V with passages such as I have cited from the Victorines bears out, in his view of the microcosm, his sense of the continuity and unity of the descending or ascending elements of the macrocosm. His view of the senses places him essentially with St. Augustine and those Platonists who insist on the integral nature of the personality and hence on the virtue of the senses, though both as poet and probably as thinker he trusts more fully the senses of the good man. Very significant for his view, because very concrete, is the great passage at the opening of the third book in which after having carried us through creation from chaos up to the coasts of light he suggests the steps of the human mind's ascent to God. For in the address to his blindness the idea of the great chain of being and the *plenum formarum* peers through the immediate and daily experience of beauty in a classical way characteristic of the tone of Milton's balance between natural feeling and symbolic Platonism.

Humanism in general and Protestantism had each its own
renewed sense of the book of the creatures: first in the idea of
the great chain; in other teleological concepts which, often in
Stoic language, urged the study of God's work in the laws of
nature, as does Hooker; and also in the immediate sense of the
beauty of nature. Protestant attitudes and emphases varied
widely. In Calvin's *Institutes of the Christian Religion* the book
of the creatures receives by prescription the first place in the
consideration how man may know God. And on the surface his
regard of the book follows the lines of Aquinas. His emphasis
is teleological. He begins with the Psalms and St. Paul; he
dwells on man as a microcosm—and on the study of physiology
in Galen—though he necessarily pauses to deny that the macrocosm can have any influence in the formation of man or in the
shaping of his destiny; and he moves on to remind us of the
great chain of being and of plenitude and of the high order
visible both in God's first work of the created cosmos and in his
secondary works of the social order.[66] He opens his theme to us
not without touches of that poetry which both experience itself
and the long tradition awaken in all who reflect upon the book.
And for a description of that first vision of God in nature which
Adam experienced he refers us to the amplifications of Genesis
by Ambrose and Basil. But though delight in the direct intuitions of experience often gleams under the opening eyelids of
the morn in Calvin, full day always shows forth the rigid logical and dogmatic consequences which must be imposed upon
that experience. It is not in his temper to dwell upon the beauties of the world as man may know them without revelation or
despite sin. In place of the ardent sense of kinship with Plato
which we find in Augustine and his followers, Calvin makes
only the grudging admission that Plato was less astray than all
his philosophic fellows; and that admission is an introduction
to the major consideration how grievously the pagans, the Epicureans in particular, have been led astray by endeavoring to

read God in nature alone. Calvin's primary concern here is lest man should be led to deny special providence. It is upon man's abjectness, upon the blindness in which total depravity has left him, that we are led to dwell. Aquinas offers humility as one of the fruits of studying the book of the creatures, a humility which places man, indeed, far down the scale, but which emphasizes his joyous sense of his participation in the great order. But to Calvin the idea of the great chain is quite secondary, merely a metaphor to the text of the Bible. To Aquinas the humanist the idea is a primary metaphysical conception which will obviate any materialistic view of the world, explicating Genesis. The material held in common by Calvin and Aquinas but marks the difference between the bibliolator and the mediaeval humanist.

Goodman in England, in a passage cited by Mr. Tillyard, illustrates the outgrowth of Calvinism. In order to assert his pessimism, he feels almost compelled to deny that the book of the creatures can be read at all. He allows educative force to the *speculum creaturarum* only because "the mind of man, which delights in nothing so much as mysteries, may make nature a ceremony and all the creatures types and resemblances of spiritual things."[67] Perhaps in that remark we have one clue to that very widespread renewal of symbolic neo-Platonism which is a distinguishing character of English thought in the first half of the seventeenth century.

Humanistic Protestantism did not share Goodman's pessimism nor his distrust of man's primary response to the beauty of the world about him. The joy of normal writers such as Hooker is less ecstatic, less sympathetic than that of the traditional neo-Platonists; their pictures may be said to be less conceptualized or less perceptive of the principle of life in the object, more aware of its immediate form. But the joy which runs through More's *Utopia* is a frank and enkindling joy. On the continent the Protestant apologist Zanchius in a passage which is close in tone to Ficino, a passage to which I have already alluded, illuminates his dry and legalistic encyclopedia of ethics and psychology with one radiant and human passage, in his preface, on man as the sole creature who returns thanks to God for all the creation, the "Secretarie of God's praise for all," as Herbert quaintly puts it. John Donne's statement on the book of the creatures in the twenty-third sermon of the *LXXX Sermons* is simply a reflection of St. Thomas' *Summa contra Gentiles,* sharpened to imaginative or contemplative intensity by a passage in the tradition of Dionysius and of Scotus' comment on him, a passage whose immediate source may well have been Raimond. It is not important for the sermon of which it is a part, being simply one point in an entire scheme which is focused on another point, the significance of the church in mediating grace to us. But it opens with a tentative inquiry into the theory of mirrored reflection which sheds light on Donne's attitude toward science. He is concerned to understand the point at issue between the old and the new science if it will reveal more precisely the specific analogy from a "science" to knowledge of God. That is all. Donne can, of course, elsewhere speak of the beauty of the flowers with the glow of a Tertullian.

The neo-Platonic reading of the book of the creatures is the version which is important for Marvell, in whom such a view developed quite easily upon a ground of Anglican Calvinism. But if we want to understand his imagination in the full context of its age, thinking of what remained outside his spirit as well as of what enkindled him, we must recall that science, too, offered a steadily more insistent reading of the book. In Hugh of St. Victor or in Bonaventura the methodology of the particular disciplines of the natural sciences might be developed within the larger *scientia* of metaphysics, even though to Bonaventura absorption in the natural sciences for themselves seemed always a danger, a danger of which Plato also had expressed his fear in the opening sections of the *Timaeus.* Hugh's statement of the hierarchy of the disciplines in their inherent relations to each other as, for instance, in the relation of observed physical fact to mathematics, is scientific. And he states very lucidly that scientific regress from a particular instance to the general case and to the laws governing the general case, and then back to the idealized particular now understood in its form and cause, the regress which many historians of thought consider to be the great contribution of mediaeval logic to the development of science. Agrippa illustrates how sympathetic magic could evolve into science better than he illustrates the evolution itself. But other Platonists at the dawn of the new science make clear how neo-Platonic conceptions of the structure of the universe, even though wrapped about in all the webs of fantastic doctrine about sympathies and symbolism, set genuine tasks for experimentation. Such doctrines of sympathy and magic, I think, Marvell did not share. The evidence that he did not is almost entirely negative. In 1672 he makes one humorous reference to cabbalism. But the significant fact in estimating his attitude toward these modes of thinking is the images of his poetry, none of which comes from particular systems of magical or sympathetic connection, all of which represent general symbolic principles of relation, order, and value, such as we find in the conception of the one and the many, or in geometry. Where his images are most particular, as in the fantastic reverie of the garden walk described in his poem on Appleton House, the tone of conscious fantasy is unmistakable, as unmistakable as the strictly rational tone of his prose later. By his day, however, science had taken a direction which isolated it from anything like Hugh's or Bonaventura's system, and the Platonism which would earlier have led him to science would no longer do so.

In non-Platonic theology Hooker's interest in the laws of nature by which God's providence orders the world might seem disposed to foster the new science, as might also the comment of Calvin on the study of physiology. And Zanchius bases his account of man, the microcosm, on the anatomy of Vesalius. But all three make a teleological assumption. And by the new science which was beginning to assert of ancient right a distinctive claim to interpret the book of the creatures, teleology, symbolism, aesthetic or devotional joy in the creatures as a primary intuition, were all attacked. Equally to be feared, because it set up a scheme which was prior to investigation, was the conception of the microcosm and the macrocosm, and the doctrine of sympathies in particular, conceptions no less obnoxious than the radical pessimism of a Calvin, a Donne, or a Goodman. Mr. Victor Harris has shown that the essential disagreements in the argument on progress and decay did not concern the empirical question whether the decay could or could not be measured, but the metaphysical question as to the structure of the universe and the method of exploring it.[68] Bacon, in the first book of *The Advancement of Learning* stresses in tones that suggest teleology the vision of God's work which will be secured by the study of his secondary providence in its scientific operation. But his care to cite Solomon as an authority on the progress which lies before science is surely meant to counter the symbolists by whom Solomon's three books had been held to be the fountainhead and prototypes of the three kinds of symbolism and is a characteristic rejection by him of their teleology. My sketch of the reading of the book, therefore, which science had now reclaimed for her own, may well close with a reminder of the sentence quoted earlier from Galileo and with a quotation from a letter of Lady Ranelagh, an intimate of Milton, to her brother Robert Boyle, in praise of the new experimental philosophy, which she believes "will help the considering part of mankind to a clearer prospect into this great frame of the visible world, and therein of the power and wisdom of its great maker, than the rough draft wherein it has hitherto been presented in the ignorant and wholesale philosophy that has so long, by the power of an implicit faith in Aristotle and the schools, gone current in the world has ever been able to assist them towards."[69] Thomas Browne in his *Pseudodoxia* and in his *Garden of Cyrus* would finally have agreed with her in reason, though his imagination loved to dwell on the older vision. Such views, by their contrast with the symbolism of Marvell's poems, help us no less than Bonaventura directly to realize the temper of his poetry.

It hardly requires saying that such a neo-Platonism as Marvell's differs radically from that of a Plotinus, a Bonaventura, or even a Ficino, in the absence of a great explicit metaphysical or logic structure to support it and in the radical simplification of its epistemology. Should the book of the creatures be read through intuition granted simply to the devout and humble heart, or through all the resources and training of the philosophical schools? The distinction was drawn clearly by Giordano Bruno, who was aware of the critical difference in the two approaches to union with God. For him, no way was possible but that of the long intellectual discipline, the long course of study and meditation, the slow and painful intellectual struggle to transform the soul, the formal steps laid down by the strictest Platonic ascent. But he recognized, though with puzzlement, the validity of the Northern way of immediate transformation, of simple withdrawal from the world and turning to love. Actually, as modern critical analysis points out, the German mystical movement rested upon the structures of both Bonaventura and Thomas Aquinas. But the emphasis of its statement did not fall there; and its communication of experiential religion did not wait upon the slow step of logical justification or intellectual discipline.

In seventeenth-century England the prevailing anti-intellectualism creates its own special condition for the renewal of Platonism and the contemplation of the creatures. And it may well be remembered here that Montaigne defended Raimond of Sebonde just at the point where systematic intellectualism had criticized him, because he gave a contemplative insight and not a rational structure. Montaigne, of course, found experience to suggest a quite different structure, had it not faith to depend on. With the English writers we are thinking of, the question is only a question of the extent of the operation of reason, not of repudiating it.

What we find there is, in fact, a conflict of views or of implications within the same writer. Marvell's *On a Drop of Dew*, for instance, seems to me to rest upon the elaborate structure of neo-Platonic psychology, and with some of the elements in his garden poetry, this systematic view is in logical conflict. Not only with the partial distrust of learning and the distrust of art there, but with the immediate and intuitive joy in nature and the absorption in her which is so much the heart of the garden poems. For the way of the Florentine neo-Platonists demands extensive discipline. Between the two there is also, as we have seen, a paradoxical difference of attitude toward the created world. And the difficulty of reconciling the two is increased when we recall that the neo-Platonic view of a Ficino had sought to dissolve this paradox by synthesis with the orthodox Christian view of the fallen state of man, whereas the more simply intuitive view was often associated in seventeenth-century England, as it had been elsewhere, with the concept of an innocence of childhood to which it should be the endeavor of man to return from his corruption by the world.[70] Such a view could draw on obvious sources in the sayings of Christ. But for all that, it is a view less readily susceptible of synthesis with Christian theology than Ficino's view, even though actually in its seventeenth-century form it was widely held by devout Christians in, for instance, the Anglican church and even if they thought of childhood as affording but a brief intimation of man's ideal state before original sin closed in upon him.

Manifestly the seventeenth century in England did not on the whole distinguish these differences in the serious theological sense of the early Fathers, the schools, and the Italian neo-Platonists. And perhaps the conflict we have noted illustrates just the point that we should dwell on most: the decline of theology and the deeply quiet orthodoxy of the faith and morals of most of the men who dwelt upon these ideas. What they wanted in a time of critical historical tension was devotion, "virtue, manners, freedom, power." Moreover the men whose views we are describing, we ought not to forget, were on the whole poets and men of letters, not philosophers or theologians—though they might be in the church. But for all that, they had their roots deep in the ground of critical views on the nature and use of the mind. Before we turn to the devotional mood, we must define Marvell's intellectual position as fully as we can and allude to the backgrounds which illuminate it.

Marvell lived in a climate of opinion in which both pietism and skepticism were so pervasive that perhaps no other reference may seem necessary than one to the "climate of opinion" itself. But the assumptions of "pietism" and skepticism are quite distinct. And I believe that the quality of Marvell's feeling will not be fully perceived unless we understand its positive intellectual justification, its Platonism in particular. Professor Lovejoy has commented ironically upon the curious fact that the idea of the great chain of being began one of its most active phases of influence just at a time when the possibility of arriving at metaphysical truth had been denied. But attitudes toward the intuition of truth other than the strictly logical discipline he implies deserve their own consideration.

It will not be ungermane to our purpose to note in passing that the terms of definition, the temper and the imaginative tone of Marvell's anti-intellectualism and of Pope's in Pope's statement of the concept of the great chain of being are very different. We are in the presence of two quite distinct phases of that general mood of limitation of reason which was coming to pervade European thought. If we would understand the idea of the great chain as an element in Pope's thought, we should cer-

tainly be helped by turning to the idea of the scale of the creatures as it appears in Pomponazzi, where it is Aristotelian and
classificatory, rather than Platonic. In this form the idea more
readily serves Pomponazzi's rationalistic this-worldliness, his
eclectic ethic of self-possession; to him already that view of the
great chain affords really the basic pattern expressed in this
whole side of Pope's *Essay on Man*. It is also later more readily
syncretized with the popular teleology springing from New-
tonian science.[71] The reaction against scholastic thought is a
common ground of both phases of anti-intellectualism. But in
Marvell, as in seventeenth-century thought as a whole from
Donne the man of religion to Traherne, from Browne to Henry
More, the temper and the intellectual ends are primarily contemplative. Their anti-intellectualism took shape within the
defining walls of the great and varied structure of early and
mediaeval theology, modified and readjusted by Calvinism and
directly or indirectly by Florentine neo-Platonism. There was in
Anglicanism a hard core of the use of elements from the structure of Thomas' thought. But the over-all English rejection of
scholasticism and marked returned to earlier church writers
with a less elaborate rational system is never to be lost from
sight. Other independent intellectual forces were, of course, at
work. One cannot assert positively that Marvell's anti-intellectualism was not influenced by subtle pressures from those de-
velopments in pure philosophy for which the age is best known
in intellectual history. But though the development of rationalism, of philosophical skepticism, of science and its metaphysical
foundations must be recalled as forming part of Marvell's background, that wider view is not really necessary to an understanding of him. It is the position of Anglicanism which is
significant.

In trying to define Marvell's assumptions in these poems, it
is reasonable to use the more explicit views expressed in his prose
of fifteen to twenty years later to know what the words of the

poems mean. For, first, the anti-Romanism of poems and prose
is manifestly a common element. Then the religious views
which Marvell held in the 1670's were not views likely to be
newly arrived at in the general religious and political atmosphere of that period by a man in Marvell's position, and moving
as he was towards conformity in the state, a conformity rooted
in the sense of the great tradition, of order, and of property;
they are, rather, views which, once they had been formed earlier
in great travail, such a man as he would hold on to unconform-
ingly; and indeed the poems themselves are the expression of
what was perhaps the critical experience of that travail. And
they are views, moreover, characteristically likely to have been
formed by any man in the civil-war years. Finally, a less certain
evidence but not negligible, he himself assumes that his intellectual views have been consistent throughout.

Marvell's anti-intellectualism may be defined in terms first of
a particular rejection of scholastic thought, winged by hatred
of Rome and a deep sense of the general futility of the unresolv-
able theological conflicts of the day on the one hand; and on
the other, second, by a profound belief in the necessity of grace
for the right functioning of reason and personality. One cannot say certainly when Marvell's ironic view of human nature
took shape; but his view of the part which it played in the intellectual history of Christendom is manifest. The conflict and
variations arising from the refinements of theological distinction
were to him clear evidence that the human mind was not intended to be an instrument to draw such distinctions. It could
make upon the basis of revelation a few clear and direct, non-
discursive, religious intuitions. For the rest, the refinements
drawn at the council of Nice were the offspring of jealousy and
of ecclesiastical rivalry, put forward only by men who could
clearly make the worse appear the better reason, and concluded
not by reason and the prevalence of the strongest arguments, but
by the contemptuous intervention of political authority. On the

other hand, Marvell's Calvinism is firm, though not dogmatic. He attacks nothing more bitterly than Parker's emphasis upon works, habit, manners, general good will, at the expense of the doctrine of grace. To Marvell's belief in the doctrine of grace, and in the immanence of grace in the operation of the mind when it forms its clearest and most basic intuitions, we must, I think, attribute his no less strong belief in toleration. He has recorded for us the deep, even the awful, impression he received from stable and sensible men, on his return to England in the late forties, of Laud's violence in endeavoring to force men's thoughts. His tone, in speaking of the Dissenters of a later generation whom he would defend from Parker, is significant. Obviously they are of a quite different class, scope of thought, and outlook from himself. But he would defend their belief in grace given immediately to the individual, in part by an appeal to the Anglicanism of the early half of the century; and therefore he must defend the integrity of their thought. Significant too is the distinction which he draws between Parker's attack upon them and Butler's attack on the Presbyterians and men of inner light. He does not merely defend Butler because *Hudibras* is a poem of great wit, though that is for Marvell a good reason to defend him; but because, I think he says, Butler attacked real abuses. Marvell, that is to say, would draw a clear line between the Calvinist view of grace, and the logic chopping, egotism, and spirit of contention of Butler's hero. He distrusts the affixing of names to one's opponents, viewing it as an affirmation of distinctions not to be drawn, as a weapon in the personal warfare of heresy-finding; hesitates himself to name men Arminians even, in a pejorative sense. Altogether, if we could bring Marvell a little earlier into affairs and could imagine him to have been in the new model army and taking part in the great debates, we must suppose him to have held just about the views held by the Puritans of the center as those views are described by Mr. Woodhouse,[72] strongly opposed to the Levellers, opposed to Presbyterian dogmatism. Perhaps like Fairfax for whom he was soon to work, he could not himself have told whether he were Presbyterian—in this case older Anglican—or Independent.

Such an anti-intellectualism, one need not point out, differs radically from philosophical skepticism. In Marvell's garden poems it turns to pietism, to an apparent distrust of all humanistic learning. But the pietism itself needs definition. It is in part a mood, but only in part. To see how it is a pietism consistent with Marvell's view of reason, and able to embrace neo-Platonic conceptions, we must look at something of its traditions, and at other contemporary manifestations of it.

I turn once again to Tertullian for the concept of reason I am trying to define both because he was widely read in the seventeenth century and because his view of the problem of intellectualism, his distinction between "dialectic" and "reason," opens classic issues. Of his rejection of systematic dialectic I have already spoken in the second chapter of this book. On the other hand his rejection of academic skepticism is equally explicit in the passages from the *De Anima* which I have already cited. And of Aristotle he says, having reference to Aristotle's denial of a mind in the infant, "Let me not overlook those who even for a little while widow the soul of the intellect."[73] All this discussion arises out of his emphasis on the Incarnation and is part also of his emphasis upon the ethical teaching of the Bible, and upon the doctrine of salvation as the primary truth and intellectual principle upon which all thought must build. That doctrine is a given truth, which it is reason for the mind to grasp because in it perfect reason is made manifest; and if the will be rectified the mind will grasp it. The idea thus connects itself with Socrates' emphasis upon the rectified will, upon definition by intuition of value. In another light, the mind's assent is seen as the act of the normal mind, the mind realizing its nature. This Stoic conception is, however, set forth with an unstoic stress on emotion. (And it may be noted that Augustine regards the apparent Stoic rejection of emotion as verbal only. They do not, he believes, reject rightly oriented love, or anger.)

The rejection of academic skepticism is equally firm and equally central in St. Augustine, St. Bonaventura, and the Florentine neo-Platonists. For that whole tradition of thought the solution to finding one's way between sophistic intellectualism and skepticism lay in St. Augustine's re-examination of the processes of thought and feeling, an exploration which led him to reaffirm the primary significance of the mind's pure consciousness of thought and of itself and to argue the existence of God from the mind's ultimate dependence upon pure Being, perfected in the pattern of Christ. His view, which permeates his *Confessions,* is perhaps most clearly seen in his *Answer to the Academic Philosophers,* the work in which he first, following his conversion, after some months of reflection, set down for himself and the group around him the intellectual principles on which his thought was thenceforth to be based. It is in the genuine form of a Socratic dialogue with his younger pupils and friends—a group chosen because it was composed of those with whom he was actually at this time living, but a group also in its members well suited to his aim of eliciting the simple revelation of the primary movement of thought. By dialectic Augustine first unveils the pure verbalism of sophistic argument.[74] Gradually as he proceeds in the debate he elicits from his interlocutors their awareness of their own assent of mind, that very assent which academic skepticism denied, until they see that that positive assent is the basic activity of their minds and is in itself the all-inclusive answer to skepticism. The answer, that is, to later Academic refusal of assent in order to avoid error. Wisdom does not need defining; we have a clear idea of it: *Cujus enim verbi in animis nostris apertiorem notionem natura esse voluit quam sapientiae?*[75] By the close of the first discourse he has demonstrated, in their examination of the discourse itself, that the mind desires positive truth and not, as the Academics hold, mere avoidance of error.

As the argument proceeds, going back and enlarging upon itself, all the impediments to wisdom, which render it necessary that in practical affairs we should live by the probable only, are allowed. But they are allowed as impediments tending to inhere in our condition only, not as impediments of purified reason. Thus from the discussion emerges the idea of that perfect wisdom which alone can have perfect consciousness of itself. This is, of course, though it is not explicitly said in the dialogue, the wisdom found on earth in Christ.

Then the certainty of the intuition of the world by the senses is affirmed despite the particular errors that they may make. For awareness of illusion proves that which is not illusion. And the clear categories and affirmations of thought, such as the disjunctive and as number, such as ideas of justice, and order, are noticed.

Finally, Augustine is persuaded to state what he believes Plato as distinct from the New Academy held, though, in the conditions existing even at the time of the first Academy, his followers concealed their views from all but the initiate. To the Socratic skill in ethics, and to Pythagoras' skill in natural and divine sciences, Plato added dialectic. He held that there were two worlds, intelligible and sensible, the former the true world, this world a wraithlike image of the other. Truth emanates from the intelligible world and is as it were refined and brightened in the soul which knows itself, though in this world never perfectly seen except by one perfect wisdom. In regard to the present world he held that opinion but not knowledge can be engendered in the minds of the unwise. And in this sensible world there are political virtues (Temperance, Justice, Fortitude, Prudence), powers similar to the true powers that are known only to a few men. But yet whatever is represented by those virtues, being of this world, can be called no more than probable.[76]

It is, I think, clear how in such a view the wise mind might be held to be able by dialectic to arrive at an intuition of the *principles* of the *Timaeus,* which are elements of primary knowledge, without its necessarily following that finite minds could arrive at particular astronomical knowledge or understand the mysteries of the infinite in detail. The consistency between this view, seen in this aspect of Augustine's thought, and his attitude towards the senses is manifest.[77]

Going forward to Bonaventura, we find a statement not only central to Christian tradition but also immediate in its bearing on Marvell, for whose lines on holy mathematics one passage in the *Hexaëmeron* supplies a precise analogue, though concept and phrase go back also to earlier Christianity. Bonaventura is particularly important to an understanding of seventeenth-century anti-intellectualism because of the full development in him of symbolic principles of thought, and because of the tension in him of the Franciscan struggle against a newly erupting worldliness, including intellectual worldliness. In Bonaventura pietistic implications of Augustinianism come sharply into the foreground, though Bonaventura is the perfecter of one of the great intellectual structures of the Middle Ages. He has been speaking earlier in the passage I shall cite of the Scriptures as a garden, an intellectual garden. In Paradise there is *no plantation save of the eternal causes.* The mind is that paradise in which Scripture is planted, and it has innumerable sweetnesses and fitting ornaments (*decores*). We must not allow the intelligence of truth to grow dark, shapeless, and deformed without its food, but we should read the Scriptures and not go out from the garden:

> Sic erit anima, ut operans et custodiens, [hortum paradisi] et faciet sibi ex ea hortum parvum in mente deliciosum. In hac sola scientia est delectatio, non in aliis. Philosophus dicit, quod magna

delectatio est scire, quod diameter costae est asymmeter: haec delectatio sic cito desinens, suo modo comedat illam. Egreditur autem de Scriptura quaedam lux, seu illustratio, in intellectum junctum imaginationi, ut non pateat egressus sapienti et hoc aspicienti intra extra, infra, supra... [These forms of study are defined; for instance, the Bible illustrates to the left by benign *flagella*.] ... Vide Noe, qui cum centum annis fabricabat arcam, et ponebat ibi quidquid habebat, tunc totus mundus ipsum despiciebat. Et dico hoc, quod rex Franciae non posset hodie talem facere, qui considerat eam secundum mensuram cubitorum geometricorum. ...

Adhuc etiam habet Scriptura arbores ad reficiendum. Illustrat autem ex his, quae sunt ex opposito. Ostendit enim nobis acies infinitas contra nos, modo per septem duces, modo unum bellum, modo multa: illud bellum est ab illo die quo "Michael et angeli ejus praeliabantur cum dracone." Imminet autem nobis triplex bellum: bellum domesticum, bellum civile, et bellum campestre.[78]

In the opening of the next sermon (XVIII), *Quomodo intellectus ordinatur ad affectum et de fructibus eorum,* he goes on to recapitulate the dangers of going too far in the sciences, which he had earlier in the fifth sermon on the Three Lights of Truth defined at more length. Truth is in its essence moral. Hence all other approaches to law and to the disciplines are false luxuriations. Approaches by *ratio physica* and *metaphysica* are false, in that they begin by positing an eternal world *because its cause is eternal,* a false view of the first cause. And so mathematics went into numerology, and natural philosophers thought because art follows nature and they knew nature, they could make gold and silver. So the grammarians erected poetic fables, rhetoricians the colors of speech, and logicians sophisms.[79] Here is the central concept of pietism as it is in Marvell and as we meet it so often in the Renaissance in dilute form when men, for instance, like Chapman, approach the mysteries of Platonism. That his conception of the soul as the *hortus conclusus* of the Song of Songs, in just this sense in which Bonaventura uses it, was current in seventeenth-century English thought there can be no question; for Vaughan makes it explicit in his *Mount of Olives:* "And at what time soever thou shalt wake me from this bodily sleep, awake also my soul in me, make thy morning-star to arise in my heart, and let thy spirit blow upon my garden, that the spices thereof may flow out." And that Marvell's *Garden* is not only a Yorkshire garden but also, in and through that warmly concrete experience, to the symbolic imagination very definitely the *hortus conclusus,* I shall show in full when we see how all the ideas I am here defining come together in his poem. Here in Bonaventura and in Augustine also more broadly is a kernel parallel to the Platonic core of Milton's damning portrait of Belial and of his defense of freedom of speech on the ground that "opinion in *good men* is but knowledge in the making."

The problem of Ficino's attitude toward intellectualism is more complex, and the answer less single and assured, because he seeks to syncretize the principles of Augustine and Bonaventura with Thomistic Christianity and with the renewed study of Plotinus. Hence in him we can find the epistemological structure of the mind's ascent to conceptual thought which I have earlier described, a structure which is often logically elaborate and which necessitates rejecting the imagination. But perhaps, on the other side, more deeply central is his exclamation that the love of the stars never carried any man to God, but only the soul's need of the absolute. Perhaps in that cry he is thinking of the dangers of Stoic materialism; possibly of Bonaventura's parallel rejection of the argument leading up to the unmoved first mover. Certainly his argument is central in explaining his use of symbolic patterns and allegory. Professor Cassirer has described at length the more comprehensive principle of symbolic thought by which Giovanni Pico della Mirandola strove to relate traditional Christianity with the other philosophies which were available in Renaissance Italy, not excluding even Paduan rationalism.[80] And he has analyzed likewise the theory of *docta ignorantia* of Nicolas of Cusa, so influential in Renaissance thought and so radically different from libertine skepticism.

Turning now to some manifestations of the intellectual temper which surrounded Marvell in seventeenth-century England. The influence of this same symbolic principle in English thought in the seventeenth century has not been sufficiently noted. Many a use of the concepts of the microcosm and the macrocosm, and of various other forms of analogy, allegory, and symbol might be simply unanalyzed remainders of older science. Many were the more serious intellectual fruits of the middle sciences of a Paracelsus or a Jerome Cardan.[81] And by serious thinkers the underlying principle of the nature of reason had been well considered. The symbolic principle which Giovanni Pico della Mirandola and Ficino used to reconcile Thomism with Platonism, with Hermeticism or with cabbalism, in England supplied for many the place of a rejected scholasticism.

Professor Hughes has penetratingly defined the complex of intuitions and traditions which moulds Donne's limitation of the intellect, suggesting at one end the relation of his thought with that of Cusa, at another the connection of his imagination with the patterns of symbolic thought renewed in the wide currency of emblems.[82] Important for Donne's view is his comment in *Ignatius His Conclave* that Copernicus might not have a place of honor in Hell because his theory might be true and because, more significantly, no man's ethics was affected, either way. Difficult as it is to reduce the irony of that work to explicit statement, Donne's subordination of all the findings of astronomy, excited as he was on the surface of his mind about those findings, to man's moral life and to his grasp on the universe through ethical reason, is clear. Or, approaching the problem of intellectual activity from the other side, Donne, like Ficino and like Gianfrancesco Pico della Mirandola, thinks of doubt about the primary ethical intuitions as a product of disordered melancholy, even while recognizing like Pico that it may also owe something to the contemporary conflict of ideas. As I have already tried to show in the earlier part of this book, Donne's mind habitually moved in the patterns of symbolic thought and the symbolic schemes opened by Tertullian and Bonaventura; if he is so strict against fantastic elaboration of Biblical allegory as to seem rational in the modern sense, that is because he so thoroughly grasped the serious core of that thought, which makes assumptions not now generally received, but which develops them with logical severity and seriousness free from fantasy. And we must not confuse his startled awareness that the particular astronomical embodiment of that picture of the universe to which his imagination was linked, might be subject to change, with a supposal that science would achieve or had a method to achieve a picture of the universe in conflict with eternal philosophy. Rather the emotional shock which can perhaps be felt in him at the disturbing of the threads by which the philosophy had been concretized in a particular cosmic myth—that emotion transfused itself into a fresh affirmation of the old philosophy, a fresh realization of man's situation in this world.

Sir Thomas Browne's famous statement half a century later must be read in the light of this symbolic principle and is very directly illuminating for Marvell.

As for those wingy Mysteries in Divinity . . . Methinks there be not impossibilities enough in Religion for an active faith; the deepest Mysteries ours contains have been not only illustrated, but maintained, by Syllogism and the rule of Reason. I love to lose myself in a mystery, to pursue my Reason to an *O Altitudo!* . . .

'Tis true there is an edge in all firm belief, and with an easie Metaphor we may say, the Sword of Faith: but in these obscurities I rather use it in the adjunct the Apostle gives it, a Buckler: under which I conceive a wary combatant may lye invulnerable. Since I was of understanding to know we knew nothing, my reason hath been more pliable to the will of Faith; I am now content to understand a mystery without a rigid definition, in an easie and Platonick description. That allegorical description of Hermes pleaseth me beyond all the Metaphysical definitions of Divines. Where I cannot satisfy my reason, I love to humour my fancy: I had as live you tell me that *anima est angelus hominis, est Corpus* DEI, as *Entelechia; . . .*[83]

Presently, almost in an aside, he rejects the Aristotelian argument from the unmoved first mover in favor of the study of the book of the creatures. Browne is, on the other hand, unlike the Italians in that he does not seek through symbolic thought to set up a comprehensive view of the world. One has no right to draw inference backward from the opening section of his *Vulgar Errors* to his earlier position when he was writing *Religio Medici;* he may obviously in the later work have reached definitions not yet clear to him in the earlier. Or he may, like Pico, distinguish between the world of science and the world of spirit. But one is tempted to think that his rejection in the later work of the whole body of emblem books as one of the great sources of popular error, on the ground that people were tempted to accept as literal fact the emblems which were only intended as symbolic inventions, may be significant in defining his earlier meaning. He would, then, have thought of Platonic symbols or myths in a rather broad and not un-Platonic way. Symbolism —Platonic myth, metaphor, Hermetic definition—affords him the basis for meditation and emotion; it is in this way, genuinely, the clue to religious insight. But such symbols do not define doctrine. His sense of the mysteriousness of the mysteries has advanced far. The matter is partly one of temperament. His implicit statement on the prerogatives of private reason, at the opening of *Religio Medici,* together with his references to natural law, place him in the tradition of the rational *via media* as Hooker had formulated it, though manifestly for Browne the bounds of reason have shrunk. His view of the Apostolic succession, his attitude toward Roman Catholicism, his whole tone, mark him as a Laudian Anglican, very susceptible to the traditions and instrumentalities of devotion. The great evidence for the truth of the Bible he finds in its ethical teaching; the evidence for Christianity in particular men is manners, good will, human devotion.

Marvell's is in contrast a Calvinist Anglicanism; and he would give a sharper, more closely defined emphasis than does Browne to the operation of grace. Hence the radical difference between his approach and Browne's to the religious divisions of the day and to the question of toleration. Nor, with all Browne's genial humanism, is his a mind of outstanding intellectual or philosophical drive. He is an artist. With that simple, good nature of his, he can easily trust to the gradual amelioration of man's condition which the contribution of science will help to make. He accepts scientific empiricism as the method for analyzing nature, for beholding the maker in the creatures. Symbolic thought, as I have already said, is no longer for him the core of an all-inclusive intellectual system. The cabbalistic interpretation of Genesis is attractive to him, but only attractive; he is aware that his symbolism is fantastic. It is the ground for feelingful mediative exercise upon the plain, accepted truths of faith. One might perhaps surmise that it was the still living imaginative remainder of the intellectual pattern in which faith had come to him in youth.

In my solitary and retired imagination

(neque enim cum porticus aut me
Lectulus accepit, desum mihi,)

I remember I am not alone, and therefore forget not to contemplate Him and His Attributes Who is ever with me, especially those two mighty ones, His Wisdom and Eternity. With the one I recreate, with the other I confound, my understanding; for who can speak of Eternity without a soloecism, or think thereof without an Extasie? Time we may comprehend; 'tis but five days elder then our selves, and hath the same Horoscope with the World; but to retire so far back as to apprehend a beginning, to give such an infinite start forwards as to conceive an end, in an essence that we affirm hath neither the one nor the other, it puts my Reason to St. Paul's Sanctuary. . . .

Beware of Philosophy, is a precept not to be received in too large a sense; for in this Mass of Nature there is a set of things that carry in their Front (though not in Capital Letters, yet in Stenography and short Characters,) something of Divinity, which to wiser Reasons serve as Luminaries in the Abyss of Knowledge, and to judicious beliefs as Scales and Roundles to mount the Pinacles and highest pieces of Divinity. The severe Schools shall never laugh me out of the Philosophy of Hermes, that this visible World is but a Picture of the invisible, wherein, as in a Pourtraict, things are not truely, but in equivocal shapes, and as they counterfeit some more real substance in that invisible fabrick.[84]

To such meditation he relates aesthetic experience:

For there is a musick where ever there is a harmony, order, or proportion: and thus far we may maintain the music of the Sphears; for those well-ordered motions, and regular paces, though they give no sound unto the ear, yet to the understanding they strike a note most full of harmony. Whosoever is harmonically composed delights in harmony; which makes me much distrust the symmetry of those heads which declaim against all Church-Musick. For my self, not only from my obedience, but my particular Genius, I do embrace it: for even that vulgar and Tavern-Musick, which makes one man merry, another mad, strikes in me a deep fit of devotion, and a profound contemplation of the first composer. There is something in it of Divinity more than the ear discovers: it is an Hieroglyphical and shadowed lesson of the whole World, and creatures of GOD; such a melody to the ear, as the whole World, well understood, would afford the understanding. In brief, it is a sensible fit of that harmony which intellectually sounds in the ears of GOD.[85]

And so, after all, Browne brings us back to our starting point in Marvell. With Marvell, despite differences of doctrine and emphasis in the two men, Browne unites in the study of that "holy mathematics" which transcends mere rationalism. But we should greatly mistake the intellectual temper of both men and of the age in general if we failed to see the Augustinian rationalism which supports their devotional mood.

In Marvell's view, symbolic thought is more entire, more rootedly significant than in Browne, though one would not say that it is a more literal intellectual truth to him. He is closer to Donne, much closer to Bonaventura. His anti-intellectualism, as I have said, goes very far in its sense of the insolubility of many theological and philosophical issues. In his later prose, no less than in his poetry, his mind turns spontaneously to the analogies of the older symbolic picture of the cosmos. But the tone of his use of such figures in his prose as well as the absence of references to a great structural system such as one finds in Bonaventura or in Ficino or in Donne's sermons leads one to feel that the symbolic patterns are for him now images and adumbrations, rather than elements in a fully defined system. But they are no mere devotional metaphors. They are insights, shoots of a still living tree of thought. Nor must a certain bantering tone in the poems and one or two mirthful allusions to fantastic and eccentric excesses of symbolism in his prose mislead us as to his attitude toward genuine symbolic thought. The analogy to guide us here is Bonaventura's condemnation of numerology and of alchemy, the rise of which Bonaventura seems to ascribe precisely to the rise of the Aristotelian organon. Marvell would not push any systematic structure, any systematic explication of correspondences, so far as had Hugh and Bonaventura. But all the more for that is Bonaventura a guide in defining the mode and the proper objects of reason. All the more does he show how we may properly grasp and be content with the basic intuition of the relation of the universe to God in the great chain and in the book of the creatures. (It is at this point, we ought perhaps to note, that Calvin would be closest to Bonaventura and of course to Augustine in rational position, though so infinitely far distant in the whole scope and color of his mind and in temper.) In *Upon Appleton House* and *The Garden* conscious intellectual command and a conscious view of the mind's steps toward truth, in the mode of symbolic thought, is present not merely in the whole tone of mind represented and in the aesthetic, but in the scheme of thought alluded to and in the participant's judgment of his experience.

Finally a passage in Henry More's commentary on the *Cabbala,* directed primarily against Puritan zeal and severity, will illustrate how wide afield men's thoughts were ranging within the "climate of opinion" and by how many ways the ideas of reason, the limits of intellect, and the character of our intuitions were approached; and again how varied a nexus of ideas was woven together to create that climate of opinion which from a distant view appears to offer a uniform hue and texture. Commenting on or defending a passage in the *Cabbala* which holds that the creation of woman is to elicit that kindly flowering joy of harmless delight in the natural life and health of the body which, if joined with simplicity and innocency, is the greatest part of Paradise man is capable of on earth, More says: "There is a truth of Sense and Experience, and it is no more to be proved by Reason, than that White is white." And in a further passage on the joy of the consensus of the soul and body in bodily health, he argues that since the soul's function is to inform a body, it is joyous to feel health. When, on the contrary, the soul-in-body is melancholy or given to sensuality it loses the sense of God and is miserable. For sensuality is incompatible with the health of the body. As in Tertullian, the connection of this concept of reason with Stoic stress on nature is clear, as also with Epicurean justification both of pleasure and of the immediate intuition.

More takes us far afield from Marvell. But he does clearly raise one question important for the whole anti-intellectualism of the age, the question of the reliability of the senses. We have already seen why it was important to Tertullian to affirm the validity of sensuous intuition, and we have seen the emphasis of Bonaventura and the Victorines upon it, even while stressing the final importance of the concept rather than of the percept.

That stress, one may surmise, would help to make their philosophy an available substitute to men of the seventeenth century for scholasticism. To Protestant thought, with its reliance upon the text of the Bible, and upon a definition of individual reason that went with that dependence and with a belief in an individual's power to interpret the text, the reliability of the senses became of fresh importance. Stress upon it is no less great in Zanchius than in the rationalist Anglican divines who in the later seventeenth century fought against fideistic arguments for Roman Catholicism, and against Roman Catholic interpretation of the sacrament of the mass. Hence though they may sometimes share the extreme quietism of Agrippa in his *De Vanitate et Incertitudine Scientiarum* in so far as it affirms the *vanity* of knowledge, it is only the first of his theses which they can accept. The fanciful passage in Marvell's *Upon Appleton House* in which he looks down upon the valley and speculates on the illusion of objects seen from the height would perhaps not have occurred except in a time actively intellectually aware of the problems involved in sensation. But the whole tenor of his poems indicates that it is not Agrippa and Montaigne who are likely to underlie his thought. Rather it is Platonic speculations on the theory of vision, such as are to be found also in the poems of Traherne, which may be in his mind. He would answer for the validity of the senses as St. Augustine had answered, and trust the same alert imagination as St. Augustine would, by the very authority of the fact that we recognize illusion. And though More's cabbalistic optimism in his work on the *Cabbala* as a whole is so alien to the temper of Marvell's Christian humanism, with its sober emphasis on ethic, the passage I have quoted from More reminds us of the common core of thought underlying the two men's affirmations of the hierarchy of the intuitions in the balanced moral personality.

I have spoken so far of the theory of knowledge. And though I have insisted that the intellectual structure of Hugh and Bonaventura carried within itself a principle of the limitation of knowledge not unsuggested in Plato's *Timaeus,* a principle which can be argued on the assumptions of that system itself to be both valid and not paradoxical, I have noticed only incidentally that the stress upon moral intuition and religious orientation in Bonaventura can with only a little shift of emphasis be tilted toward pure pietism. In that pietism Bonaventura does indeed offer to Marvell a pattern, as he had offered it to mystical theology in mediaeval Germany. But Bonaventura's pietism is still a part of a large intellectual system. And that system has a clarity and unity and intellectual scope which obviously do not pervade the thought of the poets and men of letters of the seventeenth century among whom Marvell belongs. Here in estimating Marvell's or Browne's attitude one does have to allow something for what can most tangibly be defined as climate of opinion. Theirs is not an age of the great creation of the structures of faith or discipline; it is an age at the end of a long period of making of structures, an age, therefore, in which the average man under stress turns to patterns already existing for him.

And critical, philosophical, and theological theories themselves have often in any age their starting point in experience and exist to interpret it. To understand the devotional anti-intellectualism so widespread in Marvell's age, one must reckon with the personal crises through which in that time of intellectual, social, and political conflicts so many men passed and with the experience of their own consciousness which was the fruit of those crises. Personal affirmation after disillusion must have played a very important part in defining the ideas of reason and knowledge; and in almost all branches of Christianity in the seventeenth century self-watchfulness in the individual sensibility had prepared men to value that brightly focused personal affirmation unusually highly. Vaughan's account of his own intuitions is very significant for a student of Marvell. The anti-intellectualism which we are concerned with and of which Vaughan is one most important example was already present in the Hermetic writings which Vaughan studied. But it is not to them that Vaughan owes his ultimate reconciliation to life and hence the intellectual structure of that reconciliation. The en-kindling thing for him had been the immediate experience of nature and of friendship and of family affection, coming to him in a time of special personal need. The great primary poetic things in him are those direct intuitions or re-intuitions of na-ture and of friendship, in the opening of *The Timber, The Waterfall,* "They are all gone," "Silence and stealth of days." With these intuitions, and with the recollections of his own childhood, as Mr. Martin suggests, the *theory* of the innocence and intuitive wisdom of childhood, widely current in seven-teenth-century meditations, could unite in full harmony. Several of his greatest poems express that general view, enlightened by Vaughan's recollections of his own childhood. Yet affirmation of such primary intuition once made in experience, the theory of intuition readily unites itself to traditional and formal thought of another character. The poem which I suppose we should all agree opens with Vaughan's most intense intuition, *The World,* did not arrive at its intuition simply; it closes with the affirmation that the vision can be attained only by long re-pentance and devotion channeled through the church. Doubtless the habit of devotional experience within the ritual of the An-glican church was as deeply rooted in Vaughan and as old as his primary response to the beauty of the world or the delight of af-fection. In *The Night* Vaughan uses his sense of self-possession in the nighttime as a symbol of his whole sense of self-posses-sion in withdrawal from worldly interests; and he associates his symbolic experience with that dark night of the senses and that sight of God as a dazzling darkness which is defined in sys-tematic mystical writers such as Dionysius or St. John of the Cross. In "They Are All Gone" Vaughan solves the question of immortality through the simple, immediate experience of finding a fledged bird's nest in the spring, answering, if you will, a *logical* question with a symbol, or with a metaphor-analogy like those of the Old Testament prophets, though such a symbol as they had used only to interpret *values* and *states of feeling,* not to affirm dogma. But in "Resurrection and Immortality" he interprets the Biblical visions of eternal peace in terms of the neo-Platonic scheme of the cosmos and might be summarizing the final stanzas of Spenser's *Cantos of Mutabilitie.* Vaughan is more concerned with the common theme of contemplation than with the logic and epistemology of the differing approaches to it. Marvell's crisis of feeling about the civil war is as sharp as Vaughan's, though different; and there are intimations at least of a crisis in his personal life.

Not only did these various traditions share their final object of contemplation. But to summarize what I have said in another way, they shared with all the religious psychology of the day an intensified concentration upon the individual consciousness. That consciousness was the scene and the action of that drama of the soul, the sense of which had been in Renaissance, Reformation, and Counter-Reformation so deeply renewed. It was so, whether one viewed it in its simple outgoing capacity for love of the creatures or in more complex views of the power and limitations and struggles of his mind suspended between two worlds. Hence the wish to come closer to God by an immediate intuition of the beauty of the world which he had made, and by the spontaneous upwelling of feeling, was widespread. It might even pass in the thought of the age into an articulate rejection of science and of humanistic learning. But its great energy was positive, not critical; and it was channelled particularly in the book of the creatures, the most immediate expression of the sense of the unity of all experience and of the dependence of the visible and momentary world upon the divine, which in some one of its forms entered into all the currents of sixteenth-

and seventeenth-century thought which were in any way brought into the religious stream.

In such an intuition, the return from despair to affirmation plays a part of the utmost importance. A man who has been like Marvell or like Vaughan through wearisome sciolism and through a civil conflict which has destroyed or seemed to destroy the institutions to which his deepest loyalties are attached and who has through great effort transcended those barriers of disintegration and self-consciousness in a reintegration of feeling and thought, often experiences the objects of nature with a new and special sensitiveness and in a singularly intimate relation to the energy of his own mind. It is in such a vision more their form and the energy of life in them that he sees than what we should ordinarily call their sensuous detail. As Mr. Martin says, it is this experience rather than any specific literary influence which binds Wordsworth and Vaughan together. What I mean may be felt in the quality of representation and the music of such a stanza as

> The rainbow comes and goes,
> And lovely is the rose;
> The moon doth with delight
> Look round her when the heavens are bare.

And it is this which, in another way, Marvell voices.

Yet such feeling will hardly be released without its rationale. Similar affirmations were common in the seventeenth century; and naturally they led men's minds to earlier writers who had described them and who had made them primary assumptions in their intellectual system. Thus the historical reasons which led Anglicans back to the early church Fathers and Ficino to St. Augustine were in many men no doubt supported by these psychological impulses. But each man would turn to those predecessors with whom his own deepest habit of thought and feeling was most congruous. And I believe it was precisely in such circumstances at Nun Appleton that Marvell came to lean upon mediaeval Platonism.

To round out our picture, we may glance at one or two other famous instances of pietistic anti-intellectualism, of a more purely negative sort than Vaughan's or Marvell's. In Browne the *credo quia impossibile est* was induced, it would seem, in part by the division between the sphere and method of science and the larger sphere of religion and philosophy (a division only, be it noted and not on any large scale a contradiction; for Browne held merely that science had a method of exploration, not that it had a picture of the cosmos, still less a view of the universe). In part he may have owed it to his contact with Paduan rationalism, as a reaction against it. In an emphasis of that kind upon faith he in some measure parallels Tertullian's reaction against systematic neo-Platonism and neo-Stoicism, as he echoes Tertullian's words. But the mood of adoration and wondering love does not assert itself only against intellectual doubt. And we are often led to see Browne too provincially. It is a consistent element in Platonic Christianity, and we should be astray in overemphasizing as skeptical an attitude which might seem peculiar to Browne's intellectual place in history only because we had not earlier expressions of it clearly enough in mind. As we have already seen, even the great intellectual and critical structures of Hugh and Bonaventura led to emphasis upon devotion rather than learning when those thinkers contemplated the danger that men might be turned from philosophy or theology, from contemplation, to dwell on physics or mathematics for their own sakes alone. In the lesser Victorines, aesthetic intuition and the mood of wonder play a large part. Raimond of Sebonde, again, writes his *Book of the Creatures* as an incentive to strictly orthodox religious exercise, showing man his logical place in the structure of the world, as Thomas had defined that place in the *Summa contra Gentiles*. But there are moments in his work when a simple *O altitudo* replaces rational demonstration. In the Renaissance the rise of literary humanism, and the great service humanism seeks to render this world at the expense of otherworldly orientation, define the conflict afresh. And the classical example of it is to be found in Petrarch's *Secret* where, seeking the aid of St. Augustine in overcoming the deep melancholy which possesses him, the great humanist is urged by the saint who had been always one of the great masters of his imaginative life to abandon altogether his Latin poetry and his scholarship, his belief in glory and his wish to reunite the modern world to the civilization of Greece and Rome. In England, taking account of all the other forces I have intimated, we must be sure to give due emphasis to the return to prescholastic or nonscholastic thought.

In the first part of *Religio Medici,* that which defines his rational position, Sir Thomas Browne proclaims his confidence in the study of the book of the creatures both through symbol and through science proper. In the second part he shows us another side of his temperament. Describing his religious experience and his moral attitudes he declares:

> There is yet another conceit that hath sometimes made me shut my books, which tells me it is a vanity to waste our days in the blind pursuit of knowledge; it is but attending a little longer, and we shall enjoy that by instinct and infusion, which we endeavour at here by labour and inquisition. It is better to sit down in a modest ignorance, and rest contented with the natural blessing of our own reasons, than buy the uncertain knowledge of this life with sweat and vexation, which Death gives every fool *gratis,* and is an accessary of our glorification.[87]

The same extreme otherworldly view is expressed by Sidney Godolphin in his little *Hymn,* in which, praising the attitude of wonder, he asks why we should strive at all here for partial knowledge when hereafter all things will be made clear to intelligential intuition.[88] He is but turning into a little song what Donne had expressed for the age more at large in his *Second*

Anniversary. The daily habit of our thought and imagination has so long been steeped in the detail of scientific knowledge, and in shadowy notions, at least, of scientific method and scientific orientation of thought, that it is peculiarly difficult for us to enter into the attitude of the men of the seventeenth century toward learning. That science alone, without the humanistic disciplines, will not, as its most eager protagonists hoped for it, solve all the problems of man in himself and in society is the point on which the imagination of many of us can now most readily and most fully meet with the mind of a Donne. But into the strong sense of the limits of the actual natural knowledge which will become available to men, as Hooker, Milton, Donne in *The Second Anniversary* particularized those limits, we cannot enter. It is rather by mastering science and passing beyond it into philosophy than through a denial of science, that our minds can again, on our own terms, meet theirs. But it is a great help to realize clearly the issues they were defining in their own terms. Feltham in *The Worship of Wonder* is not an obscurantist. He is merely reflecting on aesthetic emotion as one form of experience of God. Such a mood in him and in Godolphin is evidence how pervasive the attitude was.

Of course the change of Milton's attitude towards humanistic studies and science, from *Areopagitica* and *Of Education* to the rejections of *Paradise Regained* is constantly before one's mind as one thinks of Marvell. And recent definitions of his position contribute much to an understanding of Marvell.[89] Milton's dialogue on astronomy is particularly suggestive, though it cannot be exactly related to anything in Marvell, and though there is no evidence that Marvell had so specific an interest in science as Milton and Donne. Milton's answer to the problem currently under discussion whether the Biblical account of the cosmos must be taken as merely metaphorical may be fruitfully related to Marvell's thought. For the essential character of Milton's answer stands out clearly in contrast with

such works as those of Wilkins and Ross, cited by Mr. Mc-
Colley.[90] He shifts the common grounds of argument evident in
them to a different plane, to ask not what detailed fact about
astronomy now appears true, but rather what may we know,
by revelation and through philosophical intuition, about the
principle of the structure of the cosmos in its relation to God?
He has shifted to a traditional Platonic approach, in short. Perhaps his use of the words "incorporeal speed" to describe the
rate of motion we must suppose in the planets is not merely a
stroke of intensity of poetic imagination but a further revelation
of the plane of his reflection. For that word is entirely consonant
with his view in Book V, set forth in describing the life of the
angels, of the indefinable gradation from "matter" to spirit. The
limitation of knowledge which Milton sets in the dialogue
would accord well with the Platonic tradition I have been describing, and with the scope and limitation of its humanism,
though one has still to look with Mr. Hughes to Milton's disil-
lusioning experience of thirty years of history to comprehend
the great difference in the temper and in the view of positive
studies between the earlier essays and the later poem.[91]

For all that Marvell shared with Milton in the idea of reason
and the objects which ought to engage it, Marvell is an Anglican. And perhaps for normal mid-seventeenth-century English feeling Izaak Walton is a more characteristic example of devotional attitude than Milton and one closer to Marvell who illuminates him more. Walton consciously delighted to unite the
two deepest sides of his nature and to enrich his joy in his avoca-
tion of fishing by musing that the disciples were fishermen; and
he looked seriously upon the quiet and friendliness and beauty
and simple human intercourse of the country world as a real
stay against strifefulness and self-seeking, and a real adjunct to
Christian humility and love. Being old-fashioned, as well as
born in 1593, and in his simplicity and love of ritual shocked by

the new literature, Walton turns for the expression of the theme of retirement to the Renaissance pastoralism with which perhaps he had been familiar as almost contemporary literature in his childhood. Artlessly he selects its most devotional aspect, in harmony with still earlier pietistic works he may have known. Walton's piety and his interest in the literature of retirement were deepened, though his love of fishing was not created, by the civil war. But in the shaping of his piety, and his passion for pious men, it is of course rather the general sense of the decay of religion and manners and of Christian unity which counts and which brings this most Anglican of Anglicans, this devout biographer of Hooker, so close to the voice of the sects, to the mechanic preachers, and to George Fox, with the attitudes of German mystical theology always in the background. *The Compleat Angler* on another side surely owes something in form and conception to courtesy books and in that fact, by its very contrast with them in material, it serves to mark a deep change towards the sanctions of the active life, as toward the intellectual heritage which is their Renaissance background.

Marvell's anti-intellectualism, as these examples confirm, rests both upon the devotional mood, upon a moral definition of reason, and upon a sense of the bankruptcy of scholastic logic. But it is not to be taken as a denial of reason in a conflict between reason and faith; it is an affirmation; an affirmation probably owing much to such a pattern of thought as Bonaventura's. One may note at this point that the difference between the neo-Platonism of Marvell and that of Spenser is as significant as the broad resemblances between them which constantly carry us back to Spenser's attitudes for an illumination of Marvell's. This difference in Platonisms is paralleled in a way by the history of Stoicism in the Renaissance as Mlle. Zanta has described it, with its movement from the endeavor of the earlier humanists to find in Stoicism an independent morality which they could cut off from its root in Stoic metaphysic, to a later crisis in which religious thought had to reckon with Stoicism in full. The time for syncretist Platonism had passed.

The consonance of Marvell's thought with such thought as Bonaventura's is further apparent if we look a little more closely at their particular expressions of the theme of retirement and the attitude toward fame which together are another side of the same view of life. Like the distrust of the intellect, the theme of retirement and contempt of fame is so deep in the Christian tradition and so widespread in this age that it may seem rash to attempt to define any specific background for these attitudes in Marvell. Yet it helps, I think, to define his imaginative tone to remind ourselves of the development of the garden theme in Stoic thought and in the tradition of the Song of Songs, where we have already heard it running as a ground bass.

The paradox in Stoicism between man's self-dependence, to be realized only in withdrawal from the world, and his community with the whole of society and his duty to it, perhaps especially strong in Roman Stoicism, had led Stoicism to help to contribute to the Renaissance two widely different views on the active and the contemplative life. Seneca defined the difference between the Stoic and the Epicurean views when he said in his essay *On Leisure:* "Epicurus says, 'The wise man will not take part in politics except upon some special occasion.' Zeno says, 'The wise man will take part in politics unless prevented by special circumstances.' The one makes it his aim in life to seek for leisure; the other seeks it only when he has reasons for so doing; but this word 'reasons' has a wide signification. If the state be so rotten . . . ." This passage is crucial, even though Seneca affirms elsewhere that the man who lives in the world does not know his own heart. St. Augustine almost echoes him when he says in *Of the City of God* that if we are called to a place, the law of charity obliges us to take it. "In action one may not aim at highness or honor, because all under the sun is mere

vanity." But one may assume a superior position for the benefit
and salvation of one's subjects. Perhaps Herbert's *Constancie*
(surely one germ of Wordsworth's *Character of the Happy
Warrior*) might hit the mean of the balance as the seventeenth
century in ordinary mood felt it. But before the acceptance of
that mean, Stoicism had contributed its share to the Renaissance
justifications of the search for fame, so subtly different, even at
their most idealistic, from the mediaeval apology. At them we
may glance briefly, in order to feel the full flavor of Marvell's
rejection. Burckhardt defined the characteristic Renaissance attitude toward fame or glory as this-worldliness and personal ambition springing from individualism, and its characteristic literary manifestation as the collection and celebration of the lives
of great men, of which Petrarch was the trumpet in his *Triumph
of Fame*. This view might more safely be named the attitude of
literary humanism. And such a view of the claims of the active
life is quite clearly set forth by Petrarch in his *Secret* as his normal view.[92] While we are here, he offers, we are here to realize
the active life in its own terms, and so he defends his *Africa* and
its celebration of Scipio. That view received the ethical modification of its extreme this-worldliness, in sharp contrast with
a view of the human spirit such as Marlowe's in Tamburlaine,[93]
in the conception stemming from Plato that fame is the judgment of society on the deeds of good men, a conception enlarged
by Aristotle with his strong political and social orientation and
carried to the Renaissance not only by them but in all the Latin
commonplaces.[94] To this view Stoicism may well have contributed its own special emphasis on the teaching power of the
example of great men. My own copy of Lipsius' Seneca, an
Elzivir of 1640, represents on its title engraving four aspects of
Stoic thought: the four great Stoic authors at the corners; then
as the upper ornament of the page the two heroic patterns of
Stoic life, Hercules and Ulysses, with wisdom between; and below, ornamenting the stage which holds the title, a cartouche of

Honor and Virtue. The view is felt at its most humane in the mingling of Stoicism and Platonism which Cicero had reached when he says in the *Tusculan Disputations* that men do not in fear of death turn from work for the state and for the family. For the wise man regards posterity as really his concern, and a man who concludes his soul is mortal will yet attempt deeds that will not die, not from any thirst for fame, which he cannot enjoy, but from a thirst of virtue, which of necessity secures fame, even though fame be not its object. The Renaissance throwing of the greater emphasis upon the fame which society *will* award is voiced by Petrarch in a letter. Recognizing how prevalent is detraction and bidding a man in his life trust only to virtue, he yet sets as the highest goal the fame on earth that would follow man's death. That ideal, of course, informs Spenser's dedicatory sonnets and his incidental celebrations of great men in *The Faerie Queene,* and Milton's promise to the enemies whose gentle deeds shall spare him. But with all its infusion of a Stoic idealism, and despite Milton's modification in *Areopagitica* that fame is the reward that *God* and good men give to virtuous deeds, there is in such a zeal for fame no real mediation between the love of fame and the love of God. Du Bellay gave a classical phrasing of the idea in his *Defense,* but the spectacle of detraction sufficed to overwhelm the desire for fame in the members of the Pléiade. And Petrarch's habitual view in the *Secret* is given by St. Augustine the radical answer, bidding the poet reject the whole worldly endeavor, if he would truly heal the ulcerous place within of the rank corruption of melancholy. And with fame are rejected humanistic studies, just as in Agrippa the rejection of learning and the world carries with it explicitly the rejection of fame.

Courtly neo-Platonism, under the name of honor, and with explicit rejection of ambition, sought a more encompassing and spiritual justification of the active life, well defined by Miss Kelso in her study of the ideal of the gentleman.[95] Spenser is the perfect expression of that view and well illustrates how radically, despite all that he owes to St. Augustine's *Of the City of God* in his conception of history, he differs from the mediaeval view expressed by Dante when he limited Justinian to the outer circles of Paradise because he was not without that love of honor which was indeed the necessary spur to his great task, but which, drawing his desire to lean upon it, made the rays of true love in him to mount upward with less life. Spenser's knight, harboring virtuous thought and with child of great intent in his noble heart, which

> Can never rest until it forth have brought
> Th' eternall brood of glorie excellent,

feels, instead of constraint of idealism by the love of honor, the setting free of aspiration. The language in which such honor claims to be the necessary impetus towards good and against evil, borrows directly from the language in which a More and others would have expressed the social need for a belief in an otherworldly immortality. And honor, with the same this-worldly doubling of an otherworldly vision, takes on also another aspect, in which she appears as a sensitive awareness, implanted by natural law, a late and earth-born twin of conscience; the Shamefastnesse who completes the square of the dance with Guyon and Arthur and Prays-desire. In spite of the dangers of self-deception and of sentimentality involved in such a view, it was at its best no mere sophistication. At least, Guyon's rejection of Philotime for his prior and absolute dedication to the Faerie Queene, who can here hardly be distinguished from sapience, is another of those distinctions between two intentions of the soul in its actual temporal activities concealed within a single word as it is commonly used, to define which may be said to be the whole purpose of the poem, and in a sense of Florentine neo-Platonism. *Love* is only the most comprehensive of the activities thus defined and distinguished.

But the optimism of Spenser's vision could not stand. Milton's view in *Lycidas* is as far from Spenser as is Dante. Milton, it may be noted, sums up both Renaissance aspiration and Renaissance disillusion, recapitulating the entire Renaissance argument for fame and then against it, because of the blind fury and of detraction; sums it up, however, only to dismiss the whole argument by shifting to otherworldly ground.[96] Donne speaks as absolutely against fame as one would expect. Feltham in his fifteenth Resolve takes the same view.

The active life as it was defended by Spenser, and by Milton sometimes, was, we remind ourselves, never alien to contemplation, but drawing all its powers, rather, from it. Cicero, who himself dreaded leisure, in citing Scipio's words, "Never less alone than when alone," thinks of leisure and retirement as having given Scipio opportunity for those deep thoughts on which rested his entire public achievement. And Milton's Penseroso, ascending the scale through the gentler contemplation awakened in trim gardens, to the contemplation of the stars and so to Plato and to Hermes, is not setting himself apart from the active life when its turn shall come. Like his creator, he will one day see what he foresaw. In Pontanus, the Jesuit, the orientation is a little different. Teaching in his rhetoric that retirement is necessary for the writing of poetry, he draws upon the mild eclectic Stoicism of Horace and voices a commonplace of humanism. He is not at all denying the active life, but again naming the source of its strength. For the types of poetry which he describes are all directed to teach, but also and chiefly to adorn the active life. But the meaning of such a leisure to the seventeenth century is most significantly, because most positively and realistically, voiced by Bacon in his defense of the scholar in the first book of his *Advancement of Learning,* giving the stamp of actuality to the commonplace of Erasmus.

And as for the privateness, or obscureness (as it may be in vulgar estimation accounted) of life of contemplative men; it is a theme so common, to extoll a private life not taxed with sensuality and sloth, in comparison and to the disadvantage of a civil life, for safety, liberty, pleasure, and dignity, or at least freedom from indignity, as no man handleth it, but handleth it well: such a consonancy it hath to men's conceits in the expressing, and to men's consents in the allowing.

But this is that which will indeed dignify and exalt knowledge, if contemplation and action may be more nearly and straitly conjoined and united together than they have been. . . .

Where we see again the favor and election of God went to the shepherd [Abel, the contemplative life].

In Bacon we return to that mean which, as we noted earlier, one side of Stoic thought helped so much to formulate, and which reminds us how immensely much the Roman sense of order contributed to articulate the seventeenth-century sense of life.

Seneca's meditation on leisure, on the other hand, is a perfect example of that purely devotional tone in Stoicism, hardly touched by the pride of self-sufficiency, yet inimical to worldly pursuits, which brought it at moments so close to Christianity. Such a devotion might take either a pietistic tone or a philosophical and scientific direction truer to its whole intellectual structure. The fragment of Seneca translated by Marvell, on the knowledge of one's own heart possible only to the old countryman, might seem a purely Christian pietism, did we not know its source. But the Stoic garden notes in *Il Penseroso* both play a genial overtone to that melancholy which Milton finds to be the key to all self-knowledge, and which is the antecedent to contemplation, and lead on to philosophical contemplation itself by awakening interest in the stars. Milton's union of meditation on the stars with idealistic philosophy was, as he reminds us, as old as the Hermetic writings themselves. And Palingenius in his very popular *Zodiack of Life,* as I have already noted, had made the prologue to his treatise on neo-

Platonic cosmology a discipline in the garden of virtue. On the whole the scientific view was unoriented toward the active life, the devotional looked away from it. Stoicism in the first Renaissance had helped to rationalize social and political expansion by contributing to refresh and transform the ideal of a just society, reflecting the order of the universe, which is the necessary expression of the social part of man's nature and the necessary stay of his personal virtue. And this ideal Spenser hoped to realize in the Elizabethan monarchy, Milton to garner in the harvest of the civil war. But neo-Stoicism in the main came to rest on no such hopes. Rather, like its classical source, the general thinking of Renaissance Stoicism about retirement to the contemplative life in the country arose out of an immediate sense of the immitigable disastrousness and confusion of Caesar's world. The use of Stoicism differed with the differing generations. Deeply realistic about the actual world, Erasmus and More yet hoped for the creation of a great society; but only by the overthrow of existing power politics. (Erasmus sounds the note of retirement and the joys of contemplating nature only when he is defending monasticism and then in conventional language.) Theirs is an emphasis upon Stoic ethic in broad terms, not upon an individual's saving his own soul by withdrawal from the world's need; upon reason and not upon the garden. Bishop Guevara, in his *Praise and Happinesse of the Countrie-Life* a little later, characterizing enslavement to the world in terms both Stoic and Epicurean, seems with his stress upon family duties and family responsibilities to be urging rather a return to feudal society than a retreat from the world to self-dependence. Yet that sense of family duties so central to the old Roman sense of order is an element in Stoicism too. Perhaps in England Ben Jonson's Penshurst poems, though of sunny temper, have something of the same motivation. This particular stream of praise of country life is a distinctive one at any rate. Robert Herrick's yeoman-farmer family, we know, was half drifting toward the city, half turning backward to the land. In thinking of Herrick and kindred humanist poets one must think of Virgil's *Georgics,* and of the pleasures of the country as the reward for fulfilling one of the great functions of society, the making fruitful of the land. Cowley cites Virgil along with Horace; these poets of naturalistic pleasure in nature are, as they influence Cowley's own Latin poems, the source of a feeling that is derived also from the interest in nature awakened by science, as was Virgil's own. At Nun Appleton Virgil as the descriptive poet of nature, at least, would be likely to be in Marvell's thought. Though Virgil was not averse from society, description so pensive as that in the *Eclogues* and so inwoven with the idea of order lent itself readily to contemplative uses. And the few touches in Guevara upon the enjoyment of nature, while that enjoyment may be only the immediate reward of the good landlord, yet definitely evoke in a seventeenth-century mind the idea of contemplation also. And soon the wheel swings full to the other point of the compass. The significance of nature as a stimulus to devotion is enhanced when we are not merely seeking a more charming self-realization, but when we are oppressed by the evil of the world and all its ways and by the degeneration it imposes on man, and when "nature" with its simple and intuitive patterns of life is contrasted with the corruptions and sophistications of actual society. "Cursed be he who first taught the prow to furrow the sea." In his *El Villano del Danubio* in *Libro Aureo,* Guevara probed deeper than in his milder charge to the nobility, Professor Castro tells us; sought to use and partly succeeded in using Stoic primitivism as an instrument of actual politics to rescue the Indians of the new world from the conquistadores and to secure for the church the privilege of their development.[97]

In France, De Taille's poem, "Le Courtisan retiré," written at the turn of the century and said to be indebted to Guevara, though certainly not close to him,[98] is an extended and bitterly realistic denunciation of the courtier's life and of the decay of manners in the wars of religion, stressing in its picture of the court, flattery, greed, the perturbations, all the ills of the world as the Stoa and Lucian had seen them, ills from which at last the courtier retires to his chateau to enjoy the beauties of nature, to be too busy for vice, to live frugally, to be free of ambition and pomp, and to turn to God. In England even Colin Clout, after a fresh experience of the actuality of the court, retreats joyfully to the garden of the Irish Pale. Nay, as Belphoebe tells Braggadocio, and as the instruction of Calidore manifests, courtesy takes its first inward pattern from the soul that has learned to know itself in retirement. (So right is Scipio.) And for thoughtful men in the seventeenth century the torrent of actual history had again even more completely confused the problem of finding a balance of the active and the contemplative lives. Spenser had supported the sword of justice in Ireland. Marvell, in the *Horatian Ode* and looking to the fulfillment of prophecy, was momentarily intoxicated with the same sword to be lifted against both Ireland and Scotland, falling in with the general paroxysm of patriotism. Later again, after he had united his hopes to those of Cromwell and the Commonwealth, he upheld the sword of Protestant Christian power on the continent. But to those who had watched and reflected on the Thirty Years' War, and who were living through the wars and changes in England, the idea of the life of meditation must come in a different light from that which it wore to an earlier age. One thinks of Cowley, who at first united himself eagerly with those seeking composure from theological contention and political strife in the intellectual demands and practical hopes of science—using thought and words that closely echo Stoic views on science—and who presently, after the failure of the Royalist cause and then later after the disappointment of his personal hopes in the Restoration, put into practice the Epicurean life to which he had perhaps been converted in France.

For Vaughan the burden of the civil war and the struggle which led up to it can have been only one strain, though one of great importance, among the deep-seated temperamental causes which from the first made him alien among the sons of Ben, if we judge by his poetry, and unable to enter into the games of statesman, courtly lover, and capitalist. But it is worth recollecting that he translated Guevara's little treatise and that Stoic criticism of the world at least influenced a religious sensibility so far removed in its absolute ardor and visionary self-surrender from Stoic attitudes. One remembers above all the great arc of Milton's hope and thought, ending in the last line of *Paradise Regained*:

> Home to his mother's house, private, returned.

One of the most beautiful garden meditations in Renaissance literature was written by a man who grew up in the center of political woe, to help him teach himself to put aside all care for the actual world. In the *De Constantia* of Lipsius, Langius has argued with Lipsius that his seeming concern for the tragedy of war-wracked Holland is but a surrender to passion, that in reality he fears only for himself and his own loved ones. Then he leads Lipsius out into the country to his garden, that its beauty rightly meditated upon may still his perturbation and that, ending all care for the world, he may focus his sole happiness on personal virtue.

The *De Constantia* was one of the most popular books in Europe. It is likely, therefore, that Marvell had read it and was familiar with its view that virtue and care for the state are incompatible. Even if he did not know this particular book, a man of his education cannot have been unfamiliar with the Stoic view in some form including almost certainly a contemporary one. Marvell's *Garden* has so much in common with Lipsius' garden meditation in some elements of its feeling and in some elements of detail as to increase the inherent probability that he knew *De Constantia* itself. Or if not, to show forth vividly the common political and imaginative context which made their experience in some ways so alike.

I cite a passage of some length from Stradling's translation of Lipsius' *De Constantia* because it has a consonance of detail in certain elements—the green, and the retreat of the gods, but above all the radiance of tone—which suggests that this work may well have been a part of his reading at Nun Appleton. Though the translation is now readily available, it is convenient to have it immediately before our imagination in reading Marvell.

And surely (*Langius*) this your industrious care of gardens, is a labour well-beseeming and praise worthy. A labour, whereto (if I guesse not amisse) euerie good man as he is most temperately giuen, so is he drawn by nature, and addicted thereunto. An argument thereof is this, that you cannot name anie kind of delight, which the chiefe men of all ages haue more affected, then this. . . . Moreouer among the ancient Grecians and Romans, how many could I alleadge that haue cast aside all other cares and betaken themselues whollie to this studie? And they all (in a word) Philosophers and wise men, who eschewing the cities and troublesom assembliees of people, contayned themselues within the bounds and limits of their gardens. . . . Neither haue the common people dissented from the iudgement of the better sort, in this point, in that I knowe all honest mindes and free from ambition, haue euer bene delighted in this exercise. For there is in vs a secrete and naturall force (the causes whereof I cannot easily comprehend) which draweth vnto this harmlesse and liberall recreation, not onelie those that be prone by nature that way: but also such austere and graue personages, as woulde seem to despise and deride it.

And as it is not possible for any man to contemplate heauen and those immortal spirits there, without feare & reuerence: so can we not behold the earth & her sacred treasures, nor the excellent beautie of this inferior world, without an inward tickling and delight of the senses. Aske thy mind and vnderstanding, it wil confesse it self to be led, yea & fed with this aspect and sight. Aske thy senses of seeing and smelling, they wil acknowledge that they take not greater delight in anything, than in the decent borders and beddes of gardens. . . . What percing sauour? And I wot not what part of the heauenly aire infused from aboue, that it is not without cause why the Poets fayned, that flowers for the most part sprang vp first from the iuice and bloud of their gods. . . .

[Chapter III] When I had thus spoken sharplie in voice and countenance, then spake *Langius* softlie vnto me; I see (*Lipsius*) I see you loue this flourishing purple Nymph, but I feare mee you doate vpon her. You commend gardens, but so as you seeme only to admire vain and outward things therin, neglecting the true & lawful delights therof. You poare only vpon collours, and borders, and are greedy of strange Flowers brought from all partes of the world. And to what end is all this? Except it be that I might account thee one of that sect which is risen vp in our dayes, of curious and idle persons, who haue made a thing that was in it self good and without al offence, to be the instrument of two foule vices, *Vanity* and *Slouthfulnes.* . . .

Therefore I doe not contemne the beautie and elegancie of them; (as you may see for example here before your eies:) but I dissent from the opinion of these great Garden-masters, in that I get them without much trauell, keepe them without care, and lose them without grief. Again I am not so simple or base-minded as to tie or wed my self to the shadowes of my garden. I find som busines euen in the mids of my idlenes; my mind is there busied, without any labour, and exercised without paine. *I am neuer lesse solitarie* (said one) *then when I am alone: nor neuer lesse idle, then when I am at leasure.* A worthy saying, which I dare sweare had his first beginning in these selfe same gardens that I speake of. For they be ordained, not for the body, but for the mind: and to recreate it, not to besot it with idlenesse: only as a wholesome withdrawing place from the cares and troubles of this world. Art thou wearie of the concourse of people? here thou maist be alone. Haue they worldly businesses tyred thee? here thou maist be refreshed again, where the food of quietnes, & gentle blowing of the pure & whol some aire, will euen breath a new life into thee. Doest thou consider the wise men of olde time? They had their dwelling in gardens. . . . So many sharp and subtil disputations of naturall philosophy, proceed from those greene bowers. So many precepts of manners from those shadowy Achademies. Yea out of the walkes and pleasant allies of gardens, spring those sweet abounding riuers which with their fruitful ouerflowings haue watered the whole world. For why? the mind lifteth vp and advanceth it self more to these high cogitations, when it is at

libertie to beholde his owne home, heauen: Then when it is in-
closed within the prisons of houses or townes. Here you learned
Poets compose yee some poemes worthy of immortalitie. Here let al
the learned meditate and write: here let the Philosophers argue &
dispute of contentation, constancie, life, and death. Beholde (*Lipsius*)
the true end and vse of gardens to wit, quietnes, with drawing from
the world, meditation, reading, writing: and all this as it were, by
way of recreation & sport: As painters hauing dimmed their eies
with long and earnest beholding their work, do recomfort them with
certain glasses or green collours so here may we refresh our wearied
and wandring minds.

And why should I conceale mine intent from thee? Seest thou
yonder arbour curiouslie wrought with sundry pictures cut out of the
greene boughes; The same is the house of my Muses, my nursery and
schoole of wisedome. . . . So soone as I put my foote within that
place, I bid all vile and seruile cares abandon me, and lifting vp my
head as vpright as I may, I contemne the delights of the prophane
people, & the great vanitie of humane affaires. Yea I seem to shake
off all thing in mee that is humaine, and to be rapt vp on high vpon
the fiery chariot of wisdome."[99]

Yet it is from Lipsius rather than from Langius that Marvell
is enkindled, if from either. For the concern for England and
the regret for Fairfax's choice which Marvell expressed in *Upon
Appleton House* is far other than that charitableness to immediate and remediable suffering which was all that at least the
Stoic compassion of Lipsius allowed (though to Seneca himself, as we have seen, the more humane view was possible). And
Marvell, moreover, does not accept any criticism of the pure delight of his senses in the beauty of the creatures. To catch that
other element of his tone, the quality of his delight in nature
and above all the ardor of his love of virtue and rejection of
fame, mingled with absolute humility, we must look back to
another garden literature which has been threading its way
through our discussion, the literature of the *hortus conclusus*.
Perhaps, even, it had contributed to give to Lipsius' own words
about nature something of their flavor, something not quite

Stoic. But if in Lipsius there is still something of Stoic pride, and certainly the negativeness of the usual Stoic attitude toward the emotions excepting only in Lipsius' work as a whole the peculiarly Christian emotion of pity, in commentary on Canticles on the other hand the liberty of spirit and the outgoing love to God in the garden are entire. And the defense of spontaneous, unadulterated nature is there marked. One might go as far back as St. Ambrose of Milan to find the flower of the field which blossoms so much more fairly than the flowers of the garden. But I choose rather to cite an extended passage from Richard of St. Victor's *Commentary on the Song of Songs,* in which the poetic and the symbolic senses of the book of the creatures have transfused the garden of the Stoics. A fairly long illustration from that work will both reveal its tone and show a nexus of thought akin to that of the first stanzas of Marvell's *Garden.*

Horum [the just] sicut sancta erat vita, ita dulcia et suavia erant quae proferebant, vel docebant ad hujusmodi flores pervolat; ab his spirituale mel colligit, sed praecipue de flore illo singulari, id est flore qui processit de virga Jesse, *flore campi et non horti.* Hujus ordor [*sic*] floris est sicut odor agri pleni, quem benedixit Dominus. Plenus est hic ager in quo habitat plenitudo divinitatis, in quo sunt omnes thesauri sapentiae et scientiae, in quo florent justi, et in quo fructificant tam in bona vita quam in sacra scientia. Hic est ager floridus, imo plenus floribus in quo tot sunt flores, quot justi in bono fructificantes, ed extra quem non est florere, sed arescere. . . .
Hortus est anima in qua excoluntur virtutum plantaria, et spiritualium studiorum gemina. Hic hortus tunc foditur, dum in ea vitia radicitus exstirpantur, et mores convertuntur. Qui etiam tunc altius foditur, cum naturam vitiorum et origines cognoscere studet homo. Nunquam enim tepidus operator, et naturae vitiorum ignarus poterit bene mortificare vitia. Fodienda est ergo divinae passionis memoria, et clavi illi. . . . Hic hortus conclusus est sera silentii. Per silentium enim excolit in profectu et justitia, quia cultus justitiae silentium requirit. In quo se cohibet, non solum a noxiis, sed etiam ab otiosis et superfluis, quia per minima pervenitur ad majora, et per otiosa decipitur mens, et extra se ducitur, sicut dicit Gregorius. . . .

Haec igitur excludit devota anima, et contra hujusmodi hortum suum concludit. Quia vero secundo conclusus dicitur hic hortus, aliam quoque ejus conclusionem considerare debemus, non enim solum ab exterioribus periculis hunc munit et claudit, sed intus se bona sua celat, et hominibus occultat, sciens quod cum bona opera innotescunt et laudantur, mentem resolvunt et enervant. Difficile est enim aliquem laudari et venerari, et non aliquatenus laude sua delectari, vel etiam intus gloriari. Difficile est aliquem servum inutilem se reputare, dum bonorum testimonio bonus praedicatur; imo contingere solet ut deceptus laude, magis credat famae quam conscientiae. . . . Occultat vero bona sua anima devota, et claudit se contra laudes, ut has non audiat, surda ad has sicut aspis obturans aures suas ne exaudiat vocem incantantium. Incantatur enim anima laudibus, ut mala sua non videat, et de justitia fallaciter se extollat . . . inhabitet in domo Domini non manufacta, . . . Hunc ergo hortum sic conclusum fons signarus irrigat; fontem itaque signatum intelligentiam videlicet spiritualem Spiritus sancti signaculo impressam et sacrae Scripturae documentis, et Patrum exemplis munitam intellige. . . . Hoc fonte irrigantur horti hujus plantaria, quia hac scientia informantur virtutes, et bona studia, et proficiunt atque discrete fiunt. Hujus fontis sobrio potu homo in anima vivificatur, et pacem cordis consequitur. Sapere enim secundum spiritum vita est, et pax. Cujus emissiones sunt paradisus punicorum malorum cum pomorum fructibus. Mala punica rubea designant martyrium. . . . Martyrium est cum mortificamus membra nostra quae sunt super terram. . . . [There follow the names of the fruits and woods with symbolic interpretation of their meaning.] Haec est paradisus in qua versatur anima, cujus deliciis et amoenitate delectatur. Hanc paradisum in terra possidet de hac ad coelestem migratura. Primi parentes terestrum habebant paradisum, post hanc coelstem habituri si mandatum servassent. . . . Hanc paradisum [of virtue, justice, peace] emittit hortus devotae animae, et de hoc horto emittitur ad hortum conclusum supernae civitatis Hierusalem.[100]

Professor Boas and Professor Lovejoy in their great *Documentary History of Primitivism and Related Ideas* have brought together the materials on the twofold stoic attitude toward nature and art; first the rejection, on the one hand, of the luxury, the vanity, the contriving, the corruption found in the artful, whether in sophisticated man or in his surroundings, in favor of the "natural," the spontaneously poised; and second, on the other hand, that recognition of discipline, of decorum, of the use of the instrument of reason, which was a mainspring of the development of Stoicism out of Cynicism. Lipsius, in stressing the naturalness of his garden, is not only criticizing the actual social abuse of some of the extravagant Dutch tulip gardens, an extravagance symbolic of the whole condition of society which he deplores; but he is giving voice to a very old philosophical conception and to an even older conflict, or perhaps doubleness is a better word, of sensibility, present to men whenever the spirit has to adjust between the claims of its spontaneous and, so it seems, its deepest energies, and the claims of their long channeling to fruitful attainment and to social disciplines. Spenser represents a roundly Christian embodiment of the paradox in many aspects. If he is thinking of the whole life of man and his education, his voice is for nurture, as has recently been said.[101] Naturally Christian, the soul yet needs grace made available through the sacraments and through Christian education before it can fulfill its tasks in the world or be betrothed to Truth. But on the other side, if he is thinking of all the claims put forth by ambition, the love of money, conquest, luxurious living, Red Cross knows what true mede is and can answer Mammon in almost the very words of Epicurus—or of Piers Plowman:

> Frayle men are oft captiv'd to covetise:
> But would they think with how small allouwance
> Untroubled nature doth herself suffise,
> Such superfluities they would despise ....

And if he is thinking of Acrasia as the false Aphrodite, the Bower of Bliss is an artificial and corrupted imitation of nature, false like the semblance of its warder.

Marvell, then, found the idea of the virtue of simple nature in the atmosphere about him wherever Stoic attitudes permeated. Yet he phrases it with a special intensity. And one cannot fail to note in the literature of the *hortus conclusus* an expression of such feeling which brings together imaginatively in a single metaphor the threads of thought and feeling to be found in Marvell's garden poetry.

I have spoken in an earlier chapter of the dialectical design of Marvell's poetry. The debate which is the warp of so much of it is owed not more to a dialectic habit of thought than to the great intellectual conflicts out of which Florentine neo-Platonism was created. The eternal Christian warfare between flesh and spirit takes on a fresh character as the old battle with materialistic philosophies is renewed. Ficino, for one, never forgets that he is writing against the Epicureans, and the Stoics too. In this warfare the enemy also has his gardens. Palingenius cannot enter the garden of contemplation without first rejecting what he images to be the garden of Epicurus. Milton in *Comus* seems to answer implicitly, or by circumstance inevitably answers, the *précieuse* Platonism of the court of Henrietta Maria, with its sophisticated justification of sensuality,[102] explicitly, the Cyrenaic philosophy of nature. By the time of Cowley's essays, a better understanding of Epicurus had cleared up the confusion between him and the Cyrenaic defense of pleasure, and an "Epicurean" Christianity was possible to him, one especially appealing to realistic minds and those interested in science. But of that in Marvell I find no trace. He did almost certainly know the French *libertin* poetry of the first third of the seventeenth century which has recently been defined by M. Adam in his study of Théophile de Viau.[103] The writers of that poetry, blending intellectual Epicureanism and something of Cyrenaic values in a libertine thought which was given solidity by the rational criticism that Padua had launched against accepted philosophies,[104] had their own characteristic passion for solitude. They sought nature either in consolation for the disappointment of political hopes and the very real fear of extreme persecution, or as a source of melancholy and enhancement of sensibility. It was the poets of this group who, as M. Adam has shown, were influenced by Marini when he was in France, especially the poet St. Amant, learning from Marini both the art of extended description and the theory of a poetry composed of an ornament of wit play. The influence gives its distinctive character to his cult of nature, a character which determined Marvell's response.

· I have stressed oppositions and precise definitions of thought because they were so important in the intellectual life of the day and because, therefore, to remember them helps so much to an understanding of Marvell's sensibility. Yet Marvell's songs on the marriage of Mary Cromwell in 1657 (with their classical myth and pastoral names) remind us of no one else so readily as of Robert Herrick, least contentious of poets, least given to a "line." And Herrick's name in conclusion may serve to remind us of an earlier, less philosophical Renaissance feeling for nature, but even more of that Horatian temper, that spirit of reconciliation, of eclecticism, that Roman sense of order which no less than philosophical and devotional literature were at work in the age and to the pattern of which Marvell certainly responded. This Roman tone is the more important to remember because such a sketch as I have given has no special place in which to define the humanism, the spirit and form and word of the classical poetry in the field of whose magnetism Marvell had lain from early youth. Such were the winds of doctrine, the imaginative attitudes among which, while he lived in Yorkshire with Fairfax, Marvell wrote his garden poems.

Chapter Nine

THE VARIOUS LIGHT

I SHALL BEGIN MY *explication de texte* with Marvell's *Horatian Ode,* since the known dates of his political poems and the political setting in which they were written give such definite points of reference for it. It is not an easy poem to understand fully. For the political situation it interprets was one which left thoughtful men with divided loyalties; and it is the character of Marvell's poetry to reflect the complex elements of his attitude to the full.[1] The poem expresses, then, an unresolved conflict of feeling. And we know from Restoration days that the elements of that feeling which drew him to the side of the court were never fully lost. The poem begins with an overmastering sense of the virtue of Cromwell's sheer force and personal energy in themselves. It ends with a justification of force as the sole instrument which can either create order or maintain it once it is established. And so great is the significance of order that Marvell is at first ready to allow Cromwell's very success as sufficient proof that his force is heaven's flame. In this view Marvell is at one with Waller's almost contemporary poem and with Dryden's poem on Cromwell's death. And they were all in harmony with that weary, practical belief in the absolute priority of order by which, partly through the medium of Hobbes, many even of the Royalists who had fought longest and given most were soon to be reconciled to the apparently accomplished fact of Cromwell's triumph and England's meteoric rise to

international significance. Or perhaps one ought rather to draw
a parallel between Marvell and Machiavelli, as many intelligent
Englishmen then understood him. The thought of Fate in the
background of Marvell's poem and of the prevalence of fate and
justice "as men are strong or weak" is much more in the temper
of Renaissance humanism and of Machiavelli than in that of
Hobbes.[2] Yet with a difference. For the whole tenor of this
poem, as of all of Marvell's work, would show him to think
rather of the failure of character to answer to fate than of that
extreme relativeness of character to political circumstance which
Machiavelli expressed to Soderini in his letter "On Fortune and
the Times."

Such a view had not seemingly been easy for Marvell to
arrive at. For in 1647/8, in his poem on Lovelace, he had regarded the civil war as a conflict raised by selfish private am-
bitions and destructive of that civilization in which alone the
arts could live. And though his poem on Hastings' death, in
1649, does not, like others, ascribe his death to punishment
visited on England for the sin of rebellion, yet the fantastic
mockery of the classical democratic stars has at least a royalist
flavor. Even in the *Ode* itself, though we see that he had not
with some of the royalists accepted the idea of the divine right
of kings, he does regard the monarchy and Charles as the great
work of time and as having been hitherto the instrument of
justice. And we may, I think, safely look back from the later
poem in praise of Fairfax, in which he speaks constantly of the
fate which had developed the house of Fairfax, to infer that he
had a very strong sense of guiding Providence in established
order. In later years, though he was bitter in his reprehension
of the monarchy of the Restoration, and though he never later
came to take a completely royalist view of the civil war years
but maintained his defense of the Long Parliament, he repudi-
ated the concept of civil strife. He had come to feel that the
cause he had espoused in the war years was "too good a one to

have fought for." The opening lines of the *Ode* mark, then, a turn of feeling about 1650 away from loyalty to the old order, a turn which it was seemingly Cromwell who had aroused in him, though he hopes Cromwell may be the instrument of a constitutional order and not of a dictatorship. It must be remembered that at that moment no older order actually existed, and that Cromwell seemed to many the national savior against invasion from without. The poem launches at once into a praise of Cromwell's ruthless might intensified by a sense of awe at the change he has wrought.

This praise does not limit its horizon to the contemporary spectacle alone. The Renaissance habit of interpreting contemporary history in the light of the lessons of Greek and Roman civilization had not become for Marvell a mere exercise of rhetoric as it is in Dryden's poem on Cromwell's death nine years later. Whether as humanist or as positivist, Marvell took the lessons of the ancient world seriously. His opening praise of Cromwell owes much in imagery and conception, as Mr. Margoliouth and several correspondents in the London *Times* have shown,[3] to Lucan's portrait of Caesar in the *Pharsalia;* and the parallel of Charles and Pompey is in Marvell's mind later in the poem also. Yet it was for a dramatic and not an ethical pattern of character that Marvell turned to Lucan. Pompey's indecisiveness, Caesar's energy, boldness, ruthless skill as Lucan portrays them, touched his imagination to see of what sort these men were who were determining the circumstances of history. Marvell's view of Cromwell's success and of the new order he will be instrumental in creating is at once humanized and made more terrible, as is Milton's, by a passionate, though in part a blinding, religious intensity. There is in the lines on Cromwell and the state just such a confident belief in Cromwell, if not yet such a certainty that in the new order the kingdom of God is at hand, as informs Milton's passage on the harvest in *Areo-*

pagitica. In the *Ode,* this religious interpretation is explicit only in the lines,

> 'Tis Madness to resist or blame
> The force of angry Heavens flame.

The attitude is partly obscured by the Roman background of the poem and by the pattern set through the origins of its imagery in Lucan, as well as by Marvell's still divided loyalty of feeling. By the time that Marvell had written his poems to Fairfax, however, and his lines on *The First Anniversary of the Government under O.C.* his religious preoccupation and the political direction it must take has become clear. In the second of these poems, after order has actually begun to emerge, Marvell's view of Cromwell has been finally set in its Old Testament context, making clear the view half-formed in the earlier ode. Cromwell is the instrument of God, himself the servant of a parliamentary democracy, come to bring freedom, with a sword never to be sheathed, to all the kingdoms not free. Marvell is nothing of an enthusiast. But his is a mind steeped in the sense of the central revelation of the Bible. And he then shares with Milton the hope for the millennium; it is his highest praise of Cromwell that if these be the times, this man is worthy of them. As early as the *Ode* it is this sense of religious destiny, impelled no doubt also by national anxiety, which hurries Marvell into the acceptance of all that Cromwell has done: the sufferings which the Irish have endured—but which are to free them from enslavement to Roman Catholicism—and which the Scots are to undergo, the ruthless trickery of Charles to his death by the supposedly arranged flight from Hampden to Carisbrooke, the execution of the King. It can, with an even violent sense of the need of order, no matter how terribly secured, lead him a moment after the great lines on the King's death, to see in his bloody head no more than an auspicious, though terrifying, omen for the new state.

Yet from this sense of the fierce working of God's ways and of Cromwell's meteoric force which,

> Could by industrious Valour climbe
> To ruine the great Work of Time,
>
> .   .   .   .
>
> But those [the ancient rights] do hold
>   or break
> As Men are strong or weak.
>
> .   .   .   .
>
> And therefore must make room
> Where greater Spirits come,

Marvell turns, with a fulness of spirit manifest in the beauty of the lines, to that other aspect of Cromwell's character so much more in accord with Marvell's humanism. The view of history which circumstance has imposed on Marvell is overlaid upon a Horatian, a Virgilian sense of the order which Augustus has brought and in which Roman ethic may be restored. The poem opens with an echo of the Roman call from the pleasures of private life to public service; and the actual portrait of Cromwell begins on that Roman note of the farmer-citizen. For though it says of Cromwell what was the literal fact, insofar as his having been a private farmer, the light under which that fact is seen makes Cromwell the very type of Cincinnatus or more properly of Cato—the real hero of Lucan's poem:

> And, if we would speak true,
> Much to the Man is due
> Who from his private Gardens, where
> He liv'd reserved and austere,
>   As if his highest plot
>   To plant the Bergamot.

When after the lines on Charles's execution Marvell returns to the portrait of Cromwell, it is not now Cromwell's force but again his virtue and his meek service to the state which stand before us. He can both act and know, he is good and just; above all, sword, spoils, fame he surrenders absolutely to the state. They are among the most eloquent and impassioned lines of the poem. As Miss Bradbrook and Miss Lloyd Thomas have suggested, it is this vision of the state which informs the exultation in even violent order to which the poem returns in closing.[4] And if we suspect that the picture carries as much of hope as of confidence, great historians have thought that Cromwell did all that in the circumstances was possible to justify that hope.

It is not alone in its view of Cromwell's character, we remind ourselves, that the poem is complex. Marvell still felt the claims of both sides in the civil war so far as it had yet progressed. And his creation of sympathy for them both contributes as much as his passion for order to make his poem so profoundly serious when we compare it to the shallow compliance of Waller, the coldness and mundanity of Dryden. In his view of Charles he has a tragic sense from which, on the other side, the intense and visionary resolution of Milton barred the greater poet in his thought of the war.

Marvell's expression of the awfulness of the ruin of the great work of time and of the mysterious conflict between Justice and Fate, and of man's suffering, has been for many readers the greatest thing in his poem. This tragic sense is overshadowed in the poem as a whole by the fiercer political view. For Marvell must judge not only what had happened, but what was to come. But we shall not misread its temper if we remember in connection with it some of Edgar's lines in *Lear* or Agrippa's momentarily grey-lipped words to Octavius over the death of Antony:

> And strange it is
> That nature must compel us to lament
> Our most persisted acts.

The mediaeval awe and pity for the falls of great men, which had carried over also into the Elizabethan concept of tragedy, and which had there united with a moral examination into the causes of their falls, was an element always near the surface in the reading of history at that time. Mr. Margoliouth calls our attention to the fact that the account of the accusation and trial of Charles, his unspoken defense, published at Amsterdam in 1649, was called *Tragicum Theatrum Actorum & Casuum Tragicorum Londoni.*[5] But we need not go so far afield to know how Englishmen felt. Trevelyan in his *England under the Stuarts* cites Sir William Waller's letter to Sir Ralph Hopton: "My affections to you are so unchangeable that hostility itself cannot violate my friendship. We are both upon the stage, and we must act the parts assigned us in this tragedy." To this general view of tragedy, Marvell's earlier sympathy for the royalist party as the party of culture must have given a special significance. The King's political weakness is forgotten in the magnanimity of his end. Marvell's lines beat with the strong admiration which Charles's personality and the tradition which it symbolized evoked in all but the sternest of his people. And though in a moment we shall be shocked by the grim analogue which follows, into the death scene Marvell has got that nobility and devotedness in Charles's character which have been so hard for later historians not his partisans to take account of. As I have earlier suggested, he must have read with sympathy the accounts favorable to Charles published just after his death.

It is not only in the lines on justice and fate and in the description of Charles's death that tragic irony is felt. In the images a similar ironic reflection plays across the whole surface of the poem. In the lightning figure, as Mr. Margoliouth has pointed out, *side* is used doubly as the *side* of the cloud and as Cromwell's *party*. Perhaps, even, as Miss Bradbrook and Miss Lloyd Thomas have suggested,[6] the presence of the word *nurst* ought to evoke for us also the figure of the portentous birth of Caesar. Marvell had found in Lucan the figure of the lightning to describe the vehemence of Caesar's progress. In Marvell the rapid and very general metaphor used by Lucan to express Caesar's energy and destructiveness evolves into a complicated and very concrete dramatic figure which at once summarizes history in an instant, gathers together in a point Marvell's double feeling about Cromwell and about events, and awakening the thought of the common origin both of the image and of those events which it describes, leads directly into his interpretation of them.

The pun on *plot* brings the two Cromwells before us with an even more electric irony. Of the import and imaginative force of the *sad* image and of Charles's glance at the axe, I have already spoken. As we read the poem closely we become fully aware of its deeper elements and at the same time we lose something of the serene, the Horatian unity which a more casual reading may have given. And yet realizing today the full import of all that a man's zeal for order may bring him to accept, and the significance of Marvell's reservation, we feel that this poem, reflecting so sensitively the complexity of choice, has in it an element of greatness that no single view might have given and informs the wonderful energy and reserve of its music.

To set beside the *Ode* Marvell's views of Cromwell a year after Cromwell had assumed the Protectorate, and again at the time of his death, will show not only the direction of Marvell's political thought but the growth in the interval of the philosophy by which he justified it.

Between these poems and the *Horatian Ode,* Marvell had spent two years at Appleton House with Fairfax. During that period he had composed a body of religious poetry—if one may assume that *The Coronet, The Drop of Dew,* and the debates on body and soul and between the soul and pleasure were then written—or at least of poetry steeped in religious thought; and the philosophy of these poems carries over into the later Cromwell poems. But it is the political thought in *Upon Appleton*

House which here concerns us. He is living now with the great general of the first civil war who had turned aside from the course which the war was taking and retired to his country estate. Some of the most poignant, most beautiful, and most clearly focused stanzas of the poem express Marvell's anguish for England. He sees her now not with the fiery hope of the *Ode* but with much of the view he had given voice to in the poem to Lovelace, before he had been swept into Cromwell's orbit. She is a ruined garden. He acquiesces only reluctantly in Fairfax's retirement, reluctant not because he trusts the zeal of the sword but because Fairfax is the man who might have brought peace. Marvell almost certainly in this poem is to some extent reminiscent of Stoic literature;[7] and in *The Garden* one seems to hear echoes of Lipsius' *De Constantia*. But his acquiescence here in Fairfax's retirement is not at all, like Lipsius' retreat, an utter despair of the world. He believes that order can be made. But yet he admits that for Fairfax it may be right to lay down the painful task of the war by which peace sometimes comes and to perfect his personal life.

> Oh Thou, that dear and happy Isle
> The Garden of the World ere while,
> Thou *Paradise* of four Seas,
> Which *Heaven* planted us to please,
> But, to exclude the World, did guard
> With watry if not flaming Sword;
> What luckless Apple did we tast,
> To make us *Mortal,* and The Wast?
>
> Unhappy! shall we never more
> That sweet *Militia* restore, . . .
>
> . . . .
>
> And yet their walks one on the Sod
> Who, had it pleased him and *God,*
> Might once have made our Gardens spring
> Fresh as his own and flourishing.

But he preferr'd to the *Cinque Ports*
These five imaginary Forts:
And, in those half-dry Trenches, spann'd
Pow'r which the Ocean might command.

For he did, with his utmost Skill,
Ambition weed, but *Conscience* till.
Conscience, that Heaven-nursed Plant,
Which most our Earthly Gardens want.

It would seem likely that the poem was written shortly after
Marvell came to Nun Appleton, when Fairfax's retirement was
recent, and when the general hope that had looked to him was
not long dissipated. In any event the chaos Marvell pictures in
the poem reflects the times even as today they appear to historians and somewhat, we may suppose, as they must have appeared to Cromwell himself when he made his decisions. Marvell's view of the Levellers, and on the obverse his picture of the
great social order vested in tradition and the family—and by
implication supported on property—and seeking its sanctions in
religion, define in the poem the terms in which he measured
the actual disorder and cessation of function in government. It
is a picture consonant with his defense, twenty years later, of
the Long Parliament. But these terms we shall come back to
presently in their place in the poem.

The import of each poem is clear. But we may well at this
point check our reading of them and of their shifting of tone by
reference to Marvell's later comment on his part during these
years. He felt in 1670 that "the King ought to have been trusted."
Yet he defended the great leaders of the Long Parliament who
had struggled on behalf of an idea of the state based on property and of their own function in such a state. With generous
praise of Laud's abilities, he records nevertheless the impression
he had received from older men whom he knew and trusted of
Laud's ruthless drive for conformity, against men's consciences.
His own part, presently, in Cromwell's government he defends,

under attack by Parker, as an acceptance of the only government then existing, an acceptance late and reluctant. He fixes
the date of his acquiescence only at the date of his actually
taking office, ignoring or overlooking the fact that he had made
application several years earlier and had even, as Abbott says,
been temporarily employed and that he was already then on
cordial terms with Milton. But we cannot be certain that he did
not hesitate even after application. And when a man in giving
an account of his past actions remains true to essential feeling
and fact, he may be forgiven if, in the torrent of a positive plea
such as Marvell was then making at once for toleration and for
religion, he has not that calm accuracy of memory about himself which we should in other circumstances wish. More essential than these dates is his forthright defense of Milton, and his
truth to his earlier sense of the tragic complication of issues in
the years from 1642 to 1650. It was Milton's misfortune, he says,
to have been on a different side from himself on the great issue
of those years. He, that is, on his return to England sided with
those who wanted to make adjustment with the King; Milton
with the republicans and the regicides. But he would not now
see Milton persecuted for a decision so hard to make and in
which so many had erred. This account confirms our interpretation of the poems, the view of Fairfax exactly answering to it.

When Marvell himself returned to public life and to necessi-
tated trust in Cromwell, and the choice which Cromwell had
made, he had turned away from the momentary view of Cromwell as a meteoric personal force and from the blind trust in
war. He believed, as Spenser believed, though in very different
terms, that public order was a part of the great order of the
universe, and that only great characters could conceive and
maintain or re-establish that order. But the task of making it
rather than of living in the arts of peace became to him more
and more a painful burden. The view accords with neo-Platonism and with the general ethic of the age set forth in em-

blem book and in proverb. It accords even more with the deepening of devotional temper evident in *Upon Appleton House*.
From this, no less than from the forward movement of events,
may have come Marvell's renewed confidence. From about 1652
on, his view of Cromwell in its growth parallels that of Milton,
who suggested that Marvell be appointed his own assistant. In
1653, in accepting the tutorship at Eton, he had in a sense come
under Cromwell's patronage. And the two poems of 1653 *On
Blake's Victory,* attributing the chief honor of that event to
Cromwell, and the poem to Dr. Ingelo, have the character of
poems of state compliment and mark his full acceptance of
Cromwell's leadership in the task which Fairfax had withdrawn from. As Mr. Fink has shown,[8] the idea that order must
be founded, or if lost refounded, by a single great leader was
very widely held. In Marvell even more than in Milton the
sanction for this idea which he, like the classical Republicans
who looked to Venice for their model, found in Greek and
Roman history was overshadowed by the religious and philosophical sanction. When he again addresses Cromwell, he has
come to see the Protector in a neo-Platonic light, not as the man
who compelled fate by his strength but as the man shaped by
the cosmos to his task. The shift of emphasis is significant.

The two state poems on the Protector have the formal and
elaborate imagery of rhetoric proper to such poems, perhaps
even a French more than an English floridity, a rhetoric most
difficult for our age to enter into. The lengthy analysis of the
horses, to take the extreme instance, in the account of the run-
away of Cromwell's carriage is almost impossible for us to feel
as anything but fantastic flattery even after we have made the
imaginative effort of recalling the formal praises with which
Pindar's *Epinicea* open and of remembering that Marvell might
have had fresh within *his* imagination the sense of the relation
of all nature to man. The metaphysical, being metaphysical,
does not lend itself to such rhetorical uses despite the baroque

popularity in that age of metaphysical rhetoric. But though the length, the formal elaboration, and the place within the design of the images is a matter of rhetoric, the images are not like those of Dryden's lines on Cromwell's death, or like those of D'Avenant's *Madagascar,* or like those of Chapman on Prince Henry in the taste of an earlier age, mere formal or poetic invention. Through them are defined the concepts by which Marvell interprets Cromwell. This is particularly true of the first poem, which is the more metaphysical, and in which the very concrete temporal interpretation of history and character is more intimately bound up with the religious and philosophical interpretation of them. The new imagery which in that poem replaces the Roman associations of the earlier poem I have already analyzed in the seventh chapter. The figures show Cromwell as a character of a virtue as perfect as humanity, with the divine Grace, can achieve. Other kings rule pettishly according as they are swayed by personal ambition and by lack of power to plan. Cromwell rules for the people and establishes a great order. They serve the Whore of Babylon. He brings a true religion. In that view, and with the sense of a crusade, Marvell will go all the way with Cromwell in his hopes of something like a new Christian imperialism.

And yet in this later poem the ardor of the *Ode* has failed. And with the hope, the confidence, has failed also much of the larger sympathy that makes the beauty of the earlier poem. Towards other kings and other religions there is only acrimony. And of tragedy no vision. Much has been worn down by reconcilement to the facts and to the task of administration, and the sanity gained is a dry sanity. Freedom cannot in truth be won or sustained by the sword; and though without loss of trust in Cromwell himself, and indeed with added dependence upon him as parliament and other men fail, yet Marvell writes now not in hope but only in weary longing.

On the issue of freedom, in the face of the Levellers and

antinomians, Marvell has shifted with Milton, and calls in against the mass of Englishmen the distinction between liberty and license to justify Cromwell's Protectorate. Marvell still trusts the parliament with balanced parts and a free senate, but Cromwell must order the parts.

> 'Tis not a freedome, that where All command;
> Nor Tyranny, where One does them withstand:
> But who of both the Bounders knows to lay
> Him as their Father must the State obey.
>
> . . . .
>
> That sober Liberty which men may have,
> That they enjoy, but more they vainly crave: . . .

It is as the monarch of a limited monarchy that Marvell now sees Cromwell, the executive rather in a balanced state, with essentially Cromwell's own view, a monarchy in fact not too far from the monarchy which Dryden was to uphold on behalf of Charles II in the days of the struggle with Shaftesbury. If Cromwell has taken the rule from the Stuarts, it is as a great mate who in a storm seizes the helm from a confused steersman and steers his frightened shipmates off the rocks and back to the open sea. Cromwell and not the free state is the center now of all that is impassioned and visionary in the poem.

It is a Cromwell in whom the heroic element still harmonizes with the Roman virtue which Marvell had made central in the portrait of him in the *Ode*.

> For all delight of Life thou then didst lose,
> When to Command, thou didst thy self Depose;
> Resigning up thy Privacy so dear,
> To turn the headstrong Peoples Charioteer;
>
> . . . .
>
> For, neither didst thou from the first apply
> Thy sober Spirit unto things too High,
> But in thine own Fields exercisedst long,
> An healthful Mind within a Body strong;

> Till at the Seventh time thou in the Skyes,
> As a small Cloud, like a Mans hand didst rise; ...

Yet it is even more as the instrument of Providence that he prevails,

> What since he did, an higher Force him push'd
> Still from behind, and it before him rush'd,
>
> .   .   .   .
>
> Founding a firm state by Proportions true.

From current views of the Venetian constitution Marvell is separated by the primacy which he gives to religious guidance and purpose over political philosophy. If the people prove themselves equal in character and vision to Cromwell, it will be a sign that the last perfect age has arrived and that the earth is soon to fade. If not, the long slow battle for virtue on earth is still to be fought. Milton will presently gather his energies from immediate and temporal defeat to win the longer battle in the realm of thought by his poems. Marvell, one cannot but think, is unconsciously preparing himself to take part in the turn which almost all England made when, after Cromwell's death, it called back the Stuarts to save it from military dictatorship. For that and to try still by his vote and by his satires to establish this limited monarchy, this order to be achieved by good men over the slow years against the old enemies of sloth and greed in all their new forms. Already in the poem's tone the lucid and far-seeing intensity of Marvell's brief period of poetic vision is sinking into deep and voiceless chambers of his nature and leaving on the surface the somber intellectual feeling of his later years.

In the last Cromwell poem, *A Poem upon the Death of O. C.,* the wheel of Marvell's feeling is come full circle from the *Ode.* Cromwell is a supremely great man whose tragic fate it has been to be compelled to waste in war the gifts meant for peace. Marvell's trust in the immediate divine ordering of the state is gone, except as men of virtue can slowly mould the state. Perhaps the outstanding lines in the poem are the lines on Cromwell's love of his people; the satiric warning to "good" men who are irreligiously egotistical and factious; and the lines beginning "I saw him dead," which realize so vividly for us the impress of Cromwell's personality upon Marvell, even while they bring home to us the finality of the fading of the vision. The absolute plainness of these last lines answering to the darting imaginativeness of the earlier lines on Charles, gives voice to Marvell's personal grief; perhaps it gives notice no less of the change in poetic aim and method which is to come with an altered hope, or rather perhaps a substitution of fortitude for hope, and with an altered orientation to life. Yet long after the Restoration Marvell is stung to one gleam of his earlier vision of the great citizen. The bitter sense of the decay of public spirit, and of that disgust at the insignificance into which England had sunk which he shared with men of many views, yields for a moment to the old fire when he describes in thronging images the death of heroic young Douglas in the Dutch attack upon the Medway.

The metaphysical conceptions by which Marvell interpreted these years, and which give form to his poems, have emerged for us in interpreting the poems themselves. Before turning back to the garden poems, one may comment upon the consistency, within them and with Marvell's political judgments, of certain of his more immediate attitudes; they are attitudes which will emerge more clearly in the garden poems. All mark religion as a determining force in his judgments. The first is his anti-Romanism, in which he is more extreme than Cromwell. Marvell's attitude is defined sharply in terms of the issues and feelings of his own day, but it is also the attitude traditional in England since the sixteenth century, so neatly defined by Ascham and so grandiosely inwoven in Spenser's vision and allegory; by holding men's minds in bondage to falsehood, Rome is responsible for all corruption in manners and civil life.

It is in this light and with actual hopes of the ripening of the harvest even now—as, for instance, in his lines mocking the kings who do not permit the Jews to be accessible to conversion—that he praises a Christian imperialism in Cromwell. In his pamphlets, Marvell's anti-Catholicism is grounded in his anti-intellectualism, taking its rise in the common despair over the religious wars and divisions which harassed Europe and England, and resting in a long view of theological history which might anticipate Gibbon's. No more of the mysteries may be defined than is declared in the Bible and found in the Apostle's Creed. And Marvell feared, until he had read *Paradise Lost,* lest Milton not only profane and vulgarize the Biblical story, but perplex honest men by overdefining the mysteries to which understanding is blind and only hard faith can lead. To such a view Presbyterian absolutism could only be abhorrent, though Marvell remains stoutly Calvinist in his emphasis on grace. And since faith, still a vividly Biblical faith, is the cue of individual life and reason, and since no man's belief can be compelled, toleration is essential. Though Marvell does not in his poems specifically define this theological anti-intellectualism, the quietism of *Upon Appleton House,* the turning from worldly knowledge to "holy mathematics," is a branch of that anti-intellectualism and shows that his later view must have been already formed. If we apply such a view to his political judgment, the unity of his feeling is clear. The need for toleration, Sir Charles Firth judges, was a chief motive in Cromwell's determination to make order on his own lines. On the other hand Marvell's anti-intellectualism as well as all the humanistic heritage which shaped his imagination would keep him from the simple and literal bibliolatry of the sects and would determine the primacy which he gave to order, to an order in which faith could spring greenly. If I am correct in reading the devotion he expresses in the garden poems in the light of a Platonism such as that of Bonaventura, that too would be a

form in which his humanism, his love of order, and his anti-
intellectualism might readily meet. For the symbolic method of
that Platonism, in which the metaphysical foundation is prior
both to natural science and to logical discourse, gave him a
broad, an intellectual and traditional basis for *reducing* his experience of himself and the world to faith and the Bible. Such
is the ground of habitual thought and feeling from which arise
the sharper crises of feeling which wring poetry from him.

To the garden poems we may then turn, with special emphasis upon *The Garden.* That poem is so close in some detail
to *Upon Appleton House* that it was almost certainly written at
about the same time, and presumably while Marvell was still
with Fairfax. For reasons which I shall indicate presently, I
take it to be the later of the two poems, though the point cannot be absolutely settled and is not material. It is a poem even
harder than the *Ode* to understand fully, for there is, first, less
of outward circumstance to check our reading of the attitudes
involved; then the play of emotion within it is more subtle and
more complex. But there is abundant material in Marvell's
other poetry to help us understand the context of *The Garden.*
This is particularly true of *Upon Appleton House,* with its extended personal talk. How far Marvell's retirement with Fairfax was a matter of choice and how far a matter of circumstance
we cannot know. He was apparently following the occupation
as tutor which had been his first employment and which he
was to continue later for a ward of Cromwell's own. Though
one is tempted to infer that the personal need for retreat came
first and that Marvell accepted the tutorship to Mary Fairfax
as an opportunity for retirement, one has no real grounds for
such an inference; nor does it matter. The crisis which the
poems voice speaks for itself in them. Marvell was not a poet
who embodied an entire vision of life in a series of great poems.
He is one who for a brief period in a long and reserved life revealed certain of his intensest intuitions in a few lyrics that are,

slight as they are, supreme in their art. Their consistency is not
the consistency of a story or of parts ordered to imitate a whole.
It is the consistency only of a spirit of the rarest intellectual
precision and integrity, never confused by the vivid impulses of
the senses which abound in his verse, aware always of the deep
issues of feeling and value involved in any one moment. We
cannot place the Appleton poems in a spiritual biography,
though we can feel in them and in the political poems and in
the love poems a common intellectual and spiritual integrity.
We can say that in *Upon Appleton House* we have quite explicit definition of the thought which concretized in Marvell at
the time he wrote it, interrelating civil views and imaginative
life, and suggesting much as to the background of thought and
reading to which the poet related his personal experience, much
that is so implicit in the words and images of the two poems as
to be an integral part of their meanings. The poem combines a
highly formal reflective theme of compliment to Lord Fairfax
and his daughter—reflecting Lord Fairfax's passion for gene-
alogy—with an intensely personal lyric essay or meditation on
nature, the two interweaving in the theme of the virtuousness
and the delight of the retired life. The two themes may be said
to be developed in four movements. The first movement gives
us the poet's religious ideal as expressed in his interpretation of
Fairfax; the praise of Fairfax, the putting aside of the state and
the justification of retirement and of the cultivation of the
private life. This movement is constructed upon two metaphors
for order, both of which arise out of Fairfax's situation: the
figure from architecture and the figure of the garden warfare—
both figures with a devotional tradition, and particularly in
neo-Platonic literature. Fairfax has substituted the order of
charity and family life for the pomp and circumstance of a
great house; and he has substituted the marshalled harmony of
the garden, with all that it may bring through the five ports of
knowledge, for the stern discipline and array of battle. In this

movement the note of personal feeling emerges only for an intense moment in the lines on England as a garden. The second movement, throwing itself fully into the nature theme, is personal, describing the walk, the countryside, the passing of the day; through much of this passage, religious musing continues as a sort of bass or ground. The third movement returns to the original theme of formal compliment in praise of order, catching up the original figures, but in a very different tone; for this movement addresses itself to a young girl on the verge of life and not to a great administrator who has withdrawn from it. A last brief movement returns to nature in personal experience. We can best look at the complex elements of thought and feeling in the poem if we take them up in the order suggested by the poem itself.

The poem marks, in its despair for England, a revulsion from Marvell's particular religious excitement of 1650. But Marvell turns from that wasted zeal to multiple forms of quiet religious reflection and of personal religious impulse. The poem opens with a meditation *de contemptu mundi*. What need is there of a great house or of state for the wanton mote of dust? As the formal compliment to Fairfax proceeds, this view unfolds itself in a series of parallels or emblems, rising to the climax of its deep piety in the lines on Fairfax and England, and especially in the lines which, as Mr. Margoliouth points out,[9] image conscience as the sensitive plant.

> A prickling leaf it bears, and such
> As that which shrinks at ev'ry touch;
> But Flowrs eternal, and divine,
> That in the Crowns of Saints do shine.

Marvell is not quite content, however, merely with devotion. The history of the house by means of which the formal compliment is developed is made the occasion for a bitter anti-Catholic statement, perfectly in accord with Marvell's views in the Cromwell poems and in his later life. In this attack the charges of casuistry, of dishonesty of purpose, of immorality, and the objection to the theory of celibacy are the commonplaces of his age, tradition, and group, but stated with an intellectual pointedness and dramatic precision that are rare. Perhaps of a more deep significance for our understanding of Marvell's mind is his attack upon Catholic devotion. The hatred of Catholic ritual was indeed a commonplace of anti-Catholicism, often voiced, for instance, in such crude pamphlets as *The Arminian Nunnery,* that travesty of Ferrar and Little Gidding.[10] But Marvell's note is not a common one and it speaks informedly, at least as to the use of Catholic art in ritual, rather than out of mere prejudice. In stanzas xxi to xxiii there is an attack upon that use of the senses or sensual sublimation as a key to ecstasy or in ritualistic symbolism which was an important element in the devotion of the Counter-Reformation.

Of this use of the senses in literature Crashaw is the best English example. And it is probable that Marvell would have known of the center of the cult at Cambridge. He might have become particularly conscious of it during the brief days of his own reputed conversion, in which Peterhouse men were involved, or in his travels and his presumed reading on the continent. His representation of the devotional habit is a very careful one. That we may say, without at all subscribing to his attacks upon conventual perversion of sex. If the writings of St. Teresa and those about her were among his chief sources of information about such symbolism, their imagery might direct the mind of an adverse critic. The passage is particularly important not for its anti-Catholicism but because it joins with other material in *Appleton House* to show that Marvell had an intense and conscious preoccupation with the nature of the mind and with the meaning of the senses and their just use.

The next high point of religious feeling is to be found in the woodland passage. But as it is only the groundwork to the

main theme of reverie there, it must be studied as part of that
reverie, and we may for the present pass over it to the Mary
Fairfax passage. These lines take up the first movement: they
foretell the second Fairfax marriage and see in it again the renewal of the foundations of a pious society. But the mood is
altered from the opening of the poem by the garden passage
through which we have passed and by the fact that the lines
are addressed to a child just on the eve of womanhood; their
tone is at once more playful and more fancifully gay and yet
with a graver undercurrent of personal feeling. Perhaps the
garden mood and the real address of the entire poem to Marvell's pupil determined its whole temper. Marvell's view of
childhood and his command of tone in addressing a child form
one of his most poignant and original achievements. It is a
signal fruit of the classical discipline, of the religious and intellectual detachment which render so different in him the elements in the thought of the age which he shares with Vaughan.
Childhood in its innocence is the time of play, the time of nurture too; it may suggest a vision of the ideal in human nature;
but it is yet childhood and not maturity. The poem *On the
Portrait of Little T. C.* is the inevitable commentary upon the
Mary Fairfax lines. At any rate, almost from the beginning
there is an ironic burlesque tone which in stanza xxxii is almost
mock-epic and which then moving out of the indictment of
Catholicism and into the positive praise of Fairfax and retirement passes into the irony of the central warfare figure. The
lines on Mary Fairfax in a more boldly playful burlesque, echo
or restate the theme of Donne's praise of Elizabeth Drury as the
type of virtue which gives soul and order to the world. In their
view of Mary Fairfax's development and task, they parallel the
portrait of the pious lady in the sermon literature and in the
character books of the day, and in such a devotional work as
Taylor's *Holy Living and Holy Dying*. And in this they stand

in deliberate contrast with the Catholic view set forth in stanzas XIV to XIX, which is explicitly recalled to memory in stanza XCIV.

So far I have spoken chiefly of that central piety which made religion the groundwork of Marvell's thought and to him the foundation of a good society, a religion, be it noted, of spiritual conversion and not of mere ethical habit; and I have said little of the special relation of religion in this poem to the garden theme. That we must now consider, for it is what draws the woodland walk within the unity of the poem. Marvell's delight in nature for herself is very keen, and nothing in the range of English literature is more fresh with observation or more immediately conveys that freshness than the passage on the walk, particularly the description often commented on of the birds. But as his experience and his thought come together, that pure but undirected delight does not singly predominate. A series of landscapes marks a conscious literary sophistication, leading us into a fixed intellectual aim.

The revery of the woodland is twice interrupted with philosophical reflections that carry us back first to the opening of this movement and then to the first movement, though the mood has been transposed to one half fanciful, half serious; in both, seriousness and fancy are perfectly controlled in this moment of "easie philosophy."

> Out of these scatter'd *Sibyls* Leaves
> Strange *Prophecies* my Phancy weaves:
> And in one History consumes,
> Like *Mexique Paintings,* all the *Plumes.*
> What *Rome, Greece, Palestine,* ere said
> I in this light *Mosaick* read.
> Thrice happy he who, not mistook,
> Hath read in *Natures mystick Book.*
>
> .   .   .   .
>
> How safe, methinks, and strong, behind
> These Trees have I incamp'd my Mind;

> Where Beauty, aiming at the Heart,
> Bends in some Tree its useless Dart;
> And where the World no certain Shot
> Can make, or me it toucheth not.
> But I on it securely play,
> And gaul its Horsemen all the Day.

The first six lines of the first of these stanzas are surely half mirth and the more serious reference in the last two to the book of the creatures passes lightly into whimsy in the next stanza. But it is a play of the mind upon the ground of its most serious preoccupations. The reference to "natures mystick Book," the "light Mosaick" and the lines upon the holy mathematics of piety in stanza VII lead us, as we have seen in discussing Marvell's imagery and the background of his thought, to the particular literature of the book of the creatures, very possibly to the writings of the Victorines and of Bonaventura. Though lightly touched upon, nothing is more central to the structure of the poem than the explicit avowal, so inwoven by word and image with the Fairfax passage, that here in the beauty of nature and the innocence of solitude Marvell finds God as in the first freshness of creation man found him. The emphasis upon fortitude and self-possession and the immediate pleasure in the mind's freedom from passion form part of the same context as the explicit words and indeed they are made explicit in the warfare against the world and the flesh.

If we think also of *The Garden* and if we turn back to the passage I quoted earlier from Lipsius, there is much to suggest that Stoicism as well as mediaeval philosophy formed part of Marvell's reading at Nun Appleton or lay from of old vividly in his memory—the green, the retreat of the gods, but above all the radiance of tone. From Stoicism might have come in part his rejection of fame, though, as we have seen, that is not the usual way Stoicism was read in the Renaissance and Marvell's rejection is rather the absolute religious rejection. And the intensity of personal experience is very far from stoic. Into Lipsius' own passage in the garden it is true there has entered something of a Christian feeling for the creatures which brings his book close to the religious reading that Marvell is likely to have done. But that is its least stoic side. Other strains, such as distrust of sophistication and intellectualism were also widely diffused in the same way; but these attitudes, like the rejection of fame, were particularly strong in the literature of symbolic interpretation of the Bible.

Love of free nature not defaced by art is another attitude generally vigorous in Marvell.

> But Nature here hath been so free
> As if she said leave this to me.
> Art would more neatly have defac'd
> What she had laid so sweetly wast;
> In fragrant Gardens, shaddy Woods,
> Deep Meadows, and transparent Floods.

This strain, just touched on here, is a dominant note in the Damon poems, and in them, the freshness and immediacy of the poetry binds it up closely with Marvell's own experience of nature.

These Damon poems in their plots or situations, in the names they use and in part in their tone are linked with literary pastoralism. And a casual familiar reference to Guarini's *Il Pastor Fido* twenty years later reminds us how certainly Marvell must have known that literature. Yet their more dominant mood recalls one rather to the passage I have cited from Richard of St. Victor,[11] and to distinctly religious implications in the love of unsophisticated nature rather than to mere pastoralism. If we bear them in mind and if we look backward in *Appleton House* and read up from stanza I again after having read stanza x, the theme of distrust of the intellect and of yearning for a simple, primitive civilization looms large. But yet it is, on the other hand, so bound up in this poem with an English, one might

even say an Anglican, love of seemliness and order, that one
can hardly link it too seriously with the great anti-intellectualist
current in contemporary religious thought except as that current had been absorbed into Anglicanism.[12] The passage has
some breath even of the Horatian strain of Jonson and Herrick,
and is not unconnected with the Latin ideal of character which,
as we see in the portrait of Cromwell in the *Horatian Ode*, had
done so much to form Marvell's mind. And indeed, at the close
of stanza v the Roman note comes to the surface just as it is
passing into the religious note in stanza vi.

> And some will smile at this, as well
> As *Romulus* his Bee-like Cell.
>
> *Humility* alone designs
> Those short but admirable Lines, . . .

Perhaps the lines on Mary Fairfax's education best represent
the distrust of learning so far as it had become fixed in Marvell's
thought.

> For *She*, to higher Beauties rais'd,
> Disdains to be for lesser prais'd.
> *She* counts her Beauty to converse
> In all the Languages as *hers;*
> Nor yet in those *her self* imploy es
> But for the *Wisdome*, not the *Noyse;*
> Nor yet that *Wisdome* would affect,
> But as 'tis *Heavens Dialect.*

I have already suggested how the symbolic tradition of thought
supplied for Marvell a ground which was anti-intellectualistic
without being antirational.

The second strain, the distrust of art, is only implicit in *Upon
Appleton House*, in the opening stanzas. In *The Coronet* that
fear of the pride and worldliness which may lie even in religious
art found full expression. It is the poem which connects Marvell
most closely with Herbert. Distinctively Marvell's in its sen-

suousness, its precision of sensibility, its intellectual refinement, it seems to me also a precipitation of much reading of Herbert.

The wish to free religion of art, and at the same time to turn to the uses of religion the fragrant towers that had once adorned the head of the mistress, was not original with Herbert. It is an important strain in Marot, and there are innumerable expressions of it in seventeenth-century English verse. Back of it lie mediaeval attitudes rooted in earliest Christian thought. Yet Herbert made it singularly his own hope, singularly the expression of the combined simplicity and orderliness of his own temper. And in *The Coronet* it is combined with Herbert's own fear of fame and interest. Then the whole is expressed in the form of a single sustained emblem and in a free but organic combination of long and short lines, a figurative and metric combination which is Herbert's most distinctive form. To think of Herbert helps us altogether to understand the religious feeling of *Appleton House* in contrast with the attitude of the *Horatian Ode,* though we are never to forget that *Appleton House* is not so single in aim and so committed as the work of Herbert. An analogue to the last stanza of *The Garden* has been suggested by Miss Rosemary Freeman in the garden emblem book for the Virgin, *Parthenia Sacra,*[13] which I have already described among the books of the creatures. And if we think of Marvell's garden as the *hortus conclusus,* the parallel is all the more striking, while at the same time everything in the tone of the two emphasizes the Anglican quality of Marvell's work. It is the common heritage of the two books which is significant, though we should have no reason to be surprised even if a contemporary English Catholic work had contributed to awaken Marvell's imagination. For in the development of English devotional life, as Miss White has shown,[14] even the most violent anti-Catholic prejudice was no bar to exclude whatever in Roman literature was consonant with English feeling.

Like the emblem figures in the *Horatian Ode,* the emblem

figures in this Nun Appleton poem deepen the pervading piety
by their power to express with lyric fulness the immediate share
of man's consciousness in two worlds, the world of time and the
world of eternity. Marvell does not say expressly with George
Herbert, for instance, that of all the creatures man alone, by
his knowledge and love of them all, renders back to God the
love which made them; but the thought seems always breaking
through. And yet man's consciousness is not simple, as Marvell
constantly remembers. By his time, as I have already said, many
types of conceit had fallen together to create the emblem-image.
And though the dominant tone of the poem is given by the
religious symbols, there are other tones which were for Marvell
not incompatible with these, and which remind us that we are
reading a poem—a very artful poem—and not a devotional exercise. In the nunnery passage there are strains of the shimmer-
ing ingenuity of Marini and of the earlier Crashaw, possibly
of Jesuit verse, strains very likely intended in this passage to
suggest dramatically just that excessive softness which they do
in fact create; but in some of the exuberant fancies of the woodland walk there is also an enameled wit more consonant with
exploration of sensibility than with its philosophical direction
through joy in the creatures to contemplation. Though Marvell's piety is so deep, and though he is steeped in religious reflection and reading, and although he has put the world aside
and for himself passion too, *Upon Appleton House* is not wholly
committed to the eternal view, and certainly not to a simple
or narrow view of man's relation to the world. Marvell has not
polarized all his nature. Even in the midst of the seriousness
of the figures themselves and of the tradition they evoke there
is a sheer exaggeration of fancy in them which combines a
singular whimsicality with the gravity of the poem, and which
reflects the fact that it is still a poem of exploration, filled with
the wonder of man's personality. Perhaps, even, in the whole
strange, more than normal, relaxation of tension in the poem,

there is a revulsion from the intensity into which in 1650 Marvell had been swept. At any rate, philosophical and psychological speculation, political reflection, memories of his travels, delight in exploring his own personality, are running like a tide through him, side by side with devotional reading and reflection. In the second movement this personal note takes possession of the poem. It leads us to another side of Marvell's reading to which both the imagery and objective evidence serve as guides.

Among the thinkers and writers of the Renaissance who cultivated the pleasures of retirement, one important group were the libertines, who found in the country more leisure than in the world for the realization of their own instincts, impulses, and tastes, for melancholy also and scorn of the world. With this libertine literature in the poetry of St. Amant Marvell has been directly connected,[15] and he may well also have read the poems of Théophile de Viau. Lord Fairfax and his brother-in-law Mildmay Fane, Earl of Westmorland, were, during Marvell's stay at Nun Appleton, reading, adapting, and translating the nature poetry of St. Amant. Several close verbal parallels both to Fane and to St. Amant have been pointed out in Marvell's work which increase the inherent probability that Marvell too was reading St. Amant. Other parallels make it possible that he had also seen the work of Théophile. It is in their nature poetry that he is interested. Of Théophile's explicit discussion of libertine philosophical attitudes there is no reflection in this poem, though in *The Garden* I find a not improbably conscious answer to that view.

Though Marvell and St. Amant are far apart, it seems to me that Marvell perhaps owed an intense impulse to the French poet, or at least that an element in his feeling can be better understood through reference to St. Amant. I shall consider the most important of the many echoes of St. Amant's *La Solitude* which seem to have been running through Marvell's head as he wrote the poem on Appleton house and perhaps the companion poem *Upon The Hill and Grove at Bill-borow*. Since it is a question of general reminiscence, I shall give the whole of the relevant passages from St. Amant, followed by those from Marvell, with note of the particular echoes.

LA SOLITUDE

I

O que j'ayme la solitude!
Que ces lieux sacrez à la nuit,
Esloignez du monde et du bruit,
Plaisent à mon inquietude!
Mon Dieu! que mes yeux sont contens
De voir ces bois, qui se trouverent
A la nativité du temps,
Et que tous les siècles reverent,
Estre encore aussi beaux et vers,
Qu' aux premiers jours de l'univers!

. . . .

IV

Que je trouve doux le ravage
De ces fiers torrens vagabonds,
Qui se precipitent par bonds
Dans ce vallon vert et sauvage!
Puis, glissant sous les arbrisseaux,
Ainsi que des serpens sur l'herbe,
Se changent en plaisans ruisseaux,
Ou quelque Naïade superbe
Regne comme en son lict natal,
Dessus un throsne de christal!

V

Que j'aime ce marets paisible!
Il est tout bordé d'aliziers,
D'aulnes, de saules et d'oziers,
A qui le fer n'est point nuisible.
Les nymphes, y cherchans le frais,
S'y viennent fournir de quenouilles,

De pipeaux, de joncs et de glais;
Ou l'on voit sauter les grenouilles,
Qui de frayeur s'y vont cacher
Si tost qu'on veut s'en approcher.

VI

La, cent mille oyseaux aquatiques
Vivent, sans craindre, en leur repos,
Le giboyeur fin et dispos,
Avec ses mortelles pratiques.
L'un, tout joyeux d'un si beau jour,
S'amuse a becqueter sa plume;
L'autre allentit le feu d'amour
Qui dans l'eau mesme se consume,
Et prennent tous innocemment
Leur plaisir en cet élement.

.   .   .   .

XVII

Tantost, la plus claire du monde,
Elle semble un miroir flottant,
Et nous represente à l'instant
Encore d'autres cieux sous l'onde.
Le soleil s'y fait si bien voir,
Y contemplant son beau visage,
Qu'on est quelque temps à sçavoir
Si c'est luy-mesme, ou son image
Et d'abord il semble à nos yeux
Qu'il s'est laissé tomber des cieux.[16]

* * * *

Upon its crest this Mountain grave
A Plump of aged Trees does wave.
No hostile hand durst ere invade
With impious Steel the sacred Shade.
For something alwaies did appear
Of the *great Masters* terrour there: . . .[17]

* * * *

But I, retiring from the Flood,
Take Sanctuary in the Wood;
And, while it lasts, my self imbark
In this yet green, yet growing Ark;
Where the first Carpenter might best
Fit Timber for his Keel have Prest.
And where all Creatures might have shares,
Although in Armies, not in Paires.[18]

The double Wood of ancient Stocks
Link'd in so thick, an Union locks,
It like two *Pedigrees* appears,
On one hand *Fairfax,* th' other *Veres:*
Of whom though many fell in War,
Yet more to Heaven shooting are:
And, as they Natures Cradle deckt,
Will in green Age her Hearse expect.

When first the Eye this Forrest sees
It seems indeed as *Wood* not *Trees:*
As if their Neighbourhood so old
To one great Trunk them all did mold.
There the huge Bulk takes place, as ment
To thrust up a *Fifth Element;*
And stretches still so closely wedg'd
As if the Night within were hedg'd.

Compare this with *La Solitude,* stanza I.

* * * *

See in what wanton harmless folds
It ev'ry where the Meadow holds;
And its yet muddy back doth lick,
Till as a *Chrystal Mirrour* slick;
Where all things gaze themselves, and doubt
If they be in it or without.
And for his shade which therein shines,
Narcissus like, the *Sun* too pines.

Compare this with *La Solitude,* stanza XVI.

* * * *

> For now the Waves are fal'n and dry'd,
> And now the Meadows fresher dy'd;
> Whose Grass, with moister colour dasht,
> Seems as green Silks but newly washt.
> No *Serpent* new nor *Crocodile*
> Remains behind our little *Nile;*
> Unless it self you will mistake,
> Among these Meads the only Snake.

Compare this with St. Amant, stanza iv. In stanza lxv the following of the passage on the birds after the flood passage parallels the order of similar details in St. Amant.

Perhaps no one of these echoes would be significant in itself. But if we take the whole nexus of them, remembering also the probability on external evidence that Marvell knew St. Amant, it seems to me likely that the many parallels are not coincidences, but that St. Amant was running through Marvell's memory and that reading the French poet may have focused certain elements of the English poet's experience.

La Solitude and *Upon Appleton House* are, it is true, profoundly different. It is a solemn vision, almost a dream vision, of nature by which St. Amant sweeps us at once out of our common day: vast trees older than the flood, darkness, waters whose silence and whose stillness no man, no boat has ever broken. Except for the conventional reference to the flood as marking primeval time, there is no religious note and that reference is perfectly consistent with a libertine view of nature's unfolding. Of this formal picture, there is no counterpart in Marvell; but the elements of it are diffused in the ripple of his memory and the play of his fancy over the warm English countryside before him. Other formal and more traditional literary motifs follow the description of the wood in St. Amant's poem; elements which probably St. Amant owed, as M. Adam suggests, to Marino's set descriptions of landscapes, classical nymphs and wood lore, narratives. Of these there is nothing in Marvell. Nor does he, like St. Amant, nourish desolation

on an array of objects and associations of traditional sentimental
reflection and terror: ruined castles haunted by demons, birds
of darkness and ill-omened cry, skeletons of suicides dead for
love, and all that were then part of libertine melancholy and
that were to become with trappings from literary-monastic
decor the paraphernalia of pleasing melancholy in the eighteenth century.

In the series of real descriptions, however, which St. Amant
gives of tree, water, bird in the opening stanzas we have already quoted, and in the tone which pervades them, there is
material which might well have set Marvell off to the account
of his day and the walk in the woods. There is in these stanzas
of *La Solitude* an indescribable personal accent, with their
sensuous immediacy, the movement of the detail, the rapidly
shifting play of the impressions, the tone of sensibility, the
sweep of the whole, which seems to me akin to the personal
tone of Marvell.[19]

> Tu vois dans cette poesie
> Pleine de licence et d'ardeur
> Les beaux rayons de la splendeur
> Qui m'esclaire la fantaisie;
> Tantost chagrin, tantost joyeux,
> Selon que la fureur m'enflame,
> Et que l'objet s'offre à mes yeux,
> Les propos me naissent en l'ame,
> Sans contraindre la liberté
> Du demon qui m'a transporté.
>
> O que j'ayme la solitude!
> C'est l'element des bons esprits,
> C'est par elle que j'ay compris
> L'art d'Apollon sans nulle estude.

I am, it is here necessary to say, again concerned not with
sources but with realizing as many elements as possible of the
atmosphere in the light of which Marvell's poem can be most
fully understood. When Marvell read St. Amant the French

poet came to a consciousness in the roots of which were memories of other poetry of nature, as well as of the meditations of
the devotional writers. Marvell in his time and with his education, for instance, certainly knew Virgil's eclogues. The first
eclogue expresses with a penetratingly individual and modern
intensity Virgil's awareness of his own possession of the country, of peace, and of his poetry amidst tragic uprooting and
social disorder all about him. Must not this poem have been
in Marvell's recollection as he wrote of the dear isle? I think it
rises once to the surface. For does not

> But I have for my Musick found
> A Sadder, yet more pleasing Sound;
> The *Stock-doves,* whose fair necks are grac'd
> With Nuptial Rings, their Ensigns chast;
> Yet always, for some Cause unknown,
> Sad pair unto the Elms they moan,

echo "nec gemere aeria cessabit turtur ab ulmo"? Yet if it echo
Virgil, the whole stanza also reminds us how many other
threads are present in Marvell's thought. Among these, St.
Amant comes as a precipitating force, because he is a force so
close to Marvell's immediate experience and his immediate
doubts and speculations.

In St. Amant, however strikingly direct and fresh the description is in detail, it is all measured, plays its part within a
series of arranged motifs. In Marvell's poem, at the close of the
first movement, there is a sudden expression of personal feeling in the lament for England; for a moment this is put off
with the more formal rounding out of the movement in a renewed praise of conscience and a return to the formal garden
theme. And then, though he intimates an arrangement of
scenes, Marvell's fancy leaps out to play at will over the sensuous world before him, over memories of his travels, over his
current reading. The exquisite sensuous observation has been
often noted. It has a wonderful power to feel the life in the

thing looked at. One can hardly tell whether to think of it as arising from a spontaneous genius in a man returning to the countryside of his youth, or as set off by St. Amant, but quickened beyond anything in St. Amant; or as in part springing from a deliberate interest in the nature of the sensation and the percept, stimulated again perhaps by St. Amant, but more deeply by the philosophical and psychological speculations of the literature of the book of the creatures. For this last interpretation we have a parallel in Vaughan. After his essentially unfruitful time in London, and after a period of personal tension including the shock of his brother's death, Vaughan found his vein of poetry when he learned, deliberately or unconsciously or both, from the Bible or elsewhere, the power to put into words that spontaneous and integrated impression of a landscape, that flashing insight into nature, which was for him the substance on which he nourished his religious insight. We have also a little later the parallel of Traherne's speculations on the nature of experience and thought in *Jumping Over the Moon* and other poems. Such speculation, as I have suggested, may well relate to serious speculation among Platonists on the theory of vision. Certainly problems as to the nature of sensation were vividly before men's minds, not merely in such humanistic reflections on them as Montaigne made in his essays, but in Gassendi's Epicureanism and in Platonic thought as well as diffused through all Renaissance philosophy. I believe that for Marvell one line of transmission of such introspection lay in St. Amant. What he took is, of course, changed by the context into which it is brought and by the play of figure about it which is part of that context. Mr. Eliot has commented justly on the exaggeration of the metaphysical figure in this poem. Yet the style and fancy are not random in relation to each other. What might seem the mere intoxication of wit and ingenuity in the figures is rendered something utterly different by the precision and intensity of the detail of nature, by the exact description of mood. With his literary tradition, as I have already said in speaking of the *Ode,* Marvell would have thought the emblematic conceit the obvious instrument for a serious study of reverie, of associative power, of the problem of perception of the near and the distant, of the interchange of fact and thought, particularly when these were seen in a religious context. He used in his description of Douglas many years later sensuous detail and sensual implication which reads as though Marlowe's Leander were in his memory or possibly some of Marini's descriptions, and this use, where we know the passage to be of the utmost seriousness of intent, is evidence how deeply Marvell's imagination was attracted by such sensateness and yet how far he felt man's pleasure in it might be symbolic. His commentary on Catholic use of the senses, at the other end of the scale from St. Amant, has already made such speculation a part of the poem.

In the opening of the woodland movement the religious theme of the first movement carries over as a still dominant note. And it is here that Marvell may recollect St. Amant's solemn classical composition describing the mysterious and silent primeval forest. But those composed lines are broken up and transformed into the fancy and the play of wit that surrounds Marvell's sunny English scene. The new scene becomes one blended of English piety, English intimacy with earth and love of her, quaint English humourousness. The piety ripples over the scene in all the Biblical reminiscences and interpretations evoked by this land of milk and honey and in the reminders of man's humility and the bond of love that ought to bind him to nature. But these reminiscences are at least as mirthful as serious; they begin almost like the stuff for a child's play of imagination. Their tone will be precisely felt if we recall that stanza XLVII,

> And now to the Abbyss I pass
> Of that unfathomable Grass,

> Where Men like Grasshoppers appear,
> But Grashoppers are Gyants there:
> They, in their squeking Laugh, contemn
> Us as we walk more low then them:
> And, from the Precipices tall
> Of the green spir's, to us do call,

is a reminiscence of Numbers, 13, 33: "And there we saw the giants, the sons of Anak, which come of the giants: and we were in our own sight as grasshoppers, and so we were in their sight."[20]

The woodland scene and the fishing scene must not, then, be taken too seriously. Whatever larger significance the power to lose himself in nature, to become as a bird or a tree, to find complete release from tension, to *shed* his thoughts, has for Marvell, these scenes in this poem are to be read quite simply as they appear on the surface. They represent one type of experience of the many that compose the poem, and religious intention is not to be drawn into them from other parts of the poem. It has been suggested that the last lines of stanza LXXVII,

> Do you, *O Brambles,* chain me too,
> And courteous *Briars* nail me through,

should be read with Christian symbolic reference. But it seems to me that the many Christian sentiments and Christian reminiscences in the poem are quite explicit. And the very simple precision of the lines throughout the passage makes their literal sense clear. A man may be deeply religious without being at all times *devot.*

> Thus I, *easie Philosopher,*
> Among the *Birds* and *Trees* confer:
> And little now to make me, wants
> Or of the *Fowles,* or of the *Plants.*
> Give me but Wings as they, and I
> Streight floting on the Air shall fly:
> Or turn me but, and you shall see
> I was but an inverted Tree.

Already I begin to call
In their most learned Original:
And where I Language want, my Signs
The Bird upon the Bough divines:
And more attentive there doth sit
Than if she were with Lime-twigs knit.
No leaf does tremble in the Wind
Which I returning cannot find.

. . . .

Oh what a Pleasure 'tis to hedge
My Temples here with heavy sedge;
Abandoning my lazy Side,
Stretcht as a Bank unto the Tide;
Or to suspend my sliding Foot
On the Osiers undermined Root,
And in its Branches tough to hang,
While at my Lines the Fishes twang!

Marvell here gives an immediate experience that he has not drawn into any pattern of larger thought. If this were not clear from the passage itself, the following lines are surely definitive.

But now away my Hooks, my Quills,
And Angles, idle Utensils.
The *young Maria* walks to night:
Hide trifling Youth thy Pleasures slight.
'Twere shame that such judicious Eyes
Should with such Toyes a Man surprize; ...

I have drawn earlier a parallel between Walton and Marvell. Walton used the actual fishing and hedges and lavender themselves as the food of his spirit. He did not take them as symbol. And Marvell here is even more simply absorbed in the experience than Walton, if that were possible. Probably the just parallel to the lines is in St. Amant's,

O que j'ayme la solitude!
C'est l'element des bons esprits,

C'est par elle que j'ay compris
L'art d'Apollon sans nulle estude.

Or there may be an even closer one in Keats's,

Nothing startles me beyond the present moment. The Setting Sun will always set me to rights, or if a Sparrow come before my Window, I take part in its existence and pick about the gravel.

Yet the play of Marvell's thought, and his reflection on how to take experience, is not far in the background. Miss Bradbrook in her article sees the ivy lines as a possible echo of St. Amant's *La Jouyisance* and as accordingly a parody of a tradition. There is in the lines perhaps an intention more serious than a parody or rather a very serious intention expressed through parody. St. Amant and the libertines, retiring from the strife of the world into their own personalities, did not wish to be free of instincts and impulses but to concentrate upon them as what composed the consciousness. Nature was to them their individual nature. Above all they did not wish—certainly St. Amant at least did not wish—to be free of what was to men of other ways of thought the supreme perturbation, sexual delight. The country was to intensify passion. And they were not behind such erotic poets as the Latin elegists or Joannes Secundus in his *Basia* in using the forms of nature and the tactile sensations from it as suggestive enhancements of a sophisticated love.

From them on this point Marvell differed in all his feeling and thought. He had put passion behind himself explicitly, in the stanza just before this. And it may well have been within his intention in this passage to deny the sensuality and suggestiveness of these poets by re-employing their very detail in a passage of pure, intense sensuous delight in nature herself. Certainly in Marvell's poem itself, the direct and the symbolic, the sensate and the imaginative, come together in the union which is distinctive of Marvell's verse.

A fourth movement, or rather a brief coda of the poem, carries us once more away from the main formal theme in the Mary Fairfax passage and back to personal feeling. The last stanza contains the sheerest whimsy of the poem. But in the overtones of the dark hemisphere there is a reminder of the hidden beauty of the book of the creatures and of that darkness of the natural sensual world in herself from which man can turn to light. For a modern reader it carries in addition to its immediate meaning a special reminder of the multifold ways of life and views of the universe of which the seventeenth-century man was conscious. For it evokes a reminiscence of the closing of the five ports of knowledge which was to end a few years later Sir Thomas Browne's *Garden of Cyrus,* and sets him beside Marvell as one who in the hieroglyph of nature and in his friendly social impulses now rejoiced naïvely in his own personality and now was lifted up to an *O altitudo.* This then is the Marvell of *Upon Appleton House.*

I have spoken again and again of the parallel between Marvell's images and feeling and St. Bonaventura's symbolic thought. Before turning to *The Garden,* we ought to draw together what we know as to explicit systematic Platonism in Marvell's poetry. The cosmic conceptions of *On a Drop of Dew* and of the poems on Cromwell's anniversary and death mark those poems as consciously Platonic, the first very explicitly, the second by the implications of its invention. The elements of Platonism in a *Dialogue Between the Resolved Soul and Created Pleasure* had been long since woven into the texture of Christianity. But possibly a passage such as that I have cited earlier from Ficino on the imagination, as well as the whole infusion of the world of the senses into Renaissance art helps to explain the subtlety and sensuous precision of Marvell's version of the theme. If I am right in my reading of *Upon Appleton House,* Marvell has in that poem deliberately rejected self-deception as to sensuous sublimation; he has rejected libertine surrender to passion; he has not rejected frank delight in the beauty of the creatures. But it is a delight in which immediate experience passes indefinably into a concept of the meaning of that beauty. And to the organization of his feeling a reading of the Victorines and St. Bonaventura or of writers dependent upon them may have contributed. Whether *On a Drop Of Dew* and *A Dialogue* preceded or followed *The Garden* we do not know. *The Coronet* is closely connected with the first in form, and all three are close in tone and imagery. Putting these impressions together with the known date of the Cromwell poems, I suggest that the poems on Cromwell's protectorate follow *The Garden,* but the first of them at no great distance. This would agree with the obvious usual inference as to the date of that poem. To *The Garden* the literature of the *hortus conclusus* among all this reading contributes the most.

The Garden was written in a frame of mind in which profound piety was the groundwork and in a spirit deeply habituated to a Roman attitude of detachment, measure, responsiveness to the patterns of social order. Marvell had for himself given up the world. But this was not all. For at the same time he was in a state of greatly intensified sensibility. Self-awareness flooded him. He was experiencing and reflecting on the many ways in which the elements of consciousness might find direction and equilibrium. *The Garden,* like *Upon Appleton House,* reflects this complex feeling within the most precise intellectual and artistic control of its material, its specific theme as a poem.

The first two stanzas repeat in concentrated form the first movement of *Upon Appleton House,* the theme of retirement.[21] The theme is here stated first in terms of classical thought, praising withdrawal from the fame which comes through public office to the statesman and through public honor to the poet; and here tone and thought remind us of Lipsius; then in Christian terms, describing the recovery of the self from the world's stain. And here the deep imaginative influence of writ-

ing such as that I have cited from Richard of St. Victor, or
Bonaventura forms the setting for his experience, as is shown
both by tone and I believe, by the pattern of key words and
concepts. This is the religious retirement, this is the meditative
joy in the creatures of mediaeval Christian Platonism. But this
theme of withdrawal, even in the statement, breaks into that
joyous and creative sense of expansion into nature toward
which the whole poem moves. For,

> . . . all Flow'rs and all Trees do close
> To weave the Garlands of repose,

and

> Society is all but rude,
> To this delicious Solitude.

These stanzas, like all of the first four, express the transformation or conversion of the mind. And as in *Upon Appleton
House,* in the garden warfare, but more subtly and speedily in
single word metaphor rather than in prolonged simile, the poets
use double images, which are seen in one light by the world,
in another by the resolved soul.

The next two stanzas express the aversion from passion. In
them, particular recollections of St. Amant and the libertines are
still teeming through Marvell's mind, I think.

The praise of the lady's red and white and the symbolization
of all passion in it were very widespread in Renaissance literature. Spenser affords an example ready to hand; but *La Solitude*
of Théophile de Viau contains the striking lines,

> Que ton teinct est de bonne grace!
> Qu'il est blanc, et qu'il est vermeil!

The description of the beloved of which these lines form part is
set in imitation of St. Amant in the secret retreats of a forest,
the primitive haunt of innocence:

> Jamais la justice en courroux
> Icy de criminels ne cherche.

> Icy l'amour faict ses estudes;
> Venus y dresse des autels.

It is the haunt of the amorous gods; it is the haunt in which
he may enjoy Corine far from all eyes but those of Cupid. Is not
Marvell's

> No red nor white was ever seen
> So am'rous as this lovely green

an answer to this or similar passages? M. Legouis cites Spenser's *Hymne in Honour of Beautie,* stanza xi; but Spenser only
denies that it is the outward beauty which seizes us, without
condemning red and white; Spenser carries us back through
red and white to the form from which the red and white spring.
Marvell turns us sharply from all earthly love to heavenly.

The core for the meaning of *green* in this passage is to be
found in Mr. D. C. Allen's article on "Symbolic Color in the
Literature of the Renaissance."[22] Green had been in the Middle
Ages in secular thought a symbol of youth or joy—one remembers Nausicaä as a young growing thing—but also of fickleness.
But in Platonism it had become the symbol of hope. And in
mediaeval Platonism we can see the transformation taking
place, Easter absorbing the hymns of spring, and the renewal
of nature becoming the symbol of hope in the Resurrection. Mr.
Allen cites Alciati, "Spei color est viridis," and the Italian writer
on color symbolism, Giovanni Rinaldi, "Allegrezza e speranza
se la speranza istessa se adorna di verde vesta, e questo per
mostrarci che essa sola e cagione d'ogni nostra felicita e allegrezza." And Allen goes on to say green is regularly used
by the Pléiade as a symbol of hope. Even in Dante, who knew
Bonaventura, I find it approaching symbolic use: *mentre che
la speranza ha fior del verde.* M. Legouis cites St. John of the
Cross that hope is a "prado de verduraz." The contrast Marvell
here makes had already been made by Marini in his *Della
Speranza,* to my earlier citation from which the reader may

turn; though Marini's poem is a mere series of conceits upon a concept and Marvell's a personal lyric, *Della Speranza* offers a striking parallel to Marvell's theme and to his symbolism. There is also a tantalizing echo of a popular Italian saying which might have clung to Marvell's memory, and to which we are led by the later lines,

> Annihilating all that's made
> To a green Thought in a green Shade.

In Italy, candles set on altars were often colored green at the lower ends; and in the literature of color symbolism Fulvio Pellegrino (Morato) in his *Significato dei Colori e de Mazzoli,* goes with considerable antiquarian lore into the origin of this practice to prove that green is not the color of hope but of failure of hope. He certainly seems to show that the custom was the origin of some uses of the term green, as in Sonnet XXXIII of Petrarch. His own color theories he embodied in a sonnet in answer to one by Serafino. And this sonnet begins with the line, *Il color verde ridutto a niente dimostra.*[23] His sonnet, as he himself tells us, won him only ill will; and Serafino's interpretations, in which green is hope or love, remained the accepted ones. But could the line have been seen by Marvell and remembered, even while he forgot Pellegrino's interpretation, or is it the record of a popular saying that he might have heard in Italy? Carducci and Ferrari cite a reference by Leopardi to the candle and to the popular saying to explain the line in Petrarch: "Dicesi tolto della candela tinta in verde nel fine, ove guinto il lume poco sta ad esser del tolto consumato: E piu de parlar familiare." The candle itself had been cited by Daniello in his commentary on Petrarch.

The use of green in this sense of hope marks the philosophic focus of Marvell's thought in this poem. In *Upon Appleton House* in "this yet green, yet growing ark," the adjective has wider, more general connotations of living, springing life and expresses a more undetermined thought. These connotations are still present as overt ones in *The Garden,* especially in the later stanza, and keep directly before our senses the experience on which Marvell rests his thought. For that reason closer still than the passages I have referred to is Stradling's translation of Lipsius, for there symbol is only suggested, if at all, as a hovering implication of immediate experience. And closest of all in blending of experience and symbol is a passage in Hugh of St. Victor's book of the creatures from the description of the beauty of the world:

Postremo super omne pulchrum viride, quomodo animos intuentium rapit; quando vere novo, nova quadam vita germina prodeunt, et erecta sursum in spiculis suis quasi deorsum morte calcata ad imaginem futurae resurrectionis in lucem pariter erumpunt. Sed quid de operibus Dei loquimur? Cum etiam humanae industriae fucos adulterina quadam sapientia fallentes oculos tantopere miramur?[24]

In this setting, the full and precise religious implication of Marvell's term *am'rous* and its relation to the tradition of the *raptus* of profane love by sacred, which goes back to Origen, needs no comment.

Marvell's Latin version is closer in expression to neo-Latin poetry than to the French poetry he may well have had running through his memory, and the roll of the names in the Latin of the mistresses banned from the garden specifically evokes Horace, Ovid, and the elegists: Neaera, Chloe, Faustina, Corinna. But these poets had already been evoked by Théophile, for his mistress is Corine. And *On a Drop of Dew* has shown us how Marvell would think in terms of a contemporary or of an ancient tradition or idiom according as he wrote in English or Latin.[25] The carving of the names on the trees as a symbol of bringing passion into nature was running in Marvell's mind; for it is half transformed already in *Upon the Hill and Grove at*

Bill-borow. The concept was doubtless widespread. It had been used by St. Amant, in a perhaps more sophisticated way than by Orlando.

In the Latin version of Marvell's poem, it is the burning Ovidian passions of the gods which are evoked with some fulness of allusion. And the release from their fury is perhaps reminiscent of Latin visions of halcyon days. The opening line of the English stanza, "when we have run our passion's heat," in the literal sense of *passion's heat* possibly alludes, as Mr. King has suggested, to the torch of Cupid.[26] But perhaps both in the literal meaning and in the figurative picture of the race *heat* has rather the more simple and broadly symbolic meaning of the weary and consuming contest of the world and the appetites.

The religious note is, as yet, however, firmly but only lightly present in the stanza. It is the joy of art which the quiet of nature brings if she bring anything but her own joy. If Marvell had already turned his thought to Herbert and to his own *Coronet,* religion and art were not separate in his thought. But yet it is purely the classical sense of detachment, freedom, and joy in art which the lines express. And Pan will play this reed only to himself. Perhaps as Marvell wrote he remembered again St. Amant's

> O que j'ayme la solitude!
> C'est l'element des bons esprits,
> C'est par elle que j'ay compris
> L'art d'Apollon sans nulle estude,

for Marvell shares with St. Amant as much as he rejects. Perhaps only, the more general commonplace that it is in solitude that poets are inspired, a commonplace cited as such, for instance, by Erasmus in his early *De Contemptu Mundi,* in defense of monasticism and repopularized by the rhetorician Pontanus. One recalls how Pan was allegorized in the Renais-

sance, but that seems irrelevant here. One may also just fleetingly recall that Pan and his companions had had their place in
the happy garden of Bernardus Sylvestris, recall it not in specific
relation to Marvell but to remind one's self how wide and how
radical within Christian limits the justification of nature might
be. That Marvell's own poetic impulse owed a great quickening to Nun Appleton seems sure.

Then with startling suddenness we are absorbed in nature
herself.

What wond'rous Life is this I lead!

In the first stanza of the group formed by v, vi, and vii we are
still in the life of the senses. There is an almost sensual delight
in the bounty of nature to taste and touch. One thinks at once
of the fruit passage in *The Bermudas*:

> He makes the Figs our mouths to meet;
> And throws the Melons at our feet
> But Apples plants of such a price,
> No Tree could ever bear them twice.

But this vision of God's bounty is utterly stripped of the sensuous intensity of the ripe apples dropping on the head, the lus-
cious clusters of the vine crushing their wine on his lips, the
very feel of the nectaren and curious peach in the hand with
which the *Garden* stanza glows.

Many impulses meet in the stanza. It must be read first,
I think, in the light of the ivy stanza in *Upon Appleton House*.
It affirms the delight of the senses in nature; it rejects the conversion of this delight to erotic enhancement. It returns back
from passion to the pure joy in the creatures. There are two
French poems, of St. Amant and of Théophile, so suggestive for
these lines that we ought to have them in mind as a type of
thing which Marvell might well have read and which might
have contributed to his own handling of his experience.

The following lines from St. Amant's *Le Melon* indicate the sensuous delight and the tone as a whole of that poem.

LE MELON

Quelle odeur sens-je en cette chambre?
Quel doux parfum de musc et d'ambre
Me vient le cerveau resjouir
Et tout le coeur espanouir?
Ha! bon Dieu! j'en tombe en extase:

. . . .

Qu'est-ce donc? Je l'ay descouvert
Dans ce panier rempli de vert:
C'est un MELON, où la nature,
Par une admirable structure,
A voulu graver à l'entour
Mille plaisans chiffres d'amour,
Pour claire marque à tout le monde
Que d'une amitié sans seconde
Elle cherit ce doux manger,

. . . .

Baillez-le-moy, je vous en prie,
Que j'en commette idolatrie:
O! quelle odeur! qu'il est pesant!
Et qu'il me charme en le baisant!

After a brief humorous prayer that the melon may not be found to contain any of "le deaut des gens d'aujourd' huy," there is a full blazon as of a damosel or a Corine of the beauty of the interior of the fruit and a rhapsody upon its power to surpass all the precisely listed delights of the other fruits. Finally, a derivation of its growth on Parnassus introduces an extensive and not happy myth in another key and in another verse form.

Théophile's praise of the fruits is set in a more serious poem, the *Lettre à son frère,* and it is marked by tender recollection rather than by lively humorous sensibility. Lamenting his hard condition and his despair amid the ill wishes of his enemies, he

reflects that his life is in the hands of Heaven and not in theirs.
"J'espere toutefois au Ciel." Perhaps his destiny is about to
change,[27] and despite all that his adversaries can do, out of the
midst of the depression in which his senses can take delight only
in what makes them sad, he has not yet lost the hope that before
he dies he shall see Boussères and the countryside of his childhood.

> Je cueilleray ces abricots,
> Les fraises à couleur de flames,
> Dont nos bergers font des escots
> Qui seroient icy bons aux dames,
> Et ces figues et ces melons
> Dont la bouche des aquilons
> N'a jamais sceu baiser l'escorce.
> Et ces jaunes muscats si chers,
> Que jamais la gresle ne force
> Dans l'asile de nos rochers.
>
> Je verray sur nos grenadiers
> Leurs rouges pommes entr'ouvertes,
> Où le ciel, comme à ses lauriers,
> Garde tousjours des fueilles vertes.
> Je verray ce touffu jasmin
> Qui fait ombre à tout le chemin
> D'une assez spacieuse allée,
> Et la parfume d'une fleur
> Qui conserve dans la gelée
> Son odorat et sa couleur.
>
> Je reverray fleurir nos prez;
> Je leur verray couper les herbes;
> Je verray quelque temps après
> Le paysan couché sur les gerbes;

But in Marvell, we have not only turned from the fever of
the city to the tranquil friendliness of the country with a sly reminder, to a reader much versed in Renaissance discussion of
fame, with what labor fame is to be earned. His fruits are not

earned by the sweat of our brow. We have in them a joy greater than the joy of St. Amant. A gathering image of Paradise keeps suggesting to our fancy a thought which rises to the surface in the last line:

> Stumbling on Melons, as I pass,
> Insnar'd with Flow'rs, I fall on Grass.

Though the apple was the instrument of our Fall, Marvell is not thinking of that, but only of the riches of the fruits and flowers of Eden and of the earth. The cause is really woman. By her are ensnared the libertines who ought to love only the garden. St. Amant's verses suggest to us the humorous or burlesque tone, now turned by Marvell to a mockery of the French poet himself, in which we ought to read the lines. Yet with all this background in mind, to our modern ear there is something of violence in the stanza. This delight of the senses has for the moment taken possession of Marvell. And the sensuous pleasure of the garden is only a "pleasure less." Neo-Platonic concepts of the relation of this specific beauty to the ideal beauty are used just so far as a neo-Platonic view can be precisely filled with Marvell's own experience and can add to that experience, as it were, a fourth dimension of significance.

He has entered into the mind's own world, and the figures cease to be the figures of double value which in the earlier stanzas mark and keep constantly at work in the poem the choice between two worlds. The *hortus conclusus,* the enclosed garden, is the soul herself. The quaint conception "That all Animals of the Land, are in their kind in the Sea" is an emblem for the mind's possession of the forms of all things, forms through which it turns to their essence.

> Yet it creates, transcending these
> Far other Worlds and other Seas

may be read in the light of the passage from Ficino on the imagination quoted earlier, telling how things take on a larger beauty as they pass from individual objects to species in the phantasy, whence the mind receives them. *Annihilating* I take with Mr. Margoliouth in the sense of "reducing the whole material world to an immaterial thought," with something of a second meaning, considering all the world of created things as nothing compared to the hope of the eternal world brought to me by the beauty and the symbolism of this green shade.[28] He is still close to the immediate perception of the "yet green, yet growing ark" of *Upon Appleton House.* Yet his primary intention is here symbolic, marking the difference between the two poems. And the green thought is clearly that hope to which Fate's whole lottery is one blank and whose chase is

> The God of nature in the field of Grace.

The meditation on values and the definition completed, Marvell gives us in the next stanza an actual experience of transcendence, of which the meditation itself is a part. For is not the *various light* the multifold reflection in nature of the one essential Light from which nature springs? The closest analogue is that I have already quoted from Bonaventura.

> And as a certain light mixed with opacity is the way, so it is the way leading to the exemplar. Just as you have seen that a ray entering through the window is colored in various ways by the various colors of the various parts of the glass, so the divine ray shines variously in the particular creatures, and with various properties.[29]

Others may be found in Plotinus:

> That great soul must stand pictured before another soul, one not mean, a soul that has become worthy to look, emancipate from the lure, from all that binds its fellows into bewitchment, holding itself in quietude. Let not merely the enveloping body be at peace, body's turmoil stilled, but all that lies around, earth at peace, and sea at peace, air and the very heavens. Into that heaven, all that rest, let the great soul be conceived to roll inward at every point, penetrating, permeating, from all sides pouring its light. As the rays of the sun throwing their brilliance upon a lowering cloud make it gleam all

gold, so the soul entering the material expanse of the heavens has given life, has given immortality: what was abject it has lifted up; and the heavenly system, moved now in endless motion by the soul that leads it in wisdom, has become a living and a blessed thing; the soul domiciled within, it takes worth where, before the soul, it was stark body—clay and water—or, rather, the blankness of Matter, the absence of Being, and, as an author says, "the execration of the Gods."

* * * * *

Conferring—but how? As itself possessing them or not? How can it convey what it does not possess, and yet if it does possess how is it simplex? And if, again, it does not, how is it the source of the manifold?

A single, unmanifold emanation we may very well allow—how even that can come from a pure unity may be a problem, but we may always explain it on the analogy of the irradiation from a luminary—but a multitudinous production raises question.

* * * *

It must be a circumradiation—produced from the Supreme but from the Supreme unaltering—and may be compared to the brilliant light encircling the sun and ceaselessly generated from that unchanging substance.[30]

And others in the *Dialoghi d' Amore* of Leone Ebreo:

On the contrary, being unable to understand the pure unity of the divine object, it multiplies it relatively and by reflection into three, for a clear and single object cannot be impressed upon another less clear (and more complex) than itself unless its own exceeding brightness be multiplied into several lesser lights. Behold the sun, when it casts its rays upon the clouds, forming the bow: into how many colours its light is transformed by them reflecting it, or by water or a mirror. And in itself it is pure light without any colour of its own, yet it transcends and contains every other hue; so divine formality, which is perfect unity and simplicity in itself, cannot be imaged in another except by the reflection of its light and the multiplication of its formality.

Or again:

SOFIA: this sublime abstraction seems to mean that from the one depend the many separate causes. But give me an example. . . .

FILONE: I recall that I have given you a visible example of the sun and all the particular corporeal lights and colors. For though all depend on him, and in him exist as ideas all the essences of all the colors and lights of the universe, in all their degrees, yet in him they are not multiplied and divided. . . . And you see how when the pure sun imprints itself on a moist cloud opposite it, it makes the bow called iris. . . .[31]

Thus the soul of Marvell waves in its thought the various light of the creatures until she shall fly to God.

Just possibly there is in this stanza again some echo of St. Amant's *La Solitude* and of what the impulse of reading him may have contributed to this very different attitude of Marvell's.

> Que je trouve doux le ravage
> De ces fiers torrens vagabonds,
> Qui se precipitent par bonds
> Dans ce vallon vert et sauvage!
> Puis glissant sous les arbrisseaux,
>
> . . . . . .
>
> Que j'aime ce marets paisible!
>
> . . . . . .
>
> Là, cent mille oyseaux aquatiques
> Vivent, sans craindre, en leur repos,
> Le giboyeur fin et dispos,
> Avec ses mortelles pratiques.
> L'un, tout joyeux d'un si beau jour,
> S'amuse à becqueter sa plume;
> L'autre allentit le feu d'amour
> Qui dans l'eau mesme se consume,
> Et prennent tous innocemment
> Leur plaisir en cet élément.[32]

But for Marvell the creatures have become emblems. And yet not that, for an emblem is a detached object of meditation. Here at the very moment of meeting of Marvell's exquisite sensuous perception and his habitual feeling and his thought, the

bird has ceased to be an emblem and his experience of it has become an immediate psychological experience, a symbol in the
modern psychological sense of an organism of thought concretized around a particular intuition, and in the sense at least
half implied by Richard of St. Victor. His aesthetic joy in some
actual bird passes into a symbol of his soul's joy in the creation.

Thus, in a modified neo-Platonic psychology, the mind has a
vision so far as is possible while she is in this life of the divine
beauty wherein she had her origin. And yet I would not suggest that Marvell wished to describe any special religious experience. The experience he would awaken in us he describes
precisely, a tranquilizing, an enlargement, a unification of consciousness, in which what might have been only an evanescent
experience was fixed and given content by the religious thought
which entered to fill it. He interpreted it as a moment of pure
intelligential activity; in that sense an ecstasy. Yet I am con-
vinced we should be mistaken to think of it as a withdrawal
from the body in quite so explicit and, if I may say so, local a
sense as Donne describes in his poem. Rather it lies halfway
between that meaning and Milton's when he speaks of the
ecstasy of music. It is in perfect keeping with Marvell's strict
sense of the limitation of knowledge, an understanding of the
one light still only through the various lights, but an absolutely
dependable intuition; one in which the infusion of grace has
its part.

Whether in mediaeval hexaëmeral literature or in Florentine
Platonism, Platonic psychology is synthesized with Christian
revelation. And what is in neo-Platonic psychology the separation of the soul from the Divine Intelligence is in Christian history The Fall of Man and Original Sin. Are we for a moment
carried, in our recovered Innocence, back behind the Flaming
Sword? And is there in the opening lines of stanza VII a shadowy
background picture of Eden which catches up the suggestion of
stanza V?

> Here at the Fountains sliding foot,
> Or at some Fruit-trees mossy root ....

The student of English literature can hardly help looking forward to the opening of Milton's picture of Paradise and to the literature which lies back of it.

> Out of the fertil ground he caus'd to grow
> All trees of noblest kind for sight, smell, taste;
> Southward through *Eden* went a River large.

The tone of the Biblical reminiscences in *Upon Appleton House* affords a fruitful parallel. Yet if we see this picture, it is only in the barest fleeting suggestion. For *The Garden* is not an allegory of the Fall of Man. It is a lyric study of Marvell's experience. And the three stanzas have moved from imagination and a state of normal "discursive" thought in stanza v, in which the mind collects and compares many views of the world, into a state of ecstasy. It is only as the mind falls back from ecstasy that the thought of Eden becomes articulate.

And it is then an Eden from which man has long been banished, and the recollection of which only defines for him his present forlorn state.

As the moment of contemplation fades, the neo-Platonic pattern which came within the circle of the poem to interpret the contemplation moves out of view too. The condemnation of passion which has played so large a part in the poem is seen in stanza viii in one traditional mediaeval light. It is asserted with a crisp personal asperity.

> Wommannes conceil broughte us first to wo
> And made Adam fro Paradys to go.

The lines are so swift, spring so inevitably from the tide of feeling of the poem that to bring in any association from without seems heavy-handed. Yet did Marvell fleetingly and whimsically recall a rabbinic legend cited in Leone Ebreo and in

Browne, and therefore we know current, that in Paradise before the Fall Adam was an androgyne?

From this moment of wayward brooding on man's condition we return swiftly in the last stanza to the tranquillity of our Yorkshire garden. We are back in the world, a world that has become by our choice of retirement, ordered and innocent. Marvell perhaps remembers, as Miss Bradbrook and Miss Lloyd Thomas have pointed out, the books of garden emblems. But at least since Gregory of Nyssa that citizenly bee has inhabited the enclosed garden. The poet has returned also, in returning to the world, to the double image and pun.

> And, as it works, th' industrious Bee
> Computes its time as well as we.

Order is one through all the world of the creatures.

Does he remember, too, Virgil's bees? For the Latin sense of social order is not far from Marvell's thought. And does this humanist also just possibly remember his Elyot's *Booke of the Gouernour,* in which the personal and the social self are so deeply integrated? One could hardly find a more characteristic representation than in Elyot of the twofold concept of the individual in English Renaissance thought. And it is at the heart of Marvell's tradition, and of all his thought about the state. Even Venice as an example of a happily balanced state is present to Elyot's mind, as so probably to Marvell's.

For who can denie but that all thynge in heuen and erthe is gouerned by one god, by one perpetuall ordre, by one prouidence? . . . and to descende downe to the erthe, in a litell beest, whiche of all other is moste to be maruayled at, I meane the Bee, is lefte to man by nature, as it semeth, a perpetuall figure of a iuste gouernance or rule; who hath amonge them one principall Bee for theyr gouernour, . . . and with that all the residue prepare them to labour, and fleeth abrode, gatheryng nothing but what shall be swete and profitable, all though they sitte often tymes on herbes and other thinges that be venomous and stynkinge . . . .

But what nede we to serche so ferre from us, [for instances of disorder in states that try to live as it were in a communaltie] sens we haue sufficient examples nere unto us? . . . After that the Saxons by treason had expelled out of Englande the Britons, which were the auncient inhabitantes, this realme was deuyded in to sondry regions or kyngdomes. O what mysery was the people than in. O howe this most noble Isle of the worlde was decerpt and rent in pieces. . . .

The Bermudas calls for no comment in relation to the garden poems. But if my interpretation of the reading in the background of Marvell's thought be correct, what of *The Nymph Complaining for the Death of her Fawn?* Miss Bradbrook and Miss Lloyd Thomas, pointing out echoes of imagery from the Song of Songs and the implications of *deodand*, interpret the poem allegorically;[33] and Mr. Bush comments in his recent *English Literature in the Earlier Seventeenth Century, 1600–1660*, "if this have any ulterior meaning, it may be an Anglican's grief for the stricken Church."[34] With that view, recollections of the Song of Songs would well sort. To these comments may be added the note that the lines

> In this warm life blood which doth part
> From thine, and wound me to the heart

as well as in a more diffuse way some of the earlier lines, strongly suggest Crashaw's version of the mediaeval hymn, *Stabat Mater*. The rhythms also suggest Crashaw's exclamatory rhythms, and there are Marinistic overtones in the imagery. And yet the literal story is told with an actuality and precision that seem to defy allegorical forcing. In one present day reader, at least, of commentaries on the Song of Songs something of the same effect is awakened by the juxtaposition of the warm and sensuous poetry of the actual texts in Latin or English translation and the interpretations of them. Conceivably Marvell's imagination was affected in the same way. The Song of Songs was never interpreted by the great exegetes, of course, in continuous or syste-

matic allegory, except as symbolic significances might be given
to the *dramatis personae* of the formal epithalamie; but it was
translated verse by verse separately within an allegorical field,
and often with shifting meanings, the bride representing variously the Church, the individual soul, and the Virgin. Perhaps
Marvell's pastoral is to be read in that way. Possibly it is a
pastoral lyric of the symbolic parallels of which Marvell was
deeply aware, so that they pressed upon his imagination, without, however, ever verging into actual allegory. Such a reading
would accord with the sense one often has in Marvell that he
accepts elements of symbolic thought imaginatively without accepting them systematically.[35]

What, finally, of the *Dialogue between the Soul and Body,*
of which M. Legouis remarked that the body seemed to have
the last word, and of *To His Coy Mistress?* Marvell's poems, as
I have had frequent occasion to remind myself, are a series of
lyric commentaries upon life, not a philosophical poem. In his
early verse he assayed, like others of his time, what could be
said, not very seriously, from a number of points of view. But
from those exercises *To His Coy Mistress* is separated no less
by the genius—the concentration into a single effect—of its
music than by the depth of its treatment of its theme. Or one
may find that Marvell, like Yeats in our time, had never resolved the struggle to give final order to the passionate conflict
which experience and tradition had brought to his imagination, and that this unfixity of view explains his perfect imaginative sympathy with the lover. Yet Marvell and Yeats are divided by at least as much as they share; for so much which in
Yeats depended chiefly upon passionate apprehension Marvell
had steadily and detachedly assayed by the intellectual patterns
and habits of his civilization before his final passion took shape.
Moreover the garden poems, *On a Drop of Dew, The Coronet,*
the later Cromwell poems are very deeply committed. If for
a solution of the relation of these to *To His Coy Mistress* we turn

to the order of composition, we can make a surmise, though only a tentative one, as to the date of *To His Coy Mistress*. Its perfection of classical tone and diction and its imaginative relation to Catullus and Horace seem to place it near the *Horatian Ode* in time of writing. The tone of the blazon of the lady as well as the theme seem to place it when Marvell was not far out of touch with court poetry. The allowed elaboration of courtship which the mistress demands, slashed with the lover's sensuality, and pierced by the sharp irony of the close of the paragraph, might draw their immediacy of feeling from both a recollection and a mockery of court Platonism. But the seriousness of the debate is deepened when compared with the literature of court Platonism. For to the seventeenth-century ear the contest in the poem between life and time and eternity was even more sharply defined than to ours; it was just before the dissolution of the world that the Jews were to be converted. That precise religious consciousness, deepening into the somber, inverted religious echoes of the deserts of vast eternity, and, as Mr. Bush has suggested, of the ashes free from lust, and seeing so lucidly the iron gates of life, is chief among many elements, the twofold vision of the lady, the full contrasting image of chamber and tomb, the tone, the rhythms, which make the other *carpe diem* poems of the age which are often compared with it seem such dust motes in the sun compared to Marvell's lines. They give to it an intensity, a seriousness that the most explicit reading of every possible sensual allusion cannot touch and out of which we should not be surprised to see the later poems grow.

In *A Dialogue between the Soul and Body* the complaints of the body, too, are well within the range of Christian rebellion, the rebellion of an imagination deeply impregnated with Christian feeling. Its tone might be paralleled in the opening of Erasmus' *Enchiridion* in his description of the inevitable ennui of man in the world; and when George Herbert reads and sighs

> And wish I were a tree
> For sure then I should grow
> To fruit or shade. At least some bird would trust
> Her household to me, and I should be just,

he too is asking like Marvell's "body," in a weary moment and in terms very familiar to his age, that he might be spared the supreme human gift of free will for the unconscious instinctive perfection of the vegetative life. The conception of the union of body and soul in "I feel, that cannot feel, the pain" is, whether taken ironically or directly, a serious religious view.

In bringing to the fore certain aspects of the Christian tradition which contributed to shape Marvell's thought and art, I have necessarily passed over the influence of the classics and the classical tradition upon him, except incidentally. The form and design of his two poems on the marriage of the Lady Mary Cromwell and the Lord Fauconberg, probably his last lyrics, were very likely suggested by the tradition of song form. But they would remind us, if we needed reminder, how equally enduring was the impress on his spirit of the classicism which unites him with the stream flowing from the Latin poets, through the neo-Latin writers, through France, through Daniel, Jonson, Campion, Herrick, and which helps to separate him so far both from Donne and from Spenser. On its side, in diction, in traditional imagery, in that perfection of design which created the stanza of *An Horatian Ode,* and the exquisitely balanced structure of *Upon Appleton House* and *The Garden,* his classicism united with his rational and philosophical tradition to create the poise, lucidity, and control of his forms. And to his spirit it certainly contributed much of that flexibility which was the fruit of the mingling of two streams, and much of that final intellectual command of the elements of his passion and meditation which gives his poetry, within its limits, such supreme distinction.

It is perhaps but the accident of our ignorance as to the dates of Marvell's work which sets us wondering about the variety of points of view in a series of poems which are a lyric poet's expression of moments of vision, and of vision which he would himself have thought to be only partial. It may, further, well be only the false rigidity of our own conceptions of Renaissance and mediaeval Christianity which we are discovering to ourselves in the apparent mirror of Marvell, the room for skepticism, and the awareness of the role of ennui, being so large within the arc of that Christianity which included Erasmus and Montaigne, as well as Hooker. Marvell's poem on Lord Hastings is ironic and reserved in its theological statement. The very tentative poems in fashions prevailing among courtiers, which must be of about the same date, are more significant for craft than for substance. And then we come at a bound to his great poems, poems written within a very few years, poems marked equally by the certainty of their manner, the seriousness of their contemplation of their themes. And in all except the most obviously early and experimental of Marvell's poems, there is a singular unity of artistic tone. It is through this aesthetic unity that the singleness of Marvell, even in his doubt and through his varied approaches to the mystery of life, is to be felt and understood. Even if we had the dates of all his poems, we should only be watching the emergence in him of that poise of sensibility and intelligence of which, without the dating of his work, we are already aware. The same play of sense and tradition and imagination within firm and lucid intellectual comprehension comprises equally the lines on Cromwell, *To His Coy Mistress,* and *The Garden.* Of this poise both the classical and the metaphysical elements in his manner are instruments. To it they owe their perfect blending so that in reading his greatest verse, it is only by pausing and asking ourselves deliberate questions that we become conscious of the elements of his style in themselves. His integrity stands out, for instance, in comparison with a Carew, to whom the same elements supply the very stuff of his verse, rather than its mode, the classical and the dialectical exquisitely defining and arguing his assured limitation to the surface and the moment, the witty image serving only to show the dogma of accepted theology in a surprising garb. Marvell's style reveals to us the organization of a personality which, fixed in the isthmus of a middle state, insists upon the play of all the lights by which it imagines its situation, and sets its intelligence to work upon that imagination. Nowhere do we feel his quality more sharply than in his symbolism. In the use of some of the great symbolic patterns of mediaeval Platonism, Marvell is separated from Donne, and from Vaughan too, by the deepest habit of imagination, by the whole shaping influence of early education. For they grew up reading the Bible in the old schematic light, Marvell in the literal, rational Protestant way. And of all the radical divergences of thought in the seventeenth century, none is greater than that. Marvell is a rationalist, if we use rationalism in the sense of objectively oriented and critical, not readily surrendering the imagination to a great chain of symbol or extended myth. When he intimates a symbolic cosmogony or system of the world, he is always humorous or consciously metaphorical, and we are sensible that his strict limitation of reason will not let it follow far on this path toward which imagination leads the way. But where symbolic Platonism gives intellectual and grammatical form to aesthetic and moral intuition, it is for Marvell the simplest reality. As Mr. Bush has said, he did not, like Vaughan, surrender his best energies to the vision of another world; he set the longer flight for its due time. But if Vaughan has the distinction of absolute focus upon otherworldly reality, to Marvell belongs the distinction of seeing himself in the tide of time, without at all losing himself there. He preserved the world of symbolic thought not as a science but as a symbolic expression of that vision of the universe possible to man only in symbol. It best paralleled or explained, in discourse of reason, the experience of grace. We may call it a sense of the universe achieved by aesthetic intuition if we will allow aesthetic to mean no mere sensuous and perceptive delight but rather a fusing of tension; a falling into place, through the apprehension of the beauty of the world, of the values of personality; a becoming aware, by the consciousness, of its own true objects, and of the attitudes by which it may most fully attain them.

There is in Marvell a certain dryness of tone which may be related to the close precision of his diction, to the evenness of tension in his verse as compared to the rich and varied amplitude of Spenser and others earlier, of Milton in his own time; may be related to Jonsonian and to French classicism. But more significantly it may be felt as the sign of a deep reserve, a rational habit of imagination. And this has led him to be spoken of as a transitional figure, moving halfway toward so neoclassical a poet as Denham. Yet there is between them a radical difference in treatment of theme, which involves also such intimate matters of poetry as imagery and as the grammar and context of diction. In his greatest poetry, he is even farther from Denham than in his elegy on Hastings. Or one may compare his lines *On Little T. C.* with Prior's lines *To a Child of Quality,* which have some faint but significant resemblance to them in the situation of the speaker, in an almost echoing turn of words. Both poems, in situation and invention and in playfulness of tone, fall within the class of society verse. But a comparison of the points toward which the two move from that situation marks for us afresh how absolutely Marvell belongs to the great mediaeval and Renaissance structure built upon the Judaeo-Christian tradition. If we would look ahead to see Marvell in both directions of history, it is to Jonathan Swift that we must look. In Swift's irony there is a deep intellectual parallel, as well as a historical filiation, with Marvell's paradoxes, with Marvell's focus upon ethical intuition. And it is not fantastic to compare for a moment Swift's symbolic use of the popular literary forms—project, traveller's tale, fable—to express *his* paradoxes, with Marvell's use of the emblem image. Swift's, though the deeper and intenser vision, as well as the incomparably more comprehensive in its scope, is the narrower. And for Marvell, symbolic Platonism defined that immense play of imagination and thought and sensibility which the earlier seventeenth century still wished to include within the truth open to common apprehension, when reason had, indeed, moved to the strict exclusion of dogma and of the explication of the mysteries, but yet embraced a conception of grace and of the function of the imagination more otherworldly than what could be equated with common sense. And perhaps the imaginative relation of Marvell's garden poems to even so remote a work as Hawkins' *Parthenia Sacra* might serve as a symbol to remind us of all in the complex intellectual and spiritual life of the age which contributed to make it possible that he should write poems, like Sappho's in the garden of the anthology, roses, so few but so certainly great.

Appendix

POEMS AND EXTRACTS

POEMS AND EXTRACTS

IDEALLY, IT MIGHT have seemed wise to reprint for convenient reference all the elegies I have discussed in detail in Part I of this book. But to do so would have added to the bulk and to the expense of the volume beyond proportion to the value the reader would have gained. Accordingly I have refrained from reproducing all those which I have judged would be readily available in modern editions even in the library of a small college or of an amateur of the seventeenth century. Several which I have discussed in some detail and which have been reprinted, but which are not likely to be in such libraries, I have included, as a whole or in part. Of the three elegists on Hastings—Joynes, Bold, and Cave, whom I discussed together as in some sense heirs of Donne—I have selected the elegy of only one, judging it sufficient illustration.

1. From The Memorable Life and Death of ovr Late
Peerelesse Prince Henrie *by James Maxwell*

36

Lo Norths bright Star thus hath of late gone downe
In the South-point of this vnited Land:
His too swift course hath made him set too soone,
VVhen as his beames did blase o're sea and sand.

Our Orbe too base it was this Starre to beare;
For it was worthy of an higher spheare.

37

Lo the rare Pearle, that we of late haue lost,
A peerless Pearle, the Load-stone of this Ile;
VVhose worth did drawe from euery land and coast,
The eyes of strangers many thousand mile:
    But this heart-drawing stone great *Iames* his Gem
    More worthy was t'adorne *Ioues* Diadem.

38

Lo how the fragrant Lilly of this land,
The hands of Angels haue pluckt vp in haste,
Presenting it into *Iehouah's* hand;
For this Rose-Lilly did become him best:
    Saints Paradise good Lord how it adornes!
    Where floures are free from thistles & from thorns.

39

A Starre, a Pearle, a Flowre sith we haue lost,
Bright, rare, and faire, if we haue cause to mourne
God wote, man wote; loe that which cheer'd vs most
Now doth it to our greatest sorrow turne:
    HENRIE aliue did lighten euery part
    But *HENRIE* dead sends sorrow to each heart.

2. *From* The three Sisters Teares

by Richard Niccols

At length that noble Citie I beheld,
'Gainst whose broad brest the angry Riuer raues;

Yet backe repulst as being thereto compeld
He paies it tribute with his fish-full waues.

There did I heare (was neuer eare did heare
More diuers sounds) all which might yet content
The daintiest sense, to which I drew me neere
To know from whence they were, and what they ment.

And loe, I did behold, from off the shoares
Many light friggots, put into the deepe,
All trimly deckt, which by the strength of Oares
Through the swift streame their way did westward keepe.

Who in their course, like couples hand in hand,
(While their proud pennons did the welkin braue
And their shrill Musick eccho'd on the strand)
Did seeme to daunce vpon the bubbling waue.

And round about in many a gondelay,
Light-footed Nimphes and iolly Swaines did rowe,
Deuising mirth and dalliance on the way,
Not caring, how they sail'd, or swift, or slow.

So many varying and so vaine delights
Floating vpon that floud, I then did see,
Such diuers showes and such fantastick sights,
That *Thames* the Idle-lake then seem'd to be.

.   .   .   .

On you disdain'd of golden vanitie,
He dain'd to looke, and knowing sapience
To be the Garland of Nobility,
Did daily seeke your wisedomes influence,

But he is gone and few doe now remaine,
That doe not you and all your Arts disdaine.

Where are the worthies of those antique dayes,
Who woont, their Crownes and Scepters laid aside,
To girt their conquering browes with sacred Bayes,
For which their names be now eternized.
    They late did liue in him, that now is dead,
    And are with him againe rapt vp in lead.

For few doe now the sacred Nine esteeme,
That haue the gift of *Mydas* golden touch,
Science diuine, a fruitlesse thing they deeme,
And count the learned base for being such.
    O then let all that learned are lament
    His losse, whose life was learnings ornament.

  .   .   .   .

If death had giuen him leaue to lead you on,
And guide you through the crimson paths of warre,
Against the sonnes of strumpet *Babilon,*
Or those Philistines, that her Champions are,
    You with your swords were like to dig a Tombe,
    Wherein to burie all the Pride of *Rome.*

Of *Rome,* that would and will be Monster-head
Of all the world: who was so holy giuen,
That she of late with hot deuotion led,
VVould with one blast haue blowne me vp to heauen,
    Such hot hell-fierd zeale let all times know,
    Since time before the like could neuer show.

For this, had HENRY liu'd to lift his hand
To hunt from hence *Romes* Rats, that daily feed

Vpon the fat and glory of my land
And in my wounded bosome daily breed,
  I by his arme, like euer to be strong,
  Vpon the gates of *Rome* had grau'd this wrong.

For I did thinke (and who but so will thinke)
Had he but liu'd, that neuer in this land,
A fuller cuppe of glory I should drincke,
Then that which I did hope from HENRIES hand?
  For twice foure *Henries* haue beene Lords of mee,
  All which could not show greater hopes then hee.

. . . .

3. *From* Great Britans Mourning Garment

VI.

Sad Melancholy lead me to the Caue
Where thy black Incense and dim Tapers burne,
Let me some darke and hollow corner haue,
Where desolate my sorrowes I may mourne:
  And let thy heauiest Musick softly sound
Vnto the doleful songs that I recite;
And euer let this direfull voice rebound
Through the vast den: Ah dead is *Britans* light;
  Then if thy heart be with compassion mou'd
Of my Laments, come rest thy self by me,
And mourne with me, for thou hast euer lov'd
To beare a part in euery Tragedie:
  And if to plaints thou wilt inure thy mind,
  Thou neuer couldst a fitter season finde.

. . . .

X.

You sacred Forrests, and you spotles streams
That part the flowry medowes with your fall,
You water-Nymphes and Ladies of the Tea'ms,
And thou dread Thamesis, mother of them all;
   With brinish teares weep in your sandy Ford:
Weep fields, and groues, and you poore Driads weep,
The sodaine Funerall of our Brittish Lord,
Whose eyes are now clos'd vp in iron sleepe.
   Both trees, and streams, lament his loss that lov'd
Your siluer waters, and wide spreading shades,
But now is farre away from you remoov'd,
Vnto a Paradice that neuer fades,
There in eternall happinesse to remaine,
But we in sorrow here, and ceasless paine.

.   .   .   .

XVI.

I Muse from whence these forward tears shold flow
Or when our minde of secret griefe complaines,
Why though vnwilling through our eyes wee show
The inward passion of our hidden paines.
   I know our sighes are but the cooling ayre,
Wherewith our fainting heart we doe sustaine,
That els would smother in her owne despaire,
All comfort thankles breathing back againe.
But wherefore Nature should in open view,
Create two fountaines full of liuing source:
Whether so soone as we find cause to rue,
Our Passions make their generall recourse
     Who knowes? Vnlesse thereby we should reueale
     That our true sorrowes we should not conceale.

4. On the vntimely Death of the incomparable
Prince, Henry *by Sir Henry Goodyere*

First, let me ask my Self, why I would trye,
Vnmeasur'd Griefs, in measur'd lines, to tie;
Or think *poëtik Magick* should enclose
In such a Circle All-surmounting Woes.
Next; let me ask my Hearers: Will not They
Think, I take part with *Death,* what-e'r I say?
For, Thus to measure, is t' *Eclipse* this Sunne,
And re-diminish him, as *Death* hath donne.
Him let me aske; Will not *Hee* think, that This
Som wrong to Him, and som de-merit is,   [10
That I should be thus carefull to expresse
Our Losse, and leaue out His great *Happiness?*
Will not *Hee* think, that by *lamenting* Thus
His leauing of these Kingdomes and of Vs,
Wee doo not towards his new-got Kingdome striue,
Where He is *Crownd,* his Fathers both alyue?
But I'll aske none: I neither aske relief
Nor counsell now of anie, but my Grief.
Self-preseruation moues me: I shall break
If I stay, thinking still, and doo not speak.   [20
But, What? At least expresse thy Grief this way,
In saying that thou know'st not what to say:
Say, that It might be thought some pietie,
To grieue that thou griev'st not sufficiently;
As Charitie, in greatest Sinner's Case,
Admits such grief for some degree of grace.
Say, that As *Artists,* which pretend to take
Great Heights with little Instruments, doo make
Vnpardonable Errors; so would I,
His Greatnes, Goodnes, or our Miserie   [30
Thus to descriue, or who-soeuer shall
Work in this mist of Grief which shadowes all;

This Grief, that vniversally so infects,
That each Face is a Glasse whence it reflects.
For, as who doth ten thousand Glasses try,
Receiues his owne Face back into his eye:
So, if on twenty millions you light,
Each Face reflects your owne Grief in your sight;
Grief, which from vs must be deriued so,
As many Learned thought our Soules to goe,   [40
By *Propagation;* and must reach to all
The After-born, like *Sinn Originall.*
And there's now no way left vs, to preuent
This Miserie, except This Age consent
To burn all *Records of HIS Historie;*
To burn his *Tombe,* and euery *Elegie;*
To burn His *Proiects* all; and so keep hid
All that was donne for Him, and what Hee did:
That so, our Heires may neuer come to knowe
His *Worth,* Our Loss; so to inherit Woe.   [50
But, That were an uniust Impiety.
Better they suffer, then His Worth should dye.
Besides: 't were Vain; since *Nature* hath, wee see,
Fore-told All (as it were) by *Prophcie.*
She made our World Then, when Shee made His Head:
Our Sense, Our Verdure, From His Brain was bred.
And, as *Two great Destructions* haue and must
Deface, and bring to nothing, That of *Dust;*
So, Our true *World,* This Princes *Head* and *Brain,*
A wastefull *Deluge* did and *Fire* sustain.   [60
But, as Fore-sight of *Two* such *Wastes,* mad Seth
Erect *Two Columnes,* t' ovt-liue the Worlds death,
Against the Flood and Flame, of *Brick* and *Stone;*
In which he hath by his Prouision,
Preserv'd from *Barbarisme* and *Ignorance*
Th' ensewing Ages; and did re-advance

All *Sciences,* which he engraued There:
So, by *our* SETH's Prouision haue wee, Heer,
Two Pillars left; where, what so-e're wee priz'd
In Our lost World, is well *Characteriz'd.*   [70
The list'ning to this *Soueraine Harmonie,*
Tames my Grief's rage; that now, as ELEGIE,
Made at the first *Mourning,* hath bin since
Imploy'd on *Loue, Ioy,* and *Magnificence;*
So this particular *Elegie* shall enclose
(Meant for my Grief for HIM) with Ioy for THOSE.

5. A Griefe on The Death of Prince Henrie
by Cyril Tourneur

Good *Vertue* wipe thine eyes, Looke vp and see!
And wonder to behold it. Some there be,
That weepe not; but are strangely merrie, dance,
And reuell. Can the losse of HIM aduance
The heart of any man to such a mirth?
Can His graue be the womb, from whence the birth
Of pleasure riseth? *Pity them, Their woe*
Distracts 'em, and they know not what they doe.
Yet note 'em better. Be they *wicked* men,
Their shew of *Ioy* is *voluntarie* then.   [10
For now the *President* of *vertu's* dead,
Vice hopes to get her courses licenced.
Dead! T'is aboue my knowledge how we liue
To speake it. Is there any *Faith* to giue
The promises of *health* or *remedy?*
Or any *Meane* to be preserued by;
When *Temperance,* and *Exercise* of breath,
(Those best *Physitians*) could not keepe from death
The strength of *Nature?* Was HEE temp'rate? whence
(Then) Came HEE subiect to the violence   [20

Of sicknesse? Rather was HEE not inclin'd
To *pleasures? Infinitely;* still HIS mind
Was on them; *Infinitely;* For HIS *loue*
No *Obiects* had, but those which were aboue
The causes of *vexation;* such, as *done,*
Repented not the pleasures they begun,
But made them endlesse; Nothing had the might
To dis-effect his *Actions* of delight.
No; nor HIS *suffrings.* For although HEE knew,
That sicknesse came from earth to claime her due;   [30
And to depriue HIM of that fortunate
Succession to the greatnesse of the *State,*
Which HEE was borne to; *that* did likewise please
And added nothing vnto HIS *disease.*
Of HIS *contentments* heere, that was the best.
Therefore the last; that it might crowne the rest,
But these are not the pleasures that decay
The body. How hath death (then) found a way
To ONE so able? HEE was *yong* and *strong.*
Vnguiltie' of al *disorder* that could wrong   [40
HIS *Constitution.* Doe no longer hide
It, t'was to vs a *plague* whereof HEE died.
A *plague* by much more common to vs, then
The last great sicknesse. Many more the men
Who suffer in it. That which now is gone,
Was but the *Figure,* of a greater One
To follow. Since the first that e'er was borne,
A fuller number was not knowne to mourne.
For all the *old Men* of the *Kingdomes* weepe,
Since HE that promis'd by HIS *strength* to keepe,   [50
Their *children* free from *others* violence,
And by *example* from their *owne* offence,
Is taken from 'em. And they would haue died
When HE did, but for tarying to prouide

A *second* care for that they would haue left
To Hɪᴍ, of whose *protection* th'are bereft.
If we doe well consider their iust woes,
We must include our yong men too, in those,
And grieue for euer: For our old mens teares,
Are rather for the time *to come,* then theirs.   [60
If they that shall not liue to suffer much
Vnder this cause of *sorrow,* vtter such
A passion for it, *more* it does belong
To *vs* that now are *growing* to it, *yong;*
As if our *generations* had intent,
We should be *borne* to feele the *punishment.*
Now let vs *willingly* giue griefe regard,
Least we be *forc'd* to doe it *afterward,*
By *Heauen's* iust anger. Stay a little. Why
Should yong men thinke the old shall sooner die?   [70
Hɪꜱ youths great broken promise wee complaine.
Yet none was greater. And are ours lesse vaine?
Mistake not. As *Humanitie* now goes,
Hᴇᴇ liu'd a *Man* as long as any does.
For (onelie) in those *Minutes* that wee giue
To *Vertue,* wee are *Trulie* said to liue
Men, and no longer. If we recken then,
Hɪꜱ good houres, with the good of other Men;
Hɪꜱ Times whole added numbers will arise,
To his, that tels out foureskore ere he dies.   [80
To prooue this, looke as low as ere you can,
And heare the words of the deiected Man;
The *Souldier* speakes them. *Honour! Now I see,*
There is no hope that any Age will be
So good and noble as the ancient were.
None so Heroique euer shall appeare.
For if that Fate, (which cannot be withstood)
Had not decreed, there should be none so good,

Shee would not haue neglected such a worth
As His *was, to haue brought that great worke forth.*   [90
But hauing purpos'd it should neuer be,
And hearing euery where by Fame, that Hee
Was making one, she kill'd Him.—Marke his eye;
Hee weepes. *He* weepes, that can more easilie
Weepe *Bloud* than *Water.* Then I wonder, how
Or *He,* or anye other *Souldier,* now,
Can hold his *sword vnbroken;* since Hee was,
That gaue them *Count'nance.* That's the Cause (alas)
They doe not *breake* them; and a iust excuse.
They weare them *now,* to keepe them from *abuse.*   [100
For that great *fauour* now has made an *end,*
That their despis'd conditions did *defend.*
Artes too, are so discourag'd by their harmes,
In losse of Him, who lou'd both *them* and Armes,
That they would all leaue *studie* and decline
From *Learning,* if those *Naturall* and *Diuine*
Perswading *Contemplations,* did not leade
The *One* to *Heauen,* the *other* to the *dead*
(Betweene whose *parts,* they haue diuided His)
And promise, *so,* to bring them where Hee is.   [110
But I would haue their *studies* neuer die
For preseruation of His *Memorie.*
How can *that* perish? That will euer keepe,
Because th' impression of it is so deepe.
When any *Painter* to the *life,* that saw
His *presence* fullie, takes in hand to draw
An *Alexander,* or a *Cæsar;* 'his best
Imaginations will bee so posses't
With His *Remembrance,* that as Hee does limme,
Hee'l make that *Worthie's* picture like to Him.   [120
And then t'will be a *Piece* of such a *Grace,*
For *Height* and *Sweetnesse,* as that onely *Face*

Will make another *Painter*, that ne'er knew
HIM liuing, follow as the other drew.
How great a *Character* deserues HEE then
Whose *Memorie* shall but expire with men?
When a Diuine, or Poet, sets downe right,
What other Princes should bee, Hee shall write
What THIS *was.* That's HIS *Character*, which beares
My sorrow inward, to goe forth in teares.   [130
Yet some of Ioy too, mix'd with those of *Greefe*,
That flow from apprehension of releefe.
I see HIS *spirit* turn'd into a *starre;*
Whose *influence* makes that HIS owne *Vertues* are
Succeeded iustlie; otherwise, the *worst*,
As at HIS *Funerall* should proceede the *first*.
HIS *Natiue goodnes*, followes in HIS *Roome;*
Else good Men would be buried in HIS *Tombe*.
O! suffer this to be a faithfull verse;
To liue for euer, weeping o'er HIS *Herse*.   [140

6. An Elegie On the vntimely Death of the incomparable
        Prince Henry *by G. G.*

Not as the people that are hir'd to crie
And howle at euery Great-mans Obsequie:
Nor as *The Wits*, that closely wooe Applause
By curious handling This sad common Cause:
Nor toucht in *My particular* at all,
By any future *Hope*, or present *Fall*
(For, This Man's Eye was neuer cast on Mee;
Nor could I dreame that euer it should bee):
Nor do I, with the fashion, *Mourne* in *Black;*
My *Sorrow's* in my Heart, not on my Back;   [10
Where I do *weep*, because *Wee* haue no Sense
Of true *bemoaning* greatest Excellence.

With idle Rimes wee blot white spot-les papers
(Whose best vse is to make *Tobacco* Tapers).
There, striuing to out-strip each others braine.
We shew how vaine we are, to shew our veine;
Foolishly thinking, in a *measur'd* Verse,
A *Losse* beyond *Dimension* to rehearse.
When yee do write of *Loue* and *pleasant* things,
Then smooth your Lines: but, in the *Losse of Kings*   [20
When all Eyes *weep,* and all true Hearts do *bleed,*
Please no-man with a Line that he shall read.
And, of This PHOENIX, that is lately fled
To Life from hence, where all that liue are dead,
Onely pronounce, but with a voyce of Thunder,
Prince HENRY's gon: and leaue the world to wonder
What Plot of *Prouidence* it is, to showe
Such *Iewels*, and then snatch them from vs, so.

7. *From* The Mvses Teares *by Sir John Davies*

.   .   .   .

The *Doing-Horse* (all Eyes can witnesse it)
He made much more than *Do:* yet, fate so sure
As they (but where are they that so can fit?)
That back the wildest *Beasts,* yet, sit secure!
In few; no *Feate* of such *Actiuity*
As graced *Action,* and the *Actor* too,
But it (with most admir'd *Agility*)
He did past all that best, so young, could do!
With *Arts* and *Letters* hee so stor'd his MIND
That both knew all therein, y'er *Youth* could know: [10
So, *Arte* and *Nature* were as *Curst,* as *Kind,*
To *Cleaue* so to him, and to *Leaue* him so!
His *Spirit* and *Body* were at endlesse strife

Which should be *Actiu'st* in all Princely *Parts:*
For, both were full of *Grace,* as full of *Life;*
Both which winne *Glory,* with both *Hopes,* and *Hearts!*
That actiue *Spirit* his *Meditations* rais'd
Aboue the *Spheare* of GREATNES; that doth rise
From those *Perfections* that do perish prais'd,
To seek PERFECTION prais'd; and neuer dies!   [20
And, like a *Soule* (that nought on *Earth* can fill)
Seeking for al-suffizing *Aliments,*
Still mounts aboue her selfe (in *Minde,* and *will*)
Till she hath found what fully her contents:
So, his rare *Soule,* (beeing euer on her VVings,
Soone cloide with whatsoe're the *Earth* holds deere)
Sought to suffize her with eternall *Things;*
Which made her stay so much the shorter here!
The *World* could not containe her; not as He
To whose ambition *Earths* Rotundity   [30
Seem'd but an *Angle:* no; but Shee did flee
The *VVorld,* and such vaine *Pride;* yet, fled more high!
She fled to Him whose *Center's* euerywhere,
Circle no where: for, true *Eaglet,* She
On *Iustice* SONNE (her Eyes being *strong,* as *cleare*)
Still lou'd to looke, to shew her *Dignity!*
But, while She kept within her *Prison-walls*
(Or *Iaile* of *Flesh*) She, through the *windowes,* saw
To all that in *Discretions* Compasse falls;
And, ordred all that *All* by *Reasons* Law.   [40
His *Seruants* so hee swai'd (and that alone,
Himselfe beeing vnder *Tutors*) as appear'd
That they were gouern'd by some *Solomon;*
For which he was no lesse *Belou'd,* than *Fear'd.*
Reward and *Punishment* (being as the weights
By which our *Horologe of life* is mou'd)
Fell euer through Him (from Celestiall Heights)

On none, but whom true *vertue* loth'd, or lou'd!
If then, his *Priuate* in such order stood,
How had the *publike* done when hee had swaid?   [50
They had beene like for *Grace,* in likely-hood;
And (for our *Common-good*) as *Good,* as *staid!*
The *High'st* all good things hath in Essence still;
Ill, in his *Vnderstanding-pow'r;* but *Man*
Hath good things by *Intelligence;* but ill
He hath in *Essense:* for, no *Good* he can!
But He, whose *goodnesse* rauish'd him from hence,
Was *Good,* in *Nature;* by his BEING, blest:
But *Ill* he had but by *Intelligence;*
Which he, with *Grace,* corrected, being best!   [60
Some *Kings* are more than *Men* in their beliefe;
But, in their liues such *Beasts* as neuer liu'd:
The Chiefe *Offenders* than, are oft the CHIEFE:
But this, *Belou'd,* liu'd well, and well beleeu'd!

.   .   .   .

Oh! *Eloquence,* (the *Routher* of our Minde,
Swaing th' *Affects* thereof, which way it lists)
Ioyne with our *sighes* (now) like resistlesse Winds
To loose our *soules* in *sorrowes* endlesse Mists:
For *Griefe* enforc'd by *Fate,* and *Eloquence*
(Oh FORCE that still the owne desires fulfils)   [70
Than *Tyrants* sway, hath no lesse violence
Ore our weake *soules,* that worke but what it Wils!
Yet nought's more eloquent than TRVTH (most strong!)
Than our tru Grief (that seas of *sorrow weeps*)
Must mooue al *Mindes* by th' *Engin* of our *Tongue*
To floate to endlesse Woes on DOLORS *Deepes.*
Men must be wrought like *Ir'ne;* that's first made soft
With *fire,* yer *water* cooles it: *fires* of VVit
Must make them more than supple (sure, and oft)
Y'er Teares can coole strong *passions* burning-fit.   [80

Than, if my Wit were great, as is the CAVSE
Of this our *sorrow,* it should so enflame
The World with *passion* as it ne're should pause
To showre forth streames of Teares to quench the same!
But so this *Griefe* distracts it, that it can
But make imperfect Offers; it's too cold
To thaw the frozen Hearts of euery *Man:*
For *Death* (not *Dolor*) hath all hearts in hold.
Oh *words!* O *sence!* how sencelesse both wee hold
(Though most significant) that cannot curse   [90
This *Day* past execration; would yee could
(And I had you to vse) do that, or worse!
But why, O why! doe I accursed *fend,*
So curse the *Day* wherein He so was blest
For whose cause so I curse? My knees I bend,
And begge for *Grace,* sith t'was in *Minde* distrest.

.   .   .   .

8. [Elegy on Edward King] *by Joseph Beaumont*

When first this news, rough at the sea
From whence it came, began to be
Sigh'd out by fame, and generall tears
Drown'd him again, my stupid fears
Would not awake; but fostering still
The calm opinions of my will,
I said, The sea, though with disdain
It proudly fomes, does still remain
A slave to him, who never wrought
This piece so fair to wash it out.   [10
I check't that fame, and told her how
I knew her trade, and her; nay, though
Her honest tongue had given before

A faithfull Echo, yet his store
Of grand deserts, which did prepare
For envies tooth such dainty fare,
Would tempt her now to fain his fate
And then her lie for truth relate.
  But when mature relation grew
Too strong for doubts, and still the new   [20
Spake in the same disasterous grone
With all the old; my hopes alone
Could not sustain the double shock
Of these reports and of the rock:
And when the truth, the first (alas!)
That e're to me deformed was,
Escap'd the sea, and ougly-fair
Did shine in our beloved aire,
At length too soon my losse I found,
Him and my hopes together drown'd.   [30
Oh! why was He (be quiet tears)
Complete in all things, but in yeares?
Why did his proper goodnesse grace
The generous lustre of his race?
Why were his budding times so swell'd
With many fruits, which parallel'd
Their mutuall beauteous selves alone,
In vertues best reflection?
As when th' Hesperian living gold
With priviledg'd power it self did mould   [40
Into the apples, whose divine
And wealthy beams could onely shine
With equall splendour in the graces
Of their brethrens answering faces.
Why did his youth it self allot
To purchase that it needed not?
Why did perfection seek for parts?

Why did his nature grace the Arts?
Why strove he both the worlds to know,
Yet alwayes scorn'd the world below? [50
Why would his brain a centre be
To learnings circularitie,
Which though the vastest arts did fill
Would like a point seem little still!
    Why did discretions constant hand
Direct both his? why did he stand
Fixt in himself, and those intents
Deliberate reasons help presents?
Why did his well-immured mind
Such strength in resolution find, [60
That still his pure and loyall heart
Did in its panting bear no part
Of trembling fear; but having wrought
Eternall peace with every thought,
Could with the shipwrack-losse abide
The splitting of the world beside?
The universall axle so
Still boldly stands, and lets not go
The hold it fastens on the pole,
Though all the heavens about it roll. [70
    Why would his true-discerning eye
His neighbours excellencies spie,
And love those shadows his own worth
Had upon others darted forth?
Whom he with double love intends,
First to make good, and then his friends.
Why did he with his hony bring
The med'cine of a faithfull sting,
And to his friend when need did move
Would cease his praise but not his love? [80
Why made his life confession,

That he more mothers had then one?
Why did his duty tread their way
His generall Parent to obey,
Whil'st in a meek and cheerfull fear,
His whole subjection he did square
With those pure rules, whose load so light
Confesse a mother did them write?
Why did his whole self now begin
With vertuous violence to win   [90
Admiring eyes? Why pleased he
All but his own sweet modestie?
Why gave his noble worth such ground
Whereon our proudest hopes might found
Their choicest promises, and he
Be Expectations treasurie?
O why was justice made so blind?
O why was heaven it self so kind,
And rocks so fierce? O why were we
Thus partly blest? O why was he?   [100
   Whil'st thus this senselesse murmure broke
From grieving lips, which would have spoke
Some longer grones, a sudden noise
Surpriz'd my soul; which by that voice
Hath learn'd to quiet her self, and all
Her questions into question call.
She saw his soul too mighty grow,
To be imprison'd thus below;
And his intelligence fitted here,
As if intended for a sphere.   [110
His spirits which meekly soar'd so high,
Grew good betimes, betimes to die.
And when in heaven there did befall
Some speciall businesse which did call
For present counsel, he with speed

Was sent for up. When heaven has need,
Let our relenting wills give way,
And teach our comfort thus to say;

Our earth hath bred celestiall flowers:
What heaven did covet, once was ours.

9. [Elegy on Edward King]
by W. More

I do not come like one affrighted, from
The shades infernall, or some troubled tombe;
Nor like the first sad messenger, to wound
Your hearts, by telling how and who was drown'd.
I have no startled hairs; nor their eyes, who
See all things double, and report them so.
My grief is great, but sober; thought upon
Long since; and Reason now, not Passion.
Nor do I like their pietie, who to sound
His depth of learning, where they feel no ground,   [10
Strain till they lose their own; then think to ease
The losse of both, by cursing guiltlesse seas.
I never yet could so farre dote upon
His rare prodigious lifes perfection,
As not to think his best Philosophie
Was this, his *skill in knowing how to die.*
No, no, they wrong his memorie, that tell
His life alone, who liv'd and di'd so well.
I have compar'd them both, and think heavens were
No more unjust in this, then partiall there.   [20
Canst thou believe their paradox, that say
The way to purchase is to give away?
This was that Merchants faith, who took the seas
At all adventures with such hopes as these.

Which makes me think his thoughts diviner, and
That he was bound for heaven, not Ireland.
  Tell me no more of Stoicks: Canst thou tell
Who 'twas, that when the waves began to swell,
The ship to sink, sad passengers to call,
Master we perish, slept secure of all ?   [30
Remember this, and him that waking kept
A mind as constant, as he did that slept.
Canst thou give credit to his zeal and love,
That went to heav'n and to those fires above
Rapt in a fierie chariot? Since I heard
Who 'twas that on his knees the vessel steer'd
With hands bolt up to heaven, and since I see
As yet no signe of his mortalitie;
Pardon me, Reader, if I say he's gone   [40
The self-same journey in a watry one.

10. On the untimely death of Henry Lord Hastings
by Thomas Pestel

Up, Beldame *Muse!* thy Climacterick's past:
But one work more; thy lastingst, if not last.
Lord *Hastings* glorious shade before us stands,
Whose Vertue exacts this Duty from our hands:
'Twill be a Night-piece, friends: Here never seek
Lucie large-soul'd, and *Ferdinand* the meek;
Who both esteem'd it braver work and worth,
To bring this Son up, then t'have brought him forth.
He th' Exposition to their double Text,
The Glass wherein they saw themselves reflext;   [10
He, that was He, and She, and both in one,
Both she and he, all three, in him are gone.
This Sun-set all obscur'd: with Ætna prest,

Their burning Giant Grief can take no rest.
To print so black a Sorrow fair, I want
Gold-plate for Paper, Pen of Adamant.
Veils on those chief Close-mourners faces spread;
I pencil out all gentler eyes in Red
Swoln lids; as having spent their bottom-store
Of precious dew-drops, till their hearts are sore;   [20
Which fast congeal'd Balm has his Herse infixt
In Chrystal Case, with Pearl and Amber mixt.
Rare Monument! but cannot him refine,
So rich a Saint impov'rishing his Shrine.
Was he not purest, fairest, wisest, best?
All Graces magazin'd, yet unexprest.
When his bright Bodies eminence I view'd,
With such a soveraign Intellect indu'd,
So just and ponder'd Temp'rature to finde,
So early ripe, so richly matcht in Minde;   [30
Choice Gem of Nature, set in Nurturing Gold,
Exulting Fancy quick conceiv'd the Mold
Was ready now, wherein th'Almightie's hand
Wou'd cast new Nobles, and restore the Land;
Whose finest Gold, if in compare it bring,
Is sure to finde his strong *Mercurial* Sting.
He caus'd us hurl our Vows, and gave free scope
To change our Wishes into Present Hope.
But O *Sydneian!* O Blood-Royal Fate!
Great Britains curse, whose sinful, shameful State   [40
Makes all Heroick Vertue soon decay;
Which mad she throws, or just God takes away.
So fell our *Ripheus* in *New Troy,* left he
Perchance her Fires and instant Ruine see:
For will that sacred Thundrer never powre
On such a *Sodom* his revengeful showre?
Where Lust and Pride, with their five brethren stand

In bold defiance of his armed hand:
Where Lords and Gentry, mindless of white Fame,
Graceless of old, are now beneath all Shame.   [50
  Pardon, fresh Saint, to set thy shining Good
With such coarse foils, to make it understood:
To topless height, from their base depth below,
Thy flaming Pyramid of Praise wou'd grow.
But for thou joy'ft th'applause of Angels there,
How frivolous are our weak Ecchoes here!

11. On the incomparable Lord Hastings An Elegie
by Joseph Joynes

To speak thy Praises, or our Sorrows, now,
Are both impossible. Alone they know
(Exalted Soul) thy worth, who now above
Converse with thee by Intellect and Love.
Grief onely, and dumb Admiration, are
The Legacies thou hast bequeth'd us here.
This onely woful Comfort's left us now;
Our Misery's compleat: Fate knows not how,
Beyond this, to inflict another wound:
"They fear not falling, that lie on the ground["]   [10
  Not perfect Bankrupt was this Land till now,
Nor her sick lapsed desp'rate state below
The hopes of all recovery: till His fall,
We could not justly say we had lost All.
We could not say, while he was yet alive.
Truth and Religion did not still survive:
There was a Church and Academy still:
All Vertue, whilst he liv'd, they could not kill.
Justice and Honour, whatsoever's good,
Was not yet fled from Earth to Heaven. Still stood   [20
In him (that Cypher for these many yeers)

Th'opprest, and now quite ruin'd House of Peers.
All these, not lost, but outlaw'd, did conspire,
To him, as to their centre, to retire.
　　But he is gone; and now this carcase, World,
Is into her first, rude, dark Chaos, hurl'd.
Vertue and Knowledge now for Monsters go:
To grope out Truth henceforth, how shall we do?
Or finde what's Just or Sense? To whom repair,
To let us know those things have been (not are.)
Further then him, before, you need not move,　　　　[30
To learn the *Placits* of the Porch or Grove.
Or had you pleased to consult the Sprite
Of the deep *Samian,* or *Stagyrite,*
Cordova's Sage, or him that did renown
The scarce-before-him-known *Boeotian* Town,
Rome, Athens, Sybils Oracles could teach
Nothing not comprehended in his reach.
Was none so hopeful Instrument as he,
The savage World t'reduce from Levity;
Purge and restore our Manners, and call home　　　　[40
Civility to barb'rous Christendome.
For this great Work, he furnisht was like those
Upon whose sacred heads did once repose,
In shape of parted Tongues, celestial Fire:
What they infused had, he did acquire:
Unless we justly make a doubt, wheth'r He
At Eighteen could in full possession be
(Without a Miracle) of all Tongues; one
Whereof to purchase asks an Age alone.
Him in's own Language might have heard indite,　　　　[50
The Swarthy *Arab,* or the *Elamite:*
What *Athens* heard, or *Solyma,* or *Rome*
Of old, that from his tongue did flowing come:
He, that now drinks of *Tyber* or of *Po,*

Utters not that word that he did not know:
No more doth he that tastes the streams of *Sceine,*
Or those of *Celtica,* or *Aquitain.*
   He was indeed a Miracle: and we,
That Miracles are ceas'd, may now agree.
How could we hope t'enjoy him, being one,   [60
Whose new profane Opinion says, There's none?
Besides this, our own wicked Merits might
Instruct us; Twixt our Darkness, and his Light,
There could not be a long Communion.
In vain therefore, alas, did we go on,
To light his Nuptial-Tapers, and invoke
Juno and *Hymen* and the air to choke
With ecchoing Epithalms; the whilst above,
Th'Angelick Quire, enflamed with his love,
Court him from us, to those Celestial Bowers,   [70
As fitting for their Consort, and not ours.
So unto Heaven (our thoughts being fixt on Clay)
In's Fever's fiery Chariot he takes way:
The weeks first day sets forth; and six days done,
(As God had his) his Sabbath he begun.
   Thrice happie Soul! whose Work and Labour gone,
   Holds with thy Maker's such proportion.
Now whether he a Constellation be,
Intelligence, or Tut'lar Deity,
Is hid from us. 'Tis great'st part of our cross,   [80
Nothing of him to know or feel, but's loss:
Which though we could not read in leaves of Fate,
Thy Tow'rs (O *Ashby*) did prognosticate,
Which fell the dutious ushers to his fall:
There was no further use of them at all,
Since he must fall, for whose sake they had stood:
"Not be at all, as to no end, 's as good.["]
   This these Prophetick Buildings did perceive,
   And, bowing to the ground before, took leave.

NOTES

NOTES

CHAPTER ONE

1 Such an approach, assuming that the theory of poetry or formulas for poetry affect the creation of poetry, will, I am aware, be subject to question from many modern theorists of the problem of style. I believe myself that one's conception of the function and method of art, even a formal conception, is a significant element in sensibility. Whether it is so or not this study ought to contribute to show, though it will not be of any interest to those who take a radically different approach to the question, what is the poetry in a poem.

2 Any worker in this field is very grateful to Mr. R. L. Sharp for the wealth of material in his *From Donne to Dryden* (Chapel Hill, 1940) and for his many critical observations on that material.

3 On this see Richard B. McKeon, "Rhetoric in the Middle Ages," *Speculum,* XVII (1942), 1-32.

CHAPTER TWO

1 J. E. Spingarn, *A History of Literary Criticism in the Renaissance* (New York, 1924), pp. 148ff.

2 For the theory of the imitation of motives see the account of Estienne's essay on the imitation of Theocritus by Virgil and Ovid in Merritt Y. Hughes's "Spenser and the Greek Pastoral Triad," *Studies in Philology,* XX (1923), 184-215. For a full illustration of the imitation of themes and for a discussion of it, see this article and T. P. Harrison, Jr.'s "Spenser and the Earlier Pastoral Elegy," *University of Texas Studies in English,* IV (1933), 36-53; and see the introduction to Don Cameron Allen's edition, *Meres on Poetry* (Cambridge, 1938), for an account of the teaching of imitation in the schools. For convenient examples of rhetoric teaching and its formulas, the reader may consult C. S. Baldwin's *Renaissance Literary Theory and Practice* (New York, 1939), pp. 53-64, and Crane's *Wit and Rhetoric in the Renaissance* (New York,

1936), the edition of *Euphues* (New York, 1916) by Croll and Clement, and W. Ringler's *John Rainolds* (Princeton, 1940). On the influence of rhetorics and their formulas in this period there is material in Foster Watson's *The English Grammar Schools to 1660* (Cambridge, 1908) and in R. L. Sharp's work already cited; more recently, in Donald L. Clark's lucid description and analysis in *Milton at St. Paul's School* (New York, 1948). Their teachings on imagery and figures of sound have been analyzed by Miss Veré Rubel in her *Poetic Diction in the English Renaissance* (New York: The Modern Language Association, 1941). The very important bearing on the rhetorics of the theory of rhetoric as ornament is discussed in full by Pierre Albert Duhamel in his unpublished doctoral thesis, "Sir Philip Sidney and the Traditions of Rhetoric" (University of Wisconsin, 1945); see his article, since published, "Sidney's *Arcadia* and Elizabethan Rhetoric," *Studies in Philology*, XLV (1948), 134-50.

3   See the article in *Speculum*, XVII, and see also J. W. Atkins' discussion of John of Salisbury's attack on the "Cornificians" in his *English Literary Criticism: The Mediaeval Phase* (Cambridge and New York, 1943), Chap. IV. For discussion of the confusion of poetic and rhetoric and of the formulas see also D. L. Clark's *Rhetoric and Poetry in the Renaissance* (New York, 1922) and Ringler's *John Rainolds*.

4   See Mr. Atkins' account (*op. cit.,* Chap. I) of the tradition of the post-classical grammarians, and see what I say in the next paragraph on Boccaccio. It is presumably this grammatical tradition of the humanistic teaching of literature which Scaliger derides in his *Poetics* as too narrow.

5   See for instance the use of the conception of *color* in the passage cited from Gregory of Nyssa on page 44. That figure of Gregory's went right through mediaeval thought.

6   Elizabeth J. Sweeting, *Early Tudor Criticism* (Oxford, 1940), *passim*.

7   See Atkins, *op. cit.,* Chap. IV.

8   See in addition to my comment Spingarn's discussion of Fracastoro (*Literary Criticism,* p. 31), and see further his examples of theories in which ornament becomes the essence of poetry by which the commonplace is ennobled (p. 128). Fracastoro's development of Boccaccio's or Cicero's figure is perhaps best paralleled in English by Lear's plea for his hundred knights: "O reason not the need. Our basest beggars . . ." And perhaps we can today feel the humanism of the concept better in this plea for splendor of living than in a purely literary view. For Boccaccio I have used the translation of *De Genealogia Deorum,* Bk. XV, by Mr. Osgood (Princeton, 1930); for Fracastoro, the edition with English translation by Ruth Kelso (Urbana, 1924).

9   Sperone Speroni, *Dialoghi* (Venice, 1543), "Dialogo della Rhetorica," p. 123. In the last sentences, and for this reason I include them, he is defending the right of eloquence to create and appeal to emotion by the same argument which St. Augustine had earlier used.

10 *Discours à l'Académie Française.*

11 Julii Caesaris Scaligeri, *Poetices Libri Septem* (*editio secunda,* n.p., 1581; first edition 1561); *Dialoghi di Messer Alessandro Lionardi della Inventione Poetica* (Venice, 1554).

12 This seems to me the only point in the dialogue at which Lionardi draws on the specifically and narrowly rhetorical conception of poetry. Metaphors, similes, and so forth, are important in giving the color of life, but also, to some extent, as extrinsic sources of feeling in the reader. The passions, too, are primarily important as intrinsic in the imitation; but secondarily as independent stimuli of delight.

13 The theme later used by Shakespeare for the marriage masque of *The Tempest* is given as an illustration. He connects it with the political idea of a sound society.

14 Bernard Weinberg, "Scaliger versus Aristotle on Poetics," *Modern Philology,* XXXIX (1941-42), 337-60.

15 For a discussion of the scholastic conception see Jacques Maritain, *Art and Scholasticism* (tr. by J. F. Scanlon; New York, 1933).

16 J. H. Randall, Jr., "The Development of Scientific Method in the School of Padua," *Journal of the History of Ideas,* I (1940), 177-206. The scientific regress appears also in the *Didascalia* of Hugh of St. Victor.

17 Julii Caesaris Scaliger, *Exotericarum Exercitationum Libri XV. De Subtilitate ad Hieronymum Cardanum* (Frankfurt, 1576), Exercitatio I.

18 *Poetices,* Bk. III, Chap. II. On the neoclassicism of Scaliger see Spingarn's discussion in his *Literary Criticism of the Renaissance,* especially pp. 52, 134 ff., and 158. It ought not to be overlooked, of course, as I think it frequently is, that Aristotle himself laid the foundation for this view in his remark that Nature herself seems to have taught the tragic poets what verse to use, the iambic being closest to normal speech. Nor am I meaning to overlook the whole broad basis of the growth of the neoclassical idea of nature as an aesthetic norm.

19 His actual types develop, as Mr. Weinberg points out, out of Theophrastus.

20 Iacobi Pontani de Societate Jesu *Poeticarum Institutionum Libri III* (*editio secunda emendatior,* Ingolstad, 1598). I choose Pontanus not as representing simply the Jesuit view—Bencius, for instance, is Platonic—but as widely known and as widely used, at least in the digest of Buechler. The citation is from Bk. I, Chap. v.

21 In one regard Pontanus is in effect notably humanistic as well as religious. Both in his book on poetry and in his edition of Virgil he insists upon the significant representation of all the emotions, bad as well as good, and on the mixed character of the individual.

22 Janelle in his study of Southwell, *Robert Southwell, The Writer* (London, 1935), has some very interesting commentary on Pontanus.

23 Letter printed in David Masson's *Drummond of Hawthornden* (London, 1873) and cited in part by R. L. Sharp (*op. cit.*).

24 For an introduction to St. Augustine's view of expression, see the article by Mr. McKeon already referred to and the bibliography there cited. See also Fénelon's third dialogue on eloquence.

25 John Donne, *Poems* (ed. H. J. C. Grierson, Oxford, 1912), *passim;* M. Y. Hughes, "Kidnapping Donne," *The University of California Studies in English and Comparative Literature,* Vol. IV (1934).

26 Lovejoy and Boas, in discussing the use of the terms νόμος and φύσις in their *Primitivism and Related Ideas in Antiquity* (Baltimore, 1935, p. 107), refer to Cratylus' view in Plato's *Cratylus* that words are natural and not conventional, a view probably deriving from the sophistic teacher Prodicus. The view is answered by Hermogenes, who holds names to be convention only. But the authors go on to say that something of Prodicus' idea is at the bottom of the so-called dialectic method of Socrates; his method of questioning men on what words mean to them, to try to get at the meaning these words have for them, implies that words had for them a *real* meaning which they could not get at without his help. See also my later reference to Stoic concepts.

One may remember also that a view akin to that of Augustine is referred to by Longinus in a passage which the seventeenth century translated away, either as rejecting it or not understanding it.

27 McKeon, *op. cit.*

28 *De Anima,* Chap. XVII, in *Opera ex recensione Augusti Reifferscheid et Georgii Wissowa,* Pars I (*Corpus Scriptorum Ecclesiasticorum Latinorum,* Vol. XX, Vienna, 1890), p. 329.

29 *Ibid.,* Chap. XLIII, p. 372.

30 *Adversus Marcionem,* Bk. I, Chap. XIII, *Opera,* Pars III (*Corpus,* Vol. XLVII, Vienna, 1907), p. 308.

31 *De Anima,* Chap. XXXVII, p. 364; Chap. XLIII, p. 371; *De Carnis Resurrectione,* Chaps. XIII-XIV, *Opera,* Pars III, p. 42.

32 Tertullian, *Apology,* Chap. IV (Loeb Classical Library, London, 1931, p. 26).

33 From the translation by Pusey (Everyman's Library, London, n.d.).

34 Harry Austryn Wolfson, *Philo* (Cambridge, 1947).

35 For my understanding of Philo's thought and backgrounds I have depended on Mr. Wolfson's study and on Norman Bentwich's introduction, *Philo-Judaeus of Alexandria* (Philadelphia, 1910).

36 Philo Judaeus, *Works,* ed. and tr. by F. H. Colson and G. H. Whitaker (Loeb Classical Library, London, 1929-1941).

37 For a discussion of the method of rabbinic thinking, see Max Kadushin, *Organic Thinking* (New York, 1938).

38 Chap. LVI (*ed. cit.,* I, 124-25).

39 For a full discussion of the meanings of the term *logos* in Philo, see Wolfson, *op. cit.,* Chap. IV. For *logos* and speech, see note 26, above, and Zeller's discussion of the Stoic theory of the relation of words to things,

of the formation of speech, and of the significance of etymologies in discovering the meaning of words.—Eduard Zeller, *The Stoics, Epicureans, and Sceptics* (tr. by O. J. Reichel, London, 1892), p. 356.

40 *De Opificio* (*ed. cit.*), Chap. LII.

41 *De Abraham,* Chap. XII (Loeb ed., Vol. VI); cited in Bentwich, *op. cit.,* p. 84.

42 *De Opificio* (*ed. cit.*), Chap. XXVII. Δευτέρα μὲν αἰτία ἥδε λελέχθω, τρίτη δ' ἐστὶ τοιάδε. ἀρχὴν καὶ τέλος τῶν γεγονότων ὁ θεὸς ἁρμόσασθαι διανοηθεὶς ὡς ἀναγκαῖα καὶ φίλτατα, ἀρχὴν μὲν οὐρανὸν ἐποίει, τέλος δὲ ἄνθρωπον, τὸν μὲν τῶν ἐν αἰσθητοῖς ἀφθάρτων τελειότατον, τὸν δὲ τῶν γηγενῶν καὶ φθαρτῶν ἄριστον, βραχύν, εἰ δεῖ τἀληθὲς εἰπεῖν, οὐρανόν, πολλὰς ἐν αὐτῷ φύσεις ἀστεροειδεῖς ἀγαλματοφοροῦντα, τέχναις καὶ ἐπιστήμαις καὶ τοῖς καθ' ἑκάστην ἀρετὴν ἀοιδίμοισ θεωρήμασιν.

43 ΠΕΡΙ ΑΡΧΩΝ, Bk. IV (Migne, *P.G.,* Vol. XI, Paris, n.d.), col. 334. Translations of both the Greek version preserved in the anthology of Origen's work called the *Philocalia,* and of the Latin version of Rufinus are given in Origen, *Writings* (tr. by Frederick Crombie, Edinburgh, 1872, 1878), in the Antenicene Christian Library, Vol. X. I have used the version from the *Philocalia.* Both Rufinus and a Latin version of the *Philocalia* are given in Migne.

44 *Commentarius in Canticum Canticorum* (Latin tr. by Gentian Hervet), Homily I, Gregorii Episcopi Nysseni *Opera,* Vol. I (Migne, *P.G.,* Vol. XLIV, Paris, 1863), col. 776.

45 *Ibid.,* Homily VI.

46 *Ibid.,* Homily III (on Chap. I, vv. 9-13), col. 816.

47 *Ibid.,* Homily IX, col. 956.

48 Sancti Ambrosii Mediolanensis Episcopi *Commentarius in Cantica Canticorum e Scriptis* Sancti Ambrosii a Guillelmo ... *Collectus,* in *Opera Omnia* (Migne, *P.L.,* Vol. XV, Paris, 1845), Vol. I, Part II.

49 *Ibid.,* col. 1869, paragraphs 46 and 47, on Canticles, 1 : 12, 13.

50 *Eruditionis Didascalia Libri Septem* in *Opera Omnia* (Migne, *P.L.,* Vol. CLXXVI, Paris, 1854), Vol. II.

51 Bk. V, Chap. III, col. 790.

52 For a general discussion of Bonaventure I am indebted to Etienne Gilson's *The Philosophy of St. Bonaventura* (tr. by Dom Illtyd Trethowan, New York, 1938). His theory of style is discussed in Mr. McKeon's article already referred to.

53 Bonaventura, *Breviloquium,* Chap. III, in St. Bonaventura *Opera Omnia,* cura et studio A. C. Peletier (Paris, 1865), Vol. VII.

54 Bonaventura, *Illuminationes in Hexaëmeron,* Sermons II and XII (*ed. cit.,* Vol. IX).

55 *Works* of John Donne, with a memoir of his life by Henry Alford (London, 1839), III, 484.

56 *Illuminationes in Hexaëmeron* (*ed. cit.*), Sermon II; *De Reductione*

Artium ad Theologiam, ed. with an Introduction, by Sr. Emma Therese Healy (New York, 1939).

57 *Illuminationes in Hexaëmeron (ed. cit.),* Sermon 1, col. 22.
58 Walter J. Ong, S.J., has made a very significant and most lucid analysis of the underlying intellectual significance of the paradoxical play upon words in the hymns of St. Thomas Aquinas and of later poets in his tradition in an article, "Wit and Mystery: A Revaluation in Mediaeval Latin Hymnody," *Speculum,* XXII (1947), 310-21. Of particular interest is his discussion of St. Thomas' theory on the tension in linguistic expression created by faith and on the fact that this tension relates religious expression to the language of poetry. Father Ong also comments briefly on the Victorines, criticizing them from a Thomistic point of view.
59 J. B. Mullinger, *The University of Cambridge from the Earliest Times to the Royal Injunctions of 1535* (Cambridge, 1873), pp. 325, 502.
60 Title and Preface are reprinted in Migne, Joannis Scoti *Opera, P. L.,* Vol. CXXII (Paris, 1853), cols. 87-88.
61 Harry B. Gutman, "The Medieval Content of Raphael's *School of Athens," Journal of the History of Ideas,* II (1941), 420-29.
62 I have used the text in *Opera,* Vol. I (Paris, 1641). For a general discussion of Ficino's thought I am indebted to Paul O. Kristeller, *The Philosophy of Marsilio Ficino,* tr. into English by Virginia Conant (New York, 1943).
63 The full development of the metaphor from its beginning is discussed by Witelo Baeumker in *Beitraege zur Geschichte der Philosophie des Mittelalters,* III, 2, 357 ff.
64 See Gilson, *op. cit.,* throughout.
65 See his "Attic Prose: Lipsius, Montaigne and Bacon," *Schelling Anniversary Papers* (New York, 1923), and his "The Baroque Style in Prose," *Studies in English Philology: A Miscellany in Honor of Frederick Klaeber* (Minneapolis, 1929).
66 Perry Miller, *The New England Mind* (New York, 1939).
67 Documents abundantly cited by W. F. Patterson in his *Three Centuries of French Poetic Theory* (Ann Arbor, 1935).

CHAPTER THREE

1 James Maxwell, *The Laudable Life, and Deplorable Death of our late peerlesse Prince Henry* . . . (London, 1612); Sir William Alexander of Menstrie, *An Elegie on the Death of Prince Henrie* (Edinburgh, 1612), read by me in the edition of Alexander's poems by Kastner and Charlton (Manchester, 1921). See the Appendix.
2 London, 1613.
3 See Lily B. Campbell's edition of the *Mirror* (Cambridge, 1938) and

Willard Farnham's *The Mediaeval Heritage of Elizabethan Tragedy* (Berkeley, 1936).

4 Josephine Waters Bennett, *The Evolution of the Faerie Queene* (Chicago, 1942), Chap. IX, *passim.*

5 See George R. Coffman, "The Parable of the Good Shepherd, *De Contemptu Mundi,* and *Lycidas,*" *ELH,* III (1936), 101-13.

6 *Funeral Elegies upon the most Lamentable Death of Prince Henry* (T. P. for Henry Budge, 1613); *The Period of Mourning. Disposed into Six Visions* (London, 1613).

7 To look ahead for a moment, Peacham's laments can perhaps help us to understand why Henry More in the middle of the century chose the Spenserian style to embody his versification of the philosophy of Plotinus. It was not merely the neo-Platonism of Spenser which dictated his choice; but he wished the aesthetic experience of the song to awake in our imagination a first contemplative impulse which would lead us into the metaphysics of his argument.

8 *Teares on the Death of Mœliades* (Edinburgh, 1613); *Great Britans Mourning Garment. Given to all faithfull sorrowful Subjects at the Funerall of Prince Henry* (London, 1612). Fletcher's poem was published in a group of callow English poems by Stephen Hayby, John Wilson, Edward Gibson, I. P., A. B., Thomas May, Thomas Walkington, John Cozen, J. Howlet, Thomas Scampus, inserted after the first printing in the largely Latin Cambridge volume, *Memoriae Sacra Illustriss. Potentiss. Principis Henrici Walliae Principis, Ducis Cornubiae &c. Laudatio Funebris* (Cambridge, 1612).

9 For a discussion of the connections of Drummond's elegy see *The Pastoral Elegy: An Anthology,* edited by T. P. Harrison (Austin, 1939); and on its background see the articles by Mr. Harrison and Mr. Hughes already referred to (Chap. II, note 2). The Harrison volume contains both Drummond and Alamanni, his chief humanist source, and it discusses fully Drummond's relation to his continental background.

10 It is Cicero of whom St. Augustine reminds Petrarch in Petrarch's *Secret.*

11 To compare his appeal to the rivers with that in Alamanni's second eclogue is to see the difference at a glance.

12 See p. 26.

13 First published among a group of "surrepted" elegies in the third edition of *Lachrymae Lachrymarum or the Spirit of Teares, distilled for the untimely Death of the Incomparable Prince, Panaretus,* by Joshua Sylvester (London, 1613).

14 On this form and its relation to classical rhetoric, see W. Fraser Mitchell, *English Pulpit Oratory from Andrewes to Tillotson* (London, S.P.C.K., 1932). On pages 190-93 Mitchell has gathered together the material on rhetoric in Donne's sermons.

15 *Op. cit.*

16 It will be apparent how much my knowledge of "strong lines" owes to George Williamson's article, "Strong Lines," *English Studies,* XVIII (1936), 152-59, and to Mr. Mitchell's notice of the "strong-lined preachers" in his study of pulpit oratory. My conception of "strong lines" differs somewhat, however, from that of Mr. Williamson, and I should distinguish sharply between "strong lines" as they were conceived by Andrewes, Donne, and other contemporaries, and the description of them by later unsympathetic critics of them.

17 See a poem written by Thomas Pestell, who rated himself a follower of Donne, a poem in a method termed by him "strong lines." The poem closely resembles Crashaw's work.—*The Poems of Thomas Pestell,* ed. Hannah Buchan (Oxford, 1940), p. 6, "Prayr and Prase."

18 Their relationship to Donne is considered in detail by Leslie Fiedler in an unpublished doctoral thesis, "John Donne's *Songs and Sonnets:* A Reinterpretation in the Light of Traditional Backgrounds," University of Wisconsin, 1941.

19 In his *Secentismo e Marinismo in Inghilterra* (Florence, 1925).

20 For some particular details, see Don Cameron Allen, "A Text from Nashe on the Latin Literature of the Sixteenth Century," *Research Studies of The State College of Washington,* Vol. V, No. 4 (Pullman, 1937).

21 In a paper read at the meeting of the Modern Language Association of America, December, 1941.

22 London, Warburg Institute, 1939. Signor Praz cites all the comments which follow except that of Capaccio. Porphyry is not named as a medium between Alexandria and witty symbolism; but he must be borne in mind. It is at this point that the reader may most fruitfully turn back to what I have said in chapter 1 about the coalescence of St. Augustine's principles of style with the conceptions arising from the symbolic interpretation of the Bible. The following excerpt from the commentary on the Song of Songs attributed to St. Ambrose and known to the Victorines bears a striking resemblance to the later emblem in its handling of imagery and its wordplay; that is, in its combination of the natural history of the tree and the literal Hebrew etymology of its name. Commenting on *"Nardus cypri consobrinus meus in vineis"* he says: "If you inquire the place signified, it is the place where the *opobalsamum* grows. If you seek the interpretation of the Hebrew word, it means *tentatio.* Among those vines, to draw the consequence, is a wood which if it is crushed gives forth a drop of unguent, but if uncut or unbroken gives forth no such redolence. Hence the passage typifies how Christ, crucified on that wood of temptation, shed tears over the people, that he might wash away our sins, and poured forth the unguent from the bowels of his pity, saying, 'Father, forgive them.' Jesus in pity poured forth the odor of remission of sins and redemption." This interpretation is then further applied to the Christian

paradox: When the word was made man, he was poor though rich, and we are made rich by his poverty. He was powerful and offered himself to be despised. He moved the earth and hung from the rood. (Migne, *P. L.,* Vol. XV, col. 1869, paragraph 46.) The example is the more significant as an illustration of the traditional form of interpretation because in general Ambrose interprets freely and inspirationally rather than by a strict method of exegesis such as one finds consistently in Origen or in Gregory of Nyssa.

23 Hughes, "Kidnapping Donne," *Univ. of Calif. Studies in English and Comparative Literature,* Vol. IV (1934); Eleanor James, "The Emblem as an Image Pattern in some Metaphysical Poets," University of Wisconsin doctoral thesis, 1942, published in part in *University of Texas Studies in English,* XXIII (1943), 26-50. For examples of Donne's use of the hieroglyphics of Valeriano as a source for scientific interpretations see Don Cameron Allen, "John Donne and Pierio Valeriano," *Modern Language Notes,* LVIII (1943), 610-12. See also Josef Lederer, "John Donne and Emblematic Practice," *Review of English Studies,* XXII (1946), 182-200. A general survey of studies in emblem influence is given by Henri Stegemeier, "Problems in Emblem Literature," *Journal of English and Germanic Philology,* XLV (1946), 26-27. Rosemary Freeman's *English Emblem Books* (Oxford, 1948) has since been added to the valuable literature.

24 I may cite three out of a number of seventeenth-century statements to illustrate not the mere popularity of the emblem books but underlying it the recognition of the significance of this type of image, quite outside the "metaphysical" writers. Fotherby in his *Atheomastix,* published in 1622 but left incomplete at his death in 1619, says in defense of the study of mathematics: "But yet we may draw, *per obliquum dictum,* similitudes, and resemblances from both these two Sciences: geometry and arithmetic, whereby we may ascend in our contemplation, even unto divine and celestiall knowledges: as by the shape of the shadow, we may gather assuredly, the shape of the body, For as *Ficinus* hath truly observed, to this purpose; *Mathematica ita se habent ad divina, ut umbrae ad corpora.*" And he further cites Plutarch that the end of geometry is to sublime men's minds above their senses. The good bishop did not himself know much of geometry, and it would seem that he took similitude in a rhetorical sense not meant in Plotinus' philosophical view of mathematics or in an emblematic sense less serious than Ficino's number symbolism. Again, young John Dryden wrote playfully to his cousin Honor from Cambridge: "Yet though I highly vallue your Magnificent presents, pardon me if I must tell the world they are but imperfect Emblemes of your beauty; For the white and red of waxe and paper are but shaddowes of that vermillion and snowe in your lips and forehead." Whitlock in his Ζωοτόμια, published in 1654, marks a turning point in the aesthetic and the thought of

the age by accepting the literary program of Davenant and Hobbes. But he explicitly exempts the emblem from their purgation.

25　Miss Tuve's article, "Imagery and Logic," *The Journal of the History of Ideas*, III (1942), 374-400, is invaluable in insisting on the importance of logic in the literature of the time and particularly in pointing out how Fraunce gave logical interpretation to figures which we should ordinarily have thought of as mere picturesque enrichments of beauty. But I do not follow her interpretation of Donne's *Valediction* and her connection of Donne with Ramus.

26　"A Griefe on the Death of Prince Henrie, Expressed in a Broken Elegie . . . ," in *Three Elegies on the most lamented Death of Prince Henrie* . . . by Cyril Tourneur, John Webster, and Thomas Heywood (London, 1613). See the Appendix.

27　"The Influence of the *Ars Moriendi* Literature on Elizabethan Conduct," a paper read by Katherine Koller at the meeting of the Modern Language Association, December, 1941. Henry More has a statement which almost exactly parallels that of Tourneur.

28　Tourneur tells us that he wrote his elegy before the funeral. I do not know whether he had a chance to see Donne's elegy as well as other already circulating verse of Donne's or to discuss Donne's views with him. It will be noted that in the passage on Henry as a model for painters, Tourneur expresses the Renaissance concept of the artist working from the *idea* in his mind. But he twists the conception so that the *idea* is drawn from a single experience, and not from an innate concept on one hand or on the other by the mind's abstraction of it from many actual forms. This is perhaps only another way of saying as Donne has said of Elizabeth Drury that Henry represented the absolutely pure form.

29　London, 1653. Available in the edition of King's poems or in Saintsbury's *Minor Caroline Poets* (London, 1905-1921), Vol. III.

30　Webster, *A Monumental Columne, erected to the living Memory* . . . (London, 1612); Heywood, *A Funerall Elegie* . . . (London, 1613); both in the same volume with Tourneur's poem; Chapman, *An Epicede or Funerall Song: On the most disastrous Death of Prince Henry* . . . *with The Funeralls, and Representation of the Hearse* (London, 1612). Heywood will be considered presently.

31　On the general quickening of imagery at this time see valuable material and comment in Elizabeth Holmes's *Aspects of Elizabethan Imagery* (Oxford, 1929), and Theodore Spencer's *Death in Elizabethan Tragedy* (Cambridge, Mass., 1936); on Chapman in particular see Mr. Williamson's comment in *The Donne Tradition* (Cambridge, Mass., 1930).

32　*Modern Philology*, Vol. XIII (1910), cited by Miss Bartlett in her edition of Chapman (New York, 1941) with further comment.

33　On the conception of amplification here used I remind the reader again of Atkins, *English Literary Criticism: The Mediaeval Phase,* Chapter v, on Vinsauf; and Sweeting, *Early Tudor Criticism, passim.*

34 I do not associate Chapman's praise of darkness in his prefaces with the specific tradition of "strong lines" but rather with the more general conception, which came to him through humanist neo-Platonism, that philosophy is esoteric, that this fact gives the key to Greek religious and Platonic myth. His special concept of darkness may owe something to Dionysius directly or through intermediaries or possibly to Augustine on allegorical interpretation of the Bible. It has been discussed by Roy Battenhouse in "Chapman and the Nature of Man," *English Literary History,* Vol. XII (1945).

35 It deserves to be carefully studied whether there is not an allegorical element in Spenser's variations of style in his *Faerie Queene:* whether, for instance, the very plain style of the House of Holiness does not arise from its being the vision of the naked Truth. See on this Erwin Panofsky's interpretation of Titian's so-called "Sacred and Profane Love" in his *Studies in Iconology* (New York, 1939).

36 *Two Elegies, Consecrated to the Never-dying Memorie of the most worthily admyred . . . Henry Prince of Wales* (London, 1613). The first is signed Christopher Brooke, the second with separate title-page, W. B. On the backgrounds of the churchyard elements in Browne's poem, see John Draper, *The Funeral Elegy and the Rise of English Romanticism* (New York, 1929).

37 *The Muses Teares for the Losse of their Hope; Heroick and Nere-Too-Much praised Henry, Prince of Wales,* &c., by John Davies of Hereford (London, 1613).

38 See the Appendix, pp. 357–58.

39 Published in the Sylvester volume.

40 *Ibid.*

41 These are very briefly discussed by Leicester Bradner in his *Musae Anglicanae* (New York, 1940).

CHAPTER FOUR

1 With two title-pages: *Iusta Edouardo King, Naufrago. ab Amicis Moerentibus amoris* μνείας χάριν, Cantabrigiae: 1638; *Obsequies to the memorie of Mr. Edward King.* Anno Dom., 1638 (Cambridge, 1638).

2 Perhaps one ought to note that Lionardi, in whom the neo-Platonic didactic theory of art, including a discussion of allegorized myth, finds full expression, has an important passage on the function of the epithet in defining the ideal, the typical quality of things.

3 Since I am trying to understand the combined development of substance and form in these poems, I may perhaps say a word more on the actual

influence of Donne upon imagery. The influence of Donne on later poets was but one element in the broad stream of that tradition from which Donne himself drew so much. Herbert in some of his lyrics almost certainly used Jesuit emblem books (see the literature I have already referred to). One or two others of his poems, such as the introductory verses of *Easter,* appear to derive from the religious lyric of Marini, or from kindred Spanish poems not familiar to me. Joseph Beaumont was, as was shown by Austin Warren in "Crashaw and St. Teresa," *T.L.S.* (November, 1932), the first man of the Peterhouse group to become interested in the study of the life and writings of St. Teresa. Thomas Pestell, of whom I shall have something to say in my next section, one of the most ardent of Donne men, does best the type of sensuous adoration of which Donne makes no use. Marvell is a man of many European backgrounds. On the other hand the influence of Donne on Herbert's most personal lyrics needs no demonstration. The special relation of this influence to the emblem has been shown by Miss James in the thesis I have already referred to. It was from Donne also, I think, that Marvell caught the power to express the interwoven movements of thought and feeling with such subtle flexibility. And again Miss James has shown echoes of Donne, together with the use of the emblem, in Mrs. Philips' lyrics of friendship. On the other hand Pestell, as I have already noted, denominates as "strong lines" poems of sensuous adoration, thus showing that this term has perhaps been rather too distinctively associated, following Donne, with Donne. In the use of "strong lines" the symbolic or logical importance and the devotional significance of the image is clear. And in that sense, one might almost consider the images of Webster and Beaumont as "strong lines" though Beaumont's verse and diction would bar the term. Burton, too, emphasizes the significance of the image, referring to "strong lines" among tropes, strains of wit, brave heats. In Cleveland's use, which I shall presently describe, the emblematic and expressive character was gone from the image, and the key elements are as follows: the wit of its development, the lack of affective elements, paradox, "natural" diction. The wit seems to have derived, as Mr. Nethercot has noted, from school studies rather than from Donne.

4 See the preceding note and Mr. Williamson's article, "Strong Lines" (*English Studies,* Vol. XVIII), already referred to.

5 This is quite distinctively an epigram image, with witty epigrammatic development. Doubtless it had an older source; one recalls spontaneously, "Oh where/Shall Times best jewel from Times chest lie hid?" as well as Maxwell's elegy on Prince Henry, and, to look far back, *The Pearl.* My knowledge of Jesuit poetic is, of course, very cursory, and my acquaintance with the vast general field of neo-Latin epigram and elegy and in particular of Jesuit elegy is very limited. With Donne the neo-Latin epigram and Jesuit teaching had some roots in common besides the fact that Donne

probably used neo-Latin literature; no reader of Southwell and of Crashaw's early verse will forget for a moment the elements there which
parallel elements in Donne and which must spring from common traditions. But despite Jesuit development of the religious paradox, Jesuit
teaching of lay verse was essentially a worldly art. For relevant discussion,
see Pierre Janelle's book on Father Southwell, material in Mr. Croll's
essays on prose, and Jacquinet's discussion of earlier Jesuit instruction on
preaching and of the later criticism of that teaching in his *Des Predi-
cateurs du xvii⁰ siècle avant Bossuet* (2d ed., Paris, 1885).

6 They include one by Henry More and one very probably by Richard
Crashaw.

7 It is interesting to consider together Rosemond Tuve's article on Spenser's vivid recollection of the detail of allegorical figures from mediaeval
manuscripts, "Spenser and Some Pictorial Conventions," *Studies in Philology*, XXXVII (1940), 149-76, and Sir John Sandys' collection of phrases
and themes from classical and neoclassical elegies recollected by Milton
and woven into the texture of *Lycidas*, in his "The Literary Sources of
Milton's *Lycidas*," *Transactions of the Royal Society of Literature*, 2d
series (London, 1914). But whether we may ascribe the difference in the
sort of thing recalled by Spenser and by Milton to some quality of mind
in each which we may call generally the character of the poet's imagination or whether we are to attribute that character of imagination in part
to the education of the poet's mind and to what he has focused his
thoughts on, cannot here be discussed.

8 This *affection* arises from the poet's whole view, and it selects and controls his images rather than, as Dryden in part at least conceived, depend-
ing upon the images to supply the passion for that argument. See my
discussion of Lionardi. Milton uses the traditional humanist plot structure for realizing death and grief and then transcending them. Under
this poetic invention, however, this single particular action (*simplex*) is
presented to our senses.

This section of my book had been completed before B. Rajan's brilliant
article, "Simple, Sensuous, Passionate" (*Review of English Studies*, XXI,
289-301), had appeared. I am concerned here with the specific meaning
of Milton's terms in the Renaissance critical context, and the light which
that context sheds on Milton's thought. It is the significance of this critical
context that it does imply that universal view of the meaning of the particular which Milton developed to the full, as Mr. Rajan shows. Milton's
hierarchy of studies should be read in the light of the great mediaeval
schemes of Hugh of St. Victor and St. Bonaventura, as well as in the
light of seventeenth-century theory. Milton, as I have pointed out elsewhere, speaks of *reducing* the other studies to the Bible, a word which
recalls St. Bonaventura's terms, *Reductio artium ad theologiam*.

My reader will notice that I say Milton contrasts poetry to logic, not to rhetoric. This seems to me clearly what he means. As rhetoric is but the open hand of logic, the distinction is not material; but it keeps the essential categories clearer. "Passionate" also I have considered in its specific meaning. Milton's sense of the significance of poetry in moving the passions is closely paralleled by Donne's comment on his own use of the figures of sound, that the imagination must be stirred and reordered so that true opinion can replace false, at that level first. Milton's view is also within that concept of the imagination whereby Erasmus justifies the use of fables in education, and which gives the rationale for More's treatment of gold and silver in his *Utopia*. Of course the concept which would have to be formulated in somewhat the same terms throughout this long period varies in dynamic and significance in the context of each user's thought. And Milton is one of those Platonists who stress both the radical value of the good man's emotions and the illuminating beauty of the creatures.

9   A beautiful expression of the conception is found in the opening of the treatise on the nature of God and the mind by the Protestant apologist, Zanchius, perhaps the sole living passage in his dry and legalistic discussion of psychology and ethics.—Hieron. Zanchii, *De Natura Dei, seu de Divinis Attributis Libri V* (Neustadii Palatinorum, 1598).

10   In *ELH,* III, 101-13.

11   Guilielmi Hesi Antverpiensis e Societate Iesu *Emblemata Sacra de Fide, Spe, Charitate* (Antwerp, 1636): The sun in going leaves me dark. But suddenly when I fixed my eyes on the opposite heaven, I saw an unwonted joy shine.

> Parvus in occasum, sol maximus ibat ab ortu
> Grandior, hic quam quam plenior alter erat
> Hic erat in medio formosus inaniter orbe
> Luminis hic etiam veri coloris erat
> Arcus hic occidui species erat altera solis
> Altera, sole tamen, pulchrior illa suo.
> O ego, dicebam, quid euntem in deiva solem
> Conabar lacrymis hic retinere meis?

. . . .

> Sistite mortales, inamœnas sistite planctus
> Quos agit occiduo mors properata die.
> Tergite abundantes lacrymas, detergite fletus
> Quos vocat in luctus ultima vita suos.
>
>   (*Pp. 181-83*)

CHAPTER FIVE

1   *Lacrymae Musarum, The Teares of the Muses Exprest in Elegies* (London, 1649).

2   See Mr. Harrison's article in the *University of Texas Studies in English,* Vol. IV (1933).

3   The late Professor C. G. Child many years ago pointed out to his classes at the University of Pennsylvania that "metaphysical" poetry stemmed from Cambridge.

4   Perhaps one should say also that he uses not the old form of logical analysis by division, definition, and proof, but the new system of "method"; the common-sense arrangement of material set up by Ramus and his school and coalescing with the general rationalist ideal. Hall is reprinted in Saintsbury's *Minor Caroline Poets,* Vol. II.

5   So very much has been missaid about the influence of the new science in metaphysical poetry that I call attention to Hall's use of the term *geometrical* and refer the reader back to my citation from Bishop Fotherby (Chap. III, note 24) to show how neo-Platonic and traditional this use is. I have used the term *hermetic* or *neo-Platonic* in relation to Hall. He is manifestly one of the many men of his age who read in a varied lot of speculative writers and who could hold together in a loose imaginative bond conceptions which the stricter theologian or philosopher would rigorously distinguish.

6   In speaking of the classicism of Marvell's couplet, I have in mind, of course, the classicism of Marlowe, Sidney, or the French, and not the neo-classical English couplet of Cleveland or Denham.

7   Its full character becomes at once clear if we compare the lines cited with lines on the same motive from Sir John Beaumont's elegy on King James:

>   Weepe, O ye Nymphs; that from your caves may flow
>   Those trickling drops, whence mighty rivers flow.
>   Disclose your hidden store; let ev'ry Spring
>   To this our Sea of griefe some tribute bring:
>   And when ye once have wept your Fountaines dry
>   The heav'n with showres shall send a new supply.
>   But if these cloudy treasures prove too scant,
>   Our teares shall help, when other moystures want.

8   I do not mean to say, of course, that Jonson is tame. But the sheer intellectual concentration and self-possession of Jonson are very hard to imitate by men of less energy, and men who do not understand the scope of his psychological and moral views. His imitators are apt to run dimpling all the way; Jonson is as hard to imitate as Shakespeare.

9   Cyril Wyche wrote in the tradition of the pastoral elegy, in elegiac meter, Edward Campion on a Horatian model, Tho. Adams an elegiac reflec-

tion, and Ralph Montague an epigram. The latter two, as might be expected, comment upon the small-pox. The first three develop in very simple terms the themes of Hastings' virtue, of his skill in language, of his
bride-to-be, and of the marriage in heaven. None attempts anything of
the scope of Dryden.

10   What follows on Dryden has already been read at a meeting of the Modern Language Association, December, 1946, and been published in *Studies
in Philology,* Vol. XLIV (1947) in condensed form.

11   It will be remembered that Donne closes his Prince Henry elegy with
a reference to Henry's beloved. The consolation in remembrance is a
good classical theme, used by Petrarch in his second elegy and by the
author of *Great Britans Mourning Garment* in our Prince Henry series,
and listed by Pontanus among possible motives in his section on the
memorial elegy.

12   The poem proceeds by the following steps: I. Introduction: Must noble
Hastings immaturely die? (at once exordium and theme). II. Providence
and the meaning of life: *a)* Is death, sin's wages, Grace's now? *b)* Hastings' virtue and the nature of virtue; *c)* Providence: it was the nation's
sin. III. The Grief: *a)* the disease; *b)* comparison to the great dead; *c)*
the decay of the world; *d)* final tears. IV. Consolation: He will live in the
thought of his bride.

13   See besides various discussions of the development of seventeenth-century prose the materials cited throughout W. Fraser Mitchell's *English
Pulpit Oratory.* For the interpretation of them in this sense I am responsible.

14   Dryden seems to have read one line of one of the chief royalist elegies
closely enough to have remembered it thirty years later: Needham's
"drain'd/Down to the dregs of a Democracie"; or he may have looked
over the volume again at the later time.

15   Perhaps there is some light on Dryden's religious feeling at this time in
his next published poem. Written in 1650, it was in praise of a little volume of conventional devotional emblems on the Bible by a friend of his
own age, the same sort of exercises as Crashaw's first volume. It shows,
I think, that Dryden regarded the life of the *dévot* as a very special path,
and that he knew by what steps it had to be achieved. He says:

> Young eaglet . . . .
>   Making heaven thy aim, hast had the grace
> To look the Sun of Righteousness i' th' face.
> What may we hope, if thou go'st on thus fast!
> Scriptures at first: enthusiasms at last!
>   Thou hast commenc'd, betimes, a saint, go on,
>   Mingling diviner streams with Helicon.

The view is so characteristic of the time that the writer might be Cowley
thinking of Crashaw.

16 As Mr. Gwynne Evans again calls to my attention.

17 Or, as Sr. Albertus Magnus McGrath has pointed out to me, it is closer
in tone to the more commonplace Catholic manuals of holy living current in Dryden's day.

CHAPTER SEVEN

1 E. M. W. Tillyard, *Poetry Direct and Oblique* (London, 1945), pp. 77-79.

2 T. S. Eliot, "Andrew Marvell," *T.L.S.*, March 31, 1921; reprinted in *Andrew Marvell, 1621-1678: Tercentenary Tributes* (London, 1922).

3 *The Poems and Letters of Andrew Marvell,* ed. by H. H. Margoliouth
(Oxford, 1927).

4 M. Bradbrook and M. G. Lloyd Thomas, *Andrew Marvell* (Cambridge,
1940).

5 Possibly because it was written as a song. See, for instance, the special
material Herrick used in his songs; contemporary taste appeared to like
a myth or plot in a song.

6 See my earlier discussion of the genres of style, Part I, *passim*.

7 E. M. W. Tillyard, *The Miltonic Setting* (Cambridge, 1938).

8 George Sensabaugh, "The Milieu of Comus," *Studies in Philology,* XLI
(1944), 238-49.

9 Pp. 124-25.

10 Antwerp, 1645.

11 As La Primaudaye notes already in his *French Acadamie*. But the fashion
was still at its height in mid-seventeenth-century England.

12 The implication was first noted, I think, by Miss V. Sackville-West in her
Andrew Marvell (London, 1929).

13 See my discussion in Chapter II, and my more extended consideration of
the book of the creatures in Chapter VIII.

14 See Chapter III, note 23.

15 Pico, in *Opera* (Bologna, 1496); Leone Ebreo, *Dialoghi d'Amore, a cura
di S. Caramella* (Bari, 1929); Pontanus, *De Rebus Cœlestibus,* Book VIII,
Chap. II, in *Librorum Omnium,* Tomus III (Basel, 1540).

16 Margoliouth (*op. cit.,* I, 250) gives specific reference: *Timaeus,* 39 D.

17 Merritt Y. Hughes, "The Christ of *Paradise Regained* and Renaissance
Heroic Tradition," *Studies in Philology,* XXXV (1938), 254-77.

18 See Chap. III.

19 *Op. cit.,* I, 250, 251.

20 M. Bradbrook, "Marvell and the Poetry of Rural Solitude," *Review of
English Studies,* XVII (1941), 37-46.

21 For material on the *argutiae* of Spanish literature see especially Praz, *op.
cit.*

22 See Chapters I and VIII.
23 See, for instance, A. H. King, "Some Notes on Andrew Marvell's Garden," *English Studies*, XX (1938), 118-21.
24 Chapter II.
25 See various works on Elizabethan rhetoric previously referred to.
26 In Scaliger's classical tradition, of course, it *is* a comic instrument.
27 See once more Signor Praz, *op. cit.*
28 In *English Studies*, Vol. XX.
29 *Op. cit.*, I, 237.
30 Margoliouth, "Andrew Marvell, Some Biographical Points," *Modern Language Review*, XVII (1922), 351-61.
31 Cf. D'Avenant:

> But death shall lead her to a shade
> Where love is cold and beauty blind.

32 William Empson, *Some Versions of Pastoral* (London, 1935).

CHAPTER EIGHT

1 Pierre Legouis, *André Marvell, poète, puritain, patriote, 1621-1678* (Paris and London, 1928), p. 81.
2 Mgr. David Mathew, *Catholicism in England, 1535-1935* (London, 1936).
3 Abbot Suger, *On the Abbey Church of St. Denis and Its Art Treasures*, edited, translated, and annotated by Erwin Panofsky (Princeton, 1946), "Introduction," p. 21.
4 St. John of the Cross affords a significant parallel to his statement. In a brief, almost parenthetical, comment evidently made in impatient answer to what must have seemed very blind question, he says that of course one who has passed through the dark nights and made the ascent to contemplation enjoys the beauty of the world. Indeed one now has it in its entirety, for one no longer desires individual possession. His comment might serve as a text for the most significant passages in Traherne's *Centuries of Meditations*. St. John's own great though rare descriptions, in their singularly comprehensive quality, are the illustration of what he means.
5 P. 32.
6 Tertullian, *op. cit.*
7 *Quinti Septimii Florentis Tertulliani De Anima*, Chap. XVIII, in *Opera ex Recensione A. Reifferscheid et G. Wissowa*, Pars I (Prague, etc., 1890), p. 328.
8 *De Civitate Dei*, Bk. XIV, especially Chapters III-V: I have used two editions, that of G. E. C. Welldon (London, S.P.C.K., 1924) and the translation by Healey with notes by Lodovico Vives (2d ed., London, 1620).

9 *Ibid.,* Bk. VIII, Chap. IX.

10 *Ibid.,* Bk. V, Chap. V. See also Bk. XI, Chap. XVIII; Bk. II, Chap. XXIV.

11 Stephen Pepper, *The Basis of Criticism in the Arts* (Cambridge, 1945).

12 See his fear that the love of poetry may detain his pupil from philosophy and the youth's own fear that in poetry one will not find the truth (*De Ordine,* Chap. III). For ampler discussion of his fears see K. Gilbert and H. Kuhn, *A History of Aesthetics,* under the topic, "St. Augustine."

13 *De Doctrina Christiana,* II, VI, 7.

14 The chief influences upon Dionysius are said by scholars to be Plotinus and Proclus. His emphasis upon the translation of the emotions is surely related to the problem set by the Song of Songs and to Origen's answer.

15 Migne, *P.G.,* Vol. III (Paris, 1889), and the translation and commentary of John the Scot, Erigena (Migne, *P.L.,* Vol. CXXII, Paris, 1853).

16 The whole train of material things differs from the immaterial. For instance, wrath in irrational creatures is the effect of passion; but in spiritual beings, the irascible passion is to be otherwise considered: it signifies their masculine reason and immutable state, ". . . thinking indeed that these visible beauties and sensible sweetnesses of odor are expressed figures of spiritual dispensation and that mattered lights bear before them the form of immortal illumination." (Chap. II, sec. 4; Chap. I, sec. 5.) Among other grounds for his symbolic system, Dionysius is combatting the danger of anthropomorphic representations.

17 *Commentary,* Chap. I (Migne, *P.L.,* Vol. CCXXII, cols. 128, 129).

18 Rosemond Tuve, *Seasons and Months: Studies in a Tradition of Middle English Poetry* (Paris, 1933); see especially Chaps. I and IV.

19 Oxford, 1933.

20 Tuve, *Seasons and Months,* pp. 127ff.

21 *Of the City of God* (Healey, ed.) Bk. XI, Chap. IV, p. 390.

22 See p. 33. Tertullian has explicitly in mind the idea of the book of the creatures, a systematic analogy of spiritual truth in the material world.

23 Notably not in humanists like Erasmus who, as Léontine Zanta well defines it, sought in Stoicism only an independent morality. See her *La Renaissance du stoïcisme au xvie siècle* (Paris, 1914).

24 I have used S. Thomae Aquinatos Doctoris Angelici, *Summa Contra Gentiles seu de Veritate Catholicae Fidei* (Turin and London, 1901).

25 *Of the City of God,* Bk. II, Chap. III.

26 *Ibid.,* Chap. XLIII.

27 *Ibid.,* Bk. II, *passim.*

28 *Ibid.,* Chap. II.

29 Down through the seventeenth century it was, of course, an assumption constantly underlying discussions of reason and of the method of knowledge that Adam before the fall saw the broad character of the system in his immediate intuition of the particulars.

30 *Summa contra Gentiles,* Bk. I, Chap. LXXVIII and following; Bk. II,

Chaps. XLIII-XLV. On the implications of this view for art, as they are understood by Thomists today, see Jacques Maritain, *Art and Scholasticism,* tr. by G. Scanlon (New York, 1930), and *The Degrees of Knowledge,* tr. by Wall and Adamson (New York, 1938).

31 Thomas Wright, *Popular Treatises on Science Written during the Middle Ages* (London, 1841).

32 Bernardus Silvestris, *De Mundi Universitate Libri Duo sive Megacosmus et Microcosmus,* eds. Barach and Wrobel, in *Bibliotheca Philosophorum Mediae Aetatis* (Innsbruck, 1876). Commented on by Etienne Gilson (in "La Cosmogonie de Bernardus Silvestris," *Archives d'histoire doctrinale et litteraire du Moyen Age,* III [1928], 5-24), who relates it to the Chartrian school of Platonism and vindicates its full Christianity; and further by Theodore Silverstein, "The Fabulous Cosmogony of Bernardus Silvestris," *Modern Philology,* XLVI (1948), 92-116.

33 Cf. *De Administratione,* pp. 62-66:

"Unde, cum ex dilectione decoris domus Dei aliquando multicolor, gemmarum speciositas ab ex[in]trinsecis me curis devocaret, sanctarum etiam diversitatem virtutum, de materialibus ad immaterialia transferendo, honesta meditatio insistere persuaderet, videor videre me quasi sub aliqua extranea orbis terrarum plaga, quae nec tota sit in terrarum faece nec tota in coeli puritate, demorari, ab hac etiam inferiori ad illam superiorem anagogico more Deo donante posse transferri. . . .

"Opponunt etiam qui derogant, debere sufficere huic amministrationi mentem sanctam, animum purum, intentionem fidelem. . . . In exterioribus etiam sacrorum vasorum ornamentis, nulli omnino aeque ut sancti sacrificii servitio, in omni puritate interiori, in omni nobilitate exteriori, debere famulari profitemur. In omnibus enim universaliter decentissime nos oportet deservire Redemptori nostro, qui in omnibus universaliter absque exceptione aliqua nobis providere non recusavit; qui naturae suae nostram sub uno et ammirabili individuo univit, . . ."

See also especially the first five chapters of Dionysius.

34 *Ed. cit.*

35 Bk. VII, Chaps. I-XIV, cols. 811 ff.

36 *Ibid.*

37 *Ed. cit.* The distinctness of such a disquisition on the hexaëmeron from the type of pictorial elaboration set forth in Basil and Ambrose, referred to by Aquinas, popularized in encyclopedias and in Du Bartas, and discussed by scholars of hexaëmeral literature as a background for *Paradise Lost* need not be pointed out.

38 Gilson, *op. cit., passim.*

39 There is a more condensed discussion in the *Breviloquium.* The *creatura mundi* is a book in which the Trinity is read in three grades of expression, as a *vestigium* in all creatures, as an *imago* in rational creatures, as

a *similitudo* in deiform creatures, to ascend in whom, as by certain degrees of the ladder to the supreme principle, or God, the human intellect was born. See also Bonaventura's *De Reductione Artium* (*ed. cit.,* pp. 499-502):

"Secundum lumen quod illuminat nos ad formas naturales apprehendendas, est lumen cognitionis sensitivae, quod recte dicitur inferius, quia cognitio sensitiva ab inferiori incipit, et fit beneficio lucis corporalis, et hoc quintuplicatur secundum quinque sensus. . . . Itaque cum quinque sint corpora mundi simplicia, scilicet quatuor elementa, et quinta essentia, ut homo omnes formas corporeas posset percipere, quinque sensus habet illis correspondentes: . . .

"Tertium lumen, quod illuminat ad veritates intelligibiles perscrutandas, est lumen cognitionis philosophicae, quod ideo interius dicitur, quia interiores causas et latentes requirit, et hoc per principia disciplinarum et veritatis naturalis, quae homini naturaliter sunt inserta. . . .

"Quartum lumen, quod illuminat ad veritatem salutarem, est lumen sacrae Scripturae . . . manifestando ea quae sunt supra rationem; et etiam quia non per inventionem, sed per inspirationem, a Patre luminum descendit." [He then lists the four senses, the literal, the three mystical, namely, allegorical, moral, anagogic, dealing with our faith, our morals, and our end.]

"Videamus ergo qualiter aliae illuminationes cognitionum reduci habent ad lumen sacrae Scripturae. Et primo videamus de illuminatione cognitionis sensitivae, quae tota versatur circa cognitionem sensibilium: ubi tria est considerare, videlicet cognoscendi medium, cognoscendi exercitium, cognoscendi oblectamentum. Si consideremus medium cognoscendi intuebimur ibi Verbum aeternaliter generatum, et ex tempore incarnatum." [for no sensation without external image from the object.] "Per hunc etiam modum intelligo, quod a summa mente, quae cognoscibilis est in interioribus sensibus mentis nostrae, aeternaliter emanavit similitudo, imago et proles, et ille postmodum, *quando venit plenitudo temporis,* unitus est menti et carni, id est homini, quem formaverat, . . . et per illum omnes mentes nostrae reducuntur in Deum, quae illam similitudinem Patris per fidem in corde suscipiunt. . . . Si autem consideremus oblectamentum, intuebimur Dei et animae unionem. . . . quia non satiatur oculus visu. . . . Per hunc etiam modum sensus cordis nostri, sive pulchrum, sive consonum, sive odoriferum, sive dulce, sive mulcebre, debet desideranter quaerere, gaudenter invenire, incessanter repetere. Ecce quomodo in cognitione sensitiva continetur occulte divina sapientia, et quam mira est contemplatio quinque sensuum spiritualium, secundum conformitatem ad sensus corporales."

40 Sermon xi, pp. 83-84.
41 Sermon xii, p. 88.

42 Sermons XI and XX.

43 Sermon XVII, p. 110.

44 See Chapter II.

45 *Opera Omnia,* Vol. I (Migne, *P.G.,* Vol. XLIV, Paris, 1863), Sermon 1, cols. 775-76.

46 Richard of St. Victor, *In Cantica Canticorum Explicatio,* in *Opera* (Migne, *P.L.,* Vol. CXCVI, Paris, 1855), Prologue and Chaps. XXII-XXIV, cols. 405, 470-75.

47 See Chap. II, and see Helen White's *English Devotional Literature (Prose), 1600-1640* (Madison, 1931), *passim.*

48 *The Schollars Purgatory Discovered in the Stationers Common-Wealth, and Discribed in a Discourse Apologeticall* (London, *ca.* 1625), p. 54.

49 *Hexaëmeron,* Sermon VI.

50 Bk. I, Chaps XVI-XXIII (Migne, *P.L.,* Vol. CXCVI).

51 See especially A. C. Judson, "Henry Vaughan as a Nature Poet," *Publications of the Modern Language Association,* XLII (1927), 146-56; Elizabeth Holmes, *Henry Vaughan and the Hermetic Philosophy* (London, 1932); Wilson Clough, "Henry Vaughan and the Hermetic Philosophy," *Publications of the Modern Language Association,* XLVIII (1933), 1108-30; Ralph Wardle, "Thomas Vaughan's Influence upon the Poetry of Henry Vaughan," *ibid.,* Vol. LI (1936); and the chapter on Vaughan in Helen White's *The Metaphysical Poets* (New York, 1936).

52 Rufus Jones, *The Flowering of Mysticism* (New York, 1939); H. O. Taylor, *Thought and Expression in the Sixteenth Century* (New York, 1930), Vol. II.

53 For the background and development of early study of the *Cabbala* I have found much help in Joseph Blau, *The Christian Interpretation of the Cabala in the Renaissance* (New York, 1944).

54 For an account of the condensed version see E. M. W. Tillyard, *The Elizabethan World Picture* (London, 1943), pp. 25-27.

55 I have consulted the Douay version, the Latin edition (Cologne, 1617), and also a translation, *The Mind's Ascent to God by a Ladder of Created Things,* done into English by Moniales (London, 1925).

56 Mr. Kristeller, in his *The Philosophy of Ficino,* does not mention Bonaventura, but the principle of mediaty, central in the thought of Ficino, is already fully worked out in Bonaventura, as is the resulting emphasis upon man as the sole creature sharing matter who returns thanks to God for the entire creation.

57 Ficino, *Theologia Platonica,* Bk. IX, Chap. III:
"Quando animus noster, quid Deus sit, cupiens invenire, a magistris huius modi sciscitatur, phantasia praeceptor & faber nimium temerarius statuam aliquam machinatur ex quinque materiis quas aliarum omnium pulcherrimas externi sensus ipsi obtulerint, acceptas à mundo, eo tamen pacto, ut materias illas excellentiores reddat quoddammodo, quam à

mundo per sensus acceperit. Offert igitur phantasia nobis lumen adeo clarum, ut nullum aliud videri possit fulgentius. Adeo ingens, ut nullum amplius, ac ferme per immensum inane diffusum, quod innumerabilibus sit coloribus exornatum, & in circulum revolvatur, ob quam revolutionem dulcissimis resonet modulis tam implenitibus quam demulcentibus aures. . . . Sed ratio interim e summa mentis specula despiciens phantasiae ludos, ita proclamat. Cave animula, cave inanis istius sophistae praestigias. . . . Deum quaeris? accipe lumen tanto clarius lumine Solis quanto lumen Solis est lucidius tenebris, ad quod si Solis lumen comparetur, etiam si millies milliesque clarius sit, esse videatur umbra. . . . Sit deinde (si lubet) ubique praesens, non sparsum loco, sed integrum loco, cuilibet adstans, neque colorum multiplici varietate inficiatur. Splendidius enim est lumen purum, quam coloratum lumen, neque voluatur aut sonet, nolo enim moveri illud vel collidi nec frangi. Et statum esse arbitor motu perfectiorem. Auferas quoque odores, sapores, mollitiemque tractabilem, ne crassiori sit natura compositum. Hic fulget quod non capit locus. Hic sonat quod non rapit tempus. Hic olet quod non spargit flatus," etc.

58 Ernst Cassirer, *Individuum und Kosmos in der Philosophie der Renaissance* (Leipzig and Berlin, 1927).

59 See the recent commentary with emphasis upon Michelangelo's Platonism by Charles De Tolnay in his *Michelangelo,* Vol. II, *The Sistine Ceiling* (Princeton, 1945). The words, "a God creating himself," do not seem to me in the temper of the Renaissance Platonists.

60 Mrs. Bennett's interpretation of Spenser's neo-Platonism seems to me definitive.

61 I know of no finer definition of Spenser's temper than that of R. E. N. Dodge in his introduction to the Cambridge edition of Spenser (Boston, 1909).

62 An interesting modern parallel may be found in Archibald MacLeish's *Panic.*

63 If we understand artifice in this sense, we can see how Spenser—following the tradition of stoic thought—effects a reconciliation of ideas in which nurture is preferred to mere nature, when the question is viewed from that side. Habit and tradition confirm and establish what grace gives.

64 The influence of Spenser's music in the total effect he makes upon us is often divided. For his art is extremely elaborate and even its music has a certain allegorical aim. In passages in which he affirms his joyous vision, such as the descriptions of Una in the forest, Una's return to Red Cross to remind him of the grace of God, the betrothal masque, Guyon's reply to Philotime, the angels' watch over Guyon, and in passages on the pathos of human blindness and despair, his auditory images rise very clear. In passages like the cave of sleep—despite the marvellous intimation of the dreamy ease of reverie—and Acrasia's Bower, the elaborately wrought and mellifluous harmonies lack iron.

65   Between the two broad classical conceptions of creation used to amplify Genesis, that roughly derived from Aristotle and that of neo-Platonic thought (with which Stoic ideas had been already synthesized in Plotinus) which conceives a chaos created from eternity and containing the seeds of things, called into actuality by creation in time—between these two conceptions which flourished throughout the middle ages Milton would seem to have chosen the latter. George Whiting in his *Milton's Literary Milieu* (Chapel Hill, 1939) illustrates in the passages he cites a wide prevalence of the two in seventeenth-century English writing and the clearly kept differentiation. Walter C. Curry's essay, "Milton's Scale of Nature," in *Stanford University Studies in Language and Literature* (Palo Alto, 1941), carries us back to the more searching analyses of the great mediaeval theologians. But he has not yet, I think, defined Milton's tradition or his view in full.

66   Chapter 1 of the earlier version of the *Institutes;* Bk. I, Chapter v, of the versions of 1559 and 1560.

67   Tillyard, *The Elizabethan World Picture,* p. 33.

68   In his unpublished thesis, "The Seventeenth-Century Controversy over the Decay of Nature," University of Chicago, Division of Language and Literature, Department of English (1945). His book, *All Coherence Gone,* has since been published.

69   Cited by David Masson in his *Life of Milton* (London, 1881), V, 233.

70   For the full backgrounds of this discussion see L. C. Martin, "Henry Vaughan and the Theme of Innocency," *Seventeenth Century Studies Presented to Sir Herbert Grierson* (Oxford, 1938), pp. 243-55, and Merritt Y. Hughes, "The Theme of Pre-Existence and Infancy in *The Retreate,*" *Renaissance Studies in Honor of Hardin Craig, Philological Quarterly,* XX (1941), 484-500.

71   This essential difference in character is clear despite the fact that the idea of the great chain was re-Platonized and given also something of Stoic pantheism in the later seventeenth century in England and that the general attitude was through these intermediaries attached to Newtonianism. See discussions of Shaftesbury and Thomson as well as the first epistle of Pope's *Essay on Man.*

72   A. S. P. Woodhouse, *Puritanism and Liberty, Being the Army Debates (1647–49) from the Clarke Manuscripts* (London, 1938), Introduction.

73   Tertullian, *ed. cit.,* Chap. XIX, p. 330.

74   St. Augustine, *Contra Academicos,* trans. by D. J. Kavanaugh as *Answer to Skeptics* (New York, 1943), Bk. I.

75   The element of Aristotelianism in Augustine's argument is not important for us to explore.

76   *Answer to Skeptics,* Bk. III.

77   The pattern of this conception of primary intuition and its relation to faith in revelation and to the function of reason in interpreting it is tre-

mendously illuminated by the early definitions of the functions of faith and reason in Philo Judaeus, described and illustrated by Wolfson (*op cit.,* Bk. I, Chap. III).

78 *Hexaëmeron, ed. cit.,* Vol. IX, pp. 111-13:

"So shall the Soul be, as cultivator and guardian, and she shall make for herself from the Scripture a little delightful garden in the mind. In this knowledge alone is there delight and in no other. The philosopher [Aristotle] says that there is a great delight in knowing that the diameter and the circumference are incommensurable; but this delight, swiftly ending, just as its wont is, consumes the soul. But from the Scripture there proceeds a certain light or beaming forth, into the intellect joined to the imagination that does not permit the departure of the wise and this, to one who looks within, without, above, below. . . . See Noah, who, when he had been building the ark for a hundred years, and placed in it whatever he had, then was despised by all the world. And this I say to you, that the king of France today could not make such an ark, considering it according to the measure of geometrical cubits. . . .

"Besides, the Scripture has trees to refresh us. It illustrates also from things which are opposed to us. It shows us infinite lines of battle drawn up against us, now under seven leaders, now one war, now many: That war is from that day on which 'Michael and his Angels fight with the dragon.' A threefold war threatens us: war at home, civil war, and war in the fields."

79 *Ibid.,* cols. 115 ff.

80 Ernst Cassirer, "Giovanni Pico della Mirandola," *Journal of the History of Ideas,* III (1942), 123-44, 319-46.

81 Madeleine Doran, "On Elizabethan 'Credulity,'" *Journal of the History of Ideas,* I (1940), 153.

82 Hughes, "Kidnapping Donne," *Univ. of Calif. Studies in English and Comparative Literature,* Vol. IV.

83 Sir Thomas Browne, *Works,* ed. by Geoffrey Keynes (London, 1928), I, 13.

84 *Ibid.,* pp. 15-16.

85 *Ibid.,* pp. 87-88.

86 Henry More, *Conjectura Cabbalistica or a Conjectural Essay of Interpreting the Mind of Moses* . . . (London, 1713), pp. 28, 223.

87 Browne, *ed. cit.,* I, 86-87.

88 In Saintsbury, *Minor Caroline Poets,* II, 246. Essentially the same thing had been said by Beaumont in his elegy on King (see Chap. IV, p. 98).

89 I am especially indebted to work such as that of A. S. P. Woodhouse, William Haller, Merritt Hughes, Grant McColley.

90 Grant McColley, "Milton's Dialogue on Astronomy," *Publications of the Modern Language Association,* LII (1937), 728-62.

91 George Sensabaugh's study, "Milton on Learning," *Studies in Philology,* Vol. XLIII (1946), gives a valuable emphasis. But he does not give quite

adequate weight to Milton's statement in *Of Education* that what had been studied during the day was every night to be *reduced* to the Bible. The word is that used by Bonaventura to define his subsuming of all studies in theology.

92 Petrarch's *Secret,* trans. from the Latin by William H. Draper (London, 1913).

93 See Hallet Smith, "Tamburlaine and the Renaissance," *University of Colorado Studies,* Vol. II (Boulder, 1945); and Don Cameron Allen, "Renaissance Remedies for Fortune," *Studies in Philology,* XXXVIII (1941), 188–97.

94 The *loci classici* are brought together by V. B. Heltzel in the notes to his edition of Robert Ashley's *Of Honour* (San Marino, 1947).

95 Ruth Kelso, *The Doctrine of the English Gentleman in the Sixteenth Century. University of Illinois Studies in Language and Literature,* No. XIV (Urbana, 1929).

96 The Blind Fury is a characteristic figure in triumphs of Fame.

97 Guevara, *El Villano del Danubio,* ed. Amerigo Castro (Princeton, 1946), Introduction.

98 L. Clément, "Antoine de Guevara: Ses Lecteurs et ses Imitateurs français au xvie siècle," *Revue d'Histoire littéraire* (1900), p. 598.

99 *Two Bookes of Constancie,* Written in Latin by Justus Lipsius, Englished by Sir John Stradling; edited with an Introduction by Rudolf Kirk (New Brunswick, N. J., 1939), pp. 131-37.

100 Richard of St. Victor, *ed. cit.* Chapters xxviii-xxix, cols. 486–91.

101 R. H. Pearce, "Primitivistic Ideas in *The Faerie Queene," Journal of English and Germanic Philology,* XLIV (1945), 139-51.

102 See Sensabaugh, "The Milieu of Comus," *Studies in Philology,* XLI (1944), 238-49.

103 Antoine Adam, *Théophile de Viau et la libre pensée française en 1620* (Paris, 1935).

104 See Roger Charbonnel, *La Pensée italienne au xvie siècle et le courant libertin* (Paris, 1917).

CHAPTER NINE

1 Cleanth Brooks's comment on the poem, published in the *English Institute Annual* for 1946 (New York, 1947) appeared too late to be of any use to me, but it is a pleasure to find how far I am in agreement with him.

2 See besides Machiavelli's own *Discourses* and *Capitolo on Fortune,* the Introduction by Allan Gilbert to his translations of *The Prince and Other Works of Machiavelli* (Chicago, 1941). Note also the emphasis on Fate in Marvell's Fairfax poems.

3 See Mr. Margoliouth's notes, I, 236-39, for the material in full.

4. *Andrew Marvell,* p. 74.

5   I, 239. The volume contains besides portraits of the principal figures—
    Charles himself, Wentworth, Laud, Fairfax, and Cromwell—an engraving
    of the scene of the execution the moment after the act was completed. The
    stage-like effect of the platform before Whitehall is very vivid.

6   *Op. cit.*, p. 74.

7   For a discussion of Stoic backgrounds, see M. C. Bradbrook in *Review
    of English Studies*, XVII, 37–46. Her view is somewhat modified, by
    implication, in her later book. My own radical modification of it is
    discussed in the preceding chapter.

8   Zera S. Fink, *The Classical Republicans* (Evanston, 1945). My comment
    about Venetian models is based on his book.

9   I, 230-36.

10 Puritan feeling on this point as it flourished in New England is defined
    by Perry Miller, *The New England Mind*, pp. 80, 90, 107, 467ff.

11 Pp. 273-74.

12 Herbert and Vaughan, as well as Walton, are illuminating parallels to
    Marvell in this attitude.

13 In a note to Bradbrook and Lloyd Thomas' "Marvell and the Concept of
    Metamorphosis," *The Criterion*, XVIII (1938), 250, note 1. Miss Free-
    man, in her *English Emblem Books*, describes Hawkins' volume fully
    (though without reference to Marvell, since she is concerned only with
    the volume itself as a type of emblem book) and reproduces his frontis-
    piece of the enclosed garden.

14 *Op. cit.*

15 See my discussion in the preceding chapter, and see also Geoffrey Woledge,
    "Saint Amand, Fairfax, and Marvell," *Modern Language Review*, XXV
    (1930), 481-83.

16 *La Solitude*, Stanzas I, IV, V, VI, XVII.

17 *Upon the Hill and Grove at Bill-borow*, Stanza V.

18 This and the following stanzas from *Upon Appleton House*, LXI-LXIII,
    LXXIX.

19 Miss Bradbrook in her article (*Review of English Studies*, XVII) gives a
    detailed comparison of Marvell and Mildmay Fane (the possible intro-
    ducer of St. Amant to Marvell) which is of great interest. Fane, she finds,
    most decisively modifies the tradition of rural poetry by the paradoxical
    union of the ascetic and the "epicure," not really very paradoxical. But
    Fane's is poetry of moral reflection and his contemplation springs from
    that and not from nature herself.

20 A reference pointed out by Legouis in his *André Marvell*, p. 122.

21 It is hard not to write as though *The Garden* certainly followed *Appleton
    House*. It is of course possible that it marked a moment of concentration
    within the formation of *Appleton House*. But the detail of the "sliding
    foot" repeated in the two poems is likely to have gone from the literal ex-
    perience to the figurative use, as Miss Bradbrook and Miss Lloyd Thomas

have observed, and the interest in neo-Platonic psychology looks toward the second Cromwell poem of 1655.

22 "Symbolic Color in the Literature of the English Renaissance," *Philological Quarterly,* XV (1936), 81–92.

23 N.p., 1599.

24 Last, above all, beautiful green. How it seizes the mind of the gazers, when in a new spring the seeds advance in a new life, and erectly upward as if in symbols, death being trampled downward, they burst into light in the image of the future resurrection. But why shall we speak of the works of God, when we wonder so much at even the colors of human contriving which deceive our eyes with an adulterated wisdom, as it were?—*Didascalia (et. cit.),* Bk. VII, Chap. XII.

25 See pp. 163-64.

26 King, "Some Notes on Andrew Marvell's *Garden,*" *English Studies,* XX, 118-21.

27 Reference to heaven in Théophile, as Antoine Adam has shown (*Théophile de Viau*), does not carry theistic implications but a belief in Fate and in a self-developing nature.

28 More broadly, *annihilate* is a term used by St. John of the Cross to express the dark night of the senses. Sir Thomas Browne, in a somewhat cursory view, equates the term with others, including ecstasy, used by mystical writers for mystical transcendence of the body.

29 *Hexaëmeron (ed cit.),* Sermon XII, p. 88: *Sicut tu vides quod radius intrans fenestram diversimode coloratur, secundum colores diversos, diversarum partium vitri; radius divinus in singulis creaturis diversimode et diversis proprietatibus refulget.*

30 *Enneads,* IV, Tractate III, secs. 9, 10, 17, tr. by Stephen McKenna (London, 1917-1930).

31 *Ed. cit.*

32 Stanzas IV, V, VI.

33 *Andrew Marvell,* pp. 47-50.

34 (London, 1945), p. 161.

35 In his prose, certainly, one feels that the old patterns of symbolic thought spring readily to his mind, but with something of the character of an "as if." They are no longer part of a *scientia.* Perhaps the very tentative putting forth in his poem on the death of Cromwell of several views on the influence of the stars—all, be it noted, in accord with a doctrine of free-will—is a case in point.

INDEX

INDEX

and "G. G.", 94, 125-28; in Hastings volume, 125-28; in Dryden, 135, 140; theory and practice in formal tradition, 143; in Marvell, 169; Suger on, 202; in Spenser, 224; and libertines, 277; Fracastoro on, 374

Ovid, influence on neo-Latin epigram, 104; mention, 221

P ALINGENIUS, neo-Platonic cosmology, 265-66; *Zodiac of Life,* 158, 184, 265

Panofsky, E., on Abbot Suger, 185, 201-2

Paracelsus, Philippus Aureolus, 243

Paradoxical thought, and symbolism, 35; and strong lines, 74; in Sir Henry Goodyere, 83; in Henry King, 86; in Sir John Davies, 92; in Donne, 100; in Cleveland, 102; in W. More, 106; in Pestell, 119; in seventeenth-century poetry, 157; in Marvell, 174, 176, 341; in Sidney's *Arcadia,* 169; Stoicism and, 260; nature vs. artifice, 275; in Aquinas, 378

Parker, Samuel, 131, 236, 288

Pastoralism, in *Great Britans Mourning Garment,* 63-67; themes in pastoral elegy, 69-70; in elegies on. Prince Henry, 95; in Joseph Beaumont, 98-99; and Jesuit influence, 105; elements of in Milton, 107-14, 144; and classical myth, 118; before. Dryden, 129; Dryden and pastoral elegy, 134, 137; and Walton, 259; and Marvell, 302, 336

Paul, Saint, and symbolic thought, 31, 41, 44, 48

Peacham, Henry, elegies on Prince Henry, 62-63

Pellegrino, Fulvio, and color symbolism, 322

Pepper, S., aesthetics, 191

Pestell, Thomas, and Donne's influence, 115, 384; on Hastings, 118-20

Peterhouse College, and Song of Songs, 209; and Marvell, 298; interest in St. Teresa, 384

Petrarch, Francesco, as model for imitation, 12; and rising-sun image, 105; *Secret,* and St. Augustine, 256; his humanism, 144, 261; on fame, 262; praise of active life, 261; and color symbolism, 322; mention, 65

Petrus Aegidius, 76

Phantasy, in Ficino, 217. *See also* Imagination

Philips, Katherine, use of emblems, 384

Philo Judaeus, his Platonism, 37-41; principles of allegory, 166, 169

Physiologus, 34

Pico della Mirandola, Gianfrancesco, 243

Pico della Mirandola, Giovanni, conception of truth, 37; his Platonism, 163; and cabbalism, 213; and symbolism, 243; mention, 245

Piers Plowman, nature vs. artifice in, 275, 289

Pietism, and anti-intellectualism, 237-50, *passim;* in Marvell, 237, 241; in Bonaventura, 240-41; in Seneca, 265

Pindar, 289

Plato, Lionardi's use of, 16-17; Tertullian on, 31-32; and Hugh of St. Victor, 48; Calvin and, 226

Platonism (including neo-Platonism), aesthetic of, 15-20, *passim;* ascetic neo-Platonism, 30, 36; Origen's, 29-30; Tertullian on, 31-32; and symbolic thought, 37-56, 78-79, 313; Franciscan, and Nicolas of Cusa, 51; and Donne, 51-52, 93, 102; humanistic, and view of temporal world, 54; Platonic myth and emblem tradi-